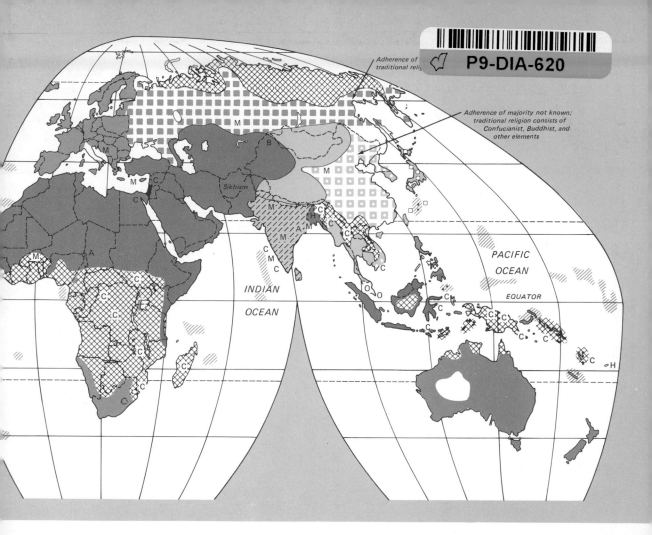

Adherence of traditional relig...

P9-DIA-620

Adherence of majority not known;
traditional religion consists of
Confucianist, Buddhist, and
other elements

PACIFIC
OCEAN

EQUATOR

INDIAN

OCEAN

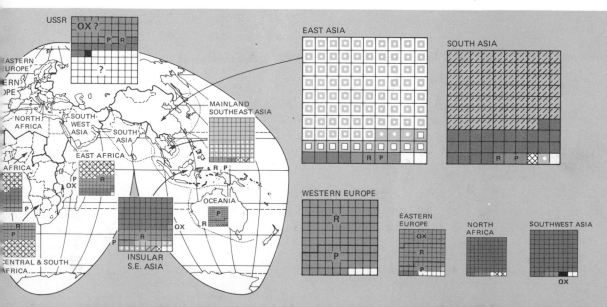

© 1974, Macmillan Publishing Co., Inc.

Many Peoples, Many Faiths

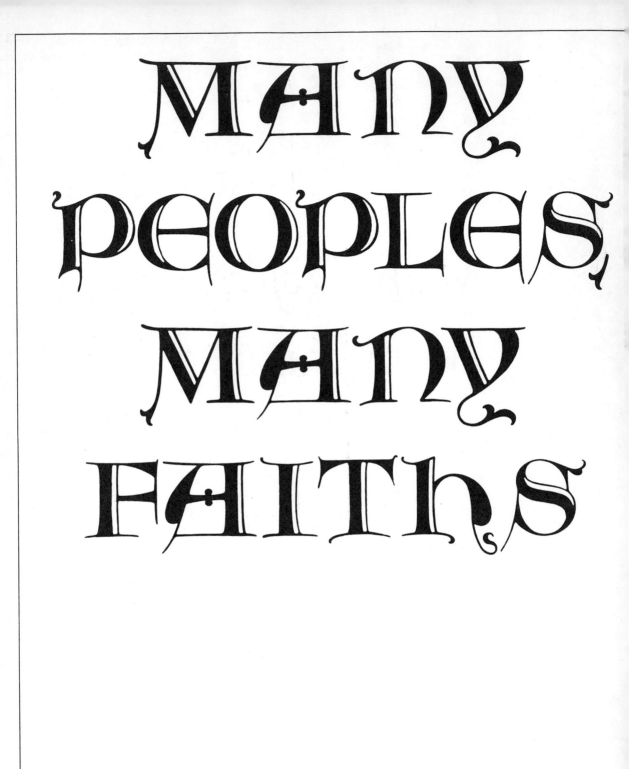

MANY
PEOPLES,
MANY
FAITHS

ROBERT S. ELLWOOD, Jr.

University of Southern California

An Introduction
to
the Religious Life
of
Mankind

PRENTICE-HALL, INC., ENGLEWOOD CLIFFS, NEW JERSEY

Library of Congress Cataloging in Publication Data

ELLWOOD, ROBERT S   1933-
    Many peoples, many faiths.

    Bibliography: p.
    Includes index.
    1. Religions.   2. Religion.   I. Title.
BL80.2.E45   291   75-37878
ISBN 0-13-555995-2

For Richard Scott Lancelot Ellwood
May his faith be always adventurous

Printed in the United States of America

10   9   8   7   6   5   4   3   2   1

Prentice-Hall International, Inc., *London*
Prentice-Hall of Australia, Pty. Limited, *Sydney*
Prentice-Hall of Canada, Ltd., *Toronto*
Prentice-Hall of India Private Limited, *New Delhi*
Prentice-Hall of Japan, Inc., *Tokyo*
Prentice-Hall of Southeast Asia Pte. Ltd., *Singapore*

ILLUSTRATION CREDITS

Page:
   1   Arthur Tress, Photo Researchers.
  13   © Paolo Koch, Rapho/Photo Researchers.
  16   Odette Mennesson-Rigaud, Photo Researchers.
  17   Bruce Roberts, Rapho/Photo Researchers.
  26   © Paolo Koch, Rapho/Photo Researchers.

Contents

Chapter 3

LIFE AGAINST TIME:
The Spiritual Paths of India 59

Chapter 4

WISDOM EMBARKED FOR THE FARTHER SHORE:
The Journey of Buddhism 105

Chapter 7

ONE GOD, MANY WORDS AND WONDERS:
Three Great Monotheistic Religions

Preface

This book is added to the several existing introductions to the religions of the world as an attempt at a new style in such writing. While striving for accuracy and depth, it is neither an encyclopedic compilation of facts nor a survey of alternative philosophies. *Many Peoples, Many Faiths* instead endeavors to encapsulate in non-technical language something of the total human experience, made up as it is of an inseparable combination of conceptual, worship, and social factors, of religious life past and present. The author hopes that his effort will implant in many readers a sense of the richness and fascination of the areas of scholarship which lie behind the presentation of this experience, and will inspire at least some to explore them more deeply.

Because of the great number of languages involved and the nontechnical nature of this book, diacritical marks and strictly consistent transliterative systems are not used for words derived from languages which do not employ Roman orthography; the principle instead has been to employ whatever standard spelling will appear easiest to the beginning student. The same attitude obtains in regard to exact historical information—dates, names, and the like—and to footnoting. Only enough is presented to provide "placing" and *examples* of the findings and resources of scholarship.

The author is grateful indeed to several colleagues who kindly read portions of the manuscript and made helpful comments and suggestions: Professors Barbara G. Myerhoff and Laurence G. Thompson of the University of Southern California; Rabbi Roy Furman, formerly of the Hillel Foundation, University of Southern California; Professor Willard Johnson, California State University at Long Beach; and the readers and editors of Prentice-Hall, Inc. For their assistance the author expresses deep appreciation; for such errors and misperceptions as may remain he takes full responsibility.

Finally, I am very grateful to my wife Gracia Fay for much support and assistance, and for many valuable suggestions, including the idea of the Thematic Charts; without her help, the book would have been far poorer than it is.

Robert S. Ellwood, Jr.

Many Peoples,
Many Faiths

ONE

UNDER-STANDING THE WORLD'S RELIGIOUS HERITAGE

Buddhist monks in Thailand watching the sunrise.

A NEW DAY
OF RELIGIOUS ENCOUNTER

The religions of the world . . . the words themselves may evoke a cinerama of images, perhaps drawn from a host of movies and novels with east-of-Suez settings. Incense and temple gongs, yogins in strange contorted postures, ancient and enigmatic chants—all these and more sweep past our inner eyes and ears. For most often what fascinates is that which is far away or long ago.

But the study of the religions of the world is no longer a matter of reading about exotic lands to which only the most intrepid travelers have voyaged. In today's pluralistic society and world community, almost any faith from anywhere is a presence and an option throughout the world. In the larger American cities, devotees of Krishna dance and chant on the streets; American Zen centers, quiet with the great peace of the Buddha, teach Eastern meditation. Christianity and Judaism in all their manifold forms have long existed here side by side, just as they have been carried by American missionaries or settlers to the homelands of Hinduism and Buddhism. There are even groups in America who have attempted to revive religions thought long dead: those of the ancient Egyptians, Greeks, and Norsemen.

Moreover, American young people in substantial numbers travel throughout the world, making personal friends of Muslims, Sikhs, and Shintoists. Even though traditional religions sometimes may seem to be losing power due to secularism and revolution, in another sense they have never been so readily accessible, in all their diversity, to everyone. It is a golden age for the study, and the interior understanding, of man's many ways of faith. Time and space easily can be made to fall away, and the archaic medicine man or shaman arrayed in bells and birdfeathers, the Hindu mystic poised deep in the Himalayas, the old Druid wizard holding high his oaken staff, all enter our lives as guests and teachers.

Hermann Hesse, in *Demian,* a novel of the spiritual quest, wrote:

> But we consist of everything the world consists of, each of us, and just as our body contains the genealogical table of evolution as far back as the fish and even much further, so we bear everything in our soul that once was alive in the soul of

men. Every god and devil that ever existed, be it among the Greeks, Chinese, or Zulus, are within us, exist as latent possibilities, as wishes, as alternatives. If the human race were to vanish from the face of the earth save for one halfway talented child that had received no education, it would be capable of producing everything once more, gods and demons, paradises, commandments, the Old and New Testament.[1]

Today, with the riches of books, travel, and experience now available, the promise of these lines can be more easily realized, at least on the level of empathy and understanding. More than once, as one explores the most alien-seeming of mankind's religious symbols and scriptures, one may find oneself saying, "This was made or said by human beings like myself. I know why they produced it; something in me has felt the same way."

When we explore the religions of the world today, then, we are engaging in human experiences both around us and in us. To talk about understanding the world's religions is to speak not only of the chronology of past events, which have made them what they are today—fascinating as that narrative is—but also of the story each is telling of ways of being human in this world, and of paths that lead to what is more than merely human.

This new day in the encounter with the religions of the world makes possible a new kind of approach. When contact with almost all religions but one's own was for most people limited to books, it was inevitable that the encounter was chiefly on the level of ideas. For many, comparative religion was comparative doctrine, or at best comparative philosophy. Its students were content to say, "The Hindus believe this," or "The Buddhists believe that," and to think thereby they understood the Hindus or the Buddhists. What little they knew about the worship practices, or style of family life, or unconscious attitudes of those who believed this or that was relegated to the realm of "quaint customs" of the sort described in travel magazines. Rarely was any profound connection made between the two levels, intellectual belief and concrete practice, to gain a full picture of the religion as a unified human experience. And if one did, that insight too might fall into a stereotyped pattern, as though "all Hindus" or "all Buddhists" were equally well-informed and equally pious in the beliefs and devotions ascribed to them.

We knew, of course, that the situation in the Christianity or Judaism many of us grew up with was not so simple. The family church or synagogue may have had its set of beliefs, its Bible, creed, confession, or catechism. At some stage we may have been taught from these documents, and may (or may not) have found their words helpful toward a meaningful relationship with ultimate things.

But the experience of church or synagogue was much more than this. In early childhood, it came as something other than a set of doctrines, and there is always something of the child in every adult.

Religion was a large hushed building with the interesting smells of incense or musty hymnals. It was a lot of music and a lot of speaking. It was stories and prayers taught by parents or teachers who wore, in those moments, a peculiarly solemn or tender expression. It was noisy children in Sunday School. Later, it was

[1]Hermann Hesse, *Demian* (New York: Bantam Books, 1970, Harper & Row, Publishers, Inc., 1965), pp. 88–89.

the site of wedding bells, thrown rice, and laughter; it was the somber place of funerals with their heavy wreaths of flowers.

Above all, perhaps, the House of God was a place deeply associated with one's biological relationships. One went to the church where family, relatives, and other people of one's ethnic background went, whether one happened to like all of them as individuals or not. It was a place where *given* relationships, as apart from relationships based on individual choice, reigned supreme.

Of course, it was understood that (at least in a free country) one didn't *have* to accept religion on this basis, and that maybe one shouldn't. Sometimes individuals, or families, abandoned the faith of their fathers and their childhood to embrace something new. They would say the new religion was intellectually more convincing, or gave a more satisfying spiritual experience. Others might cavil at this, to allege they had really joined the other church because it better suited their social pretensions. (For it was well-known that certain denominations went particularly well with certain income levels, lifestyles, and social sets.) Or, if the church-jumpers had joined a group commonly regarded as fanatic or "cultish," they might be regarded as just eccentric.

Probably both the switchers and the critics are right. People do not act with deliberate hypocrisy or self-serving insincerity in religion nearly as often as detractors of all religion allege. But human motivation is deep and complex, and no one understands all the reasons why he or she believes or acts as he or she does. A person may actually *be* a different person from his parents; his personality may actually *be* more like that of people of a different faith or social set, even though he also *wants* this to be so. He may join another faith not just to imitate people he wants to imitate, but because he really feels inside that he is more like them. If he was brought up more like them than his parents and grandparents were, that may certainly be the case.

Then there are those who are indifferent to religion, or perhaps just organized religion, altogether. Indifference to religious belief and practice, and indeed strong antipathy to it, is no new thing. The gods are doubtless as old as man, but so also are doubters of those gods.[2] While the point cannot always be made explicitly, it should not be forgotten that all the societies whose faiths are presented here also contained their skeptics and their indifferent people; these can often be documented too. The notion that irreligion is a peculiarly modern phenomenon is a modern myth. Mankind has generally been divisible into those for whom religion is intensely meaningful and those for whom it is not, plus a large middle segment willing to conform to the way the prevailing cultural winds are blowing. No easy conclusion is to be drawn from the historical facts; one can find villains, tyrants, madmen, and scoundrels among the believers, the nonbelievers, and the indifferent, and one can find persons of the gentlest compassion and the highest moral rectitude in all camps.

In passing, there is food for thought in the reflection that it is hard for most people fully to accept that indifference to religion has always been characteristic of a large part of the human race, because one of the most enduring attributes of religion in every age is a belief that the past (remote or recent) was more firmly pious than the present, a belief generally accepted even by those who reject every other claim of religion. So solidly rooted, for example, is the American belief that the era of the

[2]See Paul Radin, *Primitive Man as Philosopher* (New York: Dover Publications, 1957).

Understanding the World's Religious Heritage

American revolution, and the "good old days" of the nineteenth century, were times of widespread sober faith, that it is hard for us to accept the actual facts, which are that at the time of the Revolution only a small minority of the people in the thirteen colonies were church members, and only a quarter or so in the mid-nineteenth century—compared to over half in the midtwentieth century.

In fact, far from being a time of religious decline, the twentieth century, with its great religious innovations, ferment, and cross-cultural exposures, is an age of vitality in the religious world. To be sure, like so many past times of upheaval in religion, it is a time of crisis, even a time when the future of religion may seem to be in doubt. But religion has survived such times before, just as indifference has survived both heresy-hunting and evangelistic campaigns. No one can predict the future; all one can say is that those who do try, from the point of view of one side or another, are usually proved wrong in the long run.

All of this makes "now" an exciting time to study religion. We who come to the study of religion today bring with us expectations shaped by these times. The presence of many options, and ferment within most of them, are never just things outside a person. Most persons in our culture have inside them all the different attitudes toward religion that we have cited: association with family roots, feelings that people of the present generation are different from their forefathers, desire to find an acceptable belief, a drift toward indifference. These attitudes also can be seen acted out around us in friends and associates.

All of this also indicates how complex religion is. It is now time to try to sort out this complexity by introducing some categories through which we can try to understand and "place" the different voices by which religion speaks. We will present several sets of categories that classify, for the sake of trying to understand, the same religious phenomena in different ways. They may overlap and thereby seem inconsistent with each other; this is because none of them are "right" or "wrong," but are simply different ways of looking at the same thing. The purpose is not to confuse or make the study of religion overly obscure, but merely to show that there are alternative ways of looking at it. Just as a plumber with a complete set of tools can do more than one equipped with only a hammer, so a multiplicity of angles of vision may make one better able to understand the broad scope of human religion than a single theory. We will first look at four different kinds of religious attitudes, then two different ways of looking at the religion of another culture, then three forms of religious expression, and finally at stages of religious history. In this we will, among other things, be working toward a definition of religion—but we may not reach that point even by the end of the book. For while most people have an idea of what they mean by the word "religion"—at least until they are asked—a comprehensive and satisfying definition has thus far eluded even the wisest; perhaps it is not possible.

FOUR STYLES
OF RELIGIOUS ATTITUDES

Let us start by classifying some religious responses around us. Here are four basic religious attitudes that can be found all through the history of religion, and they are easily identifiable in American life today.

The first two are of the withdrawal type, prompting individuals to separate themselves for religious reasons from family and society and to value their own inner experiences more than what was transmitted to them by family and society. Eventually this emphasis can lead to the formation of sects and cults. The last two attitudes are basically affirmative of one's society and roots; they would be held by people who feel comfortable in broadly based religious groups that uphold the normative values of the society and are at no great odds with its culture. Note that all four of these views involve both a subjective attitude and a corresponding relation to society.

1. For some people today intensity of specific religious commitment is a very real thing. It may be more powerful than family ties; such people are prepared to break with home and kinsmen for its sake. Only in deep personal spiritual commitment do these people find integration of all that is seething within them. They are likely to gravitate toward groups in which this kind of commitment is expected. At certain times in the history of religion—the rise of Islam, the Puritan age—this sort of religion, breaking out of prior social molds, played a moving and shaking role. In the course of our survey we will find a number of groups of this type.

2. Other people are mainly motivated by a yearning for deep personal experiences of the mystical sort, for expansion of consciousness and inner well-being. For them, it is the thirst for this inward experience that transcends the family, tradition-bearing aspect of religion. They will be attracted to teachers and small groups in which techniques of changing inner consciousness are stressed. Examples are yoga, meditation, and positive thinking. Again, this quest is hardly new; the holy men of ancient India and the Taoist sages of ancient China felt the same stirrings, and through the centuries cult groups in Asia, Europe, and America have kept the esoteric and mystic flame alive.

3. Still other people move toward groups which, in their social lives, worship, and atmosphere, present an image of an accepted lifestyle—rural, suburban, or whatever—that they see as a model. This is an old function of religion, going back to those ancient myths which told of how the gods made the social and economic order, and sanctified by example or precept the several callings within it, so that the archaic hunter, fisherman, or warrior worked or fought just as had a god or hero in his myth. This role of religion counterbalances the two "withdrawal" possibilities we have discussed. By setting up positive lifestyle images related to the important socioeconomic structures of the society, religion helps to make society viable, even though in a complex pluralistic world people may move from one religious group to another to find a model that fits who they think they are. Consciously or unconsciously, people want to be with groups setting up personality images of which they can say, "That's what I would like to be like!"

4. Finally, there are people today seeking above all else to rediscover tradition, ethnic roots, and a way of being in the world which goes behind the present. In this light we can understand the revival of orthodoxy among Jews, the traditionalist movement in Roman Catholicism, and perhaps conservative evangelicalism among Protestants. This motif too calls up one of the perennial themes of religion. Religion always comes to one as something out of the past, like a memory, and carries one from the present into the past through many means: art, rhetorical phrases, ritual, or close association with ethnic and cultural heritages.

These four attitudes may be intertwined. A single person's religious life can have strong elements of two or more of them. At the same time, pluralism, with its many options, means that whichever direction one chooses, including the traditionalist, has to be a deliberate, self-conscious choice made in the face of other possibilities. This is confusing but also an opportunity. Our world cultural orientation and the new availability of the past make it now possible to understand better than before all roles of religion—as bearer of commitment, mystical experience, lifestyle models, and tradition—in other societies past and present. We are open to all religion as a human experience; we confront the religions of the world without boxes.

RELIGIONS OF THE TEMPLE
AND THE MARKETPLACE

What is religion? As we proceed to work with this basic question, let us clear the ground by saying we are only trying to isolate what human experiences, and what activities, are covered by the word "religion," so that we will know what we are looking for as we examine its role in various cultures.

We are not asking "What is true religion?" or "What do I think *ought* to be considered religion?" Questions of truth in religion, and the development of one's own spiritual attitude, are extremely important. But just as a medical student must know anatomy before diagnosing illnesses and prescribing medicines, so we should learn what religion is worldwide and has been throughout history in order to make the most intelligent possible decision about these ultimate personal questions.

Let us then narrow the question down to this: "To what kinds of human experience and activity shall we assign the word 'religion'?" Even so, the question is not an easy one. Probably no one simple definition will fit neatly over everything we ordinarily call religion. The definition will have to make contact with the four attitudes we have just described. Other images spring to mind too: temples, rituals, holy men, sacred kings, books of scripture, old men recounting tales of gods and heroes, clergy in protest marches, sacred shrines and wells, experimental services, encounter groups, and so forth. What ties all these together?

Suppose you were to visit a society completely new to you. How would you decide which of the many things you saw should be labeled "religion"? Let us imagine the main street of the capital city meandering from the port through a vast marketplace buzzing with haggling and flies. The street ends in a park set with a splendid royal palace and a temple boasting a burnished dome. Courtiers bow as high nobles and princes of the blood enter and leave the palace. Within the incense-heavy interior of the temple, priests chant with the slowness of ancient ritual, and commoners throng forward to bow before the image of a six-armed deity, present an offering of a small coin or a piece of fruit or a banner of silk, remain to pray a moment—for a sick child, for alleviation of endless poverty, for inner peace, or for eternal life in a better realm—then leave.

Back in the marketplace, you notice a strange thing happening. The merchants, who have tiny shrines on the walls of their shops and who generally end a sale with an invocation of their god, are gathered around a young man with wild laughter in his eyes, who is standing on a box orating.

Your interpreter tells you that he is saying, "I have been far out in the deserts, and there I met the real God face to face. He came to me furious as a desert sandstorm, and bright as the desert sun. He told me he is a god without hands or feet, that the image in the temple is but a hideous mockery, and that the princes who claim to be descended from God are lying scorpions."

Raising his voice and shaking his fist, the young man declares, "In the name of the true God, smash the images and crush the princes! Down with them all!"

As you walk off, you observe a couple of soldiers pushing through the crowd toward the frenzied speaker.

Where is the religion of this culture? Is it in the visible setting-apart of a sacred place in the temple, clearly demarcated by special smells, ways of singing, gestures such as bowing and making offerings, and inward attitudes of devotion and prayer? Is it marked by a special image of transhuman character such as the being with six arms? Is it in the society as a whole insofar as it is ruled by a sacred house that claims descent from the temple's god?

Or is it in the prophet who encountered the divine in all its force and dread far away from king and altar, and who now wants all that demolished? Or is it in all of these?

The definition of religion has been approached in two ways in European and American thought. One way emphasizes the temple-oriented perspective, and the other the prophet-oriented. However, there is much interaction between the two attitudes; spokesmen for one do not necessarily overlook the other. It is not a question of whether temples or prophets are "better." It is simply whether it is most useful to understanding to *begin* by describing religion as a vast set of symbols, practices, institutions, and types of persons, all related perhaps to certain feelings or states of consciousness of which the temple is a good emblem; or whether one thinks of religion as first of all an inner confrontation with the divine, perhaps unwanted, full of dread, anxiety, wonder, and obligation, typified by a prophet alone meeting the awesome splendor of a god, accepting it, and following the god's hard will even if it leads to certain death.

The first approach is basically cultural, starting with an awareness of a society's art, architecture, music, poetry, rites, and philosophy. It takes them as guides to spiritual values because it sees men and women as first of all members of a given society, drawing their values and styles of consciousness from it and its complex of art, symbols, books, and conversation. The odd protesting individual is a variable within this larger whole.

Fundamentally, this approach relates religion to man's desire to unify all of life and to make symbols of the unity. It is quite appreciative of mysticism as the capacity to experience calm, blissful, and unified inner states of consciousness— these feelings are like an interiorization of the temple, the outward unifying symbol in the community. The "temple" approach may be summarized as perceiving religions as sets of times, places, symbols, and persons which communicate a sense of the presence of the "sacred" as that which unifies and expresses all the profoundest things within and without one's consciousness.

The second—the "marketplace" or "prophet"—approach is more related to that side of human nature which makes words, which argues, which sees the

Understanding the World's Religious Heritage

separateness of man from man and of man from God. It is highly aware of the conflict between what one is and what one thinks one ought to be. It is less interested in the religion of aesthetic expression, or of feelings of bliss, than in faith for moments of crisis and decision, in the inner agonies of guilt and anxiety and moral choice.

If we were to enter a country motivated mainly by the first approach, we would be careful above all to take into account all the *phenomena* of religion (the approach ultimately becomes that known as the "phenomenological"), all that seems in a special, set-apart way to manifest the unique aura of the ultimate, whether temple or individual burning with power. Yet it is always basically descriptive, aimed at *understanding* from a vantage point outside the orbit of the religion itself, at least for the purposes of description. It may be profoundly appreciative of religion, and founded on a strong belief in the reality of religious experience. It may strive to move through description to "intuit the essence" of the style of religious life under consideration. Or it may not. But in any case it does not look at religion chiefly from the perspective of intense engagement with its claims, and the inner battle to which this confrontation gives rise.

Were we to enter the same country chiefly inspired by the second approach, we would be looking for evidences of direct religious feeling—not just of communal festive joy or habitual piety, but of individual sense of awe. We would look for those who respond to divine choice and call whether comfortable or not. We might see the throngs coming and going in the temple, but rather than their ritual gestures we would see their faces; we would note whether they were marked by passivity, or lit by a sense of the numinous uncanniness of what is sculpted above the altar, or cast down by hopelessness.

In the prophet of the marketplace we might see the real history of religion in that place happening. He was clearly shaken by the touch of the Other, although it may have given him less a radiant experience than a sense of a duty he must carry out grimly even to the death. Our main task would be to ascertain not what stories the incense of the temple told, but what was in the subjectivity of the individual people of this land—who is on fire with God, who is anxious before the mysteries of life and death, who is indifferent, what inward dramas of faith and doubt and faith again are being enacted beneath the skin and behind the eyes, and why.

Both of these approaches would unveil aspects of any religion. At the same time, it may be that one or the other would lend itself best to a particular religion, or even a particular person's experience of it. The sociologist Max Weber talked of exemplary and emissary styles of religious communication.[3] The exemplary personality is like that of the Buddha and many another saint. He is quiet, filled with divine peace, yet reveals an inward radiance which draws people around him, less for what he says than for what he is.

The emissary personality, that of the fiery prophet, is not identified with God, but comes as an ambassador of God, like Muhammad. He delivers a word of command from God, calling on people to forego their comfortable ways, repent, and obey the word he is charged to deliver.

[3]Max Weber, *The Sociology of Religion,* trans. Ephraim Fischoff (Boston: Becon Press, 1963).

Obviously each of these styles goes best with one or the other of the views of religion we have presented. Although different, each is true to part of the history of religion. In developing an overall definition of religion, and in surveying the religions of the world, we cannot just assume that either approach is prior. We cannot just take one without doing injustice to the facts of the other side.

But unavoidably in a survey like this, the temple approach will seem to be dominant. It is necessary to devote considerable space to describing the words and works of religious traditions one after the other, and to use neutral universal language in so doing in order to treat all equally. It must be left to the reader to realize that behind the descriptions lies the stuff of engagement with ultimate things—virtually every religion in this book has had its passionate converts ancient and modern, its martyrs who felt it worth dying for, its prophets and seers. Virtually every one of them presents a serious claim to the reader, and implies a choice of ultimate consequence for the rest of one's life that one could make. This may not always be stated, but the reader must always "fill in" behind the language of religious description the personal question that spiritual tradition is asking.

MAPS
OF THE INVISIBLE WORLD

The two approaches go together, for all religion has attitudes in common unshared by nonreligious outlooks. Both are based on feelings, beliefs, and attitudes which imply that humans have needs other than the physical, and live in an environment that includes more than physical reality. If people lived only to meet physical needs, an action such as "wasting" precious food to place it on the altar of gods, or "wasting" precious time on ceremonial acts, or "wasting" mental energy on anxiety about doing God's will, would simply make no sense. Even if the purpose of the religious act was, say, just to insure a good hunt, it is obviously achieving this end of meeting physical needs in a roundabout way which implies the existence of nonphysical reality.

Religion centers around those symbols, statements, and social forms which give visible expression to an invisible environment man believes to be around him, and an invisible true nature man senses to dwell within him. He wants to deal with this other reality by creating names and signs for it. In culture man makes a cosmos in which the nonmaterial is as real and as visible as stars and cheese. All these things are delineated by the phenomena that the temple approach observes.

But as the prophet approach reminds us, a particular kind of attitude also goes with this rapport with the nonphysical world. For mankind seems instinctively to feel nonphysical reality is more mysterious, more ultimate, and more powerful than the physical. It has to do with mankind's ultimate origins and most absolute relations. It has to do with that which cannot be surpassed—the point of origin beyond which one cannot go to a preceeding stage, the relationship beyond which there is none more important, demanding, or final. This relationship is more than merely the last in a series; the very fact that it is ultimate and final puts it in a special category, different in size and kind from anything coming after. Oranges may come in all sizes, but none of them look like the tree on which they all grew, or the endless horizons of the old earth in which the tree is rooted, or the boundless space which is the mother of earth and sky. So the ultimate parent must always be endless, to fill up (as it were) the void which would otherwise lie behind it.

This kind of relationship has a different "feel" about it from other relationships. Indeed, even a relation with a particularized, finite deity who is only a fragment of the invisible world and not the endless parent, like a Shinto kami, has this "feel," insofar as one senses he is at least a token of the unbounded, coming from the same place, just as even a viceroy of a king has a certain majesty. The relation is one of solemn awe, or laughing festival with sport and song, or quiet contemplation alone, but whatever the mood these moments will cloak themselves with finality; one will feel, if religion is alive, that "There is nothing more than this."

Yet religion is not just a subjective mood; it is also spelling it out in concrete expressions that bring the nonphysical realities which subjectivity feels to life in the visible, physical world. Religion is to the spiritual milieu what drawing and following maps is to the geographic environment. When man discovers new environmental factors, he wants to know how they are arrayed and where he stands in relation to them. The scriptures, temples, symbols, and holy places of religion are like the key or legend of a map. Just as a terrestial map will have signs for roads, boundaries, swamps, and mountain ranges, so the former are "pointers" that religion has set up to indicate the topography of the spiritual world.

The history of religion is the history of these maps. Just as boundaries have shifted and cities have come and gone on the maps of old earth as empires have risen and fallen, so the religious map has changed over the centuries. But certain kinds of signs remain constant. These are the symbols put on the map by the basic forms of religious expression. For while the particulars of religion take almost countless variations, there are constants in the *kind* of expression that the religious consciousness takes.

THREE FORMS
OF RELIGIOUS EXPRESSION

The sociologist of religion Joachim Wach (1898–1955) has provided one useful description of these constants. While the essence of religion may be beyond words, the religious experience, he tells us, *expresses* itself in three broad areas of human construction, which in turn engender other religious experience. These three forms of religious expression he called theoretical, practical, and sociological.[4] These categories will be referred to from time to time in this book in order to show the place and interrelationship of various of the human religious activities of which we shall speak. It will be helpful now to get a preliminary idea of what is meant by each.

[4]Joachim Wach, *Sociology of Religion* (Chicago: University of Chicago Press, 1944), pp. 17–34.

Theoretical Expression:
What Is Said in Religion

The first level of religious expression, the *theoretical,* embraces essentially the verbal expression: what is said. Religions say fundamentally two kinds of things: myth or narrative story and doctrine. In the history of religions, the term "myth" is used in a special way to denote stories which express in narrative form the central values of the society and the way it views what the world is and means. This is a usage far different from the popular denotation of the word "myth"—a fable, a story that is not true. In the history of religions, no judgment is passed on the truth of a story by the use of this word, but only a statement of its function.[5]

Practically all religions have stories which encapsulate the basic perception of the world and man's place in it in narrative form. The most important are often creation stories. They state an important view of the nature of the cosmos by, for example, whether they tell of a God who created the universe from nothing and stands outside it, or made the world by dividing up his own body in a primal sacrifice (as do some Hindu myths), and so is himself the creation.

Another important type of myth is the hero story, the story of the individual who is able to find the way back to the ideal state of the world at its beginning. He undertakes a mighty quest and experiences great anguish. But whether the model hero is a suffering saviour like Jesus Christ or a profound meditator like the Buddha says much about the central values of the community that cherishes these figures. Religions also have secondary model stories of miracles, and of major or prototypal conversions, which express its map of the spiritual world and try to bring others inside it.

All developed religions have expression in doctrine as well. Doctrines are general, abstract statements that generalize from the narratives of creation, the hero's return, and the experiences of saints and believers. Doctrines are composed when people ask, "If this is what God did on this and that occasion, what can we say that is true of God all the time?" The answers are laid out in propositional form: God is loving, all-powerful, and so forth.

In the Judaeo-Christian tradition, for example, the narrative expression is found in the Biblical account of God's creation of the world, Moses' leading the children of Israel out of Egypt, and the life, death, and resurrection of Jesus. Doctrinal expression comes in the creeds, catechisms, or general statements of church councils and theologians about the nature of God, the work of Christ, and the Holy Spirit, based on that narrative.

No problem dealt with by myth and doctrine alike is more important than that of the meaning of time. Although the subject is a partial digression, an understanding of two basic religious attitudes toward time will help to clarify a great deal that is raised in the following chapters. The difference lies in whether time is viewed as cyclical and endless, or historical and linear.

In Hindu, Buddhist, and some Western philosophies, the universe is seen as everlasting, moving through great cycles of creation and destruction and creation again. There is no ultimately meaningful goal to time and history as a whole. The

---

[5]See Gerald A. Larue, *Ancient Myth and Modern Man* (Englewood Cliffs, N.J.: Prentice-Hall, Inc., 1975).

The theoretical expression of religion in words, concepts, and doctrine is suggested by this scene of prayer and study in a Muslim mosque.

only real goal to human life is an experience of individual liberation from an existence that can only result in frustration or despair on the wheel of time. In this "cosmic" view of time, shared by some primitive religions and some very sophisticated philosophical systems, time essentially repeats itself like the turning of the seasons or the rising and setting of the sun, and since time has no beginning or end, one cannot speak of "progress' or even "history" except in highly relative terms.

But Judaism, Christianity, and Islam, in their scriptural traditions, view time as a line, beginning with the creation of the world and ending with the final judgment. In this Western, "historical" view, all the way through time there flows a purpose of which human history is a part. The acts of God in history—the creation, the giving of the Law by Moses, for the Christian the incarnation of God in Christ—are decisive events that definitively color one's spiritual life. Retrospectively, it makes a tremendous difference whether one lived before or after the Exodus or Christ—one's spiritual world would not have been at all the same had one lived in pre-Mosaic or pre-Christian times. In the cyclical tradition, on the other hand, at any time or place there are inward paths open to the center. Time is like the rim of a wheel, with spokes running in to the hub; Buddhism speaks of 84,000 paths to enlightenment.

The rapid pace of change has made linear time seem most real to most modern people, whether religious or not, whether Eastern or Western, and has shattered the world view of many traditions.

In the modern world, whether in the great religions or in a philosophy like Hegelianism or Marxism, or even in the secular notion of "progress," we think that whether one lived in the Stone Age, the Middle Ages, the twentieth century, or some future paradise makes a vital difference in almost everything subjective as well as outward about one's life, and in one's relation to God or absolute truth, inasmuch as these have been revealed in very different degrees of fullness in different ages. (Admittedly, the influence of this kind of Western thinking will be seen in the next set of categories in this chapter—the stages of the historical development of religion.) Some ideas comparable to this have obtained in the East, generally in the reverse form that says times are getting worse, and so new forms of spirituality—Tantrism, the Buddhism of faith in Amitabha—have become appropriate. But the fundamental idea of the major Eastern spiritual philosophies is that truth and reality are timeless and so stand in equal relation to all times and places, being always available to the man of will and wisdom.

In any case, religion views time as being, like the geography of temple and rite, a map of the invisible spiritual and nonphysical world; it is not ordinary chronology. Time for religion is more like memory in a human being. One does not remember with equal clarity all the millions of events that happened in one's life. A person remembers certain key landmark events that serve to define and symbolize who he or she is. It may be that some very important events in one's life are chosen to be forgotten, or allowed to emerge only in ill-understood dreams and fears. Other scenes from childhood always come forth with striking vividness when one tries to remember the past, even though they may seem trivial incidents. Similarly, religions tell accounts of their origins and pasts—accounts such as the traditional lives of Jesus or the Buddha—which like bright recollections illuminate how they now experience what they are and their mappings of the spiritual world. The theoretical form of religious expression, narrative and doctrinal, replay and interpret these moments and so unveil the religion's view of time as well.

Practical Expression:
What Is Done in Religion

The religious perpetuation of the past is a function of myth and doctrine, but it is a particularly potent function of the second of Wach's three forms of religious expression, the *practical,* which covers the visible and performed side of faith: worship, rite, pilgrimage, forms of devotion or meditation, and other personal or group activities. To stand out as especially religious actions, things done have to have an appearance that makes their religious character evident, and this is likely to be the case only if they follow patterns recognizable in the culture as "religious," neither just meeting ordinary needs in an ordinary way nor merely idiosyncratic. In other words, it will have to be a gesture that is traditionally religious, and so something which comes out of the religious past. Even clergy in protest marches are likely to wear clerical collars to show the religious nature of their actions.

For one always experiences a religion as something that has persisted through time to the present; part of the sense of expansiveness it gives is a sense of free access to the past. Even religion's visions of the future tend to be put in language that suggests a repristinated past: the descent of the heavenly Jerusalem, the coming of a future Buddha. Religious rites carry over from the past vestments, language, and the like obsolete in the rest of the culture. Thereby they gave people a larger milieu, and indeed a sense of unboundedness, by getting them outside the narrow confines of the present. At the same time this perpetuation of an idealized past serves to reinforce the values of the continuing culture it celebrates.

But it would be a mistake to conceptualize the second of the forms of expression only in terms of obvious traditional rites such as an Orthodox Jewish Passover or the Muslim pilgrimage to Mecca. In our own society, there are religious groups with colorful and highly structured rituals. But there are many others which may claim to be "not ritualistic" and have little more than a sermon or address by a leader in ordinary dress, or even just free-form discussions. Are we to conclude then that these groups have little or nothing of the second form of religious expression?

The answer is "no." If it is a religious group at all, the meeting is for some purpose connected with the experiencing and transmission of the religion, and therefore is part of the religion's message. Simplicity is as traditional, and as much a way of forging links with the past, in some faiths (like the Quakers) as ornate ceremony is in others. It is a question of what the message is.

Highly ceremonial religions say that one best transcends oneself to make contact with divine things by losing oneself in the drama and aesthetic stimulation of a mighty liturgy. Simple religions say that one best achieves the same end by the removal of all outward stimuli (except probably the spoken or sung word). Informal religions say that one attains still the same end, or something like it, where one has the greatest freedom to express him- or herself—by releasing one's inner self in prayer group or discussion or "happening," one also draws near to God.

In any case, it is clear that something is *done,* there is *praxis,* and so there is a "practical" form of expression. Whether worship is largely verbal or nonverbal, structured or spontaneous, traditional or modern, centered on one leader or highly corporate, tells important things about the group and its real view of the nature of God and man—things which sometimes are not made explicit in the formal doctrine, but which may nonetheless be unspoken assumptions that underlie much of what is really going on in this religion.

Sociological Expression: *Kinds of Groups Formed by Religion*

The forms of organization undertaken by religion, and the way they relate to the broader social context, are also part of religion's map. Generally, religion's structures fall into two types; they have already been suggested by the two types of religious responses, withdrawal and accepting of society and tradition, to which reference has been made in connection with the four types of religious attitudes.

As we have seen, religious attitudes fall into two types. These may be called the church-type and withdrawal groups. The church is the broadly based religion which represents the normative spiritual values of a society, and which most people are involved in by virtue of their membership in the society—Hinduism in India or Catholicism in Spain. This is the faith a person in a society belongs to if he or she has not made a self-conscious, adult choice to be something else. The "church" in this sense is usually a comprehensive system, allowing for individual variations and in practice not making extremely rigorous demands on everyone. In America, we would have to think of the "church" role being played in effect by a number of major denominations, which tacitly but effectively support a general American religious consensus in the minds of the majority.

Over against this consensus are the withdrawal groups, which express the experiences of those for whom personal commitment and experience are more important than the family and community functions of religion. They meet the needs of those who feel the faith or unfaith of the majoirty is not for them, and want to define themselves more sharply by making a separate choice. Those groups, such as the Amish or Jehovah's Witnesses in the Christian tradition, representing a more intense and rigorous commitment than the average to the religion which is the general tradition, are often called "sects." Groups that combine separation with syncretism, new ideas, and emphasis on mystical experience, are often called "cults."

The relation of a religion to the broader society tells its own story about the meaning of mankind's relation to the spiritual world—whether it is a wisdom

"Practical" expression of religion: beginning of Voodoo rite in Haiti. Gods will be attracted to entrance mediums by the sacred circle with its offerings.

The sociological expression of religion is suggested by this large audience drawn to a charismatic American preacher, Dr. Billy Graham.

widely if diffusely known, or whether an esoteric widsom well-known only by a few intensely dedicated people. Other aspects of the collective life also tell their stories. There is a message about both God and man in whether the group is open or authoritarian, whether the leadership is emergent and charismatic, acting out of the radiant power of the leader's own experience, or whether it works through traditional, constitutional, "rational" channels.

The Interrelationship
of the Forms of Expression

In any religion, the three forms of expression work together to form a unified experience. It is usually a mistake to think that one comes first and the others follow after. Children learn about their mother-faiths more or less through all forms of expression at once—they hear the stories, see the special atmosphere of church or temple when taken by parents, pick up the tone of social life as they play with friends and relatives who share it. Even an adult convert will probably be drawn by all three, and will participate in all three simultaneously. They unite to form a single, almost indefinable experience, which points to the ultimate nature of the holy, and becomes a part of the inner life of each person touched by it.

In the history of religion, the three keep interacting without start or stop. But they usually change at different rates. For example, in recent times many churches in America have moved rather rapidly through changes in theological emphasis (theoretical expression), but often forms of worship have changed more slowly, and sociological changes (in organizational structure and class of people attending) even more slowly than worship.

It is usually theoretical expression that changes fastest. Even when momentous change occurs in religious history with both ideological and social impact, such as the conversion of Arabia to Islam or of Britain to Christianity, it only gradually permeates the total spiritual life of the country. Folklore, folk beliefs, places of pilgrimage (perhaps with the divine names switched) linger for centuries, reaching from one era into the next. In many respects an old map of the spiritual world persists in a given culture through all changes. The Buddhism of Tibet is not the same as that of Thailand, both because their Buddhist histories were different and because the original cultures of the two countries were not at all the same. In all concrete religion, old and new intermingle: the old holy wells or mountains become shrines of new saints or buddhas; fundamental moral attitudes and family patterns change more slowly than the names and doctrines of the gods.

All of this taken together should point toward a "working" definition of religion. As we have observed, probably no absolute definition is possible. But as we explore the many faiths of many peoples, we need to know what we are looking for.

Let us start by saying we are looking for "maps of the invisible world"—for whatever indicates that there is another kind of reality than what is tangible and visible, and that the other reality influences cosmic and human events, and indeed is very close to the depths of human consciousness. Mankind wants to point toward this other reality, and must interact with it inwardly and outwardly. This is done through concepts and words spoken or in books which associate that reality with pictures and drives in one's mind, through actions which make invisible reality take visible form for a time around one and in one's society, through groups which reflect it in social configurations, and finally by making geography itself as demarcated by man-made temple and shrine bespeak the invisible ultimate presence which here and there breaks through.

But these maps inner and outer shift from one culture to another, and even from the mind of one person to another; there are temple and prophet maps and personalities. They also shift over the centuries, for this experience—religion—is never shut up for long in a box. It alternatively affirms culture and prompts withdrawal from it as new configurations appear to some on the maps. The map is brought into every present from out of the past, but this is an odd sort of map that looks a little different in whatever present it is read. All religion, therefore, is an unstable unity of past and present.

PERIODS
IN RELIGIOUS HISTORY

The changes in religious life implicit in the foregoing statements have happened, for religion is never static. We now come to the final way of categorizing

Understanding the World's Religious Heritage

religious phenomena, according to the period in which it flourished or from which it derives. This historical approach, however, can easily become the most deceptive of all. It fits in with the linear time concept, which, as we have seen, is particularly modern but is only one way of viewing time. It can easily be taken to imply a gratuitous concept of progress by which "later is better"—but whether or not one accepts this as true depends on values independent of historical periodization itself.

Most important, the historical approach can impede religious understanding because it is a frame of reference very different from the way most religious people in the present, and virtually all in the past, have understood their religion. Most people participating in a Jewish or Christian service do not give much thought —even if they know—to which hymns and customs are ancient, which are medieval, and which are modern. Until recently, the majority of people, being illiterate, had not the slightest idea outside of mythic accounts about the origin and historical development of their religion—to them it came in the form it was practiced in their village as a single, seamless totality in the present. Whether a rite was old or new, Stone Age or sophisticated, made little conscious difference if its origin was outside living memory. Historical analysis would have to be handled with great caution if it were to be used as a way of understanding this kind of religious life.

Nonetheless, we will present a set of periods in the history of religion, and moreover most of the material on various religions will be organized in basically historical form—giving the life of founders or the teaching of original scriptures first, then the development of doctrine and devotional patterns, and so forth. All in all, the historical approach does seem to be the most useful, better for all its dangers than any evident alternative.

First, history does represent the way we in the modern West tend to think when we approach the academic study of something like religion. We want the historical questions answered early on—until they are we do not feel we have enough of a "grip" on the subject, a clear enough "picture" of it, to ask anything else. Whether this is ultimately good or not, it is the way we approach social phenomena. When we hear about Confucianism, we want to know about Confucius and his life, then about his influence, even though a traditional Chinese would have experienced his influence before knowing about the great sage's life.

In this book we will often try to give something of this realism by starting with cultural impressions, then going on to answer the historical questions they will stimulate.

Second, history provides a convenient way to deal one by one with the many components—the different scriptures, beliefs, rites, and so forth—of any developed religion. They have usually come from different times. By taking them in this way they provide an object lesson in how religions change and grow—a process people can see around them, too, when they learn what to look for.

Third, the historical approach offers a far greater expansion of awareness in the study of comparative religion than does a merely contemporary slice; one can image not only what is going on today, but also medieval pilgrims and Stone Age wizards. The fact that a modern religionist may not be consciously aware of the time period background of his usages may not mean history is wholly irrelevant to understanding his experience—perhaps nonetheless he changes time-gears in devotional moments, slipping back into a medieval or Stone Age world, and knowing something about these worlds helps us to understand him now, and increases our ability to appreciate what he is doing. For another thing that must be remembered is that the history of religion is largely cumulative—when a new period, or even a new religion, comes it does not so much replace what went before as just add another layer on top of it, while the former still continues to live, perhaps with changed name and role. In the Middle Ages (and today) there persisted with various rationales customs such as Christmas trees and Easter eggs, which stem from the pre-Christian world of archaic hunters and agriculturalists.

Knowing about all these things is fascinating and can lead to various sorts of useful understanding—if we always bear in mind that it is only one dimension of religious understanding, and can be very misleading as a guide to understanding how religious people actually understand themselves and their faith.

Following are periods in religious history worldwide, starting with earliest man.

Hunting Religion

The earliest human society of which we can speak is that of hunters and gatherers. Typically, spiritual power is focused in the sky, the world of animals, and the ecstatic individual. Often a "high god" above made the world and sustains it. A very deep relation exists between man and animal; beasts have spirit as does man, and to take them they must be enchanted, propitiated, and respected. The human custodian of spiritual power may be the shaman, an individual who has gained mastery over spirits and who knows the paths of the dead by means of a great initiatory experience. Commonly the initiation of all members of society is important too; life is seen as a series of stages through which one passes, gaining appropriate power at each. Birth and death are likewise stages in this endless cycle, and the land of the dead is thought of as similar to this, though the ghosts of ancestors are potent and feared.

Agricultural Religion

The development of agriculture was as great a landmark in religion as in economic history. The transfer of attention from the forest to the planted field meant that the earth, as mother of all, grew in significance as the high god faded. Moreover, the development of agriculture brought home anew the relation of death to life, in the seed which seems to be dead but is born anew. Animal and human sacrifice to the powers of fertility, cannibalism, and initiatory mysteries reached a high point in archaic agricultural society. Initiation was particularly practiced among the men, as though to counter the newfound feminine spiritual power of the earth mother. Spiritual life became more and more tied to the cycle of the seasons, marked by spring planting rites and the autumn harvest festival.

Ancient Empires

One result of agriculture was a great increase in the amount of population that could be sustained by a given tract of land in fertile areas. Moreover, the population was sedentary, bound to soil and the seasonal round. This in turn made possible and inevitable trade on a large scale, the growth of towns, and the unification of large areas into great political units, which a small but mobile elite based in a major urban center could control. These were the ancient agricultural empires, like those of Egypt, Mesopotamia, India, or China. Their first religious results were enhancement and sophistication of motifs of archaic agricultural religion. The sacred king, like the pharaoh of Egypt, acquired an immensely exalted spiritual position as one who is initiated through a mystery of death and rebirth parallel to that of the plant, and who performed the rites of spring and harvest. Polytheism reached an apex, for it is really a result of the union of a number of tribes, each with its own patronal deity, into a single society, and also of heaven being made to imitate the increased compartmentalization of human labor in the city and the bureaucratization of earthly government.

Religion Responding to History

Other, more deeply creative forces were also at work. The growth of trade and new imperial social organization led to writing, chronicles, and intercultural contact. Out of all this arose glimmerings of historical awareness—the realization that time seems to move irreversibly in one direction, that things have changed and will not change back. This discovery of history is always a crucial challenge to religion. Because religion points toward self-transcendence, it must somehow show that historical change is not the last word—that even if the old timeless world of the hunter or the planter's seasonal round is passing, something stands above history. Responses to history follow four main strands listed below, sometimes separated and sometimes intertwined.

Epic. One possible response is to accept history but to see in it the unfolding of a purpose implanted in it from the beginning—the triumph of a particular people or dynasty, the defeat of the powers of darkness by the true God. Much of the great narrative literature which grows out of the era of the discovery of history has this basic motif: the Old Testament, the Kojiki in Japan, the Aeneid. In these the historical experience of wars and conquests, empires and disasters are part of a narrative with a beginning and a happy ending.

Ritual. Another response is to keep certain rites, especially those of a court, a city, or an official priesthood, unchanged as a sort of frozen perpetuation of the past before the discovery of history and a symbolic area of experience untouched by it. In ancient Rome, the institution of the Vestal Virgins and the sacrifices of the city's priesthood remained virtually unchanged through all the historical vicissitudes of the empire. In ancient Japan, an imperial princess was sent far away from the court, to the vicinity of the Grand Shrine of Ise, where she avoided all Buddhist practice and even words. She represented the court before the great ancestral deities as Ise, not as it was but as it would like to be seen by the gods, as she took her place in the classic purely Shinto rites of the Grand Shrine.

The Religious Founders. The most consequential event of this era, however, was the emergence in the ancient world of the great international and national religions built upon the work of individual founders. Only a half-dozen or so persons have filled this awesome vocation, which has made their names more powerful in history than those of countless kings. They are Moses, Zoroaster, the Buddha, Confucius, Lao-tzu, Jesus, Muhammad. It is interesting that out of the hundreds of thousands of years humanity has lived on this earth, all the major religious founders have lived within a span of less than two millenia—between Moses in the thirteenth century B.C. and Muhammad in the seventh century A.D. In each case their work, sometimes only after several centuries during which their transformation of values was quietly permeating an older society, resulted in a new state, empire, or cultural wave that marked the emergence into history of vast populations.

The founder-religions—Judaism, Zoroastrianism, the Chinese faiths, Buddhism, Christianity, and Islam—have in common that they see in the life and words of the founder the exemplification and perfect statement of the ideal human life, and also in some way see him as empowering his followers to live it. Buddhism, Christianity, and Islam, especially, see the founder's religion as being transnational and transcultural, and have demonstrated this by missionizing it across many boundaries and seas. The founder-religions, especially the missionary ones, are clearly a particularly creative sort of response to the discovery-of-history experience. By making the life of a single individual the pivot of history, they acknowledge its irreversible movement and at the same time give it a sharply focused central axis. By emphasizing the drama of a single and unique life as the bearer of revelation, they show that now, in the more complex, diversified, and chancy life of a "modern" society, the creative individual and not just the immemorial custom of a tribe is what counts.

Yet at the same time, they are religions and emerged in a time when traditions were still strong. They provided foci around which all manner of things new and old were consolidated—they all have expression on many levels, from folkways to philosophy to eccentric individualism. They could only have come into being in their historical form after or along with the development of writing, large political systems, and international trade. These have been their bearers—all make much of scriptures and political implications. Yet the founder-religions have come to be, in varying degrees, greater than particular times and places.

Wisdom. Another path to transcending the onslaughts of history is through absolutizing states of consciousness or angles of philosophical vision in which the timeless shows its incomparable superiority over time. In India, at approximately the same time as the emergence of the founders, the tradition which was to become Hinduism produced texts such as the Upanishads and Bhagavad-Gita; in them the central theme is the unity of the individual self, who seems to suffer the vicissitudes of time and space, with the absolute who changes not. These books, representing the composite wisdom of many sages, mark much the same era as the founders in other traditions.

Even in the founder-religions, a reaction in favor of mysticism and wisdom tended to set in by a few centuries after the founder's day, and the same was true where polytheistic worship persisted. In either case, the wise urged a perspective that saw unity beyond the many gods or the comings and goings of founder-teachers. In the West, Neoplatonic, Stoic, and Epicurean philosophy fulfilled this role. In Judaism, books such as Proverbs and the apocryphal Wisdom of Solomon personified wisdom as a maiden greatly to be desired and through whom God made the world; to know her is to know the inner mystery of the way things work. In the same manner, from around the first century A.D., Mahayana Buddhism personified wisdom, Prajnaparamita or the "wisdom that has gone beyond," a sort of perfect intuitive insight, as a goddess to be worshipped and desired. Christianity, especially in the Greek theologians and mystics, and Islam also, went through a stage in which the deepest emphasis was on understanding with mystically illumined insight the eternal realities of God and his relation to man and the creation which underlay the particulars of the revelation through Jesus or Muhammad.

The wisdom movements all had in common a highly sophisticated restatement of motifs of the shamanism and initiatory rites of the earliest religion: belief that through proper psychological procedures one can obtain perception into the inner laws of the cosmos and thus power over them. For this reason, wisdom religion is also an ancestor of modern science.

Medieval Devotion

Wisdom mysticism, however profound, did not allow for a full expression of emotional feeling. The Middle Ages in both Asia and Europe brought to flower a piety in which feelings of rapturous love and identification with god or saviour were pre-eminent. We speak of the love of Christ and the Virgin Mary in the devotion of medieval Europe, of passionate Sufi mysticism in Islam, of Krishna and other Hindu gods in India, and of Kannon and Amida in East Asian Buddhism. These movements, in which romantic love and religion interfuse, bespeak a new individualism and sensitivity in their stress on the feelings of the devotee. They were generally accompanied by rich artistic expression in images and paintings of the beloved deity.

Modernity

The real roots of the modern situation in religion go back as far as the end of the Middle Ages, and are typified by such developments as the emergence of Pure Land Buddhism in Japan and the Reformation in Christianity. In both cases, emphasis was put on salvation not by involved spiritual practices or feelings, but by a simple act of faith, which could be made as effectively by layman as by monk or priest. What this really implied was a new exaltation of the secular world and the individual in it. The gradual breakdown of peasant culture based on the agricultural round meant a loss of the charisma of traditional saints and priests and of the spiritual unity of communities, and with it a sense for the spiritual richness and complexity engendered by wisdom and devotion with their occult rites and fervent asceticism.

Later reform movements in Islam and Hinduism went the same direction as those in Christianity and Buddhism in rejecting the wisdom and medieval devotional approaches in favor of the supposedly plain and nonpriestly original teachings of the faith. One reason for the early modern reaction in the direction of simplicity and faith certainly is the modern realization that man can do much to control and exploit his world, through trade and technology, but to so do he must have a religion which can be practiced in the midst of worldly work, and so validates it. The modern faith cannot be too tied to a peasant outlook, or be too demanding of time or emotional energy, or too appreciative of mystical or emotional rather than rational and pragmatic states of mind.

However, this was not all that shaped the modern religious consciousness. This state of spiritual awareness is a welter of diverse and highly contradictory themes. The very trade and technological departures liberated by the religions of faith eventually began to undermine them, for they led to intercultural contact and scientific discoveries that made people wonder about the basis of faith. The new knowledge combined with the new secular freedom led to what is called "liberalism" in religion, essentially the statement of religious attitudes so as to fit with the normative social and scientific values of the cultural context.

Liberalism has, in turn, provoked its share of reactions, such as "integralist" Catholicism and fundamentalist Protestantism. In non-Western cultures the "crisis of modernity" has been exacerbated by the fact that it has meant coping not only with new social and scientific ideas, and the changing conditions of life brought about by industrialization and urbanization, but also with an alien dominant culture, the Western—often brought by colonial masters. There traditional religions have responded, as in the West, in ways ranging from rigid rejection of the new, to reformism based on traditional principles like that of Gandhi, to supporting militant nationalism as in the Japan of the 1930s and 40s, to lending support to radical revolution as have some Buddhists in Communist China.[6]

It is clear, then, that religion is today in a state of flux and transition. But this has always really been the case, although it has not always been quite so readily apparent. Yet all the way through each stage has been melting into the next; there are always constant themes in religion, but their ways of expression shape themselves anew to some extent in each generation. The process is a complex interaction of prophet and temple, of withdrawal and old or new social norms, working through expression in word, act, and group-formation, expressed through symbols or concepts which may be as old as cave art, or discovered only yesterday.

EVERY RELIGION
A COLLECTION OF TENSIONS

It should never be forgotten that any actual religious tradition has within it something of all that has been presented. Buddhism, Christianity, Islam, and the rest have in them something of the temple and something of the prophet, something of withdrawal from culture and something of affirmation of it, something of the Stone Age and something of modernity. Each may have special emphases, and each person within each may have his or her own emphases, but it needs to be grasped that all sides are there all the time. The categories presented can be helps in understanding, but they are not slots in which anything "out there," practiced by real living people, can be neatly dropped.

This should not surprise us if we recall that we ourselves are not just one thing all the time either. We may affirm parts of our culture and reject parts of it; we too may have something of the past and something of the present in us; we slowly change over the years. Every actual religion is not merely an abstraction, but is

---

[6]See the discussion in the epilogue by Robert N. Bellah, ed., in *Religion and Progress in Modern Asia* (New York: The Free Press, 1965).

rooted in the minds of thousands or millions of people fraught with such complexities; the religion may partly serve to simplify the complexities, by setting up models and priorities, yet it cannot help but reflect them as well. Each religion turns out, in fact, to be not a simple solution to the basic tensions of life, but a particular way of configuring them. It takes the chaotic complexities of human existence, and make emerge out of this morass patterns, sets of polarities and priorities, which help the individual to live in the midst of complexity.

In the same way every religion throughout its history and in its full spectrum of expression will form more of a pattern, a configuration, than a straight line. Each religion has its own sets of polarized attitudes toward acceptance or rejection of environing culture, toward the past and present, toward ordinary as over against ecstatic consciousness. It reflects, in other words, the great complexity and diversity of human experience even within one tradition. What distinguishes one religion from another is not only the unique founding and formal doctrine of each, but also the particular way each sets up its tensions and patterns—the particular points it lays out on its compass.

Certain areas of tension run through all religion. In virtually all we find individuals and movements representing polar positions on these axes. A good example is the "temple" and "prophet" matter. Others are intellect versus feeling (trust to reason or to emotive experience as guide to truth), tradition versus innovation, affirmation versus rejection of culture, indigenous versus imported religion, finding the good in human society versus finding it in nature. But the symbols and personalities and concrete historical events which express these tensions in actual religion are manifoldly varied.

To illustrate each religious or cultural tradition as a collection of tensions a series of Thematic Charts are included in this book. They should help the reader conceptualize the basic framework within which each tradition is working, and how its leading figures and ideas relate to each other. There is nothing absolute, of course, about the reduction of each tradition to two pairs of opposites, or in the particular terms which have—through a combination of arbitrariness and reflection—been selected to demarcate each chart. It is hoped, in fact, the reader will make his own refinements; like all schematizations, the charts are cruder than reality. But schematizations also supply signposts, and symbolize that there are currents and prevailing tensions in reality which otherwise might be lost in its infinite multiplicity.

These charts, unlike the time-line charts, are non-historical; their thematic relationships and polarities exist within each major spiritual tradition across time as well as across denomination and sect lines. But it should be remembered that virtually nothing of significance that ever appears in the long history of a religion is ever really lost. Some whiff or savour will survive to keep it a putative part of every subsequent configuration of that tradition: Vedic rites can still be seen in India; even Protestant churches still sing medieval hymns.

It is time now to turn to the religions of mankind themselves.

TWO

THE SACRED IN SKY AND SOUL

Prehistoric and Primitive Religion

Jemez American Indians in traditional costume for a ceremony in Gallup, New Mexico.

SURVIVALS OF
THE FIRST HUMAN FAITHS

Behind the panorama of great religions with their founders and histories and systems—and behind much else in modern life as well—hangs the backdrop of primitive religion. It is the religion of peoples without writing, who live in very small social units like tribes and clans. The term "primitive" is somewhat unfortunate in that it could be taken to imply a negative evaluation, suggesting the culture is undeveloped and so of little sophistication or worth. This is not true: the "primitive" cultures of today have behind them as many years of development as the "advanced," and many of their concepts are far from naive or irrational. It is only that for them sophistication has run in other directions than in those societies which have put it into writing and constructed large social organizations.

The substance of primitive religion is tremendously varied, for the roster of primitive tribes and cultures, each with its own gods and rites and attitudes, is almost endless. We are not thinking only of that dwindling number of living primitive cultures in the Amazon basin, central Africa, or New Guinea, but also of the ranks of peoples down through the ages with comparable cultures and religion—including the ancestors, up to a couple of thousand of years or so ago, of most "civilized" peoples. The "primitive" is not merely exotic—it underlies every culture and every living religion as well.

Because the primitive religious scene is so immensely varied, this chapter cannot hope to cover it in a systematic or culture-by-culture way. The chapter is impressionistic and rather nonhistorical, although we will take note of the religious significance of one important event in prehistoric "history"—the emergence of agriculture. But generally our approach will be thematic, drawing from cross-cultural data to illustrate certain of the great motifs of primitive spirituality. Not all of these motifs are shared by all primitive cultures, of course. For specific data on particular cultures, the reader is referred to the literature of anthropology.

Mircea Eliade has used the expression "cosmic religion" to refer to a religious outlook largely coextensive with the religion of archaic hunters and farmers but with continuations down to the present.[1] Cosmic religion, he tells us, has little sense of history or of what was discussed in the last chapter as linear time. It finds and expresses sacred meaning in aspects of nature and human life—seasons, sacred rocks or trees, the social order, birth and death—without linking them to historical personalities or written documents as founder-religions do. Although the situation is full of ambiguities, reflecting on the cosmic religion experience is a good way to start meeting the primitive spiritual world.

Primitive cosmic religion includes festivals of seedtime and harvest, and the sacred trees and mountains around which the earth seems to pivot. It is the overlaying of our world by an "other world" of gods and goblins, of elves and spirits of the returning dead. Primitive religion is the rites of hunting and archaic agriculture in a world where "everything is alive." It is the ecstacies of shamans who are believed to be able to control spirits and travel in trance to heaven or the underworld to recover strayed or stolen souls, or intercede with the gods.

The world of primitive religion seems very remote to us at first glance. Yet many of its motifs, when communicated in fairy tales or African masks, come across as hauntingly beautiful or nightmarishly powerful. They hit one unexpectedly with all the impact of a half-remembered but very important scene from a dream or early childhood. Then again, countless survivals from the world of cosmic religion, from Christmas trees to the Muslim pilgrimage to Mecca, continue to flourish as much as ever with somewhat transmuted meanings. It could be argued that most popular religion, whether in Buddhist, Christian, or Muslim lands, is only a partially altered cosmic or primitive religion under another name.

Christmas, for example, is a festival of a religion deriving from the era of the discovery of history and commemorates a historical event, around which all history is believed to turn. But consider the Christmas symbolism—a celebration of light at the darkest time of the year, the inauguration of a new year, an ornamented tree representing a "cosmic tree" symbolizing the mystical center of the earth and way of access to the divine world. This is not only pre-Christian in origin, but expresses the cosmic religion kind of emphasis: the spiritual experience produced by the turn of the seasons, the sacred meaning of landmarks of nature like trees and mountains, the sheer immediate evocative power of symbols like light and glitter, the perennial importance to spiritual life of family and the sacred, set-apart time of festival.

Then there is our orange and black feast, with its atmosphere of jack o' lanterns and tales of witches amid frost and falling leaves. Perhaps the oldest holiday that is a part of general American culture is Halloween. It is almost a pure survival of primitive cosmic religion, and incorporates no small number of its themes. On this night, children masked and costumed as ghosts, witches, and devils, or as pirates, cowboys, or mobsters, visit homes to receive candy with the threat of "tricks or treats."[2] Pranks ranging from soaping windows to putting a farmer's wagon on top

---

[1]For the meaning of the term "cosmic religion," see Mircea Eliade, *Cosmos and History* (New York: Harper and Row Publishers, 1959), and *The Sacred and the Profane* (New York: Harper and Row Publishers, 1961).

[2]For further anthropological discussion of the American Halloween, see Victor W. Turner, *The Ritual Process* (Chicago: Aldine Publishing Company, 1969), pp. 172–74.

Main Themes of Primitive Religion

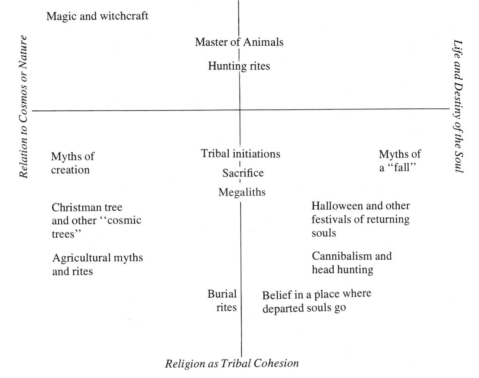

The Individual Religious Specialist

Shaman's vision flight

Shaman's contact with
gods and departed souls

Shaman's initiation

Magic and witchcraft

Relation to Cosmos or Nature

Master of Animals

Hunting rites

Myths of
creation

Tribal initiations

Sacrifice

Megaliths

Myths of
a "fall"

Life and Destiny of the Soul

Christman tree
and other "cosmic
trees"

Halloween and other
festivals of returning
souls

Agricultural myths
and rites

Cannibalism and
head hunting

Burial
rites

Belief in a place where
departed souls go

Religion as Tribal Cohesion

Thematic Chart I.   Here we see several of the aspects of primitive religion mentioned in the text set in a pattern which illustrates some possible ways of seeing their interrelationship. The chart shows that primitives, like all people, saw themselves related to the cosmos or nature, yet also as possessing something, symbolized in the concept of a soul, transcendent to nature and having a different destiny; and that religion served both to bind communities or tribes together, and to provide scope for individuals like the shaman with a special calling in relation to the sacred.

of his barn are also sometimes part of Halloween. There are costume parties with spooky decorations and traditional games like bobbing for apples.

Perpetuated into Christian times as the eve of All Hallows or All Saints Day, Halloween was originally the autumn festival of the ancient Britons and their Druid priests called Samhain. It was the Celtic and Anglo-Saxon New Year. Like festivals of harvest and New Year's everywhere, Samhain had motifs of settling accounts, kindling a new fire, the harvest moon, the celebration of first fruits, and the return of the dead to visit the living. It suggests a temporary return to the chaos before the world was created and thereby the release of the dark and uncanny denizens of chaos. Behind children's masks of woodwoses and witches, behind "tricks or treats" and bobbing for apples, lies the ancient cosmic religion orientation toward the turn of the seasons, rather than a historical event, as where reality is revealed. For an important motif of cosmic religion is a feeling that the turn of the year is like a clock running down and coming virtually to a stop just before it is wound up again on New Year's Day. New Year's is like a recurrent Day of Creation to cosmic religion, and so the preceeding eve is like replunging into that precreation flux when there were no controls. Thus the coming out of dark, grisly entities on Halloween, the ancient New Year's Eve, and our tradition of getting drunk on the modern New Year's Eve. In ancient Rome, the end-of-the-year festival was the Saturnalia, when masters and slaves exchanged roles in a gesture of turning upsidedown the ordinary structures of society.

Another holiday celebrated mainly by children—May Day—continues the pre-Christian spring festival of ancient Britain, known as Beltane. As Halloween in the fall bore a mood of night, moon, the dead, and unwholesome visitants, so May Day is a celebration of day, sun, flowers, and all that is bright, warm, and fresh, although also supernatural. Dancing around the maypole was an ancient practice to encourage fertility; may baskets were gifts of the bounty of the enchanting White Lady who rode through the land awakening the miracle of spring. A center of this belief was the town of Banbury in central England; until modern times the visit of the White Lady was enacted on May Day in a pageant culminating at the ancient market cross in the town square. As the old rhyme has it:

> Ride a cock horse to Banbury Cross,
> To see a fine lady on a white horse,
> With rings on her fingers and bells on her toes,
> She shall have music wherever she goes.

Long after Christianity came, in fact, May Day celebrations were held in Banbury in which youths would gather boughs and make garlands, a maypole would be set up, and a girl would be chosen May Queen (formerly representing the goddess of fertility), and would ride to the festivities on a white horse.

It is interesting that the most colorful survivals of cosmic religion, May Day and Halloween, are kept mainly by children. Part of the world of primitive religion indeed seems childlike: wearing masks, keeping special days, belief in spirits, magic places, and gestures. Moreover, there is a sense in which the culture of children is always conservative. It retains lore in fairy tales, games, and holidays which has lost power in adult culture.

But it would be a grave mistake to think of primitive people as childlike. Adults among them are adult; primitive myths and symbols are saturate with evidence that they have passed through adolescence, experienced adult sexuality, married, had children of their own. All these experiences are marked by rich ceremonial, and permeate the rites of spring and harvest, and the tales of the gods. Primitive people think as rationally, and handle ideas as complex, as any modern adults. Their symbol-systems often convey as much complexity of information and insight as pages of writing, or even mathematical equations.

Moreover, survivals like Halloween and May Day contain only a few of the themes of primitive religion in its fullness. They suggest a typical (at least in temperate climates) seasonal emphasis, but the pantheon of gods and the full relation of the religion to society is less evident. Our holidays are, after all, only bits and pieces of forgotten faiths. (Though as we have seen, popular religious practices everywhere are continuous with primitive religion, just as Judaism and Christianity are shot through with cosmic survivals, often in their most appealing aspects, the art, symbols, festivals, and folkways.)

But we must now approach the world of primitive religion in its fullness. This is a world spanning hundreds of thousands, if not millions, of years. Beside its empire the mightiest of the organized literate religious systems seem puny, of short time and small space. It is difficult to bring this diversity together. Not only are we dealing with countless cultures, but even within one culture, the major motifs flow in and out of each other; slicing them up into categories does violence to the actual unified experience. Although primitive religions do have rational world views expressed through rite and symbol and society they do not have the formal written ideological statements which in other religions are all-too-tempting pegs for interpretation. We have to see what the unified experience and the particulars alike are themselves saying. Clifford Geertz has written that primitive religion:

> . . . consists of a multitude of very concretely defined and only loosely ordered sacred entities, and untidy collection of fussy ritual acts and vivid animistic images which are able to involve themselves in an independent, segmental, and immediate manner with almost any sort of actual event.[3]

What we shall be examining, then, is images, and it is images—symbols, gestures, sacred art, and the mighty figures of myth—which stand out like giant hieratic forms in the world of cosmic religion. It is from the accounts of heroes in story, from masks, from priests in the midst of a hunting rite, from carvings of ancestors, and paintings on rocks and caves, that cosmic religion is learned. All of these go together to make up a cosmos in which spirit and matter are thoroughly interwoven, and everything is more than it seems as myth, rite, and art make the invisible visible. In this cosmos man's life is only complete in his total relationships—with family, tribe, ancestors, the Other World, and all spirits here and beyond.

[3] "'Internal Conversion' In Contemporary Bali," mimeographed, 1961, p. 3. Cited in Robert N. Bellah, *Religion and Progress in Modern Asia* (New York: The Free Press, 1965). p. 176.

The Sacred in Sky and Soul

S. G. F. Brandon has emphasized that religion is "the expression of man's fundamental instinct to seek security from the menace of time."[4] The ability to think in time categories is absolutely basic to what it means to be human. Mankind classifies events as past, present, or future.

Animals (and infants) apparently are aware only of the present apart from unconscious patterns of behavior based on past experience, for without the kind of concepts supported by language it is difficult to categorize thoughts into "memories," "present experience," and "future expectations." Gods, presumably, are above the need for such categories and see vast aeons as one. But mankind is bound to time while highly aware of it.

This time consciousness has given man an advantage of tremendous consequence, for he can learn from the past and plan for the future. He does this both magically and practically. But awareness of time has another and darker side—a human being is also aware of the inevitability of his or her own death. The overcoming of mortality—or rather giving voice to that in man which cannot believe in his mortality—is the object of the timeless images of art and myth. Through the three forms of religious expression—in mythic heroes, in the special time and external recurrence of rite, in social bodies that survive the individual—man creates forms and pictures in the mind so "strong" they stand out as more powerful than that which time bears away.

Most prominent of these images may be those of the time of human origins and the gods of that time, for there if anywhere is mastery of time and death. At the same time, primitive man is aware that the world is far from perfect, and that if the creation was meant to be good something must have gone wrong. Often an original or ultimate god will be portrayed as having made the world, but now seems to have little concern for mankind except perhaps to enforce the moral law. A deity like this is spoken of as a *deus otiosus*—"hidden god."

Sometimes a myth, comparable to the Garden of Eden narrative, accounts for the separation of man from primordial closeness to his creator. With the separation, death enters the world. The natives of Poso, Celebes Island, Indonesia, said that originally the sky where the creator dwelt was very near the earth, and he would lower gifts down on a rope to his children. Once he thus let down a stone, but the first men and women were indignant at such a useless gift and refused it. So the creator pulled it back up, and lowered instead a banana. This they took. But the creator called to them, "Because you have chosen the banana, your life shall be like its life. Had you taken the stone, you would have been like it, changeless and immortal."[5]

Or, the creation itself may have been accomplished by lesser deities. Among the Semang, a simple hunting culture in Malaya, it is said the high god, Karei, lives in

---

[4]S. G. F. Brandon, "The Significance of Time in Some Ancient Initiatory Rituals," *Studies in the History of Religion,* X (Leiden, Netherlands: E. J. Brill, 1965), 40.

[5]James G. Frazer, *The Belief in Immortality,* quoting A. C. Kruijt, I (London: Macmillan and Co., 1913), 72–73.

the sky and his wife Manoid in the earth. Their children are Ta Pedn, Begreg, Karpgen, and a daughter Takel; the thunder is Karei playing with his children. Karei's son, Ta Pedn, created everything; Karei himself made nothing. Karei merely enforces, as a firm and inexorable father-judge, the moral law. He requires that transgressors make a blood-expiation. It is said in fact among the Semang that Ta Pedn is good, but Karei is evil.[6]

Many myths from around the world give essentially the same message: at first mankind was deathless and close to divinity, but something was not right. Either, as with the Semang, there was a difference of attitude within the household of the gods, or as in Poso a mistake occurred, perhaps some seemingly minor and accidental thing—making a wrong decision when all the facts were not readily apparent, the cruelty or heedlessness of a single human, animal, or bird among all that breathed in the teeming garden of creation. Yet this single mistake changed everything, and brought to pass that all future generations would live far from God and near to death.

But this does not mean that abiding things or the invisible world is gone, only that they are farther away and the maps need to be clear. So between mankind and the ultimate, invisible points of reference are living ladders. Gods and ancestral spirits are rungs on the ladder. The great importance of ancestral spirits, who often blend into the great gods, is that in them two of the most potent wellsprings of religious awe—death and the figure of the father—are combined. They are images of fathers, uncles, and grandfathers who are all the more powerful and dreadful now that they have passed through the mystery of death.

Indeed, it is characteristic of many peoples to believe that the supreme god who created the earth is remote from our affairs, and that it is really the finite but far more involved ancestral or nature spirits with whom we have most to deal. The Luguru of East Africa, for example, say that the earth was made by the High God Mulungu, but he is not normally concerned with human affairs. He is given no prayers or sacrifices; they are made rather to the *mitsimu,* or ancestral spirits. One native authority said:

> *Mitsimu* are the spirits of our grandfathers who died, of our grandmothers. Some people say these are *mitsimu*. They bring sickness to a person for his faults. Also, as I say, when your maternal uncle . . . departs and bequeaths you his name there must be a supernatural event, then they say the name is seeking a person, his maternal uncle's name, then they say that's *mitsimu*. Or suppose you want to go to Dar es Salaam, and you ask permission from your maternal uncle and he says "You can't go!" and you say "I'm going!" and then he says, "All right, you'll see for yourself!" Then where you are going there is sure to turn out some danger. From the *mitsimu*.[7]

In this matrilineal society, the chief authority figure is the maternal uncle, who is superior even to one's father or mother. Thus the authority of the ancestral spirits

[6]Paul Schebesta, *Among the Forest Dwarfs of Malaya* (London: Hutchinson & Co., 1927), pp. 185–87.

[7]James L. Brain, "Ancestors as Elders in Africa—Further Thoughts," *Africa,* XLIII, no. 2 (April 1973), 130. Reprinted by permission of International African Institute, London.

is chiefly aligned with the maternal uncle. But they are more than just glorified uncles. The mitsimu are personages with the numinous enchantment of the divine haloing them; they are part of the invisible world. The appearance of omens, such as a solitary unusual animal, is said to be a warning from them. Places of awe and dread, like a burial ground, a deep lake, an underground river, or a striking hilltop, are thought to owe something of their uncanny feel to the presence of these haunts. The mitsimu are not mediators between the passive High God and men, but independent powers, working according to the lights of their own path in the cosmos. The Luguru universe is pluralistic; although Mulungu may have created all souls in the remote beginning and so there is an ultimate principle of unity the powers now work all on their own. Yet they are not merely chaotic, for the ancestors work in support of the familiar and traditional values.

CIRCLING PATHS
THROUGH LIFE AND DEATH

The existence of these ancestral spirits reminds us that life is generally felt to be everlasting, and ultimately independent of existence in the flesh. The invisible world begins with an invisible entity within the self, which really *is* the self, which perhaps lived before entering this body, is able to leave it on occasion, and will probably live elsewhere afterward. It may, in fact, return after death to the original lost unity of earth and heaven. These almost universal convictions imply belief in a soul.

Mankind has a deep intuition that mind is more than just a moist membrane secreting consciousness, doomed to blank out utterly with biological death. Rightly or wrongly, the way the human being *experiences* consciousness suggests that cognition has some principle of being independent of the physical brain, even though they work in tandem for the present. A person finds, for example, that his or her consciousness can contemplate the beginning, transformation, and ending of all things outside the self, but can accept the notion of his or her own beginning and extinction at best only abstractly, rarely with felt conviction. Instead, consciousness experiences itself as something without start or stop, as that which just *is,* a mirror over which all sorts of images and fantasies are tumbling nonstop. This manner of self-awareness must have given rise to the concept of spirit or soul, really just names for consciousness as it experiences itself to be an independent "isness" working and perceiving *through* the body. And if the soul is not the same as the body, perhaps it can find the way back to a primordial unity with its origins, which the body cannot.

Yet, while traditional man is generally clear on the validity of the soul concept, his experiences of his own and other souls are tremendously mixed. The spirits of the deceased (like his own) seem sometimes dark and vindictive emotional forces, sometimes calm and happy sprites around the hearth, sometimes in faraway paradisal realms. These inconsistent data are reflected faithfully in his convoluted ideologies and myths dealing with the soul and afterlife. Sometimes there is a belief in two souls, one which departs this world for good to go to an alternative one, and another soul which troublesomely remains behind to exact worship, speak through mediums, and exercise vengeance on those who do not honor it enough.

Other peoples postulate three, four, or even more souls with separate destinies that make up the complexity which is a human being. Still others postulate several different stages in the afterlife to account for the different potentialities of soul they intuit. These may include remaining around the place of burial for a few days after death, inhabiting the family shrine for some longer period, going to a heavenly world, passing (or failing) various tests and judgments, and later reincarnation in this world.

A simple expression of soul belief is that of the Langalanga, a Melanesian people of Malaita in the Solomon Islands, who follow a life of fishing and tuber agriculture. An anthropologist who studied the Langalanga reports that they have no explicit cosmology or creation myth at all, nor belief in any supreme gods. They acknowledge only circulating spirits who indwell successively animals, ancestors, and men. People, they say, have two souls; after death the *agalo* remains around the village; the *kwasi* goes to an island on the east end of Guadalcanal. The latter is the Langalanga heaven, but it is just like the world the deceased left. Once there, the kwasi has no contact with his relations back in Malaita, but lives on this isle of the dead just as he did before, building houses and tilling gardens. The ''souls'' of his possessions go with him after death.

The agalo souls, on the other hand, become ancestral spirits, and receive all the reverence and attention their kind always exacts. They can speak through mediums. If they feel neglected, they can cause people to fall ill. In this circumstance, the medium will probably report that the agalo wants a pig. The ritual sacrifice of pigs is a transaction between men and the ancestral spirits; with each twist of the rope used to strangle the victim an ancestor's name is called out. Certain persons in the society are believed to have powers of witchcraft; this depends on power received from an agalo. There are also nonancestral inhabitants of the invisible world, however; the sharks in the bay are thought to be quasi-divine protectors, and offerings are made to them of the entrails of slaughtered pigs.[8]

Here is another concept. On Yap in the South Pacific, it was said that after the individual has died, his soul lingers in the neighborhood of the burial until the body decays. Only then is the soul light enough to ascend to heaven. Heaven is presided over by Yalafath, creator of the world. He has a big house in heaven, but it is actually only a sort of hotel, for when the soul has been in heaven long enough for its earthly odors to wear off, it returns to earth as a ghost. Then the ghost may punish people who did not honor its burial sufficiently.[9]

The heavenly world is often thought to be in a definite geographical direction, commonly that of the setting sun: the coast of Guadalcanal; the Western Isles, Avalon, or the Hesperides of European lore. In any case, going there is a transition amounting to rebirth into a state comparable to that of humankind before the primal separation from the time of origins, and so the soul's great journey is also the way

[8]Matthew Cooper, ''Langalanga Religion,'' *Oceania,* XLIII, no. 2 (December 1972),.113–122.

[9]James G. Frazer, *The Belief in Immortality,* 3rd ed. (London: Macmillan and Co., 1924), pp. 165–69.

back. Here is the account of the soul's progress to the Other World, according to the Thompson River Indians of British Columbia:

> The country of the souls is underneath us, toward the sunset; the trail leads through a dim twilight. Tracks of the people who last went over it, and of their dogs, are visible. The path winds along until it meets another road which is a short cut used by the shamans when trying to intercept a departed soul. The trail now becomes much straighter and smoother, and is painted red with ochre. After a while it winds to the westward, descends a long gentle slope, and terminates at a wide shallow stream of very clear water. This is spanned by a long slender log, on which the tracks of the souls may be seen. After crossing, the traveler finds himself again on the trail, which now ascends to a height heaped with an immense pile of clothes—the belongings which the souls have brought from the land of the living and which they must leave here. From this point the trail is level, and gradually grows lighter. Three guardians are stationed along this road, one on either side of the river and the third at the end of the path; it is their duty to send back those souls whose time is not yet come to enter the land of the dead. Some souls pass the first two of these, only to be turned back by the third, who is their chief and is an orator who sometimes sends messages to the living by the returning souls. All of these men are very old, grey-headed, wise, and venerable. At the end of the trail is a great lodge, moundlike in form, with doors at the eastern and the western sides, and with a double row of fires extending through it. When the deceased friends of a person expect his soul to arrive, they assemble here and talk about his death. As the deceased reaches the entrance, he hears people on the other side talking, laughing, singing, and beating drums. Some stand at the door to welcome him and call his name. On entering, a wide country of diversified aspect spreads out before him. There is a sweet smell of flowers and an abundance of grass, and all around are berry bushes laden with ripe fruit. The air is pleasant and still, and it is always light and warm. More than half the people are dancing and singing to the accompaniment of drums. All are naked but do not seem to notice it. The people are delighted to see the newcomer, take him up on their shoulders, run around with him, and make a great noise.[10]

Several important motifs are apparent in this vivid passage—the western location of the land of the dead, the barriers to be crossed, the guardians, the possibility of some souls being sent back, and of communication between the two worlds. Note especially the paradisal quality of the Other World with its overtones of return to the spontaneity and innocent sensuality of childhood, a theme reinforced by nudity reminiscent of the Garden of Eden.

Thus in the lore of primitive religion, the mysterious world of the ancestors and the dead impinges upon that of the living, and confrontation with death is near the heart of religion. In fact, the oldest clear evidence of human religiosity is in connection with the problem of death, its grisly awesomeness and the power of those who have passed through it yet are believed to live, and the matter of the trails the dead must take.

The earliest human skeletal remains in China and Europe, 300,000 and 100,000 years old respectively, indicate separation of the skull from the body of the deceased. In the Chinese case, that of Peking man, the skulls of the dead may have

[10]H. B. Alexander, *North American Mythology* (Boston: Marshall Jones Co., 1916), pp. 147–49.

Stonehenge, on Salisbury Plain, England.

been carried about as a talisman by the living. In the European, they were preserved at a shrine. (These discoveries have given rise to rather lurid theories of cannibalism and headhunting. But other anthropological reflection has pointed out that these practices are generally found only in fairly advanced levels of culture, being mostly associated with the world of archaic agriculture. The closest parallels of these prehistoric usages may be among very primitive peoples such as the Andaman Islanders, who carry the skulls of their dead about with them as an expression of faithfulness and attachment, and because the dead are believed to be benevolent spirit-helpers.[11])

The same concern for the dead is shown by later remains in which the bones are stained with red ochre dye. The famous "Red Lady of Paviland" found near Swansea, Wales—actually a man about 25 years old who was buried some 18,000 years ago—is a skeletal remain with bones of a rich deep rust color. Associated with the skeleton are rods and rings made from the ivory of mammoth tusks, and seashells of the same red ochre. Perhaps the shells were symbolic food for use on the road to the Other World. Red, the color of blood and life, probably indicates hope for new life. The same hope doubtless lies behind the frequent practice of burial in a crouched, fetal position—a return to the womb of mother earth in expectation of rebirth.

[11]Johannes Maringer, *The Gods of Prehistoric Man* (New York: Alfred A. Knopf, Inc., 1960), pp. 17–22.

The Sacred in Sky and Soul

This journey requires its gateways and milestones, and human society requires its monuments. As technology advanced, maps of this invisible world took more and more impressive shape in architecture and sacralized geography. Thousands of years later, also in Britain, circular symbols appear, built about 1800–1400 B.C. At Stonehenge in southern England, bluestones up to 30 feet high have been arranged in two concentric circles surrounding two horseshoe-shaped series of stones. The circles orient man to the physical universe, for they have a definite astronomical significance—the entrances to the circle are directed toward sunrise at the summer solstice and sunset at the winter, as well as other celestial events.

At the same time, they are landmarks on the map of the invisible world. The Other World and the astronomical cosmos blend into one whole. Stonehenge has a relation to the dead, and the Other World to which the dead go. Burials and cremations have been found at the site. Moreover, the Stonehenge arrangement contains five trilithions, or sets of three stones with two upright and one laid across the tops to form an arch; these may represent a burial cairn with five chambers, or ritual doorways to another realm.

Like the Great Pyramid of Egypt, Stonehenge can be seen as a scientific instrument of the most sophisticated sort known to the culture and a religious temple combined. It is as if a cyclotron or a Mount Palomar Observatory were united with a cathedral, and the rituals of worship were inseparably blended with the procedures of observation to express a unified religioscientific world view.[12]

Primitive cosmic religion places mankind in the universe as a part of a pattern or set of cycles. It draws up a map of the invisible world, which makes the cosmos a home for mankind, a place where we are supposed to be, as a segment of a great family of forces and spirits. The point of all its symbols and festivals is to *demarcate* the currents and eddies in the stream of space and time, and so show that there is a pattern. This is well illustrated in the words, also about circles, which an American Indian is recorded as speaking:

> You have noticed that everything an Indian does is in a circle, and that is because the Power of the World always works in circles, and everything tries to be round. In the old days when we were a strong and happy people, all our power came to us from the sacred hoop of the nation, and so long as the hoop was unbroken, the poeple flourished. The flowering tree was the living center of the hoop, and the circle of the four quarters nourished it. The east gave peace and light, the south gave warmth, the west gave rain, and the north with its cold and mighty wind gave strength and endurance. This knowledge came to us from the outer world with our religion. Everything the Power of the World does is done in a circle. The sky is round, and I have heard that the earth is round like a ball, and so are all the stars. The wind, in its greatest power, whirls. Birds make their nests in circles, for theirs is the same religion as ours. The sun comes forth and goes down again in a circle. The moon does the same, and both are round. Even the seasons form a great circle in their changing, and always come back again to where they were. The life of a man is a circle from childhood to childhood, and so it is in everything where power

---

[12]Work by Alexander Marshack has indicated that time notations based on the lunar periods, probably used to set festivals, go back at least 25,000 years into the Upper Paleolithic. See Alexander Marshack, *The Roots of Civilization: The Cognitive Beginnings of Man's First Art, Symbol, and Notation* (New York: McGraw-Hill Book Co., 1972).

moves. Our tepees were round like the nests of birds, and these were always set in a circle, the nation's hoop, a nest of many nests, where the Great Spirit meant for us to hatch our children.

But the Wasichus [white men] have put us in these square boxes. Our power is gone . . .[13]

Very often the circle includes pre-existence, and so belief that the journey to the Other World and return back is a cycle repeated over and over obtains in some societies, like Yap. Among the Australian Aborigines, life really begins in the Dream-time—the Other World, which is at once the original time of creation, the sky, where one goes in dreams and visions, the home of the departed, and in a more partial and mystical sense the time of sacred festivals and dances.

In the Dream-time of the beginning, godlike ancestors deposited the souls of all the living in "spirit wells" near mundane watering holes, or else the souls came from a great serpent underground, or down from the sky above. In any case, they are sent into the world from a sacred, Dream-time origin, and are received by the earthly parents in a mystical experience. Birth, however, is like a "fall" from the Dream-time, for it is obviously unsatisfactory without the dream side, which has now become ephemeral and invisible. So the Dream-time is made visible in myths, in the rock paintings that illustrate the sites of the spirit wells with pictures of the Dream-time folk, by association of social units with totem animals who are links to the invisible world, and by ceremonial. Again we see how the three forms of religious expression working together construct a strong link between this world and the Other, mapping out the latter and making it "visible" in rite, symbol, and sacred geography. Above all, through the series of initiatory ceremonies, which mark particularly the life of a boy and man, one moves further and further back into the Dream-time and receives its power so as to effect an ultimate transfer to it after physical death—whether permanently or as part of a continuing cycle the Australians seem to have no fixed doctrine.[14]

But we must now move from an abstract consideration of such spiritual beliefs as the soul, the Other World of the gods and the dead, passage between this world and that, and cycles of life and death, to see how they are experienced in such typically fundamental institutions as initiations and shamanism.

INITIATIONS

For most primitive cultures, life is a series of initiations, and it is through them that its most meaningful signs of status are bestowed, as well as the deepest mysteries of the ultimate meaning of human existence revealed. Birth and death are themselves initiatory experiences and so part of the series; the great ceremonial initiations enhance, ratify, recapitulate, and prepare one for what is imparted by these two deepest of all sacred mysteries.

[13]John G. Neihardt, *Black Elk Speaks* (Lincoln: University of Nebraska Press, 1961), pp. 198–200. Copyright © John G. Neihardt, 1932, 1961. Reprinted by permission of John G. Neihardt Trust.

[14]See A. P. Elkin, *The Australian Aborigines,* 3rd ed. (Garden City, N.Y.: Doubleday and Co., 1964), pp. 168–71, and Mircea Eliade, *Australian Religions: An Introduction* (Ithaca: Cornell University Press, 1973), especially pp. 64–65.

Birth is like a repeat of the primal "fall," and death—if well handled—a return to what was before the fall. Every stage between these two, then, is a progressive reversal of the fall. The earlier initiations of boys and young men, therefore, are fundamentally repeats of the ordeal of birth, as it were to do right this time what was done wrong the first time. Later initiations to higher degrees by older men may show them becoming more and more spirits and terrifying ancestors, and also more directly impart to them the secrets and powers they will need to pass the guardians of the Other World.

Appropriately, initiation is a painful trial, like birth and death. Among the Papuans about Finsch Harbor in New Guinea, the initiation ceremony for all youths was held every ten to eighteen years, and the boys who underwent it ranged in age from four to twenty. The central feature, as in many such rites around the world, was circumcision, or more exactly a ritual death and redemption of which circumcision is a lasting token.

At the appointed time, the young candidates are taken by the men of the tribe into the forest. The bull-roarers—flat elliptical pieces of wood, which when twirled make an unearthly roaring sound—are booming. Significantly, the word *balum* means both bull-roarer and ghost. The women of the tribe look on from a distance, anxious and weeping, for they have been told the boys are to be eaten by a balum or ghostly monster, who will release them only on condition of receiving a sufficient number of pigs. The women have therefore been fattening pigs since the ceremony was announced, and hope they will be adequate to redeem their sons and lovers. There must be one pig for each initiate.

Australian Aboriginal rock painting of female spirit.

Deep in the forest, the boys are taken to a secret lodge designed to represent the belly of the monster. A pair of eyes are painted on the entrance, and roots and branches betoken the horror's hair and backbone. As they approach he "growls"—the voice of more hidden bull-roarers.

The pigs are sacrificed and eaten by the men and boys, for the monster demands only their "souls." The boys enter the lodge and undergo the circumcision operation. They remain in seclusion three or four months living in that long hut, inside the "monster." During this time they weave baskets and play two sacred flutes said to be male and female and to be married to each other. No women may see these flutes, and they are employed only during such sacred seasons as this.

At the end of the seclusion period, the boys return to the village, but in a special manner which bespeaks festival and rebirth. They are first taken to bathe in the sea, and then are elaborately decorated with paint and mud. As they go back to the village, they must keep their eyes tightly shut. An old man touches each on the forehead and chin with a bull-roarer. They are then told to open their eyes, and then they may feast and talk to the women.[15]

Arnold van Gennep, in his classic work *The Rites of Passage,* demarcates three stages in typical rites of transition—ceremonials that handle crossing territorial boundaries, pregnancy and childbirth, marriage, funerals, and enthronements, as well as formal tribal initiations. Van Gennep divides rites of passage into three parts: separation, transition, and reincorporation. The rite of separation is evident in the taking of the boys into the woods with the bull-roarers booming and the women weeping—gestures of separation forever from a former state of life, like a death. The stage of transition, also called *limen,* liminality, or marginality, is perhaps the most mysterious and interesting of all the stages. A period passes in the heart of a rite of transition when the subject is in a cut-off, sacred, yet powerless and perhaps hidden state, divorced from his past but not yet incorporated into his future. This is the state of the New Guinea initiates after they have entered the jaws of the monster and are living for several months in the hut which is his body, playing the mysterious flutes. Finally, there is the stage of reincorporation, evidenced by the great procession of the boys, with eyes shut, back to the village, and followed by feasting and talking with women.[16] Victor Turner has recently explored further the role of the liminal state in both archaic and modern society. He develops in particular one important aspect of liminality—those persons, from monks to clowns, for whom the sort of sacred and free and powerless separation which the initiate transits through becomes a *permanent* way of life.[17]

Another important element of the New Guinea initiation is the implied antagonism betwen the sexes. A desire to deceive the women about what is going on, and so to make fools out of them, appears to be even more blatant than the deception of the boys, who are soon enough brought into mysteries of which the women must never have knowledge. The women—whether they are really fooled or not—must act as though they honestly think their boys are in danger of the monster. (Of

[15]Frazer, *Immortality,* pp. 250–54.

[16]Arnold van Gennep, *The Rites of Passage* (Chicago: University of Chicago Press, 1960).

[17]Turner, *Ritual Process.*

course, there is real danger—some boys do not survive infection from the circumcision operation, and are said to have failed the test and been taken by the monster.)

Moreover, the desire on the part of the men to enact institutionally and ritually what women *do* naturally and biologically—give birth—is evident. One wonders how much of all culture has psychological roots in masculine desire to emulate feminine birthgiving through artificial creation—ritual, art, architecture, science, as well as tribal initiation. In the archaic initiation of boys, birth symbolism is sometimes extremely pronounced—the novices may literally crawl through the legs of the men in imitation of birth; subincision, or the making of ritual wounds on the boys in imitation of female anatomy, may be practiced.[18] It is as though by appropriating more and more female as well as masculine power—through these rites, through the sacrifice of pigs provided by the women—one acquires a sort of invincible hermaphrodite quality that will prevail in this world and the next.

In the New Hebrides island of Malekula, where a similar Melanesian culture obtains, the men spend their lives undergoing a series of higher and higher initiations, as they are able to obtain the requisite pigs (raised by the women) for sacrifice and feast. These achievements are memorialized in the imperishable tusks of the boars, and by wooden markers like totem poles in the courtyard of the men's lodges; these become ancestral gods. By the spiritual power of the pigs a man is enabled to pass the toils of Lehevhev, the terrible spider woman who guards the road to the Other World. In the highest of these degree-rites the initiates are garbed in masks and ghostly white webbing, as though they were already sacred ancestors with the dread power of one who has passed from death into unearthly life.

Besides these tribal rites there are also special individual initiations. For some peoples, in fact, the initiation of all young men was more individualized than in New Guinea; the Pawnee young man was expected to remain alone in the bush until he personally received a dream or vision of his guardian spirit. There are also particular sacred individuals, especially kings and shamans, who are set apart by distinctive movements of the sacred.

Those who have seen the coronation of the British sovereign or read about it will recall that this rite also demarcates clearly van Gennep's three stages. There is separation when the monarch leaves the palace for Westminster Abbey in an ancient coach. The liminal state is reached when the king or queen kneels alone before the altar during the long and awesome celebration of the liturgy by the Archbishop of Canterbury. Finally, the new sovereign is "reincorporated" into the structure of society with his or her new role as he or she is proclaimed king or queen, and returns to the palace amid cheering throngs.

One of the most archaic royal rituals to persist into the modern world is the accession rite, called the *Daijo-sai,* of the Japanese emperor. At the Harvest Festival of the first full year of his reign, the new sovereign proceeds to an area on the grounds of the old imperial palace in Kyoto, where two identical thatch lodges of prehistoric style have been constructed, together with auxiliary buildings. Toward evening, he enters a hall called the *kairyu-den* ("eternal flow hall") where he bathes and puts on a long white robe of linen. He advances in a solemn procession to the

[18]See Bruno Bettelheim, *Symbolic Wounds* (Glencoe, Ill.: The Free Press, 1954).

two lodges, his feet bare and treading on a mat unrolled before him and rolled up behind him. He enters the two lodges, one before midnight and one about 2 a.m., performing in each a long-secret rite. He offers food and rice wine to unnamed deities, and sips a bit of the wine himself. After the solemn nocturnal ceremony, the emperor and court enjoy several days of banquets, whose entertainments and customs became progressively less sacred and more amusing and secular.[19] Once again, the three stages of a rite of transition stand out clearly, as does the creation of an alternative world by architecture and rite where contact with gods is possible and the social structures of this world are validated.

SHAMANS

There are those who are singled out by the divine to receive special ecstatic powers for dealing with spiritual things. These are the persons called shamans or, less precisely, medicine men or witch doctors. In the Thompson River Indian account of the road to the Other World, we read that the deceased saw special paths the shamans took to the Other World to intercept lost souls. This is characteristic, for the shaman above all is one who, on subtle planes of perception or soul travel, moves freely between this world and the other. He knows the geography and dynamics of the invisible world. Thus he can serve as guide of the souls of the dead, and also as healer and interceder.

The word "shaman" is Siberian, and it is in that land of endless birch and evergreen forests, broad rivers, cobalt skies, and dark subzero winters that its classic form is found, although shamanism, or closely related phenomena, appears in most parts of the earth. Indeed, it could be argued that shamanism is the prototype of much of the religious world.

Let us look at a few shamanistic performances, and try to understand what some of shamanism's common features are.

The Altaic shaman in Siberia wore brown leather and elaborate decorations of metal discs, birdfeathers, and colored streamers. He entranced himself by beating a drum rhythmically for hours, sitting astride a bench covered with horsehide or a scarecrow-goose, and the beat of the drum was the pounding of the hooves or wings of these spirit-steeds as they bore him to the Other World. Finally, the shaman would dismount and, flushed with ecstasy, climb nine steps notched in a tree trunk. At each stage in the ascent he would relate the difficulties of his journey, address the gods of that level of the heavens, and report what they were telling him about coming events. Some of the episodes were comic, such as a burlesque hare hunt on the sixth level. The shaman's scenario is generally enacted with a rich dramatic sense for the right combination of spectacle, mystery, suspense, comic relief, and exalted sentiments. When the Altaic shaman had gone as high as his power permitted, he concluded with a reverent prayer of devotion to Bai Ulgan, the high god, and collapsed, exhausted.[20]

[19]See Robert S. Ellwood, Jr., *The Feast of Kingship: Accession Ceremonies in Ancient Japan* (Tokyo: Sophia University, 1973).

[20]Mircea Eliade, *Shamanism: Archaic Techniques of Ecstasy,* trans. Willard R. Trask, Bollengen Series, LXXVI, Bollengen Foundation (1964), 190–97.

Peter Freuchen, in his *Book of the Eskimos,* describes a shaman's seance he attended.[21] He emphasizes that the shaman, named Sorqaq, prepared seriously for the exercise by fasting and meditation on the cliffs. Sorqaq was to contact a god who dwelt beneath the earth to find out why the tribe had been suffering a series of accidents. Nonetheless, he opened the session by telling those who attended that they were a bunch of fools for coming, that nothing he did would have any truth in it, and so forth. The audience responded with cries of belief and encouragement. The shaman then sat naked upon a sealskin on a ledge in the igloo, and his assistant bound him tightly with sealskin thongs. His drum was placed beside him. The lights, except for one small flame, were put out.

Then Sorqaq began to sing, and his voice grew louder and louder. Soon it was accompanied by the beat of the drum, and the rustle of the sealskin—which seemed to be flying about the room. The awful din rose to a crescendo, with everyone joining in the singing. Sorqaq's own voice became fainter and seemed to be coming from farther and farther away.

The assistant suddenly put on the lights. Freuden noticed that the audience was ecstatic—eyes gleaming, bodies twisting to the music of the shaman's song—like participants in a revival. Even more remarkable, the shaman himself was gone, his place on the ledge empty save for the drum and sealskin! Among the crowd the spiritual intensity grew, with people experiencing seizures and speaking in strange words, including a special seance language in which persons and objects are referred to by alternative terms.

Then the assistant announced that the shaman was returning. People went back to their seats and the lights were put out. The assistant told with what difficulty Sorqaq was swimming through the rocks beneath. His voice was heard growing in volume, and once again the drum sounded louder and louder, and the sealskin crackled in the air. The room quieted after Sorqaq returned, and he was seen once again seated on the ledge tightly bound in straps. He told what he had learned: "To avoid more tragedies, our women must refrain from eating of the female walrus until the winter darkness returns!" (Freuchen remarks that because they are considered basically unclean, it is almost always against the women that the taboos are directed.)

After the performance, Sorqaq said to Freuchen, "Just lies and tricks. The wisdom of our ancestors is not in me. Do not believe in any of it!"

These accounts should make evident that the shaman is distinguished from other types of religious specialists, such as the priest or the sorcerer, in part by the dramatic quality of his performance with its semispontaneous appearance and the fact that the shaman seems to, and often does, undergo the psychic and physical changes attendant upon altered states of consciousness. Anthropological work has brought to light that taking hallucinogenic plants, such as the fly-agaric mushroom in central Asia and plants of the datura family in the Western Hemisphere, is a part of shamanism in many cultures.[22] The altered state of consciousness and the visions of

[21]Peter Freuchen, *Book of the Eskimos* (New York: Fawcett World Library. 1965), pp. 168–71.

[22]See, for example, Peter L. Furst, ed., *Flesh of the Gods: The Ritual Use of Hallucinogens* (New York: Praeger, 1972); Michael J. Harner, ed., *Hallucinogens and Shamanism* (London and New York: Oxford University Press, 1973); and Barbara G. Myerhoff, *Peyote Hunt: The Sacred Journey of the Huichol Indians* (Ithaca: Cornell University Press, 1974).

the shaman, however valid spiritually in the context of the culture, are often facilitated by the well-known effects of these drugs.

That is not the case with all shamanism, however. Trance-induced altered states of consciousness, in which radically nonordinary perception and audition are obtained, are quite possible without the aid of drugs. Trances of this sort are often accompanied by violent trembling, swelling, discoloration, and berserk behavior, as well as divine utterance. Sometimes seemingly superhuman strength is attained; Tibetan shamans have been reliably reported to be able to twist strong steel swords into knots while in this state. But afterward the performer will be so exhausted as to sleep for days, and such shamans are said, in fact, to be generally short-lived.

The shaman is also distinguished by a related factor, the nature of his "call." Other religious functionaries may have entered into their role by heredity, choice, or apprenticeship. But in the case of the shaman, although these factors may play a part, the important point will generally be that he has passed through a powerful spiritual ordeal of selection, testing, and "remaking" by divine beings themselves. Above all, he will probably receive an assisting spirit, who gives him supernormal powers and control over other spirits.

Here is a vivid account of the manner in which the Eskimo shaman received his power:

> The *angakok* consists of a mysterious light which the shaman suddenly feels in his body, inside his head, within the brain, an inexplicable searchlight, a luminous fire, which enables him to see in dark, both literally and metaphorically speaking, for he can now, even with closed eyes, see through darkness and perceive things and coming events which are hidden from others: thus they look into the future and into the secrets of others.
>
> The candidate obtains this mystical light after long hours of waiting, sitting on a bench in his hut and invoking the spirits. When he experiences it for the first time "it is as if the house in which he is suddenly rises; he sees far ahead of him, through mountains, exactly as if the earth were one great plain, and his eyes could reach to the end of the earth. Nothing is hidden from him any longer; not only can he see things far, far away, but he can also discover souls, stolen souls, which are either kept concealed in far, strange lands, or have been taken up or down to the Land of the Dead.[23]

One could move from this kind of experience to that of, say the Buddha at the moment of his enlightenment, when it was not a question of an illuminating spirit entering him from outside. Rather, for the Buddha, all gods and spirits fell into secondary roles beside the pure, radiant, conceptless, horizonless, marvelous openness in which all thought of self vanishes. Reportedly, one who attains Buddha-consciousness, or Hindu liberation, is able to see all the intricacies of all lives past and present, and to be in seamless subjective union with horizonless infinity.

The process of becoming a shaman is sufficiently violent to cause Mircea Eliade to speak of it as an "initiatory psychopathology." The future shaman's career begins typically with a "call" from a god or spirit, perhaps the primordial master

---

[23]*Shamanism: Archaic Techniques of Ecstasy,* by Mircea Eliade, trans. by Willard R. Trask, Bollingen Series LXXVI. Copyright © 1964 by Bollingen Foundation. Reprinted by permission of Princeton University Press from pages 60–61.

shaman, in the form of "voices" or strange impulses or seizures. For a time, unable to escape from a supernatural world for which he is not prepared, he may be tormented by cruel spirits in his head and body. He may suffer extremes of anxiety and fey rapture, wander about the village in a dissociated manner, have fits, be unable to eat or drink, even become criminal. He is, in a word, what we would call insane.

But in terms of his own culture, he is one marked by the gods as a possible candidate for a mighty vocation. However much he may want merely to be "normal," that can never be; the gods will not let their fingering-out of a person be scorned. He must either serve them, or face the unspeakable terrors of their punishment in mind and body.

Even so, he will not necessarily succeed in becoming a shaman. There is a great test that lies ahead. He is already in the spiritual world. Now he must acquire power to master it. He has no choice; he must master it, or it will destroy him. He can acquire this power only with the help of one who has it. He must find an initiator, either a great shaman in this world or a supernatural ally in the other, who will impart to him the techniques of control. In our terms, he must conquer his sickness and make it work for him. It must continue to produce knowledge-giving visions of the spiritual world, or the subjective world if one prefers, but only when he requests it to do so. His must become an insanity he can turn on and off at will, so as to learn the things only this state can teach but not be enslaved by it.[24]

To arrive at this kind of control the novice must pass through a catharsis which is virtually a death and rebirth. Alone in the wilderness, in sickness, as aide to a senior shaman, he meets his crisis. Among the Eskimos it is said that the future shaman must take out all his bones and count them; among the Australians that his soft viscera must be replaced by organs of quartz.

But however exclusive his call, shamanism is not lacking the sociological dimension of religion. The future shaman's spiritual attack, private as it is, is also a phenomenon expected in his society, and has a conventional interpretation and resolution. Moreover, once the shaman has passed through his initiation, he has a role traditional in the society which frequently has great prestige.

However genuine the call, the role—partly because of the conventional expectations—is not without an element of showmanship or even fraud, as the Eskimo shaman Sorqaq intimated. Perhaps his point of view was the same as that of Quesalid, a shaman of the Kwakiutl Indians of British Columbia, who told the anthropologist Franz Boas the story of his life. Quesalid said that he started out as a skeptic and associated with shamans to learn their tricks and expose them. Invited to join with them, he learned plenty: sacred songs, how to induce trances and fits, how to produce seeming magical feats by sleight-of-hand, and much else. In the meantime, knowledge of his training spread, and he was invited by a family to heal a sickness.

Despite Quesalid's disbelief, he felt constrained to accept; the healing was a success. As more triumphs followed, word spread that he was a great shaman. Knowing such things as that the "sickness" he pretended to suck out of the ill

---

[24]See Eliade, *Shamanism*, and Andreas Lommel, *Shamanism: The Beginning of Art* (New York: McGraw-Hill Book Co., 1967), pp. 11–12.

person's body was actually made of down he had previously concealed in his mouth, Quesalid was at a loss how to interpret to himself what he was doing. Finally, he came to feel that the healings worked because the sick person "believed strongly in his dream about me," and he apparently felt that the deceptions were justifiable insofar as they helped people believe. Nonetheless, he proved the superiority of his method in competition with shaman colleagues, and was contemptuous of most other shamans as charlatans, saying he had only known one he thought was a "real shaman," who employed no trickery he could detect and who would not accept pay.[25]

Yet the shaman's mind is a convoluted, complex thing, a mixture of his own unusual psychology and community expectations. Perhaps one should take both his claims to marvelous powers and to being a fraud with equal caution. We noted in the case of the Eskimo shaman that his opening protestation that what he did was all lies and attenders were fools for believing in him had an obviously ritual quality about it—it was apparently a stage the seance had to go through. The disclaimer only evoked from the audience eager affirmations of belief and pleas to begin.

It may be, too, that in talking to visiting explorers and anthropologists, shamans do not always express the full extent of their belief in the religious reality of the shamanistic experience. Knowing quite well that the inquirer does not accept or understand that reality, the shaman conforms to what he thinks are the expectations, and makes himself appear clever and "modern" by exposing it all (confidentially) as a bag of tricks to one whose comprehension goes no further than this—just as he gives different explanations of convenience to his own people and shaman colleagues.

Many people—shamans included—would rather be considered clever charlatans than pious fools. Yet there is also evidence scattered through the accounts that shamans have possessed powers similar to those reported in Western psychical research, as well as genuine medical skills and techniques of psychotherapy,[26] and serve as important custodians of cultural lore—as knowers of the songs and poetry and myths of the people. They are creators of art and poetry *par excellance* from out of the depth of their experience with things of mind and sould.[27]

The shaman, then, is not to be disparaged. Claude Lévi-Strauss suggests that what he does is create an alternative world, one structurally just as plausible and internally consistent as the ordinary world, which his clients enter. In it his magic works because it is integral to that world, and in that world the suffering of a patient is also acceptable because it has a meaning, as witchcraft or initiation.[28]

[25]Franz Boas, *The Religion of the Kwakiutl, Columbia University Contributions to Anthropology*, X, part II (New York; 1930), 1–41. Summarized in Claude Lévi-Strauss, *Structural Anthropology* (Garden City, N.Y.: Doubleday and Co., 1967), pp. 169–73.

[26]See E. Fuller Torrey, *The Mind Game: Witchdoctors and Psychiatrists* (New York: Emerson Hall Publishers, Inc., 1972); Robert J. Beck, "Some Proto-psychotherapeutic Elements in the Practice of the Shaman," *History of Religions*, 6, no. 4 (May 1967), 303–27; and Robert S. Van de Castle, "Anthropology and Psychic Research," in *Psychic Exploration*, ed. Edgar D. Mitchell (New York: G. P. Putnam, 1974), pp. 269–87, with extensive bibliography.

[27]See Lommel, *Shamanism*.

[28]Lévi-Strauss, *Structural Anthropology*, pp. 181–201.

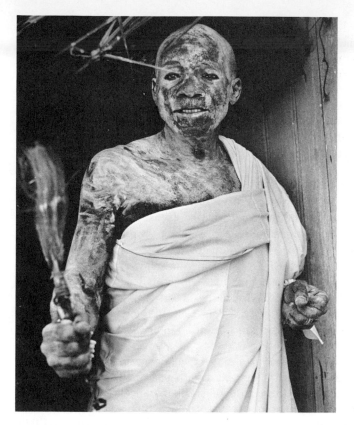

"Witchdoctor" of the Ewe tribe, Ghana. The magico-religious healers popularly called "witchdoctors" or "medicine men" are actually shamans or have shamanistic traits.

The shaman, moreover, seems to know that certain supports of his art are sleight-of-hand illusions, yet also does genuinely believe in his spirits and gods, and in his power to communicate with them and to heal. He does not think it wrong, therefore, to use a few deceptions on a technical level to create an atmosphere of the supernormal in which belief is facilitated, and his spirits can work more easily.

There are variations in shamanism. One major distinction is between the "traveling" shaman, like the Altaic and Eskimo already presented, who goes to the distant heavens or underworld in his trance. The other is the "possession" shaman who, as it were, draws the gods to him rather than going to them, being possessed like a medium by gods and spirits in his performance, and letting them speak through him.

A good example of the latter are the *miko,* or shamanesses, of Japan. Now disappearing, they played a substantial part in the popular religion of Japan in the past. They are found today mostly in the far northern part of the island of Honshu; every summer they gather there for a sort of convention on Mount Osore ("Mount Fear") on the upper tip of that island. The Japanese shamans of this type are all female, and what is more, are all blind or nearly so. All were initiated into the vocation of shamanizing as young girls. While it precluded marriage, unlikely for a blind girl in any case in traditional society, it did provide a respected place in the village for girls who otherwise would have had slim prospects.

Blind girls became apprentices of older shamanesses at six or eight years of age. After a strict training involving fasts, cold-water ablutions, observing taboos, and learning shamaness songs and techniques of trance and divination, they were initiated.

For this rite, the novice wears a white robe called the death dress. She sits facing her mistress and other shamanesses; these elders sing and chant formulae and names of deities. Suddenly the mistress cries, "What deity possessed you?" When the candidate gives the name of a Shinto god or Buddha or bodhisattva (who will thereafter be her main supernatural patron), the mistress throws a rice cake at her, causing her to fall onto the floor in a faint. The elders then dash water onto her head as many as 3,333 times. Then they lie beside her and revive her with body heat. When she comes to, she is said to be reborn; she exchanges the death dress for wedding apparel, and a traditional Japanese wedding—with the traditional exchanges of cups of sake nine times—is performed. The new shamaness is the bride, her deity the groom. Next a great feast of celebration follows, shared by relatives and friends of the new medium; she demonstrates her proficiency at communicating with spirits of the dead. For a week following, as a sort of divine honeymoon, she may live alone in a shrine of her deity.[29] Van Gennep's three stages of rite are beautifully evident in this scenario with its "death," rapture, and "reincorporation" feast.

While doing field work in Japan in 1966, the author visited a shamaness who consented to give me a "reading." One wall of the main room of her small house was taken up with altars, Shinto and Buddhist alike, reflecting the syncretistic nature of popular religion around the world. She sat on the floor facing the altars and sang in a sleepy, mystical tone as she swayed back and forth, going into a light trance. Then she called on the help of the sovereign gods, giving out a list of popular Shinto and Buddhist figures, and calling on the patrons of the local mountains and region. Next she received her modest payment, worked the 500-yen note in her hands slowly, and placed it on an altar.

After this, she called down the guardian deity of my family, whom she said was Fudo, a bodhisattva prominent in popular Buddhism. He gave me such warnings as that I was in danger of having a cold in the next ten days, that my wife would become ill in the middle of the year, and a doctor from the south would help her to recover. This directional emphasis is doubtless due to the influence of Taoist geomancy, or the plotting of auspicious and unlucky directions, on folk belief in both China and Japan.

Next the spirit of my grandmother was summoned. The miko had some diffidence about this request, since she had never before summoned a non-Japanese spirit. But she proceeded, and the shade of my American grandmother spoke in Japanese, and as though she were an oriental ancestral spirit.

She started by saying, "Except when it is difficult, offer me water. In this matter I am not happy. The good faith my grandson would show in offering me water as a parting gift would make me happy." She continued, however, to say that although a good doctor was not called when she died, she had had a long enough life and had no regrets; she was now happy in heaven, but wanted to be remembered

[29]Ichiro Hori, *Folk Religion in Japan* (Chicago: University of Chicago Press, 1968), pp. 203–6.

more by offerings of water, presumably at the small shrines of Buddhas and ancestral spirits found in a corner of a traditional Japanese home. She inquired about relatives, gave such advice as to watch out for pickpockets on vehicles, made a few minor prophecies, and promised to be with me.

The shamaness said nothing of much evidential value, but the session did provide a vivid insight into the shaman's role: to serve as a meeting ground between this world and the other, and as a reinforcer of popular spiritual lore. The altars and references to many faiths indicated that she was not tied to the systematic beliefs of any faith, but was rather alive to the presence and powers of gods and spirits of any sort. She knew, so to speak, the secret short-cut paths to the Other World, and seemed to link them. One got a feeling that (as for me) the real value of what she did was in the performance, with its atmosphere of mystery and belief in the survival of the deceased, rather than in the somewhat banal things the departed were made to say. In all this she was in the great tradition of shamanism.

ARCHAIC HUNTERS

Religion past and present concerns itself not only with crossing the bar to the Other World, but also with human needs here. Modern churches not talk only about salvation, but also offer prayers for harvest and good industrial relations. People have always viewed what is understood to be the source of their lives materially and subjectively to be at least a symbol, more likely the very presence, of the divine: the animal for hunters, the plant for agriculturalists, the king as giver of order for the ancient city and empire, the psychological sense of selfhood in the great ethical and salvation religions of individual decision and experience.

Thus the relation of the archaic hunter to his game is far from mere exploitation. It is an important part of his religious life; going into the field, tracking, and killing the animal is, so to speak, an act of interplay with spiritual forces and in this respect comparable to going to church or temple. Even though some tactics of the archaic hunter may seem cruel and ruthless, he sees his relation to the animal as that of one power or soul with another. To take the animal requires the consent of the animal in some sense, or that of his divine masters, due propition for the wrong done him, and proper magic to make it happen at all.

It is necessary to prepare spiritually for a great hunt. Ceremonies set the hunters apart. Rites such as drawing a picture of the animal sought and charming it strive to attract the game, even as apologies to the animal may be offered. As the hunters leave for the field, a sacred silence may be observed; while out, they may observe taboos of diet, remain continent, talk in a special vocabulary. They may stir up the animal's attention with a ritualized dance to draw it into an ambuscade, or wait for it by a watering hole with a yoga like quietude. When it is taken and devoured, the remaining bones may be treated with respect, for the animal's soul may return to see how its remains were treated, or mystically animate the bones to make them magical instruments of great potency. Killing, in other words, entails all sorts of responsibilities. This is a different world of man-animal relations from that of the modern slaughterhouse, or of many a modern sportsman with his high-powered rifle, telescopic sight, and desire for a "trophy."

Archaic hunters frequently believe in a divine "master of animals" who has control over the forest, or of a major species, and is able to "open" or "close" the forest, making game available or impossible to find. Among the Naskapi Indians of Labrador, for example, the Caribou Man is said to live in a world of caribou hair as white as snow and deep as mountains. These mountains comprise the immense house of the Caribou Man, who is white but dresses in black. He is surrounded by thousands of caribou two or three times normal size, both live caribou and caribou ghosts. The animals pass in and out of his caribou paradise, along paths lined several feet deep with hair, and shed caribou horns, as the Caribou Man releases them into our ordinary world for the proper use of man.

No human is allowed within 150 miles of the Caribou Man's house. But yet it is said that a hunter who really comes to know the ways of the caribou, so that he can virtually think like one and share its life, and who observes all the rules in his hunting, such as not taking too much game and respectfully using every part of an animal he does kill—such a man becomes almost one with the Caribou Man, and is always given what he needs.

When the Naskapi shamans address the animals, they say, "You and I wear the same covering and have the same mind and spiritual strength." This attitude governs their understanding of the animals which are so crucial to their survival in a harsh climate. Souls of animals circulate; the ghosts dwelling with the Caribou Man are waiting to be sent back into the world in fleshly bodies to be killed once again. It is therefore important that mankind live in reverent harmony with the biological and spiritual ecology of nature. Animals treated rightly will "play the game" and return to offer themselves as game to man again; those who are not will be an enemy, now and hereafter.[30]

A comparable view of life is reflected in the bear sacrifice of the Ainu, a hunting people who live on Hokkaido, the northernmost island of Japan. They believe that an Other World reflects this one virtually as a mirror image; life circulates between it and here. When it is night here it is day there, and so forth. From time to time the Ainu took a small bear cub. It was raised in their village and treated with great affection, like a spoiled child. When it had nearly reached adulthood, it was killed and sent back to the Other World in a long and elaborate rite, which was the greatest event in Ainu religious life. Before being sacrificed, the young bear was solemnly addressed. It was told that it had been sent into the world to be hunted, and to remember how much care and love was showered upon it. They begged it not to be angry, but to realize what an honor was being conferred upon it. They said that it was being sent back to its parents in the Other World, and asked it to speak well of the Ainu before them. Finally, they begged the bear to come back into the world to be sacrificed again.[31]

ARCHAIC FARMERS

The beginning of agriculture perhaps at several places some 10,000 years

[30]Frank G. Speck, *Naskapi* (Norman: University of Oklahoma Press, 1935), pp. 83–84.

[31]See John Batchelor, *The Ainu and their Folk-Lore* (London: Religious Tract Society, 1901), pp. 483–95, and Joseph M. Kitagawa, "Ainu Bear Festival (Iyomante)," *History of Religions,* I, no. 1 (Summer 1961), 95–151.

ago, and the subsequent spread of the practice of planting and harvesting, produced perhaps the most far-reaching religious changes of any transition in the history of religion. In many ways we are still living in the age set in motion by the development of agriculture: the modern city is an extension of the village of the first sedentary planters. At least until the present century, the average person almost anywhere in the world was a peasant living close to the soil and seasons, whose life and values were more like those of the archaic, Neolithic agriculturalists than of contemporary technological society. It may be that today, as we finally move away from the world shaped culturally by the peasant farmer's way of life into a truly urban world of computers and space travel, religious changes as marked as those that separate the archaic farmer from the hunter will eventuate.

What was the development of agriculture, and why was it so important? First of all, it may seem strange that it should have taken man something like a million years to make such a seemingly simple and obvious observation as that seeds could be planted in the spring to produce plants in the fall where one wanted them, and that animals could be kept around the house. Second, it may seem just as strange that such a clearly mundane, economic matter should have such far-reaching religious significance as appears to be the case. In fact, these paradoxes are very instructive of the profound relation between religion—or, if one prefers, world view—and culture, and conversely of the deep impact such things as economic system and social organization have on religious forms. Each does much to determine what is, at least psychologically, available in the other sphere.

That it took mankind so long to discover such a simple thing as planting, despite the fact that he always needed food and that trees and herbs were setting examples by "planting" themselves all around him every year, shows the close relationship between what one expects to see because of one's concept of the way the world is, and what one does, in fact, "see." For the hunter, with his magic and attention focused on the dramas of the animal and the shaman, his faith centering around the master of animals who opens and closes the forest, plants and especially tiny seeds would be merely part of the background of life, scarcely noticed and never studied. The relation between seeds and new plants, even of those whose fruits he took or which his animals ate, would not have occurred to him. (Who knows how many more clues to unknown but equally important aspects of reality lie all about us every day, but are not "seen"—and may not be for another million years—because our expectations about what there is to see closes our eyes even as we look directly at them!)

Every world view model opens up some possibilities and makes inaccessible others, which must wait for a different age. The world view of man as hunter made possible a deep appreciation of the mysteries of animal life and man's spiritual as well as material interaction with it. Yet so much did the hunter see the human state as that of a being who wanders about the face of the earth under the sky, going whither the guardians of the forest direct and accepting what they choose to give, that it could not occur to him to "see" the possibilities of sedentary habitation on one small piece of land deliberately worked for all it could produce. The difference in attitude is well expressed in the words of an American Indian who, when urged by the United States government to take up farming on a reservation, refused in these words:

You ask me to plow the ground! Shall I take a knife and tear my mother's bosom. Then when I die she will not take me to her bosom to rest. You ask me to dig for stone! Shall I dig under her skin for her bones? Then when I die, I cannot enter her body to be born again. You ask me to cut grass and make hay and sell it, and be rich like white man! But how dare I cut off my mother's hair?[32]

These words were spoken in the last century, but they are an echo of the Paleolithic mind. For they come from the world which was before the discovery of agriculture—and they give us a hint of why for many peoples the introduction of agriculture seemed to be a kind of loss of innocence, or "fall," and its practice a way of life which, if more productive than hunting, was also somehow haunted by a sense of guilt that agricultural man felt but could never quite express save in myth and rite.

We do not know exactly how the discovery of planting took place. With its development the religious focus shifts to earth and tilled field for its metaphors. It shifts to the model of the plant, which "dies" in the autumn to provide life for others, and then through the surviving seed comes back to life after a sort of burial in the spring.

But even though the introduction of agriculture resulted in considerable advancement in human living standards and culture, its discovery seems half-consciously often to have been regarded as an unlocking of forbidden knowledge, or to have involved a crime, a murder, which although it may have brought mankind wealth was spiritually a second "fall," putting humanity still further away from the gods and the primal innocence. (The second offense in the Bible after that of Eden was committed by Cain, tiller of the soil.) It will be said that the first plants were "stolen," or that the culture-hero who introduced agriculture was a trickster or rebel against the primal gods, or that the first plants came from the body of a slain but innocent maiden.

Thus in the Kojiki, the ancient Japanese mythology, it is related that the moon-god, Tsukiyomi, came down to earth and, going to the home of the food-goddess, requested something to eat. She gave him a meal, but he considered it all repulsive food. In his anger he slew the food-goddess, and found in her body all sorts of food plants of a new sort—rice, beans, and so forth. These Tsukiyomi took back to heaven, and the High Goddess Amaterasu said they would be for planting in the broad and narrow fields of heaven and earth.

A myth from Ceram, in Indonesia, relates the same experience to the *dema*, divine creators and helpers who lived with man in mythical times. It tells us that a hunter long ago found a coconut on the tusk of a boar he slew. That night he was commanded in a dream to plant it. Immediately it grew into a great tree, and shortly after a girl-child was born out of the tree after the hunter had spilled blood on it accidentally. He named her Hainuwele; in three days she was of marriageable age. Hainuwele then attended a great dance. For nine days she stood in the midst of the dancing area and passed out gifts to the dancers. Nonetheless on the ninth day the

[32]James Mooney, "The Ghost-Dance Religion and the Sioux Outbreak of 1890," *Annual Report of the Bureau of American Ethnology,* XIV, 2 (Washington 1896), pp. 721, 724. Cited in Eliade, *The Sacred and the Profane,* p. 138.

dancers dug a grave, put Hainuwele in it, filled it in, and continued by dancing on it.

When Hainuwele did not come home the next morning, the hunter sensed that she had been murdered. He found the body, cut it into pieces, and buried the pieces in different places. The interred pieces gave birth to previously unknown food plants. The hunter carried Hainuwele's arms to a leading dema, Satane, who took them into the dancing ground, drew a nine-spiral figure with them on the ground, and went to the middle of it. She said, "Since you have killed, I will no longer live here. I shall leave this very day. Now you will have to come to me through this door." Satane vanished through the mystic spiral into another mode of existence, and since then men have been able to meet her only after death—after the agriculture-giving murder, the demas have no longer lived in companionship with humans.[33]

Through stories like this, a grim basic principle came to affect the agricultural world view even more than the hunter's: the principle of death for life. Agriculture seems to have brought out a new and darker sense of the interconnection of death and life. The interconnection was not unknown to the hunter; the Naskapi believed that by a reverent treatment of the bones of a slain beast, the soul of the animal could be influenced to return and offer itself again. The Ainu believed that by sacrificing the precious bear cub they could persuade it and its relatives on the Other Side to return and replenish the supply of game.

But in agricultural society, all of this becomes more accentuated, often reaching a point which seems to us a grisly and perverse preoccupation with ritual death, animal or human. Religious headhunting, cannibalism, human sacrifice, and large-scale animal sacrifice are not genuinely primitive, but are usually associated with agricultural societies and are a part of the mentality to which it gave rise. The meaning of sacrifice for early agricultural society can be ascertained by a few examples.

The Naga tribes of northeast India, archaic agriculturalists, were famous as headhunters. Heads from neighboring tribes were sought on several occasions—to grace the funeral of a chief, to settle blood feuds, as an aspect of attaining manhood. A male could not marry until he had taken a head. Heads were presented at the harvest festival to placate the ancestral ghosts, and in some Naga tribes were placed on poles in the fields of growing crops, so that the life-power of the severed head would flow into the food plants. Headhunting was always undertaken with religious preparation; participants perform special rituals, and remain apart from women both before and after a hunt.[34]

The relationship of headhunting to agriculture is even clearer in the case of the Jívaro of the upper Amazon. A Jívaro male who had taken and shrunk a head would perform a dance with it and two female relatives, usually his sister and wife. He would hold the head in his outstretched hand, and they would hold on to him as they danced; this would empower these women to gain greater productivity from the crops and animals it was their province to tend. The dance seemed to make power

[33]Mircea Eliade, *Myth and Reality* (New York: Harper & Row Publishers, 1963), pp. 104–5.

[34]T. C. Hodson, *The Nàga Tribes of Manipur* (London: Macmillan and Co., 1911), pp. 104–5.

flow from the head through the husband, and then through his sister and wife into the crops. After this rite the head was no longer powerful and could be discarded like a squeezed lemon.[35]

The Khonds, a tribe in Bengal, offered a human victim to the earth goddess. The sacrificed person was supposed to be a volunteer, but was often bought from his parents as a child. After he had been set apart for this grim vocation, he lived happily for years. Like the Ainu bear cub, he was well treated and looked upon as especially consecrated. Finally, at a great festival, also marked by an orgy to promote fertility (another important aspect of agricultural religion), the victim was decked with butter and flowers. The tribesmen danced around him, praying loudly for good crops and weather. After he was drugged with opium and killed, the priests cut his body carefully into pieces; these were buried with great ceremony in the fields to promote fertility.[36]

In Fiji, a tuber agricultural society, captives taken in battle were killed as sacrifices. As in many other places, it was considered auspicious to place a human sacrifice under the foundations of a new building, or to kill a victim in connection with the launching of a new boat. Or, victims taken in war were baked and distributed throughout the victorious kingdom for a feast. Chiefs prided themselves on how many men they had eaten. In all of this, it is clear that human sacrifice means a transfer of power from the victim to the sacrificer or his works, a concept adumbrated in the murders that mark the beginning of agriculture in myth.

The sedentary character of agriculture in itself effected extensive changes in religion and culture. Because cultivation can sustain far more people than hunting and gathering on the same acreage, the advent of agriculture led to a marked increase in population in fertile regions. Inevitable results of this and related factors were the emergence of towns and cities, elaborate trade relationships, extensive division of labor—a flourishing agricultural economy could support not only the farmers, but also various tradesmen, craftsmen, rulers, priests, and even a few scholars and philosophers. Finally, the susceptibility of the agricultural routine to commerce, taxation, and control led to writing and the ancient empires in which civilization as we know it emerged. The religious products of this new economy were far-reaching: elaborate polytheism mirrored in the heavens the new extensive division of labor and the coming together of many tribes; sacred scriptures were a first result of writing; even more far-reaching was the result of the leisure of priests, scholars, and philosophers.

But now we are getting into the historical springboards of leaps out of primitive religion altogether. We must return to more immediate products of the discovery of the plant as miraculous life-giver. The sedentary farmer's closeness to the cycle of the plant made him extremely aware of the turning of seasons, especially planting and harvest. Out of this came such festivals as May Day and Halloween, associated with seedtime and harvest.

---

[35]Michael J. Harner, *The Jívaro: People of the Sacred Waterfalls* (Garden City, N.Y.: Doubleday and Co., 1972), p. 147.

[36]Mircea Eliade, *Patterns in Comparative Religion* (New York: Sheed & Ward, 1958), pp. 344–45.

Sedentary agriculture also gave women a new importance. Perhaps it was women who first discovered planting; in any case, it is common in archaic farming societies for the men to continue going out on hunts (for game or heads) while the women maintain the tillages around home, which actually supply a large part of the food. (Indeed, in many societies, possibility including modern Europe and America, the real economic base is domestic plants and animals, but the exploits of the hunt and war provide unique, though economically irrelevant, symbols of masculine status.)

Life in villages made the role of women as symbol of place, home, and social continuity important. More significant, the common association of earth and plant with mother and child made the spiritual power of the feminine grow with the growing importance of the soil and plant. Countless of the great goddesses of antiquity—Isis, Demeter, Ishtar, Kali, Amaterasu—clearly stem from the powerful agricultural mother of archaic farming culture.

These developments did not fail to produce reactions on the part of the men. Some of the men's initiations which are kept most secret from the women and which most obviously imitate women's mysteries, such as those from New Guinea, emerge from archaic planting societies. Sometimes these movements take extreme shape, in their reassertion of the remaining masculine virtues of group loyalty, strength, warlikeness, and spiritual skill, such as headhunting or the Leopard Society of West Africa. One men's society in Melaesian New Britain, the Dukduk, traveled from place to place with the function of enforcing the law in a rough-and-ready way wherever they landed.

An interesting penultimate reaction of masculine interests is megalithism, or the erection of giant stone monuments like Stonehenge. A period of making bigger and bigger constructions of this type as temples, observatories, or tombs occurs in many parts of the globe just before the breakthrough to ancient civilization. They are found in England, Malta, China, and Japan, and are succeeded by even greater edifices, such as the pyramids and zuggarets of Egypt, Mesopotamia, and Meso-America. It is as though the megalith were an extension of the custom in many men's lodges of erecting great totem-like figures as memorials of initiatory feasts and of ancestors.

The last overt reaction is what has been called the Patriarchal Revolution. At the onset of the ancient civilizations, whether in Egypt, Mesopotamia, India, or China, we see a vigorous assertion of masculine primacy in powerful sovereigns, and a corresponding suppression of feminine religious figures, whether queens, goddesses, or shamanesses. In China and Japan, we read of early edicts forbidding or limiting the work of various sorts of priestesses; the sexless asceticism of early yogins and Buddhist monks says the same thing, in different words, as the ascendancy of the pharoah who made Isis, the great goddess, his throne, but who identified himself with the male Ra and Osiris. We may ask ourselves whether now, after several thousand years, the pendulum is swinging again toward feminine values in religion and culture.

Three

LIFE AGAINST TIME

The Spiritual Paths of India

THE FACE OF INDIA

I first entered India by plane from Kabul. I left the windswept, mountain-guarded capital of Afghanistan with its icy rivers, mosques, and scarfed and tur-baned tribesmen bearing ancient rifles. I followed, at jet speed, the track over the famous Khyber Pass of countless invaders and pilgrims from the hard but exhilarating highlands of central Asia, where man seems an ant under vast mountains and cold skies but where magnificent horsemen and warriors are bred. With them, I dipped down into the heat-thick air of the Ganges basin. Long before, at the dawn of history, Indo-European cattle herders had taken the same trail, and after them Alexander and his Greeks, Huns, Turks, and the cavalry of the opulent Mughul emperors.

Indeed, in Afghanistan I had seen one evening the gardens of Babur, founder of the Mughul Empire, cool and leafy in a dramatic mountain glade, almost a fragment of a Muslim heaven, and recalled how after conquest had taken him to sultry Delhi the homesick monarch had yearned for this spot. Others had come over the passes for reasons other than physical spoils, for India has never failed to draw seekers of all sorts: Chinese monks seeking authentic scriptures of the Buddha, the Enlightened One, that son of India whose *dharma* had half-conquered the Middle Kingdom; God-intoxicated mystics of Islam who were partly to conquer India in turn.

As I winged over Pakistan and toward the Indian heartland, the dry, bare, scowling humps of the Hindu Kush Mountains were suddenly no more. It seemed the earth itself had dropped away, or been smoothed out with an iron like a sleeve. Flat fields of watery green, veined with placid rivers and ponds shimmering with heat, peeked through the lazy summer clouds. Here and there a straight narrow road or railway gave furtive hints of human planning and industry; more often were villages and towns sprawled out into amoebalike shapes.

Like me, most international travelers today arrive in India by air, landing at one of the teeming, steamy cities in the Ganges basin or along the coast—Delhi,

Dates	General Historical Context	Personalities and Movements	Sacred Literature
1500 AD	Bangladesh 1971— Independent India, Pakistan 1947— British rule 18th century–1947 Mughal Empire 1526–1761	Gandhi 1869–1948 Akbar r. 1556–1605 Nanak 1470–1540 fdr. of Sikhs	Guru Granth Sahib
1000 AD	Small states, many Muslim ruled Delhi sultanate (Muslim) 1211–1398	Kabir 1440–1518 Ramanuja, d.1137	
500 AD	Small states, largely Hindu	Growth of Hindu Tantrism Shankara 788–822 and Advaita Vedanta	Tantras
1 BC/AD	Gupta Empire in N. 320–540 ; classic Hindu period	Rise of Bhakti Decline of Buddhism in India Nagarjuna c. 150	Puranas Lotus Sutra and other later Mahayana sutras Bhagavad-Gita Laws of Manu
500 BC	Mauryan Empire 321–185 Invasion by Alexander 326	Ashoka r. 273–237 Buddhism prestigious First Buddhist Council c. 480 The Buddha 563–483	Yoga Sutras Heart Sutra and other early Mahayana writings Later Upanishads Buddhist Tripitaka Early Upanishads
1000 BC	Urban civilization beginning in Ganges basin; Kashi (Benares) prominant	Mahavira c. 540–468	Aranyakas Brahmanans
1500 BC	Consolidation of Indo-European supremacy in N. End of Indus Valley civilization		Later Vedas Rig Veda

Bombay, Calcutta. The air terminal will be located some miles out of the city, and the visitor will get his or her first impression of this fabled land riding in a bus or cab through a brief patch of countryside and then the messy environs of the metropolis.

At first, visitors may be quite disappointed, if their expectations about India were shaped by that genre of literature and art in which it emerges closer to Oz than this earth. They will see a dull flat land of green fields and brown dust or mud, depending on the season. The landscape will be suffused, if it is clear, with glaring heat and light, yet for all the brilliance the scenery seems to give a drained, faded impression, as though too much sun had leached it of certain stripes of color. The monotony of the softly verdant fields is broken only by clumps or rows of stolid trees, or slow muddy rivers, or the dull white of humped cattle, or tiny homes and shops all drab with dust, rust, and water stains.

As the visitor enters the city, another experience envelops him. He or she is lost amid labyrinthine crooked streets, open-air shops, houses of earth and corrugated metal, rain-browned official buildings. The narrow ways are thronged with oxcarts, horse-drawn wagons, countless bicycles, ancient buses and trucks, and once in a while a chauffered auto. On the most important streets as well as the byways, traffic may be backed up as a whitish inviolable cow ambles along or stands still, staring at the bustle of the human world with placid, indifferent eyes.

Above all there are people—women in many-hued saris, men in pants and pastel shirts, half-naked children. People are jammed into the streets like water being forced through a narrow funnel, jammed into buses and trains until they hang onto the railings and windows, crowding in and out of buildings, sometimes flaring up at each other, sometimes moving as though it were all a great dance.

On the surface, then, India may give an impression of drabness and grubbiness, not to mention the depressing signs of extreme poverty and hunger too often apparent. Families live and die in culverts or pallets on the streets; there are emaciated children and animals, thin adult faces deeply lined with toil and malnutrition, hawkers and beggars in public places. India is indeed a harsh land, given to cruel extremes of flood and draught, heat and cold. The virile climate racks the tired overworked soil year after year, and wastes the far too many people who swarm its face.

But for all that, one does not get the feeling of a sad, listless land or people. As soon as one's eyes and ears truly focus, vitality pops up everywhere like bright eyes from behind veils: craftsmen vigorously hammering metal, the glint of copper and brass in shops, lurid movie posters, the shining faces of children running and playing. Rather than listless, India is a country of strange and violent extremes. Everything—beauty and horror, life and death, rapture and anguish, love and callousness—goes to unbridled extremes here more than anywhere else; the beauty is more extravagant and the horror more horrible than in more temperate lands.

When I first left India after three weeks, I felt emotionally exhausted, as one does after passing through a major personal joy, crisis, or grief. India had been, in a real sense, all three. For life and beauty, I recalled warm eyes, flashing smiles, festivals full of colored streamers, bejeweled elephants and palenquins, vigorous and sinuous dances. For grief, there was a madwoman lying ranting in the middle of the highway, ignored or left to her dream by the passersby; the ragged begging children; the indigents sleeping on streets in their thousands night after night. India was not so much an interesting experience, in the casual sense, as an intense and unforgettable vision. As in a high dream, a door had opened a crack to let me glimpse something of an alternative world where the extreme potentials of human life in all directions—ecstasy, madness, depravity, extremes over which we in the West so often draw a veil—were starkly revealed.

Underlying these extremes and pervading them all is a great fact: the religion of India. For India has an intricate invisible geography. It runs like girders beneath the dusty surface. Everywhere one sees the signposts of religion's map of this invisible world—bright temples of such unusual shapes as to seem almost botanical, little wayside shrines smeared with ochre and sprinkled with flower petals, sacred rivers lined with pilgrims and smoking funeral pyres, holy men covered with white ash and painted markings and matted hair, cheap prints of startling divine beings with elephant heads or multiple arms. These religious outcroppings of the Other World are like jewels embedded in the ravaged face of India, like breakthroughs of a vein of emerald beneath a sere terrain.

UNDERSTANDING HINDUISM

The religion of the great majority of the people of India is Hinduism, and its guideposts of the invisible world have a distinctive flavor. The first real Hindu temple I visited was not in India, but on the island of Fiji, where many people from India have settled. The air was humid and heavy; the fane was by the side of a road, and was largely open-air. I first saw a large *lingam,* the half-phallic pillar which is the expression of Shiva. He is the absolute from which all cosmic energies, creative and destructive, derive; like sexuality, he is sheer life-force, able to give the most stupendous joy and excruciating pain, to make and rip apart; and set is the bearer of the genetic molecules, our closest organic equivalent to a deity's eternity.

In the presence of the lingam, I reflected that the Indian world view is deeply biological, tending always in the end to see the cosmos as a great living organism; it is not brain but virile sexuality which sometimes plays the God-part in this map of this organic cosmos, for in India it is finally not ratiocination that leads us to God-realization or grasping the oneness of the organism, but flashes of intense joy so sharp, or prolonged calm so steady, that we forget time and self-consciousness. This is what God is, too, whether under the name Shiva or some other, for in India God in his fullness has commonly been regarded as not different from what the consciousness of a man or woman is at its most starlike: God has there been called Being, Knowledge, Bliss—Sat-Chit-Ananda—all at once. The body has more pungent ways than thought to enact the One; why should they not become his symbols?

The lingam is not only sexual. Set as it is upon an oval base called the *yoni* (a name for the female organ), it could also be the flame in a lamp, or the axle of a wheel, or even the sun-packed heart of a spiral nebula—all symbols appropriate to

God. Nor is it only the sexual process that suggests the heat of God's work in the world, for the meaning of food also points to God—as does incense and jewels and everything that is, in its own way. But especially food, for we are all in the cycle of begetting and eating, and being begotten and eaten. The basic life processes are forms of oxidation, and thus forms of burning, but at a slower rate than flame—a realization represented for the Hindu by the sacrificial fire of the brahmin priests, and the funeral fire, which reduces one's physical side to ashes at the end. The ascetic, covering his body with white ash and letting the fire of his desires burn out, only speeds up the inevitable process for the sake of efficiency in letting the other side surface.

The Shiva lingam on Fiji was surrounded by open grillwork. Offering pans of colored rice were put in front of the stone pillar, attracting squadrons of birds who flew through the grill to peck at it. Outside, facing the lingam, was an image of Nandi, the bull who is always Shiva's animal companion. Behind the bull was Ganesha, the elephant-headed son of Shiva, a great deity in his own right as remover of obstacles worldly or spiritual. The base of his statue was piled with rotting fruit, the remains of many offerings.

Another temple building stood a little way off. At first I did not go near it, for a priest, naked above the waist, was leading several sari-clad ladies in worship, and I hesitated to intrude. I later returned to gaze into the cavelike sanctuary. My look met the oval white spectral eyes of a black figure. A single oil lamp scarcely more than outlined the shape, but the eyes in that gloom were incredibly luminous; they have followed me since. This was Krishna, the marvelous child, divine lover, and hero. His languid poses, his impudent charm, his effortless omnipotence fascinate India because they are like the beguiling paradoxes of God. He is God himself, and when he came to earth long ago to counter the decline of righteousness, he brought with him the whole sensuous and rapturous ambience of his highest heaven—slow rivers, gemlike flowers cascading everywhere, the frolics of the *gopis,* or milkmaids, who eternally love him, all under a moon as big as one remembered from an endless childhood summer evening.

Legs flexed and eyes half-closed, Krishna would sound his flute deep in the woods, and the gopis, burning with intermingled human and divine love, would leave their legitimate husbands and dash into the forest of delights to revel with the young god. For the devotees of Krishna agreed with the troubadors of the Age of Chivalry in the West that extramarital love is a closer simile than the nuptial tie for the love of the worshipper for God, since the former is a passion freely given for the beloved's sake with no heed for the cost in shame and suffering, while the latter was (in old India and medieval Europe) probably a legal bond arranged in childhood by the families without regard for the individual's feelings. Deep in the forest, Krishna would dance with the milkmaids, miraculously multiplying himself so that each would think she alone was his partner. Or he would hide himself and make the gopis seek for him, sorrowing, that the celebration might be all the greater when he was found. Or he would steal the devotees' clothes while they were bathing in the river, to have them show their pure trust by emerging naked.

As an adorable but mischievous infant, too, Krishna was given to transcendent

Main Themes of Religion in India

The Affirmative Way

Community temple
worship

Bhakti: Krishna,
Shiva, etc., worshipped
as means to liberation

Household worship

Tantrism

Laws of Manu

Kabir

Bhagavad-Gita

"Karma-yoga"

Buddhism

Jainism as a religion

Upanishads

Institution of
Sadhus or Holy Men

Shankara

Yoga

Jain monks

The Negative Way

The Cosmic and Social Order (Dharma)

The Individual's Liberation (Moksha)

Thematic Chart II. The religious traditions of India, especially Hinduism, can be comprehended if it is seen that, like other religions, they strive to cover two often-divergent objectives, sanctifying the social order and providing a path to inward liberation for individuals wholly absorbed in the spiritual quest. The means can be thought of as twofold also: these poles are also not unique to Indian experience, but perhaps each has never been expressed as extremely as there. The Affirmative Way means using things found in the realm of the many as means to the One; it is the employment of art, images, rites, temples, the social order, etc., to raise one's love to the infinite. The Negative Way is the ascetic way of denial; it finds the One by taking away all things that in their multiplicity and separateness are not the One.

pranks. He once ate some dirt, and when his irritated mother opened his mouth to check on it, she saw there the entire universe. He once stole some butter, but when his exasperated mother sought to tie him up in punishment, no matter how much rope she used it was never quite enough. In all this Krishna was as capricious and infatuating as God or a coy lover, for God also seems capable of playing cruel tricks on man, yet we, like the gopis, continue to run after God, accept his opalescent moods, and feel something in us lifeless till we have once danced in abandon with him.

The crude paintings on the walls of the temple with the ghost-eyed Krishna told of these stories; there the milkmaids forever danced toward him in eager joy. Around the temple of this timeless passion ambled half-naked children, domestic animals, and countless birds.

In this temple and many others in India itself, I was struck by the continuity I felt between the temple and the riotous, rotting organic life around it. The Western church is usually dead but for cut flowers, and tightly sealed against all nonhuman life. But through feast, sacrifice, or offering, the throbbing and dying life of the universe flows in and out of the Hindu temple like a vast tide of monkeys, cows, birds, flowers, and fruit. Indeed, the temples themselves, with their knobby outrè shapes, seem almost more botanical than architectural. Like Hindu society itself, they grow out of the soil of India like prodigious plants, reaching away from nature yet still linked to its maternal arteries.

Betty Heimann has suggested that it is to the *biological* flavor of Hinduism to which one must turn for understanding.[1] This is a deep insight, even if Hinduism presses biology much beyond where others might set man and nature, or mind and body, over against each other. But as in the lingam of Shiva, the biological and the divine are one unity. I have written elsewhere:

> Hindu society is not a contractual state, but a great organism. By means of the caste system, every individual finds his place through the biological process of birth and contributes to the whole like a cell of the body . . . The fantastic numinous Hindu gods, dwelling in the dark cavelike interior of the temple (called the *garbha* or "womb"), are uncanny just because they are forms half-remembered, surfacings from the subtle deeps where mind grapples with such biological demigods as parents, sex, food, and shadowy recollections of the womb and the magically omnipotent infant. Yoga requires a skillful and persistent combined engineering of physiological and psychological forces. It says these two are ultimately one. It suggests the goal, *samadhi*, blissful unconditioned awareness, is the epitome or ultimate objective of the unceasing biological process. It is a total unveiling of that consciousness and perception which life seems to want, free of the limitations life ordinarily imposes. This attainment is, for Hinduism, the real transcendence. To Hinduism, the meaningful dualism is not of man and nature, or of mind and body, but of the infinite or unconditioned and the finite or conditioned. Mind, the unconscious, human society, and nature are all part of a biological continuum, all on one side of the dualism, because they are all alike conditioned; only the breakthrough which sees them all at once and so makes the many one moves to the other side. It is no blasphemy that birds and gods

[1]Betty Heimann, *Facets of Indian Thought* (London: George Allen and Unwin, 1964).

Life Against Time

share the same offerings; it symbolizes they are alike in the circle of conception and consumption.[2]

This polarity is expressed in the basic polarity in Hindu thought and life, that between *dharma* and *moksha*. Within the union which is life and the cosmos, these are the two lenses through which it ideally can be seen: as dharma, or the cosmic and social order; and from the perspective of moksha, or the state of liberation or unconditionedness.

The word "dharma," related to our "form," is one of those terms so broad as to require more an intuition than a precise definition. It suggests the total order of the world as it is: the laws of nature like gravitation and day and night, called *rita,* and flowing out of it the social order of human civilization, and finally the rites of the priests which sustain both. But dharma also implies righteousness in the sense that it means moral behavior which is in accord with the way things are. Man and even the gods of nature can rebel against dharma, though they cannot escape the consequences that dharma imposes through *karma*, or personal retribution, just as one could attempt to defy nature by jumping off a cliff and trying to fly, but would be met by the consequences. Finally, dharma includes ritual usages that uphold the great cosmic-social order by demarcating caste and sustaining the work of creation through "feeding" the divine forces that move it.

Actually, seeing the world as dharma means regarding life as ritual. It means that one suppresses one's individualistic predilections to harmonize with the swing of the total pattern, so that the world becomes like a great dance. There are rituals for rising, for brushing one's teeth, for bathing, for eating, for love, for study, for worship. One's personal dharma, *swadharma,* his or her particular steps in the great dance, are determined by his or her individual birth and karma. Karma, related to our word "car," suggests activity and refers to that chain of cause-and-effect set in motion by one's deeds in the world, which sooner or later, through inexorable laws of justice built into dharma, rebound to perpetrate and affect one's own future. As one sows, so one reaps. Retribution or reward will include (but is not limited to) the state in which one is reborn—as a monarch or slave, a god or a dog.

This is dharma, the realm of endless and ultimately self-correcting change driven by striving and cause-and-effect in which we dwell. It is an interesting level, but in the end wearisome. However, it is not necessary to remain forever running with its tides and tossed hither and yon by the self-made waves of karma. There is always the possibility of leaping aboard a raft and skimming to a different level altogether, to a state as opposite to it as land to water. This is moksha, "leaping out," finding liberation. It is the final quest, after all other quests have run out.

According to the Laws of Manu (c. A.D. 100), there are four basic goals that motivate people: pleasure (*kama*), gain (*artha*), righteousness (dharma), and liberation (moksha). Each has its own place, and indeed its own "rituals," such as those for the first in the well-known *Kama-sutra.* But all except the last finally exhaust themselves in craving for something beyond that level.

[2]Robert S. Ellwood, Jr., *Religious and Spiritual Groups in Modern America* (Englewood Cliffs, N.J.: Prentice-Hall, Inc., 1973), p. 217.

We may imagine a young man starting out in life motivated mainly by pleasure—a playboy, a hedonist. But after a whirl at this he finds that pleasure alone, without direction or purpose beyond today, gives one a sense of disintegration. He feels that if he keeps up that way of life he will just keep wanting more and more to provide the same satisfaction, and that he will finally end up enslaved, more anxious to avoid losing pleasures and their symbols than enjoying them.

So next he decides to try instead for some real goals: getting ahead, making money, getting a big house and car (or, in ancient India, a chariot). This is the second stage, artha, and in time this goal is increasingly well met.

But still the man senses a certain inner disquiet. There is a quality of self-respect, or of desire for the respect of others, that he does not have. He wants not only to be successful, but also to be substantial, a solid, respectable citizen, a community leader. He wants to exemplify and uphold dharma in this world. So he becomes active in the P.T.A. and Chamber of Commerce, and perhaps even gets into politics—highly motivated, of course. (Or, in ancient India, he is active in the *panchayat,* the local governing body of his caste, or is a faithful ritualist, or even a gracious and just king.)

Yet, when a busy day is done and he goes to bed, he may later wake in the middle of the night with an empty, despairing feeling, as though he were all straw and gnawing rats inside. What he is doing is good, yet somehow it means nothing, or rather it would mean nothing if it is all that people do, age after age, generation after generation, getting nowhere because it all has to be done time and time again, for all eternity. The big questions are now unavoidable: Why does nothing fully meet the unquenchable yearning in mankind? What will become of me in the end? What is the real purpose of life and why is it so hard to discover? Who am I, anyway? He is now ready to tackle the last goal—moksha.

In India, these developments ideally would be in tandem with the four *as-hramas,* or stages of life: student, householder, hermit, renunciant. But the first three goals—pleasure, gain, and dharma—would be dealt with in the householder stage, since the student was expected to practice continence and application, and was under obedience to his father and teacher. Then, after he had seen his first grandchild or his hair had begun to turn gray, he could retire to a hermitage to begin the quest for moksha, and culminate it by becoming a *sannyasin,* or renunciant, a wandering monk free from all ties. His wife could accompany him if she desired. Of course, not more than a small percentage of the people of India, largely upper caste, have followed this regimen, and frequently the "retirement" of the last two stages is actually to a private room within the house. But the tradition is still alive, and answers to something universal; one feels many westerners would be happier by accepting that in the last half of life pleasure and gain should be put aside in favor of another quest, which can be repressed but deep inside becomes more and more insistent.

There are many paths to moksha, bespoken by the many temples and teachers. There is the way of Krishna through his garden of supernal love, the way of Shiva and the cosmic power of his lingam, and the ways of yogins outside of all such temples. In India, the quest would be undertaken under the guidance of a *guru,* a spiritual guide who would initiate the seeker into the path he was qualified to impart and direct him along it. Later we will examine some of these paths.

Let us first look ahead to the goal. It may be given many labels: God-realization, identification with the absolute, supreme bliss, cosmic consciousness—but it is perhaps best spoken of by those more negative terms such as release, liberation, or freedom. For it is really beyond all concepts and labels. It is simply freedom. Not freedom in any political or individualistic sense, but inner freedom from *everything* that circumscribes or conditions the sense of infinity one has within; that is, from all relation to the cause-and-effect of karma within or without. One is to rise above and master all this, to become as lithe and free as sunlight and cloud in the sky. Then one knows the answer to the secret of who one really is.

The prevailing Hindu answer is that, in the great quiet of meditation, in hearing the sonorous words of scripture, in the joy of devotion, the realization comes through that there *is* only One—Brahman, God—and that, as the Upanishads say, "Thou art that."

Phenomena and ideas like these are some of the signposts on India's map of the invisible spiritual world, and show ways in which the three forms of religious expression weave in and out of each other. We have seen hints of the two levels of theoretical or verbal expression: the myths of Krishna's delights, the symbolic potency of Shiva's lingam; and beyond them a flash of doctrinal putting-it-together in God as One and beyond time, and in the four stages of life, and the polarity of dharma and moksha which explains our fascination with these myths and symbols even in the midst of life. For the temples and images and myths are like reminders of moksha when we are not yet there; they are like colored glass between this world and the Other, letting us see the light from the moksha side.

In these same temples we see something of the practical or worship expression: altars yeasty with life, multiformed images, priests. We have also seen suggestions of the main streams of Hindu sociological expression: the caste system which is the foundation of dharma in practice, the four stages of life which define duties and possibilities within society, and the devotional movements which have centered around the gods such as Krishna, Shiva, and others. It now remains to examine Indian religion in more detail by putting it into historical perspective.

THE RELIGION
OF THE ANCIENT ARYANS

The Indus Valley, in what is now Pakistan, was the scene of a remarkable civilization around 2500 to 1500 B.C. Two cities some 400 miles apart, Harappa and Mohenjo-Daro, together with some smaller towns and villages, comprised it. Each city was laid out on a grid plan, and the houses, although virtually identical and severely functional, were technologically advanced; the plumbing has been equaled only by that of the Romans and the modern world. The writing of this culture has not been deciphered, and there are many mysteries about it, not least in its religion. The cities contain no obvious temples, though each does have a cloisterish complex with a pool perhaps used for ritual lustrations on high ground above it; it may have been the stronghold of a powerful priestly order. There are enigmatic religious motifs on many of the seals and small art objects that have been found; these suggest a mother goddess, as one would expect in a highly sedentary agricultural society like this, phallic gods, sacred bulls, and in one case a deity in perhaps a yogic meditation posture. Some scholars have theorized that the sides of Hinduism which center around Shiva, bulls, the mother goddess, water ablutions, and yogic techniques come out of an indigenous culture related to that of the Indus Valley.[3]

But around 1500 B.C. a new people entered India. They conquered the cities of the Indus Valley. Being but simple nomads they did not replace them with a comparable material culture for many centuries, although spiritually they brought a different but equally impressive complex that was to provide the formal foundation of intellectual Hinduism. These were the Aryans, cattle herders who apparently came out of central Asia across the famous Khyber Pass into the hot plains. They are of Indo-European stock like most of the European peoples, and their Sanskrit language is related to Greek, Latin, Irish, German, and English. We have already seen cognates in our language to Sanskrit words like dharma and karma.

The Aryans, very different from the Indus Valley folk, were an active, simple-living, and aggressive collection of tribes. The Vedas, the fundamental official scriptures of Hinduism, start out with the hymns and rituals of their priests. They splendidly reflect freshness of vision, heroic masculine virtues, and ritual precision.

Aryan society seems to have been composed of three classes: the brahmins or priests, the kshatriyas or warriors, and the common people. Each had its own pattern of life; of primary interest now are the brahmins. The group of words related to "brahmin" appear to come from a root meaning a magical force or spell.[4] From the earliest times, words of power that encapsulate the essence of a god or line of force in the cosmos, and so can be used to control it, have been employed by shamans and wizards. The brahmins used them in connection with their sacrificial rites; just as through words of power and sacrifice the gods made the world, they said, so by words and sacrifice the gods could themselves be controlled. Thus the sacrifices controlled the gods, and the brahmin priests controlled the sacrifice, making them like higher gods themselves, participating in the cosmic sorcery of the great master-magician himself, whose dreamings construct the world.

But this is getting ahead in the story. The oldest and most important of the Vedic scriptures is the Rig Veda, hymns to the gods sung while sacrifices were being presented; parallel to it are sets of songs and chants for auxiliary groups of priests and of charms called the Sama, Yajur, and Atharva Vedas respectively. These Vedas in turn have sets of commentaries called the Brahmanas, Aranyakas ("Books

[3]See A. L. Basham, *The Wonder that Was India* (New York: Grove Press, 1959), chapter II.

[4]There is a collection of similar words, confusing at first, which are built on this root. Brahma is the creator god of some Indian mythology. Brahman (the neuter form) is used in philosohpical writing from the Upanishads on to refer to the impersonal Absolute. The Brahmanas are sacred ritual texts that are part of the Vedas. Brahmans are the priestly caste, presumably so-called because they possessed mysterious and magical power like that by which the world is sustained. For the sake of clarity, in this book the common spelling "brahmin" will be used for the priests.

of the Forest Schools''), and Upanishads. They offer ritual instructions but also, over the centuries, present more and more philosophical reflection on the meaning of the rites.

The original gods of the Aryans were vital, flashing, brilliant beings of sky and storm. They dwelt in the three levels of the known cosmos—sky, atmosphere, earth—and those of the middle level moved vigorously about.

The most popular deity was Indra, prototype of the Indo-European warrior and comparable to Thor in Germanic mythology. He wielded a thunderbolt and dwelt in the atmosphere where the action is. He was accompanied by the Maruts, a boisterous band of warrior-companions who rode chariots like the armies of ancient India. Every dawn was a victory for Indra. Abetted by the morning sacrifices of the priests, he and his Maruts would arise and defeat the demonic powers of darkness. Indra consumed countless cattle and, in preparation for heroic exploits, vast lakefuls of the sacred drink soma. Indeed, it was he who had originally found and taken soma from high in the mountains. Like a Wagnerian hero, Indra slew the monster Vritra in mythical times, but finally as his age gave place to another was superseded by other gods closer to the heart of wisdom.

The Vedas present Dyaus—whose name is obviously cognate to the Latin Deus and Greek Zeus—as sky-father, but he is shadowy and remote, virtually a *deus otiosus*. Equally mysterious is the vague but profound-seeming figure of Aditi, light (or mind) beyond shadow or stain, and mother of the gods. Then there are two sky gods of somewhat more concrete personality, Varuna and Mitra, kingly figures whose main task is the upholding of rita, the cosmic laws. There are few female figures; such as there are, like Aditi and Ushas, the Dawn, seem passive and indistinctly conceived although the subject of lovely hymns. It is as though Aryans thought naturally in the ways of the masculine world—unlike the Indus Valley people with their fertility goddesses—and so the feminine appears as something rare, surprising, provocative, but elusive, like a maiden in a high window just glimpsed by a questing knight.

In a sense, however, all the bright gods of the Vedas are elusive; all are described interchangeably as shining and benevolent, and each is addressed in turn as though he were the only deity, until finally we come to wonder if there is just one god who bears a series of names and parts. Yet there is a tremendous vitality and sense of personal forces at work in the Vedas. Nowhere is this paradox more apparent than in two further deities, Agni and Soma.

These are deities of the rituals. They are only barely personified, but extremely important. Agni, whose name is cognate with the Latin *ignis* and our "ignite," is fire. Fire is, as we have seen, the crucial mystery in the cycle of conception and consumption that keeps life in process; all its transitions, from sex through eating to death (in which we are eaten in turn, whether by microbe, worm, or tiger) are various gradations of oxidation, that is, of fire. This lively magician of life and death is Agni, and he is the central actor in the drama of the sacrifice, which miniaturizes the universe. On earth, it is said, he is fire; in the atmosphere, lightning; in the sky, the sun. Existing in principle in all strata, he is also the quick messenger of the gods; he bears prayer and sacrifice to them.

Same is the drink of power and immortality which the gods consumed, especially Indra, and which was also manufactured, offered, and consumed in the sacrifices. It had an exhilarating, empowering effect: Indra fortified himself with Soma for the battle with Vritra; on another occasion he felt frenzied, exalted, as though he had passed beyond earth and sky, and asked himself rhetorically if he had been drinking Soma. The brahmins also sang:

> We have drunk the Soma, we are become Immortals,
> We have arrived at the Light, we have found the Gods,
> What now can hostility do to us, what the malice of mortals,
> O immortal Soma!

The question arises: What was Soma? The juice that is presently used in brahmin ceremonies under the same name does not produce any such effects. Many suggestions have been made. R. Gordon Wasson has argued that Soma was made from the fly-agaric mushroom, a hallucinogenic plant still employed by shamans in central Asia to induce altered states of consciousness. He points out that the cryptic Vedic allusions to the plant from which Soma is made nowhere speak of root or leaf, and in other respects seem compatible with the mushroom. Wasson also suggests intriguingly that the reason the secret of the original Soma was lost is that the fly-agaric only grows high above sea level; as the Aryans penetrated farther and farther into India, it was necessary to substitute for it.[5]

To understand Hindu thought, it is necessary to glance at what actually went on in the brahmin rites. It would be a great misconception to imagine a gorgeous ceremonial along the lines of a high mass, or the processions and offerings of later devotional Hinduism. For while the brahmin rites required much preparation and many priests, outwardly they were quite plain. They were performed out of doors, but often under a temporary shelter, in a quiet place with only the priests and the lay patron who was paying for them present. Three fire pits of different shapes, representing earth, atmosphere, and sky, and a grass-lined pit for preserving oblations and utensils, were dug. Offerings of butter, vegetable, or flesh were placed into the fires; the simplest offering was simply pouring melted and strained butter (*ghee*) from two spoons slowly into the fire. While the offerings were being presented, other priests would chant the proper hymns; sometimes still another would just stand in the center meditating on the whole procedure, unifying it in his thought.

Yet these relatively undramatic acts had to be done precisely right. The fuel and the fires were built with immense care as to detail; if a single syllable of the hymn was mispronounced or a single gesture wrong, the rite might be stopped and started all over again from the beginning. Much in contrast to the effusive and half-spontaneous dances and rapturous playlike swingings of flowers and food, lamps and water, of the later devotionalism, here all is crisp, sharp, small, and exact. It had much the atmosphere of a modern laboratory experiment.

[5]R. Gordon Wasson, *Soma: Divine Mushroom of Immortality* (New York: Harcourt Brace Jovanovich, Inc., 1969). See also R. Gordon Wasson, "What Was the Soma of the Aryans?" in *Flesh of the Gods,* ed. Peter T. Furst, pp. 201–13.

Indeed, the Vedic rites were a sort of science; while the premises may have been different from ours, the old brahmins saw themselves less as enthusiastic lovers of their gods than as technicians making precise adjustments in the cosmic order to correct an imbalance or produce some desired result. For the sacrifice was nothing less than "making the world" and calling into life the gods who rule over it; the purpose then was to meditate on what the cosmos is like and to make adjustments in it in such a way as to keep it on course or direct its power in desired directions: prosperity, the inauguration of a king's reign, a son, long life, immortality in heaven.

It was as though a reducing lens had been held up to the cosmos. The sacrificial spread was a miniaturization of the universe as a whole, made much smaller and its processes correspondingly speeded up. The fire was the destruction and transmutation of material—food—through heat that keeps the universe going. The words of the chants, the mantras, or "thought-forms," were sounds whose "vibrations" were in tune with the gods and the subtle currents of reality itself. On this "laboratory" world the priests performed their delicate technical operations; the rites keeping the universe on course and helpful to man were like making tiny adjustments in a tremendously huge and intricate machine, perhaps only turning a single screw a quarter of a turn. But a trained technician, who knows exactly what he is doing, can by such minute modifications make the difference between whether the machine works as desired or not. So the brahmin priests understood their ritual activities.

But as time went on, as the brahmin sages pondered over and over the meaning of the rites, new questions arose. They thought of the web of vibrations, which the mantras and the miniaturization process seem to suggest, as orchestrating the universe. The whole was like a magic web that held the universe of men, gods, and substance together, "the thread stretched out on which these creatures are strung together" (Atharva Veda 10:8:37), and within even this "the thread of the thread," the fundamental unity, subtle beyond all sight yet inextricably there, beneath the world's romping multiplicity—Brahman, originally the power of the màntric charms that hold the world in course. Upon this secret the brahmin priest, who supervised and by his thought unified the sacrifice, was to meditate.

Other questions concerned Agni, the sacred fire. Fire is at the center of the world, and so of the sacrifices—but is it only the fire that burns visibly? What of the fire that burns within a person's own body—the fire of joy, of concentration, even of fever? Does this make the person also an altar, and a world?

In brahmin thinking, the sacrifice was "interiorized" to pave the way for philosophy and yoga.[6] *Tapas*—interior heat—was generated by the real sacrifice, which was within one. Through the asceticism of fasting and concentration one built up tapas, and this power could be used by the adept to bless or curse, or gain cosmic vision. For the person *was* now the cosmos; one replaced with oneself the cosmic sacrifice; all without was also within, the greater in the smaller and the smaller in the greater. This is the secret of the Upanishads, the last and most philosophical commentary on the Vedas.

[6]Mircea Eliade, *Yoga: Immortality and Freedom* (New York: The Bollengen Foundation, 1958), Chapter III.

The texts called Upanishads are presented as words about the inner or final meaning of things which would be imparted by a father or master to his most advanced pupils as the culminating stage of their learning; they are not for beginners, for until one has had enough experience of life, or has matured enough to ask the right questions, they would be only empty sounds. Far from preaching it broadcast, the wise preserved Upanishadic wisdom jealously for those ready for it. The ten to sixteen principal Upanishadic treatises, composed in the centuries around 500 B.C., were not published or taught widely, but passed on orally in secret at the right times.

Thus the Chandogya Upanishad tells of a brahmin father who sent his son to study in a forest school. When the son returned, full of pride in his Vedic scholarship, the father deflated his son's ego and increased his wisdom by telling him of a further knowledge, "that knowledge by which we hear the unhearable, by which we perceive the unperceivable, by which we know the unknowable."

This arcane knowledge was that as different things made of clay or gold go by different names, they are still clay or gold, so all things are One Existence under many names. At the beginning this One Existence thought to himself, "Let me grow forth." "Thus out of himself he projected the universe; and having projected out of himself the universe, he entered into every being. All that is has its self in him alone. Of all things he is the subtle essence."

And the father adds the crucial words about the One to his son: That Art Thou.

Other analogies are used in this passage: one honey is made from nectar gathered by bees from many flowers; all rivers flow into one sea. The One Existent is the invisible essence of all things, like the "nothingness" at the heart of a seed of a giant tree. And after each example of the essence, the father repeats: That Art Thou.

This essence is Brahman. The great inner knowledge which the wise ones of the Upanishads came to is "Atman is Brahman." Atman is the innermost self, the "soul"; Brahman is the universal One Existent. "He is pure, he is the light of lights." All persons and all things are really Brahman, taking many shapes like fire taking the shape of every object it consumes, or air the shape of every vessel it enters.

As the Svetasvatara Upanishad puts it beautifully:

> O Brahman Supreme!
> Formless art thou, and yet
> (Though the reason none knows)
> Thou bringest forth many forms;
> Thou bringest them forth, and then
> Withdrawest them to thyself.
> Fill us with thoughts of thee!
>
> Thou art the fire,
> Thou art the sun,
> Thou art the air,
> Thou art the moon,
> Thou art the starry firmament,

Thou art Brahman Supreme:
Thou art the waters—thou,
The creator of all!

Thou art woman, thou art man,
Thou art the youth, thou art the maiden,
Thou art the old man tottering with his staff;
Thou facest everywhere.

Thou art the dark butterfly,
Thou art the green parrot with red eyes,
Thou art the thundercloud, the seasons, the seas.
Without beginning art thou,
Beyond time, beyond space.
Thou art he from whom sprang
The three worlds.[7]

The movement from Veda to Upanishad is well expressed in the Katha Upanishad. It begins with the account of a young man named Nachiketa. Nachiketa's crusty old brahmin father presented a sacrifice of the Vedic sort in which he was supposed to offer all his possessions, but was careful to present only old and scroungy cattle. The boy, shocked by this, told his father he also was one of his possessions, and asked him to whom he would give his son. The irritated parent responded that he would give him to Yama, the ancient King of the Dead.

Nachiketa, taking this very seriously, proceeded to the home of this king, Death. Death was not at home, forcing Nachiketa to wait. When he returned, Death in compensation offered the sincere young brahmin three wishes, which he agreed to fulfill.

The first two wishes are clearly rooted in the traditional Vedic world. Nachiketa asked first that his father's anger would be appeased; this wish concerned the finite social relations of patriarchal society. Second, he asked to know the fire sacrifice that led to heaven, for as we have seen the power of the sacrifice extends from this world to the next. But this was only a finite matter too, for life in the Vedic heavens is extended only as long as the warping of cosmic energy by the rite lasted. Depending on one's skill and power, it might assure bliss for a very long time, but being just a matter of technical craft, it would ultimately wear down, for within the cosmos there is no such thing as perpetual motion or energy.

But the third question was a shift to another level of discourse. Nachiketa said, "When a man dies, there is this doubt: Some say, he is; others say, he is not. Taught by thee, I would know the truth. This is my third wish."

Understanding the thrust of the question, that Nachiketa is probing the fringes of an entire new spiritual world from that of the Vedic rites, and might well be ready to enter it, Death parried with him. He went through the time-honored conventions of the master seeming to frustrate and discourage the novice to test him. He informed Nachiketa that the gods themselves find the answer hard to understand, and urged

[7]Swami Prabhavananda and Frederick Manchester, trans., *The Upanishads: Breath of the Eternal* (New York: Mentor Books, 1957). Copyright © 1957 by the Vedanta Society of Southern California), pp. 123–24. Reprinted with permission.

him to select some other favor. He urged him to select sons, cattle, elephants, gold, a mighty kingdom, celestial maidens so beautiful as not to be meant for mortals.

But Nachiketa stood fast, pointing out that these things are only grasped for a fleeting day, then vanish like smoke . . . in the process, they wear away the senses. How can one desire them, he asked Death, who has once seen Death's face? There is a secret of imperishability and immortality which is beyond them, he insisted, and would not yield till Death had imparted it.

Inwardly well pleased, Death confirmed that there is another secret, one that cannot really be taught at all, but can be caught from a true teacher by the student who is truly prepared: that the true Self within is the imperishable, changeless Brahman, the One beyond and in all these forms and changes. The mantra, or sound, which expresses Brahman himself, and whose recitation can give rise to his consciousness, is OM. The King of Death continues:

> The Self, whose symbol is OM, is the omniscient Lord. He is not born. He does not die. He is neither cause nor effect. This Ancient One is unborn, imperishable, eternal: though the body be destroyed, he is not killed.
>
> If the slayer think that he slays, if the slain think that he is slain, neither of them knows the truth. The Self slays not, nor is he slain.
>
> Smaller than the smallest, greater than the greatest, this Self forever dwells within the hearts of all. When a man is free from desire, his mind and senses purified, he beholds the glory of the Self and is without sorrow.
>
> Though seated, he travels far; though at rest, he moves all things. Who but the purest of the pure can realize this Effulgent Being, who is joy and who is beyond joy.
>
> Formless is he, though inhabiting form. In the midst of the fleeting he abides forever. All-pervading and supreme is the Self. The wise man, knowing him in his true nature, transcends all grief.
>
> The Self is not known through study of the scriptures, nor through subtlety of the intellect, nor through much learning; but by him who longs for him is he known. Verily unto him does the Self reveal his true being.
>
> By learning, a man cannot know him, if he desist not from evil, if he control not his senses, if he quiet not his mind, and practice not meditation.[8]

The Self—Atman who is really Brahman—is the only Being, the Sole Existent, the One Mind. He is everywhere yet indivisible. Brahman alone exists; all else floats insubstantial on the face of the shoreless ocean of his being, wisdom, and bliss, like reflections in an unstained mirror. Yet the ordinary consciousness grasps only the things and not Brahman, for the simple reason that Brahman *is* the consciousness, just as the eye cannot see itself or a pliars grab itself. Brahman plays hide-and-seek with himself in the world, indwelling the myriad things while elusive to human thought and dream. Why? None of us groping about in the world of the many can fully know, just as a man inside a house can only know incompletely the whole plan and shape of the structure. He would have to step through the door and look at it from outside as well.

The sages of India tell us there are doors which the wise and intrepid can find.

---

[8]Ibid., pp. 18–19.

As the end of the above passage tells us, it is through meditation, that is, quieting the senses and the mind, that the door to the infinite dimension can be unlatched. For it is the play of the senses and the mind which turn one away from one's true nature—Brahman—to the phantasmagoria of many things to which feeling and thought attach themselves like leeches.

It is as though a play had been going on for a very long time—not weeks and weeks, but countless years. It has been going on for so long that the actors have forgotten they are merely playing parts, and have come to identify themselves with the parts. They think that when one actor murders another, the victim is really dead, and the red gore on the floor is not ketchup but real blood. They think that when two members of the cast fall in love, or break up with tears and angry words, that these are absolute and final realities of life, not just events woven into the web of a greater drama with higher purposes beyond their ken. So the show becomes so mad, with the actors' involvement and anxiety rising out of control, that the prompter behind the stage must send out messengers to remind them that it is only a play . . . to remind them who they really are.

This is like the Upanishadic view of the world. The messengers are like the great sages who remind us of how things really are, the *rishis*, or seers, who composed the Vedas, the God-realized teachers who bring students into Brahman consciousness in all ages. But the difference is that in the Upanishadic vision there are not many actors, but one actor—the One Mind—who is playing all the parts and is also the prompter. He who is playing the part of the one you love—and also the one you hate, and the stranger to whom you are indifferent—is none other than the Self, of whom our outward-directed thoughts have been forgetful.

One other message from the Upanishads: The Mandukya Upanishad tells us that the Self, as consciousness, has three aspects . . . and beyond them, a fourth.

The first is the ordinary waking consciousness. It is you or I walking down the street, perceiving other objects and people as outside of oneself, and thinking of oneself as separate from them, while enjoying the pleasures of the senses.

The second aspect is the mental nature turned upon itself enjoying a mental world created within the head. It is the dreaming state of consciousness, and by extension the worlds of imagination, fantasy, and the deep archetypes of the unconscious. The images which dance behind the curtains of the mind in this state derive from things remembered by the senses and so come from outside, and except in advanced yogic states they are more or less out of control—we cannot usually tell ourselves what to dream. Yet although the second is not a divine state of consciousness, but rather an inward turning of the first, it does have some similarity to Brahmanic consciousness; it is one mind growing a whole world of bright and transient forms, which do not exist elsewhere, out of itself.

The third aspect is the self in deep sleep without dreams. When all forms external and internal vanish into formlessness, and mind and sense are still like a windless lake in the midst of night, one enters the third state. Significantly, it is called the Prajna state. Prajna means wisdom, not in the sense of factual knowledge about all sorts of things, which obviously would not apply, but that sharp, intuitive insight that simply *knows,* without the confusion of words or ideas from the world of the many. And what is known in this way, *all* that is known in this way, is Brahman.

In an important sense, then, the deep-sleep-without-dreams state is closest of these three to Brahman-consciousness. A fundamental principle of Hindu and Buddhist philosophy is that all outward, particularized perceptions and concepts, such as one has in the waking state, are really limitations. If you are thinking about one thing, or a thousand, there are still millions of things you are not thinking about, and the very things you are thinking about cut you off from them, and so limit you. Only when this part of thought is quieted does the mind become like Brahman's— thinking of nothing in particular, and so horizonless, infinite, in tune with the All.

Woman praying at a Hindu shrine. Note offering trays.

In deep sleep one is functioning just on the biological plane—and so becomes an integrated part of the dance of the atoms and galaxies, without being cut off by any individualizing thoughts from this infinite play of Brahman.

One could ask if all this means is that Brahmanic consciousness is like a return to the womb, or even a wish for extinction. Certainly deep sleep is like a nightly return to the womb, or a miniature death, and it is well-known that in every human being there is somewhere a deep undertow that desires the womb, or death. The unborn infant in the womb dwells in a world in which it is, to its knowledge, the only being, secure in warmth, darkness, moisture, delight. Is not this like the state

Life Against Time

of Brahman, Sole Existent, and so impervious and unthreatened—and like the state of the mystic in Brahman-consciousness?

Of course, there is probably strength in periodic return to the womb, or to the other state in which no outward harm can come—death. Through the womb one can make contact with one's true parent, the universe; the womb was our link with the universe, for through it we tied in with the billions of years of life that made us, and with the universal sources. Compared to these billions of years one's brief conscious hour on the stage is of little magnitude. In the profoundly biological thought of India, this is important. Through the womb comes the gift of the quasi-immortal genetic molecules, crafted over thousands of centuries; it is not without meaning that we spend one third of our time in sleep, back in the womb at the forge of our making, psychologically speaking. We may also do this, we are told, more deliberately and purposively in meditation. The gods themselves, in India, dwell in the womb of the temple, and sit on lotus thrones, which are also womb symbols. As for death, it may also be well that we make his advance acquaintance knowingly and comprehendingly, for we will know him better as the scenes of the drama shift— and like the fetus, he also seems beyond change or harm, and one with the infinite universe.

Yet the infant is born into this world. It leaves its world of total darkness for ours of half light and half darkness, of day and night, joy and sorrow. In the womb it is acquiring organs of whose use it has no glimmering: hands and feet, eyes and ears. It passes through a process which must seem to it like a death, but we on this side say, "Joy! A child is born into the world!"

In this world of half light and half darkness too, the wise say, we possess capacities of which we have little prescience: inexplicable drives to achieve and love even at risk to this flickering life, yearning for the infinite. These capacities are intended for use in another stage, which follows another birth that seems like a death in that it is an erasure of the manifold enchantments of the mind and senses. This is birth into the world of full and seamless light, the Brahman world.

That this end is really the fulfillment and opposite of the womb, though an end which has more than passing familiarity with the beginning, is the message of the fourth state. For the Mandukya Upanishad tells us that the true Self, AUM, is the unification of all three other states. It is the state of a person who walks through the world bearing the gifts of all three. He or she has the fearlessness and sense of oneness with his universe-home of the womb, or of one dead, or of Brahman. He has under his control all the delights and occult powers of the inner dream world. Yet he lives and works with acute capability in the outer world, for he knows things as they really are, down to their roots. In the vision of the Upanishads, he and he alone is a complete human being.

A TIME
OF SPIRITUAL FERMENT

The spiritual movement of India around the fifth century B.C., which produced the "interiorization of sacrifice" of the Upanishads, produced other equally important results. Then as now, the culture of India was neither a monolithic unity nor divided into watertight compartments. Like America but more so, it was a mix of many colors; individual components can be distinguished, but at the same time the mixture as a whole is slowly stirring, blending, and receiving new inputs.

The Upanishadic vision is only one element in this mix. As the epitomizing expression of the classic lore of the most prestigious scholarly class, the brahmins, it enjoys a unique status and would be accepted as authoritative, along with the rest of the Vedic literature, by all who consider themselves orthodox. But to think that it is *the* tool by which Hindu culture is to be interpreted, or that it plays a role in Hinduism exactly parallel to the Koran in Islam or the Bible in Christianity, would be to oversimplify grossly.

Nothing is that easy in Hinduism. Although reference to the Upanishads greatly illuminates the mentality that underlies India's gods, art, and institutions, one who tried to understand what he or she saw happening in an average Hindu village temple or pilgrimage center solely on its basis would be quickly at sea. It must be borne in mind that, through the centuries, the great majority of the people of India, illiterate and provincial, doubtless never heard much of the teaching of the Upanishads. Indeed, as we have seen, these scriptures were considered unsuitable for any but advanced upper caste students, and were restricted until quite modern times. Chinks of their light might have reached the peasants through the lips of wandering holy men, or veiled in myth or song, but the people would know them as treatises no more than they knew the Sanskrit language to which the Vedas, including the Upanishads, were traditionally confined, unwritten but passed privately by rote from brahmin teacher to disciple.

So it was that at the time the Upanishadic vision was crystallizing, much else was happening as well across the dusty face of India. Although its cities were shattered, much of the Indus Valley culture persisted, with its religious emphasis on fertility, the mother, purity, and (presumably) mystic states of consciousness attained by techniques of the yogic sort. Doubtless this heritage did much to influence the direction which the Upanishadic culmination of Vedism took. Not only did the Aryan thinkers in India move toward mystical monism rather than monotheism as in Iran, but a doctrine as central to later Hinduism and Buddhism as reincarnation appears first in the Upanishads. In the earlier Vedas it is in very rudimentary form, and can be supposed to be largely a contribution of the indigenous culture.

It was a time when the Aryan conquerors were pressing across northern India, and had established control virtually to the Ganges delta. No great unified empire had as yet arisen, although Aryan kingdoms large and small patchworked the sub-Himalayan plain. Material civilization was still scanty, but spiritual and philosophical cultures were vigorous and moving ahead rapidly.

Spiritual teachers strolled from village to village in the company of bands of disciples, even as do *sadhus,* or "holy men," in India today. Typically, they would walk in the morning, arriving at the destination by noon, when they would beg food. In the afternoon they would rest and meditate; in the evening the townsfolk would gather around. The visitors, intriguing and the subject of much local talk because they came from "outside," would pay for the hospitality they had been afforded with spiritual instruction—and doubtless also by telling news. The next day, unless a local magnate persuaded them to stay on as his guest, they would leave—possibly taking with them a local lad or two who had been impelled by a combined itch for adventure and hunger for higher things to leave home in the company of the peripatetic master.

Their teachings were wide-ranging and circumscribed by few dogmatic presuppositions, for these teachers were not brahmins defending the Vedic tradition, performing the sacrifices, and interpreting them now on Upanishadic lines. The brahmins were still mostly priests retained by courts or living in their own communities, hardly likely to go wandering among the common folk. But the new teachers, from other ranks of society, were looking for truth everywhere. One might be saying the world was created, another that it is eternal; one might be saying all is mind, another that there is nothing but matter.

One assumption that they shared in common, however, was that philosophical teaching was not to be merely abstract, but was to aid in attaining a state of inner liberation. Each school should imply a spiritual path, and so could be tested empirically. Most, even many of the so-called materialists, advocated methods involving extremely rigorous self-denial and self-control.

One teacher, Vardhamana, called Mahavira ("Great Hero"), c. 540–468 B.C., was the founder of the Jain religion, which now numbers about 1½ million adherents in India. He, or at least his followers, taught that there is sentient, feeling life in all that exists—humans, animals, plants, even stones, dust, and air. The "souls" or particles of life are bound up in these material shells as a result of karma, a sort of substance that coats them as a consequence of action based on desire. Desire produces actions toward particular objects, and thereby "grows" the material organs it needs to attain them. If you want a piece of candy, you need an arm to reach out and grab it, and a mouth with which to eat it. The karmic laws of the universe, according to Jainism and other Indian philosophies, say that in such matters you get what you want—but then you have to live with it. You now have a body so that you can enjoy candy, but you are trapped in that body, with all its limitations and capacity for pain—and you will have a very hard time getting out of it.

According to Mahavira and the Jains, as it was action that got one into the predicament, so it must be its opposites—quietness and abstention—that begin to reverse it, as well as suffering induced by asceticism, which wears down the karmic shell until it collapses and finally the soul breaks free, floating up to the top of the universe to enjoy an eternity of bliss and omniscience. Inflicting suffering on another soul, however, through cruelty or indifference or even apparent necessity, adds to one's burden of karma—for this reason Jains go to great lengths to counter the callousness of the world toward life. They strain water to keep from swallowing tiny organisms and screen lamps to keep moths from the flame. They maintain homes for unwanted animals and hospitals for injured birds, and are strict vegetarians. Monks go nude or wear only white sheets, pluck out their hair by the roots, and otherwise practice rigorous asceticism, in very rare instances to the point of starving themselves to death.

But although the lives of the monks may be austere, Jainism has other sides. Jain temples are among the most exquisitely beautiful in India, and Jains have played a most creative role in the letters and philosophy of their land. Mohandas Gandhi, and through him such Americans as Martin Luther King, were deeply influenced by Jain teachings about harmlessness and nonviolence. Moreover, the Jains, typically merchants and bankers, are a very wealthy and highly educated class in India today.[9]

Gautama Buddha, a younger contemporary of Mahavira, was among the many who roamed the eastern Ganges valley with him. Many wanderers are now forgotten, but two, Mahavira and Siddhartha Gautama of the Sakya clan, called the Buddha, are not. Both founded faiths which have persisted through twenty-five centuries; both have symbolized for many the highest conceiveable human state; both have structured the lives and blessed the deaths of innumerable spiritual children through the ages. Both moreover were of similar background; each was the son of a minor non-Aryan, indigenous ruler afforded more or less honorary warrior-caste (kshatriya) status; each was considered by his followers to be the last of a great chain of mighty teachers. Indeed, similar legends are told about the nativity and life of both, so much so that scholars once wrongly concluded they were the same person going by two names in two different religions.

Yet beyond this, their destinies differ, and far more so do the destinies of the two faiths. Jainism, profoundly Indian, has remained remarkably unchanged in teaching and practice through the ages, but at the price of remaining small and restricted to India. Buddhism has reached hundreds of times the numbers of Jainism, has spread over vast continental areas, has exfoliated into incredible diversities of sect and practice—and, again in contrast to Jainism, essentially died out in its homeland (although it has had something of a modern revival there) while spreading from Siberia to Ceylon, and from the Caspian Sea to Japan, not to mention its influence in the West.

While Mahavira taught a way of stern denial and control, the Buddha called his path the "Middle Way," for it was a spiritual tack of dwelling in the calm spot of equilibrium between all polarities, such as asceticism and indulgence, love of life and desire for death, even being and nonbeing. The Buddha, we are told, had been brought up in luxury and had tried the extremes of fasting and asceticism, but came to see both sides as forms of egotism. It should not be supposed, however, that Buddhism is any sort of easy-going, moderation-in-all-things philosophy. To find the exact spot of equilibrium where one is in precise balance with the universe and so has all power is no easy act of spiritual archery. It involves neutralizing all the outward and subtle desires that keep us shooting impulsively this way and that, scarcely seeing the target, much less hitting the bullseye.

Although the Buddha and Buddhism are discussed in detail in the next chapter, it is important here to place the inception of Buddhism in its historical time and place, for despite the fact that Buddhism was to become the spiritual foundation of lands and ages remote from the India of the fifth century B.C., the Buddha was a son of India and of the special style of spiritual ferment of his day, as well as having much more to give. It can be observed too that Buddhism prospered in that India, doubtless because of its close relation to the indigenous tradition and the moderation

---

[9]See Mrs. Sinclair Stevenson, *The Heart of Jainism* (New Delhi: Munshivam Manoharlal, 1970; Oxford University Press, 1st ed., 1915), and William de Bary, *Sources of Indian Tradition* (New York: Columbia University Press, 1958, 1966), Chapters IV, V.

and attractiveness of its monks. They found favor in the homes of the mighty. In particular, they won the support of the Emperor Ashoka (c. 273–37 B.C.), one of the noblest rulers of all time.

Ashoka unified northern India and then under Buddhist influence ceased to make war, proclaimed tolerance for all beliefs, and noninjury to life. He reportedly sent the first Buddhist missionaries outside India, to Ceylon, Southeast Asia, and the West. While Ashoka was personally nonsectarian, supporting and approving worthy teachers of whatever persuasion, evidently the Buddhists were closest to his heart. His patronage gave Buddhism a prestige which, extended by various later kings, it was to enjoy in India for upward of a thousand years.

It is not clear to what extent India *was* Buddhist between around 300 B.C. and A.D. 400, but many of the greatest intellectual leaders and most prestigious educational institutions were Buddhist, and Buddhism set the tone and subject matter of the greatest of art and architecture in those days. Of course, the masses of people were in no sense exclusively Buddhist. At best they listened to Buddhist monks, offered flowers and fruit at Buddhist temples, and went on Buddhist pilgrimages, without neglecting the gods of tribe and caste or the ministrations of the brahmins either. But this is typical of the way things were and are in India.

Indeed, to understand Buddhism it is helpful to realize that there is a sense in which one can say that Buddhism has seldom been *the* religion of a society, for it deals with personal liberation and not much with religion's role of legitimizing social institutions like family and government. In "Buddhist" countries these are often taken care of by other traditions—Hindu, Confucian, Shinto. Nor is Buddhism intolerant of Hindu or other gods; it is glad to acknowledge them so long as they are seen as pupils of the Buddha, "teacher of gods and men," as well. Rather, Buddhism is really the *sangha,* the order of Buddhist monks, dwelling *in* a society providing guidance for those ready for it, quietly available.

Yet there were ways in which Hinduism and Buddhism were consciously or unconsciously competitive. Even in the high tide of the Buddhist period, the Hindu tradition was providing responses and alternatives to the Buddha's way which would eventually supersede it in India itself, at the same time tremendously enrichening and broadening the appeal of Hinduism in order to answer the questions raised by the Buddhist experience. But in so doing Hinduism capitalized on the older tradition's strong points as a total religious expression: its concern not only with liberation but also with the organization of society, the pluralism of spiritual paths and stages implicit in its polytheism. Let us now examine this new post-Buddhist Hinduism.

THE NEW HINDUISM

One Hindu response was the Laws of Manu (c. 100 A.D.), which as we know was a systematization of the Hindu view of society containing the teaching about the Four Ends of Man and the Four Stages of Life. The Laws also rationalize the caste system by speaking of the four great divisions of society, called *varnas* (literally "colors")—brahmins or priest-scholars, kshatriyas or rulers and warriors, vaishyas or merchants and craftsmen, and shudras or peasants. It is said that they come from different parts of the body of the primal man; brahmins from the head, kshatriyas from the arms, vaishyas from the thighs, and shudras from the feet.

In all of this, the Laws of Manu are clearly trying to deal in a unified way with the two great but hard-to-reconcile poles of Hindu experience—dharma and moksha, or one's duty in society and liberation. So the two are seen as appropriate concerns for different stages of life, and through the caste system the social many is made manifestly compatible with oneness through the image of the great social organism, with each cell and organ playing its part.

What would one do during the course of seeking liberation? Can Hinduism compare with Buddhist meditation on this count? One important answer is given by the Yoga Sutras of Patanjali (c. 100 A.D.).[10] Buddhism had emphasized introspective meditation, with analysis of sensation and consciousness; the Yoga Sutras return to India's deeply biological, psychosomatic understanding of the nature of man as the background for liberation. Thus, hatha yoga, the physical yoga of postures and breathing exercises, plays a major role in the spiritual quest, for rightly understood breath and body are indispensable tools. Brought under control of spirit as precision instruments, they can facilitate states of consciousness that evoke the goals of spirit.

The goal of the yogin, the practitioner of yoga, is control of the modulations of the mind; in other words, *kaivalya,* "isolation," independence of the anxiety and limitations imposed by interaction with the changing world of sight and feeling and fantasy. This is done by getting the mind and body strictly under control by the exercises, and then using this control to withdraw attention from the outer world, so that the inner light shines unimpeded.

According to the Yoga Sutras, the process is comprised of eight steps, called limbs.

The first two are positive and negative moral rules aimed at a life of quietness, gentleness, and purity, for one's manner of life must be prepared and purified before yoga can hope to succeed. Releasing its potent spiritual forces into an unworthy vessel can, in fact, be most dangerous both to the individual and society.

Then comes the two steps of asana, or posture, and pranayama, or breath control, in which the psychosomatic powers are lined up to move in the one direction of liberation.

After the yogin gains control of his own bodily and emotional house in this way, the stage of the disengagement of the senses and attention from outer things becomes possible. This makes for acute inner, subtle ways of awareness. Just as a blind person develops especially sharp touch and hearing, so yoga tells us that when *all* the gross senses are withdrawn, other undreamed-of capabilities latent in man begin to stir, so that when they come to be mastered by the yogin he has awareness of things near and far, and ability to use occult forces, beside which the ordinary

---

[10]Swami Prabhavananda and Christopher Isherwood, *How to Know God: The Yoga Aphorisms of Patanjali* (New York: Mentor Books, 1969); Eliade, *Yoga,* and Alain Danielou, *Yoga: The Method of Reintegration* (New York: University Books, 1955).

Life Against Time

senses and capacities are as an oxcart to a rocketship. The Yoga Sutras tell us how to read minds, walk on water, fly through the air, make onself as tiny as an atom, be impervious to hunger and thirst, and so forth.

But these powers, doubtless tempting to many, are to be given up for an even greater goal—true liberation. This is the work of the last three steps, which are interior: concentration, meditation, and samadhi. Samadhi is the absolutely equalized consciousness of perfect freedom.

Both of these responses, the way of society and the way of the yogin, are brought together in the greatest Hindu statement of the period, the Bhagavad-Gita. Also composed somewhere around A.D. 100, it is really a section of the mighty epic called the *Mahabharata,* which has to do with a great war between cousins over the succession to the throne of an Aryan state. But the Bhagavad-Gita, or "Song of the Lord," can stand by itself once its setting is understood.

King Arjuna, whose charioteer is the heroic god Krishna in human form, is about to lead his army into bloody battle against the foe. Apalled at what he is about to do, Arjuna pauses in deep moral distress. The book is a series of answers that Krishna gives the king in his irresolution. It is discourses on why Arjuna can and must fight, but its implications go much further than this; the pacifist Gandhi greatly treasured this book, taking it as an allegory of the nonviolent struggle against injustice and for spiritual purity.

Krishna's first answer is along the lines of Upanishadic thought. He emphasizes that there is no reality behind talk of life and death, killing and being killed:

Some say this Atman	Unborn, undying,
Is slain, and others	Never ceasing,
Call It the slayer:	Never beginning
They know nothing.	Deathless, birthless,
How can It slay	Unchanging forever.
Or who shall slay It?	How can It die
Know this Atman	The death of the body?[11]

But if it does not make any difference, the question could be asked, "Why kill instead of not killing?" This Krishna answers, in effect, "Because you are a kshatriya, a warrior, by birth and caste, and therefore fighting is your role in the drama of the universe; there is no honorable way you can shirk it, and right is on your side since the enemy has gone against dharma."

Further questions arise. Does this mean, then, that one born a warrior has no hope for salvation comparable to that of the brahmin whose hands are unstained with blood and who enacts the mystic sacrifices? Does it mean that he whose place in society makes it almost mandatory that he stay in the world cannot compete with he who is able to become an ascetic or a yogin?

No, replies Krishna. It is all a matter of how one lives in the world. The object is to become one with the Absolute, so that nothing in one's thoughts or deeds separate

[11]Swami Prabhavananda and Christopher Isherwood, *The Song of God: Bhagavad-Gita* (New York: Mentor Books, 1951), p. 37. Copyright © 1944, 1951 by the Vedanta Society of Southern California. Reprinted with permission.

one from him. But if Brahman is truly All, the world of the activist is just as much God as that of the recluse. Brahman is expressed through dharma as much as moksha if he is truly All; in the caste laws and all of life's stages together. One can realize God in acting as much as in meditation, if one's actions are as selfless as meditation and as passionless. Krishna teaches Arjuna the secret of karma-yoga, yoga in the midst of doing. The point is to be in the world impersonally, objectively, doing not out of personal desire for the fruits of one's actions, but fearlessly and dispassionately, as it were by proxy for someone else, motivated solely by the duty and righteousness of the act. Then, with one's feelings not getting in the way, one's actions are a part of the great dance of the cosmos, of the life of the whole social and natural organism, and are as quiet and far-reaching as meditation.

> You have the right to work, but for the work's sake only. You have no right to the fruits of work. Desire for the fruits of work must never be your motive in working. Never give way to laziness either.
> Perform every action with your heart fixed on the Supreme Lord. Renounce attachment to the fruits. Be even tempered in success and failure; for it is this evenness of temper which is meant by yoga.
> Work done with anxiety about results is far inferior to work done without such anxiety, in the calm of self-surrender. Seek refuge in the knowledge of Brahman. They who work selfishly for results are miserable.[12]

Traditionally, karma-yoga was interpreted in a highly conservative way to mean that one must accept the role given by caste. Some modern Hindus, however, see it instead as a view which liberates one for bold and selfless acts of service to mankind, however risky, unpopular, or likely to fail—if one is acting out of impersonal righteousness, rather than for the gratification of pocket or ego, these considerations do not matter.

A philosophy like this does not satisfy all the spiritual needs of most people. However noble it may be, by itself it has a quality of dry resignation that does not answer man's thirst to *know* God. Yet something like karma-yoga can be an invaluable preparation for what seems to be its opposite, a religion of deeply felt awe and love in the presence of God. For only the person whose ego-self is unobtrusive can know God in any case.

This reflects the spiritual progression of the Bhagavad-Gita. After the Upanishadic and karma-yoga stages, the dialogue moves more and more into a sense of a mystical presence, nearer than hands and feet, which is with the one who had given up all selfhood to serve.

> Now I shall tell you
> That innermost secret:
> Which is nearer than knowing,
> Open vision
> Direct and instant.
> Understand this
> And be free for ever
> From birth and dying
>
> With all their evil.[13]
> Who burns with the bliss
> And suffers the sorrow
> Of every creature
> Within his own heart,
> Making his own
> Each bliss and each sorrow:
> Him I hold highest
> Of all the yogis.[14]

[12]Ibid., pp. 40–41.

[13]Ibid., p. 79.

[14]Ibid., p. 67.

More and more too something new in the tradition, a sense that the realtionship of the individual and this presence can be one of love, and that love is greater than success or failure in keeping the formal obligations of law and rite.

> Great is that yogi who seeks to be with Brahman,
> Greater than those who mortify the body,
> Greater than the learned,
> Greater than the doers of good works:
> Therefore, Arjuna, become a yogi.

> He gives me all his heart,
> He worships me in faith and love:
> That yogi, above every other,
> I call my very own.[15]

The greatest spiritual explosion, however, is yet to come. Nearness and love, in place of philosophy and duty, lead to a radically different relationship between mankind and God, and one far more analogous to the relationship of personalities than of man to natural law. Moving into this spiritual sphere, Arjuna culminates the discourse by asking to see Krishna in his full splendor and glory. Krishna obliges:

> Then . . . Sri Krishna, Master of all yogis, revealed to Arjuna his transcendent, divine form, speaking from innumerable mouths, seeing with a myriad eyes, of many marvelous aspects, adorned with countless divine ornaments, brandishing all kinds of heavenly weapons, wearing celestial garlands and the raiment of paradise, annointed with perfumes of heavenly fragrance, full of revelations, resplendent, boundless, of ubiquitous regard.
>
> Suppose a thousand suns should rise together into the sky: such is the glory of the Shape of Infinite God.
>
> Then the son of Pandu [Arjuna] beheld the entire universe, in all its multitudinous diversity, lodged as one being within the body of the God of gods.
>
> Then was Arjuna, that lord of mighty riches, overcome with wonder. His hair stood erect. He bowed low before God in adoration, and clasped his hands, and spoke:

ARJUNA:

> Ah, my God, I see all gods within your body;
> Each in his degree, the multitude of creatures;
> See Lord Brahma throned upon the lotus;
> See all the sages, and the holy serpents.

> Universal Form, I see you without limit,
> Infinite of arms, eyes, mouths, and bellies—
> See, and find no end, midst, or beginning.

> Crowned with diadems, you wield the mace and discus,
> Shining every way—the eyes shrink from your splendour
> Brilliant like the sun; like fire, blazing, boundless.

> You are all we know, supreme, beyond man's measure,
> This world's sure-set plinth and refuge never shaken,

---

[15]Ibid., p. 69.

Hindu temple at Jabalpur, India. Note "tank" or body of water for religious ablutions and community washing.

> Guardian of eternal law, life's Soul undying,
> Birthless, deathless; yours the strength titanic,
> Million-armed, the sun and moon your eyeballs,
> Fiery-faced, you blast the world to ashes.[16]

Here we see Krishna (as Vishnu), brighter than a thousand suns, express through endless multiplicity the same infinity which can also be expressed as the One, Brahman. God is here represented by the myriad things, and among them he is as an enthroned sovereign. But God as infinite series or infinite multiplicity also brings out the dark side of God: infinite series expressed through time as well as space; and in time all things perish, so God appears as destroyer—"By me these men are slain already," Krishna says a little later of Arjuna's foes. Hence this vision too is a justification of Arjuna's fighting, and of much more as well.

Yet God as personal being, with whom one can have a relationship of knowledge and love, and who moreover comes among people as friend and brother like

16Ibid., pp. 91–93.

Krishna, engenders a new spiritual sensitivity too. It was a theme emerging in both East and West; at about the same time this narrative was composed, Paul was writing, "We have seen the glory of God in the face of Jesus Christ."

ADVAITA VEDANTA
AND TANTRISM

A little later, new and sophisticated philosophical schools emerged to restate Hinduism's ancient wisdom. One was Advaita Vedanta, which may be rendered "Nondualism in the Vedic tradition," of the great Shankara (A.D. 686–718). Commenting on the Upanishads, Shankara brought home in radical metaphysical language its intuition that there is only one reality, Brahman. Brahman only exists; all else—every idea, form, and experience—is "superimposed" on Brahman owing to our *avidya,* ignorance of the true nature of reality. What we see ordinarily is *maya,* often translated "illusion," but this would have to be understood in the right sense, for maya is an appearance of Brahman and so is not unreal. The world is really there; it is not on a level with the pink elephants of the proverbial drunk. But it is not seen for what it is. Shankara liked to use the simile of a man who saw something lying on the ground and jumped, thinking it was a snake; he looked again, and saw it was only a piece of rope. In the same way, we really see something when we see the world, but misapprehend what it is we see; we think it is really many separate things, when actually it is "nondual"—it is but one "thing," Brahman.

Shankara's influence on the practical side of Hinduism was comparable to his philosophical influence. He reformed and promoted monasticism, establishing four great monastic centers of learning in the quarters of India. He tried to modify the harshness of caste distinction, and encouraged devotion to the Hindu gods as aspects of the One. In all this, although he would not admit it was a goal, he was establishing Hindu parallels to the intellectual monasticism, subtle nondualist philosophy, and conditional devotion to Buddhas and bodhisattvas of Buddhism.[17]

Another movement starting in these centuries cut across both Hinduism and Buddhism, and deeply affected the course of both. That is the complex and mysterious set of spiritual attitudes and practices called tantrism. It is a road to enlightenment through powerful initiations, "shock therapy" techniques, the negation of conventional morals and manners, magical-seeming acts and chants, and use of sexual imagery and ritual. Tantrism seeks through "radical" means to induce powerful consciousness-transforming experience, while preserving something of the "technical" aura of the old Vedic rites.

[17]On Shankara and Advaita Vedanta, see Eliot Deutsch, *Advaita Vedanta: A Philosophical Reconstruction* (Honolulu: East-West Center Press, 1969); Eliot Deutsch and J. A. B. van Buitenen, *A Source Book of Advaita Vedanta* (Honolulu: University of Hawaii, 1971); Y. Keshava Menon and Richard F. Allen, *The Pure Principle: An Introduction to the Philosophy of Shankara* (East Lansing, Mich.: Michigan State University Press, 1960), and Swami Prabhavananda and Christopher Isherwood, *Shankara's Crest-Jewel of Discrimination* (New York: Mentor Books, 1970).

One reason why tantrism's origins and teachings are so obscure is that it has often been the province of raffish and obscure segments of society, who have expressed through it reaction against the current religious "establishment"— brahmins, princely rulers, Buddhist monks. It presented itself to left-out people as a secret, "underground" path far more potent than the official teaching, if one were bold enough to reject conventionality by accepting it. If the adept, it says, does not shrink back or go mad at its "steep path," in a single lifetime it can bring him to a state of realization and power which would take countless lives by ordinary means.

Roughly, the procedures of tantra are this: The novice is initiated into the practice of a particular tantric path by a guru; this impartation of power is said often to be physically felt and is extremely important. Being empowered, the aspirant then seeks identity with a deity like Shiva or Kali through magical evocations of the god's visible presence, visual fixation on diagrams (*mandala* and *yantra*) of his powers, recitation of mantra which encapsulate his nature. By becoming one with the divinity, the aspirant hopes to share his or her cosmic realization and omnipotence.

In this process, the tantrist seeks to experience the god as the totality, the unity beyond all opposites—like male and female—indicated in the unity of god and consort-goddess.

To do this, one may liberate oneself from "partiality" by getting outside of structure—living independent of caste and morality. In some tantric traditions, in specific rites "forbidden" things, like meat, alcohol, and sex were partaken of, either symbolically or actually. Sexuality, in particular, is important to tantrism, not only because of the "shock therapy" effect of sexual rites, but also because it is a tremendous evoker of energy, which the skilled practitioner can then sublimate to the spiritual quest, and because it is a symbol and sacrament of the tantrist view of reality. In Hinduism, the male tantrist identifies himself with a male deity like Shiva, the absolute, and his female partner with Shiva's consort, Shakti, who is the phenomenal universe; as the couple unites, they mystically unite the absolute and the universe in a flash of ecstasy.

But the rite cannot do this sacramentally, nor can moral reversal be spiritually efficacious, nor the sexual energies be transmuted, until the novice is well advanced in one's tantric sadhana, or path. Unless, for example, one has truly negated one's self and identified with the god, sex is merely lust and not participation in divine mysteries.

Tantrism had an influence far beyond the schools which taught it in its strictest form. All Hindu worship on a serious level is now likely to show some influence of tantra, if only in the use of yantra and the repetition of the name and mantram of the deity over and over.

The important concepts of kundalini and the chakras come out of the tantric tradition, although they are represented today in most yoga. They are an interiorization of the Shiva/Shakti dynamic. The kundalini, or "Serpent Power," is a feminine energy believed to dwell, coiled three and a half times, at the base of the spine. Through yogic techniques of posture, breathing, and concentration, the kundalini is awakened and aroused to be drawn up the spinal column. In the process it "opens" six chakras, "circles," or lotus-centers of dormant psychic energy located along the spinal column at the solar plexis, heart, neck, and so forth.

This, together with the withdrawal of senses from the outer world incumbent upon yogic practice, is said to produce remarkable states of awareness. The final objective, however, is only achieved when the kundalini reaches the inside of the skull, where, with a psychic explosion, it awakens a ten-thousand petal lotus, which grants cosmic consciousness and God-realization. The awakening brings into the light an entire world within the head, replete with its own miniature mountain, lake, and sun and moon, and in its midst Shiva is enthroned.[18]

DEVOTIONAL HINDUISM

The early Middle Ages were times of realization of both the social and devotional promise of the Hindu reactions to Buddhism. In the process, Hinduism became a system integrating all the population of India into a loosely knit organism providing for a multitude of spiritual drives and social needs. New tribes and peoples throughout the land were brought into the system by being recognized as branches of major castes; thus thousands of subcastes, or *jati,* were created. The folk-gods of all these people were recognized as representations or aspects of one of the great gods of Hinduism—who by now owed as much or more to the indigenous traditions as to the Vedas. To these gods, devotion, the service of a loving heart, weighed more than legal righteousness or ritual.

Accounts of these gods, their myths and words and methods of worship, are presented in books called *Puranas,* deriving from the early Middle Ages. The devotional gods rejoice in colorful images and pictures, often being many-armed or animal-headed; they enjoy lavish temples and dramatic processions. It is this Hinduism which most moves the average Indian, and is most conspicuous to the tourist.

As a spiritual path, devotionalism is bhakti—the way to liberation or moksha through losing one's egocentricity in love, love for the chosen god. Love is, for most people, the human drive in which one most readily forgets (if only now and then) self-centeredness. In these moments, one's feelings go outside of one's self to share in the subjective life of another human being through caring and empathy; it is a start, at least, in losing one's finite selfhood and expanding awareness toward the Infinite, and the best many of us do. Why not, then, bhaktists say, utilize this drive to propel the ultimate quest, for loss of self in the divine? Through the love of gods which one can visualize and adore, but who are themselves not separate from the absolute, one shares their nonseparateness, for one becomes what one loves.

The greatest theologian of bhakti was Ramanuja (born c. 1017). Although trained in Shankara's nondualist Vedanta, Ramanuja was of strong religious bent and a devotee of Vishnu. He criticized Shankara's system as both inconsistent and

---

[18]See Rai Bahadur S. C. Vidyarnava, trans., *Siva Samhita* (Allahabad, India: Lalit Mohan Basu, 1942); Eliade, *Yoga;* and A. Bharati, *The Tantric Tradition* (Garden City, N.Y.: Doubleday Anchor Books, 1970).

spiritually unsatisfying. If everything is Brahman, he argued, but this is not known because of avidya, ignorance, then this would mean that the ignorance lies in Brahman himself. Better to postulate a different model for the relation of universe and God than veiled identity—an organic model in which God is like the head, and the cosmos the body, the two inseparable and interacting but having distinct modes of life. In this theistic system, God is personal and loving, and souls, in lifetime after lifetime, can respond to his love and grace, and by purifying themselves through bhaktic worship, draw near to him until they gain blissful eternity very near him in a paradisal heaven. Through highly sophisticated philosophical argument, Ramanuja defended the religion of the love of a personal god, which was and is the faith of the great majority of his countrymen.

The devotional gods are best thought of as belonging to two families—the Vishnu family and the Shiva family. The difference can be thought of in this way: Vishnu and his religious system are somewhat like the Western concept of God, in that the masculine figures are heroic and dominant and the feminine rather demure; Vishnu as God represents not so much the cosmic totality as the forces on behalf of order or righteousness. He descends from highest heaven whenever righteousness declines in incarnate form, working to restore good in the world.

In the Shiva system, God is above all simply the absolute and so the union of all opposites—creation and destruction, male and female. Shiva and his consort goddess thus have equal prominence, and she is far from unassertive. But although they may appear in visions, they are not usually claimed to be born incarnate among men.

Vishnu, it is said, slept over the cosmic ocean on a great serpent made up of the remains of the last universe before this one was formed; time is immense cycles of divine sleep and waking. When it came time for the cosmos to be made again, a lotus grew out of Vishnu's navel, and on the lotus appeared Brahma (not to be confused with Brahman), the creator god. He defeated the imps of chaos, and fabricated the world. Then Vishnu uprose, seated himself in high heaven on a lotus throne with his consort-goddess Lakshmi (fortune). The serpent arched his hoods over the divine sovereign to make a canopy; the lesser gods attended him.

But as time progresses, the set moral order of the world (dharma) declines and the power of demons grows. To counteract the latter, Vishnu periodically enters the world in bodily form; these are called his *avataras,* or descents. The most popular list gives ten: as a fish, a tortoise, a boar, a man-lion, a dwarf, Parasurama (a brahmin hero), Rama, Krishna, Buddha, and Kalkin, the incarnation yet to come.

The most important are Rama and Krishna. Rama is the hero of the *Ramayana,* a great epic very popular among all classes in India and Southeast Asia as well. It relates that Rama was a prince of the ancient city of Ayodhya, but owing to intrigue was wrongly exiled from court. His brother and faithful wife Sita accompanied him as he went to live a simple life deep in the forest. But Sita was abducted by the demon Ravana, and carried off to his palace in Lanka (Ceylon). Assisted by the monkey-army, and especially the mighty monkey hero Hanuman, Rama waged war against Ravana and prevailed. He received back his wife, was reconciled to his father, and finally presided over a long reign of peace and paradisal prosperity.

While Rama does not seem to have been considered divine at first, and his devotion did not become really popular until fairly recent times, he is now firmly established as an incarnation of Vishnu. He remains, however, essentially God as supreme human ideal: gentle, brave, devoted. Sita is the supreme model of the traditional India wife, utterly pure and loyal. Hanuman's loyalty is also extolled; in north India his shrines are quite common, and in some cases he is shown with his breast torn open to reveal Rama and Sita reigning in his heart.

We have already spoken of devotion to Krishna. He appears in three basic moods: as the marvelous infant, the divine lover, and the great hero of the Bhagavad-Gita. His name means "The Dark One," and much of his worship, especially the agricultural and erotic elements, derives from the culture of the darker indigenous peoples. His commonest title is Govinda, popularly regarded as meaning "Cowherd" or "Cow-finder," and because of attempts of the king, Kans, to kill him he was brought up by a plain cowherd family. The homely tales of his youth are full of milk, butter, and the warm smells of a cattle byre. In this simple and relatively innocent world Krishna is delightfully naughty and much beloved.

Here it was that as a child Krishna ate the dirt and stole the butter. Here it was that he grew to manhood, and as a young man would play his flute in the woods, enticing the shepherd girls to share his divine delight. The *Srimad Bhagavatam,* the classic text of the life of Krishna which beautifully combines a luminous simplicity with hints of the divine profundity beneath its surface, tells us:

> Sri Krishna is the embodiment of love. Love is divine, and is expressed in many forms. To Yasoda his foster-mother, the God of Love was her own baby Krishna; to the shepherd boys, Krishna was their beloved friend and playmate; and to the shepherd girls, Krishna was their beloved friend, lover, and companion.
>
> When Sri Krishna played on his flute, the shepherd girls forgot everything; unconscious even of their own bodies, they ran to him, drawn by his great love. Once Krishna, to test their devotion to him, said to them, "O ye pure ones, your duties must be first to your husbands and children. Go back to your homes and live in their service. You need not come to me. For if you only meditate on me, you will gain salvation." But the shepherd girls replied, "O thou cruel lover, we desire to serve only thee! Thou knowest the scriptural truths, and thou dost advise us to serve our husbands and children. So let it be; we shall abide by thy teaching. Since thou art in all, and art all, by serving thee we shall serve them also."
>
> Krishna, who gives delight to all and who is blissful in his own being, divided himself into as many Krishnas as there were shepherd girls, and danced and played with them. Each girl felt the divine presence and divine love of Sri Krishna. Each felt herself the most blessed. Each one's love for Sri Krishna was so absorbing that she felt herself one with Krishna—nay, knew herself to be Krishna.
>
> Truly has it been said that those who meditate on the divine love of Sri Krishna, and upon the sweet relationship between him and the shepherd girls, become free from lust and from sensuality.[19]

This is the very heart of Krishna bhakti devotion—this loss of self in the divine through the rapture of passionate love, until oneself, others, and the

[19]Swami Prabhavananda, *Srimad Bhagavatam: The Wisdom of God* (New York: Capricorn Books, 1968), pp. 199–200. Copyright © The Vedanta Society of Southern California. Reprinted with permission.

whole world become Krishna. His favorite among the milkmaids was the lovely Radha, whose image often stands beside his. However, he could not continue forever on earth—although he does in his heavenly world—in these pastimes of a divine youth. The time came for him to take up arms, slay the wicked king Kans, take over his and later another kingdom, and work against the forces of evil. He slew demons all over India, took part (as we have seen) in the great battle of the Mahabharata, during which he delivered the Bhagavad-Gita. He was a worthy and magnificent ruler; a princess of Berar, Rukmini, became his chief queen among 16,000 wives, and he had 180,000 sons.

This happy estate, however, was not to last. In a scenario typical of European mythology but oddly unique in India, Krishna's chief men fell into a drunken brawl, and soon had the whole capital city in a tumult. Krishna's brother, chief son, and best friends were all slain in the rioting. Unable to stop this disintegration into chaos, Krishna left to wander dejectedly alone in the woods. There a hunter accidentally killed him as he sat meditating; like Achilles, his heel was his only vulnerable spot, and there an arrow struck. Krishna is the only Indian god to die.

Krishna's story, then, begins with a divine infancy, flight, and murder of innocents reminiscent of Christianity, and ends on a note more suggestive of Greek tragedy or some bleak Nordic myth than mystic India. But in between the aura of divine mystery about the pranks of infancy and the dalliance of love evokes the warm maternalism and poetic passions of India.

Devotion to Vishnu and Krishna takes equally expressive form. Vaisnavas, devotees of Vishnu or one of his forms, tend to be vegetarian, and flesh offerings are not used in the worship, only plant and dairy products. Some mark themselves with a V-shaped symbol on the forehead and perhaps upper arm.

Hinduism may take very austere forms in the case of renunciants who "interiorize" it all, and worship without priest or temple. But it has never entertained much the Puritan idea that there is something virtuous about making ordinary worship drab. Rather, India (outside Buddhism) tends to feel that genuineness is found at extremes; whatever path a person takes, it should be taken all the way, with the abandon of the mystic or the lover, for greatest benefit. Ascetics may starve their eyes and ears as they starve their bellies, striving to find God in the all by negating him in any particular form.

The bhakta, the devotionalist, goes the other way and characteristically follows it without restraint; using the particular, the charming Krishna or the enigmatic Shiva, as stepping-stones of love to the all. This is the Hinduism of the temple, where nothing is spared of lights, music, flowers, jewels, pomp, incense, and offerings to create an atmosphere of kingship, love, and heavenly delight, which takes the worshipper out of the ordinary and into the transforming circle of the sacred. Images of the god may be sheathed in gems worth a royal ransom; on festivals the bejeweled deities may be taken through the streets on festooned elephants or giant chariots.

Above all in the worship of Krishna, devotees lose themselves in graceful dance and chanting to exciting music. Women place images of the infant Krishna in tiny cribs and, calling themselves "mothers of the god," rock him back and forth as an expression of love. In devotional services, often images of Krishna and Radha are put together on the swing the bride and groom share in Hindu weddings, and are rocked back and forth. Always, the motive is put in terms of casting aside self-restraint and just asking, "What more can I do to show my love? What more can I do to please the beloved god, to make myself his indulgent mother, lover, or companion?"[20]

The **Shiva** family has a different feel about it. Instead of sunny Vishnu and playful Krishna, here is a fierce ascetic crowned with the mysterious moon, or a wild dancer whose hair is serpents, or one whose presence is simply the heavy stoney pillar of the lingam. Rama was allied to an army of monkeys, but Shiva is companioned by a retinue of ghosts, and instead of the decorous Lakshmi or the charming Radha, his consort may be the grim Kali, of bulging eyes and tongue hanging out to lap the blood of her victims.

Yet Shiva and his family are also deities of immense power, mystic depth, and ultimate goodness. The difference is that while the Vishnu family, like the Western monotheistic God, represents in the divine all that is good, the Shiva family represents simply the all, the totality, the union that lies beyond all dualities of matter and spirit, creation and destruction—their "goodness" is in the wisdom which comes from initiation into this ultimate unity.

Shiva is descended from the deity of the Vedas named Rudra. A crossgrained god who lived off to himself in the mountains, and who sang and danced in his solitude, Rudra could capriciously bestow healing herbs or send an epidemic. Worshippers called him Shiva ("Auspicious One") more in fearful hope than trusting love, for his lonely power was great. Shiva seems then to have assimilated much of the mystic and yogic divinity of non-Aryan religion. By the latest of the Upanishads he already is the all—and, indeed, to those who lack the eye of wisdom, the universe itself does seem to sing and dance like a mountain madman with more zest than moral precision.

Shiva, serpent-entwined, is a much more enigmatic figure than Vishnu; one is less sure how to read his subtle, ambivalent smile. His three most important representations are as the Lord of the Dance, the Master Yogin, and the Lingam. As Lord of the Dance, he dances with perfect equilibrium and pounds his drum down through all the changes of the world, until the time comes for an age of the world to end; he then beats the drum louder and louder until its vibrations shatter the cosmos into its primal elements.

As Master Yogin, he is seated high in the Himalayas, on skull-faced Mount Kailas, his body covered with the white ash which is a symbol of the ascetic's burning-away of passion. He is seated on a tiger-skin pallet; his symbol, the trident staff, is in place beside him; the holy Ganges river leaps off the topknot of his long

---

[20]See Milton Singer, "The Great Tradition of Hinduism in the City of Madras," *Anthropology of Folk Religion,* ed. Charles Leslie (New York: Vintage Books, 1960). The spirit of Krishna devotion is evident in the "Hare Krishna" movement in America, with its fervent bhaktic singing and dancing. This movement derives from a Krishna devotional tradition started by Sri Chaitanya (c. 1486–1533) in Bengal. He and the movement regard Krishna as the supreme, personal God, and not as just an avatar of Vishnu or an expression of an ultimately impersonal Absolute like Advaita Vedanta.

matted hair. He is sunk deep in meditation, and his concentrated thought is what sustains the world; if he were to cease his mentation for even a moment, the world would begin to vanish like a dream, and "leave not a rack behind." The story is told, in fact, that once his consort came up behind him and playfully put her hands over her husband's eyes—but removed them in a hurry when she saw the mountains and forests fade, and the sun and stars start to blink out.

Or as the cosmic Being, the sheer life-force and sole reality which underlies all that is, Shiva can be simplified and abstracted still further, to the still upright column of the lingam . . . the pivot on which the wheel of the universe turns, or the phallus of an unquenchable will to live.

As Shiva represents absolute Being, his consort-goddess, called his Shakti or Power, is the whole of the phenomenal world, in all its bounty, danger, and change, forever wedded to the Absolute. She is thus a being of fierce splendor and power, and equal to Shiva just as in an even deeper sense the two are one. She is the fullness of the Eternal Feminine, the Great Mother and Mistress in all her moods, and she goes by countless names.

As Parvati, she is the world at rosy dawn, nature at its gentlest and loveliest. As Annapurna, she is the bountiful mother, the goddess of food and abundant harvest. But as Durga, the coloration shifts a bit; Durga is good for she slew a mighty demon, but the Great Goddess in this form is more chancy-looking: she proudly rides a lion and wields a great sword.

Finally, in the form of Kali, she is also good and the object of the devotion of mild and sapient saints. But she is good in a dark way which only the wise can understand, for on the face of it she is time and death. She bears a sword, and carries the severed head of a victim said to be a demon, killed out of mercy lest his bad karma become too weighty. Her tongue hangs out, around her waist are the arms of other victims, and their severed heads are garlanded around her neck. She is dark, often standing or dancing on the prostrate white body of Shiva, the passive Absolute whose energy she draws upon. She is worshipped with offerings of male goats slain in her temples, and in the past has been presented human sacrifice.

All of this expresses that Kali is the phenomenal world of time, change, and multiplicity. In it all that comes into being is sooner or later destroyed. So it is said that Kali will give birth to a child, fondle it at her breast, and then wring its neck.

The ways of Kali are not pleasant to contemplate, and one may wonder why such a goddess would be worshipped. Although the deities of other traditions, including the Western, also have their black sides, India is unrivaled in exuberence of expression of both the light and dark colors of the sacred.

But there are those who say that until Kali is fully understood and loved, one cannot truly find peace or know God, for peace and God are beyond the vicissitudes of creation and destruction, and one must confront them and pass through them first. They say Kali is standing there with her blood and her victims, and one cannot simply go around her; one day a person on the way to liberation must face her squarely, if not embrace her. Indeed, centering around Bengal there is a spiritual tradition called Shaktism, which focuses on the worship of the Great Mother; forgetting even Shiva, they hold that in Kali alone is the power of the universe and the wellspring of bliss.[21] Goddesses are also the main objects of worship in many villages.

Another style of devotionalism emerged at the very end of the Middle Ages on the spiritual frontier between Hinduism and Islam. The faith of Muhammad was then coming into India in force together with Muslim rulers. Eventually as much as a fifth of the people of India—the present populations of Pakistan and Bangladesh, plus a scattered minority in the Republic of India—became Muslim, drawn by Islam's practical advantages, the greater simplicity and human equality of this faith without image or caste, and the attractiveness of many of its Sufi preachers and mystics.

However, the majority of Hindus, especially of higher caste, remained Hindu and indeed became very conservative about it. The meeting of two cultures alien to each other, like Islam and Hinduism, produces two kinds of reaction. Some, generally the great majority, will respond with a conservative withdrawal into his or her own culture or faith. Especially if also politically subjugated, one will say, "They can take everything else from me; they will not take my faith," and cling to it all the more tenaciously and inflexibly. The ultratraditionalism for which Hindu society was famous until recently—rigid adherence to caste, rite, and the authority of past models—was not so much the heritage of the great creative periods of ancient India as a response, understandable in context, to the more recent centuries of Muslim and British rule, when it was the only possible vehicle for a Hindu sense of identity.

For others, the confrontation of faiths effects a different reaction. These are sensitive souls who say, "If one faith claims one truth, and another a different truth, then is not everything we have taken for granted thrown into question? Perhaps reality is instead a truth beyond them both." There were some, from the great Mughul emperor Akbar (r. 1556–1605) to lowly weavers and washermen, who out of this situation were driven to adore a God beyond all particular places and rigidities of orthodoxy. The wandering ecstatic of a God in all persons and places, who is loved in a bhaktic way, became a new and attractive style of pilgrim. A good example is the poet Kabir (1440–1518). Alluding to the Kaaba in Mecca, the center of Muslim devotion, and Mount Kailas in Tibet, venerated as the abode of Shiva and a place of Hindu pilgrimage, he sings:

> O servant, where dost thou seek Me?
> Lo! I am beside thee.
> I am neither in temple nor in mosque: I am neither in Kaaba nor in Kailash:
> Neither am I in rites and ceremonies, nor in Yoga and renunciation.
> If thou art a true seeker, thou shalt at once see Me; thou shalt meet Me in a moment of time.
> Kabir says, "O Sadhu! God is the breath of all breath."
>
> It is needless to ask of a saint the caste to which he belongs;
> For the priest, the warrior, the tradesman, and all the thirty-six castes, alike are seeking for God.
> It is but folly to ask what the caste of a saint may be;
> The barber has sought God, the washerwoman, and the carpenter . . .

[21]See Ernest A. Payne, *The Śaktas* (Calcutta: YMCA Press, 1933), and John G. Woodroffe, *Shakti and Shakta* (Madras: Ganesh, 1951).

Hindus and Moslems alike have achieved that End, where remains no mark of distinction.

If God be within the mosque, then to whom does this world belong?
If Ram be within the image which you find upon your pilgrimage, then who is there to know what happens without?

Hari is in the East: Allah is in the West. Look within your heart, there you will find both Karim and Ram;
All the men and women of the world are His living forms.
Kabir is the child of Allah and of Ram: He is my Guru, He is my Pir.[22]

A comparable mystic poet was Nanak, founder of the Sikh religion, which today numbers some eight million. Nanak (1470–1540) had, like Kabir, strong ties to both the Muslim and Hindu traditions. He had an ordinary upbringing and marriage, but when he was about thirty he left his family to heed a call to the renunciant life. Then, when he was about fifty, a decisive special vision was granted him. God above and beyond human places and faiths came to him, Nanak said, and pledged him to worship and teach faith in his Divine Name.

The god of this revelation was neither the god exclusively of Islam or Hinduism, but the one all-powerful, loving God who is above them both, who makes no unfavorable distinctions among mankind as to creed or caste, but rather looks into the heart. He may be called by any name—Brahma, Rama, Hari, or Allah—so long as the worshipper recognizes that he is not limited to any of them. Sikhs love above all just to call the Lord Sat Nam, the True or Absolute Name. The repetition of his name is itself true devotion, and equal to any pilgrimage to Mecca or Benares—in submission to it lies freedom. Here we see a fruitful combination of the fervent, loving devotion of bhaktic Hinduism and the strong Islamic concept of submission to a personal and sovereign God.

Nanak spent the rest of his life, surrounded by disciples, as an itinerant poet and minstrel of this God. Here is one of his most expressive poems:

Those who believe in power,
Sing of His power;
Others chant of His gifts
As His messages and emblems;
Some sing of His greatness,
And His gracious acts;
Some sing of His wisdom
Hard to understand;
Some sing of Him as the fashioner of the body,
Destroying what He has fashioned;
Others praise Him for taking away life
And restoring it anew.

Some proclaim His Existence
To be far, desparately far, from us;
Others sing of Him
As here and there a Presence
Meeting us face to face.

[22]Rabindranath Tagore, trans., *Songs of Kabir* (New York: The Macmillan Company, 1917), pp. 45–46, 112. Hari is a name for Vishnu. Karim means a Muslim wonder-working saint. Ram is, of course, Rama. A Pir is a Muslim Sufi teacher comparable to a Hindu guru.

Life Against Time

To sing truly of the transcendent Lord
Would exhaust all vocabularies, all human powers of expression,
Myriads have sung of Him in innumerable strains.
His gifts to us flow in such plenitude
That man wearies of receiving what God bestows;
Age on unending age, man lives on His bounty;
Carefree, O Nanak, the Glorious Lord smiles.[23]

Nanak believed he had been called to serve as the guru, or teacher, of this faith in the true God. After him, a succession of nine more gurus bore his authority. After the tenth and last, the Holy Granth, the Sikh scripture comprised of poems of Nanak, Kabir, and others took the place of a living teacher. The story of how Sikhism became inevitably another religion, instead of a faith beyond all religion, and of how its history led it to some extent from the poetic and mystical rapture of Nanak to become a movement that came to exalt the manly, military virtues, is a colorful and fascinating one. But it cannot be told here.[24]

THE PRACTICE OF HINDUISM

The long past we have looked at is still present in India. Much has been poured into the melting pot of Indian culture over the centuries and millenia, but little (except Buddhism) has been lost. The earliest continues alongside the latest.

[23]Trilochan Singh and others, *Adi-Granth: Selections from the Sacred Writings of the Sikhs* (New York: The Macmillan Company, 1960; London: George Allen and Unwin, © 1960; reprinted New York: Samuel Weiser, Inc., 1974), p. 30. Reprinted by permission of George Allen and Unwin, Ltd. and Samuel Weiser, Inc.

[24]See John Clark Archer, *The Sikhs* (Princeton: Princeton University Press, 1946).

Portrayal of Ganesha, the elephant-headed god who is son of Shiva and remover of obstacles, with his consort. From Nepal.

As jet planes whine over modern Delhi or Bombay, brahmin priests still chant the Vedas and prepare the ancient fire rites. Hindu worship and social expression, while capable of change, move at a slower rate than intellectual or historical forces. Let us look at some of these phenomena.

In a devout Indian household, especially of the upper castes, the day begins early. It is understandable that dawn should seem the most apt time for worship in India. Not only is it natural that one should turn to God at the beginning of a day's activities, but the Indian dawn has a special quality. Except in winter, the day soon enough becomes wearisomely hot, muggy, or dusty. But for a short time, just before and during sunrise, it is as though an enchantment had fallen over the ancient land. The air is limpid, fresh, and inviting; dew gems the grass; all is as still and hopeful as the deep meditation of Shiva just before a new world streams forth from his thoughts. At this hour, the head of the household arises, splashes himself with water, and going out on his porch or rooftop says the Gayatri mantram, the morning hymn to the sun. He may place on his body sacred marks, indicating of what deity he is a devotee, who represents his "chosen ideal."

He then proceeds to the household shrine of the chosen deity. There he presents morning worship: he ritually chants praise and mantra of the deity, presents cups of water, washes the image, offers food cooked by his wife. He may also study and meditate. If the household can afford it, the rites may be performed by a retained brahmin; otherwise, they must be done by the head of the household.

The household, in fact, is the real center of Hinduism, although of course its religious life is rarely seen by the foreign visitor, unlike that of the spectacular temples. But many devout Hindus never go to public temple. They express their faith through home customs and rites; to follow the home rites of one's caste and lineage is expected for social standing, at least in such matters as coming-of-age and marriage; worship at the temple is much more a matter of personal preference.

In the upper castes, there are samskaras, or sacraments, which mark the stages of life for boys, and would be marked by appropriate family ceremonies with a brahmin officiating: birth, the child's first eating of solid food, first haircut, attainment of manhood when he is invested with the sacred cord.

No occasion is greater in Hindu family life than a wedding. For a woman, it is the decisive event in her life. She has no separate sacramental initiations; her marriage is the great initiation that sets up her spiritual framework. After marriage, it is with and through her husband that she formally worships the patron of the household—although women worship in the temples with other women. The wife does not worship at the household shrine, but prepares the offerings the husband presents, and in a deeper sense worships the god of whom her husband is family priest in her husband, since priest and god become identified.

A Hindu marriage is a long, exhausting ceremony lasting several days. There are offerings, formal meetings of the two families and of the bride and groom (who if of very traditional families would not have seen each other prior to the wedding day). There are vivid rites such as the bride and groom sitting together on a swing, and later binding their hands to each other, the groom saying, "I am heaven, thou art earth."

Funerals, on the other hand, are not generally performed by brahmins, at least of high status. Although a member of a class of funeral priests may officiate, the chief functionary at a funeral of a man is the deceased's eldest son, who lights his father's funeral pyre, and when the skull becomes red-hot, cracks it with a stick. Bodies are brought from all over India to the banks of the Ganges, especially at Benares, to be burned; the ashes are thrown into the sacred river. Even if it is not possible to bring the body to Benares, the ashes may later be brought to that site.

All these rites suggest indirectly some of the great themes of Indian thought, and point to both unities and tensions in Indian culture. The funeral fire reminds us of the Vedic sacrificial fire, and tells us that death is but another stage in the cycle of conception and consumption through which the sacred fire dances. The sacramental structure of life, and the role of the eldest son, suggests the organic, biological view of life of which we have spoken.

Another usage which does so is the caste system. Caste presents its own paradox: on the one hand, it suggests the organic unity of life; on the other, a desire for symbols of separateness—each group in its own place, not eating or mating with those outside a small unit. The basic dynamic in caste is the purity-impurity tension.

Although the ancient classification of society had only four great orders, the practical division of modern society is into thousands of *jati,* literally "births," with their own caste rules. They range from various types of brahmins through bankers, silversmiths, and farmers down to the "untouchables," to whose lot fell tasks such as sweeping, washing, and tanning hides.

The real principle of division is not occupation, as many think, but commensality—who can cook food for whom, who can eat with whom, and by extension who can marry whom, or, for that matter, can even come near whom without pollution. It is a question of realtive purity and impurity. One is made impure by contact with a member of a lower caste—sharing water or food, being touched by the lower one's spittal. These contacts would require ritual purification. A basic principle is that products of the body pollute; thus barbers and washermen, handling hair and grime from human bodies, are low on the caste scale.

So far we have dealt with aspects of the organic, dharma side of Hindu life— birth, marriage, death, caste. But even here, since caste itself is founded on a sense of the pure versus the impure, we get a glimmer of that basic thinking in terms of dualisms or polarities which carries up to the distinction of dharma and moksha. The moksha possibility is exemplified in other highly visible aspects of Hindu society: the holy man and the temple. But as a sort of transition to the Other Side, there are things which are simply pure and purifying; they stand as symbols of transition, on the borderline between the realm of dharma and that of moksha, and probably go back to days before the dichotomy of the two levels went beyond thinking of the impure and the pure. Two examples are water and the sacred cow.

There is a "tank" of fresh water by every temple not on a stream, river, or ocean, and the main places of pilgrimage, like Benares, are near rivers or the sea. The Ganges, flowing past Benares, is the most sacred water of all, streaming from the head of Shiva, and Hindus in the millions throng to it to bathe.

An unforgettable sight confronting every traveler to India is the innumerable white humpbacked cows wandering freely about streets, marketplaces, and all but the busiest sections of cities. The gentle-eyed beasts, often no better fed than the masses of Indians but safe from slaughter, frustrate one as their slow ambling holds up traffic, but they are as much a part of India as the dust itself. The sensitive observer may see, in their warm and much-beloved frames which appear in the most unlikely places, a different concept of the relation of man and animal from the Western, one of living together rather than of superiority of man over beast. The cows all belong to someone, to whom they supply milk, and dung for fuel and plaster, but they seem also a public symbol, which indeed they are. They suggest the warm maternalism that India adores. Mohandas Gandhi, with his keen, non-Western perception, once remarked that the cow is really the most universal Hindu symbol, and cow protection its most expressive principle. Hindus, he said, may agree on nothing else, but they unite on the veneration and protection of the cow, a token of maternity, simplicity, nonmaterialism, and nonviolence. The products of the cow—its milk, urine, and dung—are purifying and used in purificatory rites.

Visible reminders of the moksha side of things are the numerous sadhus, the holy men of India. Virtually every Hindu village and homestead may from time to time have strange, yet familiar, visitors. They may be sons of the house or village, or from far away, but they will no longer be bound by family ties or have any claim other than charity upon the support of anyone.

The sadhu has in principle cut himself loose from society to be free for the greatest of quests. For what he represents—even if personally unworthy—he is welcomed and fed, his blessing sought and his curse feared. Sadhus have no centralized discipline like that of Western monastics, although most do acknowledge the absolute authority of their own guru, or in a few cases of an order. A sadhu may in turn establish his own "family" after the spirit, for disciples may join him and devout laymen may seek him out to become his spiritual pupils. To these the sadhu becomes formally a guru; he initiates them into his method, be it Vedantic, Tantric, devotional, or whatever. He takes on the burden of the disciples' karma, and becomes their means of grace; followers worship the "lotus feet" of their guru. As the means to God for them, he becomes their personification and presence of God.

The way of life among sadhus varies greatly. Some wander as of old from village to village, teaching and begging. Some frequent temples and pilgrimage sites, where they seek alms and instruct in the appropriate devotions. Many are childlike, jovial spirits, going in merry bands from festival to festival. Others are unspeaking recluses deep in the woods, known only to a few who supply their meager needs. Some are charlatans, some are crazed, some are wise and learned, some true saints. Some were born to the holy life and have really followed no other. Some were prominant in business or civic affairs, and only made the renunciation late. Some are devotees of Vishnu, wearing the V-shaped marks; others of Shiva, and cover themselves with white ash. Traditionally, the ochre robe is the token of asceticism; some wear it, others rags, others nothing at all. Some shave their heads, others wear hair and beard as long and matted as old vines. But all are part of the pageant of Hinduism, and are venerated by traditional Hindus. Insofar as they are God-realized, they *are* God, for they have become transparent to the God within, who is as much God as God anywhere. God is believed to be nowhere more present and visible than in the forms of his Great Souls; to venerate them is to venerate God Their diversity, and the strangeness of some of them, only bespeaks the mystery and infinity of the Divine Sea whose waves creast in his lovers.

The temple, through the medium of art and architecture rather than of a human life, also bespeaks the other side. Even as one approaches it, one senses the approach of another kind of realm. Here are lively people progressing upward in festive mood, and here are special shops selling flowers for offerings. The temple may be alive with monkeys and birds, with sacred cows grazing on the lawn, but it is also a throne room, and a brilliant image of the deity or a lingam stands toward the back. The arrangement and schedule of the temple are those of a king in his court. The deity is awakened in the early morning with conch trumpets, given his meals with regal ceremony, presented entertainments of music and dance. There is even a siesta in midday when the curtains about his throne are closed. At regular hours he holds court; then his subjects come with their gifts, most commonly wreaths of flowers, which are handed to a priest, naked from the waist up, who takes them and tosses them over the image. He receives a token payment, and often bestows on the worshipper a touch of color on the forehead as a blessing.

The interior of the temple is splendid and colorful, suggesting the heavenly delights of the pure realms of the gods, who in turn shatter like prisms the clear light of the Absolute into these gay colors. The gods too suggest that beyond mere purity is the playful delight of the divine, rolling out world after world. This warm and vivid atmosphere, of a piece with India's rain and sun, remains deeply impressed on a visitor long afterward.

Hinduism has undergone slow changes in modern times, as it has all through its long history. Just as earlier problems were the meetings of Aryan and indigenous cultures, and of Hinduism and Islam, so the basic problem of thinking Hindus in the nineteenth and twentieth centuries has been the meeting of Hindu and Western values. How can the ancient faith respond to Western science, education, democracy, and the economic and social dislocations they bring? How does Hinduism fit in among the religions of the world? Dealing with questions like these while living in two worlds at once led Hindu intellectuals to produce a fascinating array of new philosophical and spiritual options, some of which have had considerable influence in the West.

One great influence was Ramakrishna (1836–86). Not an intellectual himself, this Bengali was in many ways a traditional Indian saint and mystic, deeply devoted to Kali the Great Mother, able to go into deep ecstatic trance, profoundly aware of God in all things. Yet he was also aware of modern religious pluralism, and after experiencing several religious traditions, including Islam and Christianity, from within to his own satisfaction, he taught that all religions were of the same essence and paths to God-realization. Disciples of his, particularly Swami Vivekananda (1862–1902), brought his message to the West. In his writings and in the work of the Ramakrishna Order, he did much to make Vedantic Hinduism and the mysticism of Ramakrishna an intellectually vigorous and compassionate faith relevant to the modern world both in India and the West.

Undoubtedly the most significant of all modern Hindus was Mohandas K. Gandhi (1869–1948), who led the movement for Indian independence through "soul force," the nonviolent resistence by noncooperation, demonstrations, and fasting, which Gandhi drew from the Jain's ahimsa and the Bhagavad-Gita's karma-yoga.

In the life of Gandhi, as in all else, we see the Indian religious tradition working once again to weave together in a new pattern the two realms where it has seen and known the one God—the social order and the infinite within the self.

FOUR

WISDOM
EMBARKED
FOR
THE
FARTHER
SHORE

The Journey of Buddhism

Statue of the reclining Buddha, at the hour of his physical death and full attainment of Nirvana. From Ceylon.

A RELIGION OF TRANSFORMATION
OF CONSCIOUSNESS

Buddhism is many things. On the flat Ganges plains east of Benares, it is an ancient enshrined tree, said to be a scion of the very tree under which he who is called the Buddha, on the night of a full moon, ascended through the four stages of trance and attained full, perfect, and complete enlightenment. In southeast Asia, it is steep-roofed temples, rich in gold and red, which house conventionalized images of the same Buddha, perhaps standing to teach, perhaps in the seated meditation posture of enlightenment, perhaps reclining as he makes his final entry into Nirvana. The images will probably be gilded, gleaming with transcendent golden light, and the figure's eyes will be half-closed and enigmatic. Around his head may be a many-pointed crown, or simply a burst of flame. Outside the temple, saffron-robed monks of the Blessed One walk with begging bowls, seeking alms.

Or, in the snowy Himalayas, Buddhism is a prayer wheel, a cylinder on an axle inscribed with a mantram such as "Hail the Jewel in the Lotus," and set up on a roadway or around a temple to be spun by passing pilgrims. It is an old Zen monk making tea or contemplating the rocks in his monastery garden. It is vigorous, dynamic young people in modern Japan, organizing rallies that combine Buddhist chanting with marching bands and rock concerts.

What is it that ties this tradition together? Buddhism is not rooted in a single culture area as is Hinduism, but is an international religion, a movement *introduced* in historical time into every society where it is now at home. It has deeply pervaded these cultures and deeply identified with them. But the perceptive observer never quite loses awareness that, on the one hand, this religion is not identical with all the spiritual life of the culture, and on the other hand, that it is a movement wider than the culture, and has brought in gifts from outside.

All of this gives Buddhism a somewhat different atmosphere from the Hindu context out of which it emerged to combine something of the Indian spiritual tradition with very different cultures. Instead of the rich, heavy "biological" flavor of Hinduism, of which we have spoken in the preceeding chapter, Buddhism has a more psychological thrust.

What is distinctive about Buddhist altars is that, instead of portraying the archetypal hero, mother, or cosmic phallus, as do Hindu, the image communicates a unified psychological state—profound meditation, warm compassion, or even unambiguous fury against illusion. Buddhist practices, too, are focused on strong and clear states of unified consciousness. Either they produce clear states, or they draw power from beings who have achieved unfettered clarity.

Given this fundamental psychological thrust, let us briefly look at Buddhism in terms of the three forms of religious expression. We shall examine them in reverse order.

The basic sociological fact in Buddhism is the samgha, the order of monks. It is not a unified organization throughout the Buddhist world, and its structure and role vary. In modern Japan it is often no longer even celibate. But almost always where there is Buddhism, there are men and women who have given up "natural" life and its goals to take formal vows which orient life in another direction, the realization of a different state of consciousness from the ordinary. Inseparably from this purpose, they are teachers and bearers of Buddhist tradition, and by their distinctive garb, monasteries and temples, and way of life they make the Buddhist presence unavoidably visible in the midst of society.

Buddhist practice is, as has been indicated, immensely varied. But it centers around three foci: the imaged ideal of the Buddha, the transformation of consciousness, and the transformation of karma or practical destiny. The Buddha is revered and presented to the world as the fully realized being who thereby teaches and epitomizes the true nature of all other beings; he attained realization through accepting the destiny to which he had been born and which he had himself purposed in previous lives, and through profound psychological self-analysis and self-control. Buddhist practice for transformation of consciousness works in the same way and so is most fully expressed in meditation, but also includes chanting and ritual. But the Buddha and other beings who share aspects of his state are also masters of the karma which shapes our present and subsequent lives, for perfect self-realization gives omniscience and reshapes the flow of currents in the karmic ocean. Interaction with the Buddha, with his symbols, with the samgha, and following the ordinary moral teachings which come out of his awareness, exposes people to waves that reshape destiny for good even in those who do not formally work to transform consciousness; theirs may be equanimity here and a better rebirth as a king or sage or god.

Buddhist theoretical expression centers around the same three foci: it is concerned with the meaning of the Buddha, the transformation of consciousness, and the interacting work of karma in this and other worlds. Above all it is psychological in point of departure, for it is concerned with the analysis of human perception and experience. Buddhist thought is not a vague diffuse mysticism, but a sharp precise intellectualism, which delights in hard logic and numerical lists of categories. It holds that ordinary life is unsatisfactory for it is based on ignorance and desire, resulting in inability to realize that there is no real "self." All entities within the universe, including human beings, are impermanent compounds that come together and come apart. The answer is a different kind of mind, a wisdom mind, which finds the middle way between all attachments, uniting all opposites—being, like the Buddha,

Main Themes in Buddhism

Buddhism as a religion for society

Village temple

Theravada	Mahayana
Celebration of Wesak and other popular festivals of Buddhism	Seventh month celebration of returning spirits in China and Japan
	Lotus Sutra
Merit-making lay Buddhism	"Pure Land" Buddhism
	Nichiren Buddhism
The five precepts The four "unlimited" virtues	Idea of the Buddhahood of all things
	Bodhisattva idea
	Idea of three Buddha "bodies" and devotion derived from it
Four Noble Truths	*Tibetan Book of the Dead*
	Zen
The Theravada Samgha	Heart Sutra
	Nagarjuna's "Void" teaching
	Vajrayana or Tantric Buddhism
Arhat concept Vipassana meditation	Chod ritual

Buddhism as a means for liberation for individuals

Thematic Chart III.   Here we see that the fundamental tension in historical Buddhism is between the religion as a way for individuals, like the monk on the arhat or bodhisattva path, to seek absolute liberation from conditioned reality; and the fact that as the dominant religion of nations and cultures it has also had to serve ordinary men and women. Mahayana and Theravada Buddhism, however, have handled this tension in different ways.

free of partiality toward any segment of the cosmos—and is therefore, in its unclouded clarity, open to all omniscience, all skill, and all compassion.

We shall now look at the life of the Buddha, to see how these themes are expressed in the traditional account of his quest and achievement.

THE LIFE
OF THE BUDDHA

At the beginning of the tradition of which all these forms and much else are branches lies the life of one man, Siddhartha Gautama, of the Sakya clan, called the Buddha, dated by modern scholars approximately 563–483 B.C. The Buddha was born, according to tradition, at Lumbini, today about where the border of India and Nepal lies north of Benares. His father was ruler of a tiny state in the foothills of the Himalayas.

Tradition has it that a wise old brahmin came to the court and, observing certain remarkable signs on the infant's body, predicted the wonderful child would become either a world emperor or a Buddha, that is, an Enlightened One and World Savior. The father, being more political than spiritual in orientation, preferred that his son follow the world emperor option. Realizing that if the gifted boy saw the suffering of the world, he would be so moved by compassion that he would prefer to save mankind from pain than rule from a throne, the king determined to shield him from any sights of ill. He built Siddhartha Gautama glorious pleasure palaces, equipped with everything to delight the heart of a young prince, from chariots to dancing girls. All was surrounded by a high wall.

There the future Buddha matured, married, and had a son. But even unbroken amusement palls eventually, and the prince persuaded his charioteer to take him for rides down the road toward the nearby city. He took four trips in all, and saw four thought-provoking sights: an aged man, a man suffering in agony of a hideous disease, a corpse, and finally an old wandering monk.

After this, Siddhartha saw even his dancing girls in a different light, and large disturbing issues clouded his mind.

What is the meaning of life, he asked himself, if its initial promise of joy ends long before its dreams can possibly all be fulfilled, in the old age in which one totters backward into infantilism again, or in sickness which can reduce a man or woman full of zest and hope to the state of a howling animal, or finally to the apparent blank extinction of death? How can one be delivered from this ghastly witches' revel of birth, fancy, and pain?

Siddhartha did not know, but he knew that until these questions were answered he could no longer live for anything else than finding their answers. The last sight, the itinerant monk with his staff and begging bow, inspired him with the idea of a life wholly dedicated to finding the answers he sought. Not long after, in the middle of the night, the prince kissed his wife and son farewell without waking them, and slipped off with his faithful charioteer to the banks of a river. There he exchanged his fine raiment for the coarse garb of a renunciant. He then proceeded alone on the great quest.

In his search he sampled the web of paths to realization which crisscrossed the spiritual map of India. He talked with brahmins. He worked with two teachers of trance meditation, and went the route of extreme asceticism, getting down to one grain of rice a day, and becoming so emaciated that his ribs and spinal column stood out as if he were a walking skeleton. But he found that neither philosophy nor fasting and self-control alone brought what he desired. He gave them up and went back to a moderate diet.

Then, late one afternoon, as he wandered not far from the banks of the Ganges, he felt that the time had come. Purchasing a pallet of straw from a farmer, he seated himself on it under a huge fig tree. He placed his hand firmly to the ground and swore by the good earth itself he would not stir from that spot until he attained complete and final enlightenment. All night he remained there, sunk in deeper and deeper meditation. Mara, the evil one, buffeted him with furious storms and sweet temptations, but a wave of the Blessed One's hand was enough to dispel them. His consciousness refined itself by moving through four stages of trance, beginning with the calmness of the passions that concentration brings, and ending with transcendence of all opposites. He also passed through several stages of awareness. First he saw all of his previous existences. Then he saw the previous lives, the interlocking deaths and rebirths, of all beings, and he grasped all the karmic forces at work; the universe became like a mirror to him. Finally he saw with full understanding what principles underlay this web and how extrication from it is possible. He saw the mutual interdependence of all things, and how egocentric ignorance leads sentient beings inevitably through desire to suffering, death, and unhappy rebirth. The Four Noble Truths (to be discussed later) appeared in his mind: All life is suffering; Suffering is caused by desire; There can be an end to desire; The end is in the Eightfold Path.

Siddhartha Gautama was now a Buddha, an "Enlightened One" or "One who is awake." He is also called the Tathagata, an expression difficult to translate, meaning something like "He who has gone thus," in the sense of "He who has passed beyond all bounds; one cannot say where he is but can only point in the direction he went"—referring to his overcoming of all "conditioned reality" in his enlightenment to become, one might say, "universalized." He was one with the universe itself and not any particular part of it in principle, even though, of course, he continued to have a physical body. (Another title commonly used in Asia is Sakyamuni, Shaka or Shakamuni in Japanese, meaning "Sage of the Sakya Clan.")

After remaining in meditation many days, he arose and went toward Benares. On its outskirts, in Sarnath, the "Deer Park," he met five ascetics with whom he had been associated before. He preached to them about the Middle Way and the Four Noble Truths. They were converted, and became his first disciples.

As he wandered about teaching, other disciples came to join him, until there was a band of some sixty accompanying the Enlightened One. Upon entering the Buddha's order, each took the "Three Refuges" or "Three Jewels": I take refuge in the Buddha; I take refuge in the dharma; I take refuge in the samgha. The dharma here means the Buddha's teaching; the samgha is the order of monks. Thus the Three

Jewels affirm that the Buddha is the supreme embodiment of the potential of human life; his teaching tells how he can be emulated and what his wisdom is; the order is the custodian of the Buddha and dharma for future generations and the social context in which the potential can best be reached. We see here Buddhism taking the three forms of religious expression: there is an intellectual teaching; an emerging object of worship and a formal act of submission; there is a sociological expression, the samgha, which today is probably the oldest continuing nonfamilial social institution in the world.

The life of monks was strictly governed by rules, of which the basic ten are prohibitions against 1) taking life, 2) taking what is not given, 3) sexual misconduct, 4) lying, 5) drinking liquor, 6) eating after noon, 7) watching dancing, singing, and shows, 8) adorning oneself with garlands, perfumes, and ointments, 9) sleeping in a high bed, and 10) receiving gold and silver. (These rules are still followed by Buddhist monks although sometimes are intrepreted in an allegorical sense in northern traditions. Devout laymen often undertake the first five.)

The Buddha's ministry, which lasted forty-five years after his enlightenment, was generally successful. Of those to whom he preached, many were said to have become arhants—fully liberated beings who will suffer no more rebirths. Since being a Buddha is unique, the arhant state is the spiritual goal of the Buddha's preaching. When the band of disciples reached sixty, he sent them out as missionaries. Thousands came to the Buddha or his disciples seeking lay or monastic initiation, many from the highest ranks of society. Sometimes whole tribes or ascetic orders were converted at once. In time an order of nuns was established. Valuable pieces of land were given the order.

There was, of course, opposition. Certain brahmins murmured against the Buddha's doctrine. One disciple, Devadatta, egged on by a hostile king, became a "Judas" and tried to kill the Buddha, but his plots were foiled by the sage's perception. The Buddha's end finally came from eating tainted food; he died meditating in great peace surrounded by his disciples, passing again through the stages of trance, imparting final wisdom to the samgha, such as "Be ye lamps unto yourselves," and "All compounds are transitory." Breathing his last, he then transcended all particularized existence and joined Nirvanic consciousness.

This is the story traditionally told of the Buddha. Much of it is legendary, or a reading back of later Buddhist developments, but it is nonetheless important for it presents the image of the Buddha that shaped the 2,500 years of Buddhist history.[1]

BASIC BUDDHIST TEACHING

When the Buddha returned to preach to the five ascetics in the Deer Park after his enlightenment, he preached to them the Middle Way. When they first saw him and recognized him as one who had been with them but had left, they mocked

---

[1]On the life of the Buddha, see E. J. Thomas, *The Life of the Buddha as Legend and History* (London: Routledge and Kegan Paul, 1927), and the shorter summary in Richard H. Robinson, *The Buddhist Religion: A Historical Introduction* (Belmont, Calif.: Dickenson Publishing Company, Inc., 1970).

him as a pleasure lover who had gone back to soft living. But when he opened his mouth to speak, they could not resist a wisdom which went beyond their mere pride in denying the flesh.

Of the Middle Way he said:

> Those foolish people who torment themselves, as well as those who have become attached to the domains of the senses, both these should be viewed as faulty in their method, because they are not on the way to deathlessness. These so-called austerities but confuse the mind which is overpowered by the body's exhaustion. In the resulting stupor one can no longer understand the ordinary things of life, how much less the way to the Truth which lies beyond the senses. The minds of those, on the other hand, who are attached to the worthless sense-objects, are overwhelmed by passion and darkening delusion. They lose even the ability to understand the doctrinal treatises, still less can they understand the method which by supressing the passions leads to dispassion. So I have given up both these extremes, and have found another path, a middle way. It leads to the appeasing of all ill, and yet it is free from happiness and joy.[2]

The Middle Way becomes on its deepest levels an attitude that seeks to find the delicate, infinitely subtle point of absolute equilibrium between all extremes and polarities, from the obvious balancing off of asceticism and self-indulgence, to the recondite metaphysical reaches of eschewing attachment either to life or death, to desire for being or desire for nonbeing. Everything comes in pairs of opposites, the Buddha taught, in our world of partialities, multiplicity, "conditioned reality." The senses, the desires, the unexamined life get "hung up" on one side or the other in these pairs of opposites, thinking one side or the other is "better." The way of wisdom is to balance them off to be one with the totality that includes them both instead of just a part—and so have the permanence and invincibility of the totality. The man of wisdom is stable like the sky, not just like clouds now blown this way, now that, and finally dissipated.

The Four Noble Truths go deep into the psychological analysis behind the Middle Way idea, and the process to attain perfect equilibrium and totality. In his Deer Park sermon, the Buddha went on to say:

> What then is the Holy Truth of Ill [Suffering]? Birth is ill, decay is ill, sickness is ill, death is ill. To be conjoined with what one dislikes means suffering. To be disjoined from what one likes means suffering. Not to get what one wants, also that means suffering. In short, all grasping at any of the five Skandhas involves suffering.
> What then is the Holy Truth of the Origination of Ill? It is that craving which leads to rebirth, accompanied by delight and greed, seeking its delight now here, now there, i.e. craving for sensuous experience, craving to perpetuate oneself, craving for extinction.
> What then is the Holy Truth of the Stopping of Ill? It is the complete stopping of that craving, the withdrawal from it, the renouncing of it, throwing it back, liberation from it, nonattachment to it.

[2]Edward Conze, *Buddhist Scriptures* (Harmondsworth, Middlesex, England: Penguin Classics, 1959), pp. 55–56. Copyright © Edward Conze, 1959. Reprinted by permission of Penguin Books Ltd.

Wisdom Embarked for the Farther Shore

What then is the Holy Truth of the steps which lead to the stopping of Ill? It is this holy eightfold Path, which consists of right views, right intentions, right speech, right conduct, right livelihood, right effort, right mindfulness, right concentration.[3]

These Truths can be summarized as consisting of two pairs. The first is:

All life is suffering (or ill, or pain, or anxiety, or bitter frustration).
Suffering is caused by desire (or craving, or attachment).

This pair is the analysis of the ordinary human condition: a mad circle dance, fueled by ignorance, of suffering and desire chasing each other. The more we suffer, the more we want things to assuage or distract. The more we get, the more does anxiety that we will lost them, and frustration at the transience of all things, build up further suffering. And so around and around.

Thus the good news in the second pair:

There can be an end to desire.
The way out is the Eightfold Path.

Buddhism is sometimes thought of as a pessimistic religion, but that is so only in its assessment of the ordinary life governed by the play of the first two Noble Truths. Buddhism is one of the most optimistic of religions in its vision of the ultimate potential of mankind once that syndrome is broken. For the third of the Noble Truths says the syndrome of suffering can be ended by the stopping of craving; at this point the vicious circle can be halted. One can throw sand in its gears and pull the plug on its turbulence.

Desire, then, is the vulnerable point at which the circle can be broken. It is vulnerable because there is something we *can* do about craving. Craving or desire, the Buddha said, is like a fire, and any fire requires fuel. If fuel is taken away, the fire must die down. The fuel of the fire of desire is the many things to which the senses are attached. How does one pull back the senses from these attachments? By concentration or meditation, the last and culminating point of the Eightfold Path, which focuses one's awareness on something other than objects of desire, and so lets the senses quiet down from burning for things they can never really have.

What is the goal of meditation? Ultimately, it is Nirvana, the state absolutely transcending all pairs of opposites, and so all "conditioned reality," by the blowing out of all flames of attachment. In Nirvana, all conditioning, including the notion of being a separate individual self, is gone utterly beyond.

It must not be supposed that Nirvana is simply a state hardly distinguishable from annihilation. It is rather the opposite—universalization, the falling away of all barriers so that the mind becomes undifferentiated from horizonless infinity. This is a statement of psychological quality, rather than ontological as it probably would be in Hinduism. But the full, attractive, positive nature of Nirvana must be stressed. The word Nirvana is said to mean "extinguish" or "blow out," like blowing out a

[3]Conze, *Buddhist Scriptures,* pp. 186–87.

flame, yet it does not mean disappearance in a negative sense, but rather the blowing out of all the fires of desire which constrict us. It does not mean extinction of consciousness, but extinction of the desires that cage and enslave consciousness. Our present consciousnesses are usually bound up with relishing sensory input and the accompanying mind-fogging cravings and self-delusions. It is virtually impossible for us now to know what Nirvanic consciousness, genuinely free of all this, would be like. Nirvana is truly the opposite of life as we know it. But for all that, or rather because of that, in Buddhist literature it is portrayed as the Otherness which is utterly desirable, a sparkling and golden light, calm beyond all imagining.

Nor is the quest for Nirvana escapist. Far from being less alive, active, or useful, the person passed into it, if one can so speak—or brought near to it—is far more, infinitely more, of all of these, as well as blissful to an unlimited degree. But one simply cannot express in any words the meaning of these statements. All language comes out of making distinctions, and so is bound up with the pairs of opposites that rack the conditioned world. Nirvana is beyond all opposites; what is left, so to speak, when the last of them are surpassed. Therefore, although we know from the unsatisfactory nature of life within attachments, contraries, and conditions that Nirvanic transcendence would be supremely desirable and glorious, words cannot tell what it is, only what it is not, and those who have been there can only smile.

Nirvana is not merely an enhanced personal existence, as if it were just a heaven gained by good merit. As we have seen, in both Hindu and Buddhist philosophies, personality or separate existence are finally viewed not (as we in the West tend to think) as vehicles for expanding awareness and joy, but as limitations. However much one may learn, see, and experience, infinitely more is unlearned, unseen, and unexperienced. For the separate self is conditioned by being in some particular time and place, has a limited lifespan, and even the most brilliant human mind can comprehend only so much—a few grains of sand on the beach of the sea of the infinite universe.

In meditations leading to Nirvana, a different tack is taken—not the instrumental mind trying to comprehend through the senses and reason, but the awareness trying to break through their finitude. This can be done; sense and reason are a ring of fire whose fuel lines can be cut. Meditation does not destroy the mind, but opens it up completely by breaking down the barriers, so that one simply is the Nirvanic ocean, and rides the tides of the infinite like a surfer riding the waves. Nothing cuts him off from infinity, so he sees, thinks, knows, does to an unlimited degree.

This is the state claimed for the Buddha after his Enlightenment. He still walked the earth, but in a Middle Way manner, making no karmic waves, and at the same time his infinitely attuned mind was able to know all and see all. An ordinary-sized human being, so perfect was his equilibrium that he could, like the operator of a perfectly adjusted lever, work incalculable results. It is said that, deep in meditation late at night, his mind would move like a searchlight through the world, find people in spiritual need, and transport himself through his power over matter to that point, or even to several points simultaneously, to help.

When the Buddha died, or rather attained Nirvana absolutely, according to

Wisdom Embarked for the Farther Shore

Buddhist belief an effect occurred which can only be called an implosion on the spiritual level. An implosion is the opposite of an explosion; it is what happens when a vacuum is suddenly created, and all surrounding molecules of matter rush in to fill the void. The Buddha made no karma actively, as we do trying to grasp at things to fulfill desires. But his passing was like an implosion in the karmic field—suddenly there was nothing there—and a stream of karmic force—good karma—is still rushing in striving to enter the gateless gate through which he had passed.

The best way to go in the direction he went, of course, is to meditate, emulating the means he used to get there. Next best, if one must act, is to act in ways that harmonize one with the onrushing waves of this stream flowing into the implosion void, and let them bear one along. This is the meaning of being a Buddhist, accepting the "Three Refuges." It is the meaning of the ordinary acts of kindness that follow the four "unlimited" virtues winning rebirth in a very high heaven: unlimited friendliness, unlimited compassion, unlimited sympathetic joy, unlimited even mindedness. It is the inner meaning of the merit-making acts of lay people toward the meditative monks, such as giving them food, clothing, and donations. It is the meaning of acts of pure devotion that win good merit, like having sutras read, gilding images of the Buddha, burning incense, and offering flowers at shrines.

NO SELF

One of the fundamental points of Buddhist psychology, and a key to understanding the whole system on a deep level, is *anatman,* "no self." This Buddhist teaching can be compared to the Upanishadic doctrine that the atman, the innermost self or soul, is really identical with Brahman. The Buddhist negative expression anatman, or no self, is a difference of emphasis rather than a contradiction, for if the self is simply the one universal Brahman, it is also "no self" in any individualistic sense. But the difference points to the Buddhist tendency to psychological analysis rather than ontological statement.

Reflection on the idea of no self provides a line of insight into the meaning of the Four Noble Truths, the Middle Way, and the Buddhist experience. This is because the *fundamental* craving or desire that keeps us in the suffering-desire syndrome is the desire to be a separate individual self.

The first Noble Truth, that all life is suffering, tells us that there is something unsatisfactory, something of anxiety, frustration, bearing a sense of incompleteness, about all of life as it is ordinarily lived. (It does not mean that all life is excruciating pain, or that there are no pleasant moments. The Buddha, who supposedly lived his first twenty-nine years in a round of extravagant pleasure, could hardly have said that. But what he does say is that there is something frustrating and unsatisfactory in all of life, and this gets worse and worse.)

The Second Truth tells us the reason for this sense of inadequacy in ordinary life is that we are always trying to cling to things—objects, persons, ideas, experiences, and so forth—which are partial and not permament, and so keep us in anxiety lest we lose them, as sooner or later we shall. Yet nonetheless we want to grasp.

The conclusion can only be that somewhere we have acquired a distorted idea about the whole nature and possibilities of human life—that we are basing life on a false premise. And just as when you try to do a complex mathematical problem with the wrong formula, sooner or later everything will begin to come out wrong, so it is with human life. According to Buddhism, the false premise which underlies all other delusion, suffering, and grasping, is that one is a separate, independent, individual self—rather than a transitory compound of several elements completely interdependent with the whole universe.

Buddhism teaches that instead of being a "self," in the sense of a separate,

Row of Buddhas outside a temple in Bangkok, Thailand. This is the posture of enlightenment, symbolized by the flames on the heads and the hand gestures.

enduring "soul" stuck in a body, we are all compounds made up of several different constituents. The five parts that make up a human being are called *skandhas;* the word *skandha* means "bundle" and reminds us that these constituents themselves are collocations of dharmas, the pointlike primary particles which flash out of the void. The human skandhas are: form (the physical shape), the feelings, the perceptions (the "picture" the mind forms out of data transmitted by the sense organs), the inherent impulses (karmic dispositions), and the background consciousness. Note that both physical and psychological entities are brought together.

Wisdom Embarked for the Farther Shore

The problem is that when these five entities get together, they interact in such a way as to make the "person" think of him- or herself as a separate individual self. Actually, although understandable, according to Buddhism this is a misreading of the data.

Consider what happens when you, as a collection of the five skandhas, walk down the street and meet another such collection. You interpret everything in terms of reinforcing the illusion that you are a "self," yet a moment's analysis would show how false this premise is.

As you walk, you could think, "I must be a separate individual self, for my physical body gives me the impression of being a detached unit, self-propelled and separate from other objects as I walk past them." (Not really true, for even the physical body is in continual and necessary interaction with the environment—breathing, eating. It is only a certain debatable perspective that makes us include the stomach when we say "myself," but not the field that grows the food it digests, or the sun that makes it grow.)

As you see the other person, you could say to yourself, "I must be a separate individual self, or else why would I perceive that unit out there as other than myself." (But it is not really "I" who sees the other; it is just a phenomenon of light waves hitting sensitive nerves. The skandha of the feeling senses then stimulates the skandha of perception to form a mental picture on the basis of this data.)

You may react emotionally to the person you see—with joy and desire if it is a person you love, with anger if someone you dislike. You may say, "I must be a separate individual self, for if I were not who would be feeling these emotions of joy or anger?" (But these feelings are not a "self"—they are just something that comes and goes like billowing waves in response to data fed in by the senses, interpreted by the perception, and probably conditioned by the karma of patterns of behavior toward that person, or similar persons, carried over from the past along with much else.)

Finally, you may say, "I must be a separate individual self, since I am aware of all this." (But the human capacity for self-consciousness is not itself a "self;" it is just the skandha of consciousness which accompanies physical form, feeling, perceptions, and impulses—for it can neither generate nor erase the latter four, but is just a mirror in which they reflect as they act and react.)

Through such analysis as this, Buddhism concluded that we are not separate individual selves, but collections of elements temporarily brought together, and bound to break apart. A life which disregards this fact is basing itself on a false premise, and can experience only the anxiety-craving syndrome as it faces old age, sickness, and death.

Nonetheless, this collection perversely *wants* to be a separate individual self. From birth on a human being asserts selfhood as the real reason for most of what he or she does. The newborn baby cries as if to say, "I must be a separate individual self, or else who would be crying and who would be hungry?"

Through life, one wants to learn, wants to achieve, wants to be loved, wants to accumulate goods, acquire fame, become a saint, win life in heaven—all for one-self, all as though to say, "I must be a separate individual self, for if I were not, who would be learned, famous, beloved, immortal?" Nevertheless all these· dreams bring their own syndromes of anxiety and craving, and the body and perhaps the mind falls apart before they more than begin to be fulfilled.

The Buddhist would put the question another way: "*Who is* rich, famous, wise, holy, immortal? A name? A process? A set of memories? None of these are a *self.* Is there any *one* who can be abstracted from the round of rising and falling feelings and forms of a human life, who is independent of the continual flux of the universe? If there is no *one,* then we cannot properly think of the recipient of wealth, fame, wisdom, and so forth—but just that *there is* wealth, fame, and wisdom, or *there is* perception, anger, joy, but not as things to be grasped, or which anyone can grasp. For the Buddha's final words are reported to be, "All aggregates are transitory"— every compound, including the human, is unstable and will come apart.

The reason is karma, the force of universal action and reaction that keeps everything moving and changing. The activities, and even the mental images and thoughts, which you desire to perpetuate yourself as a separate individual self, set up "waves" in the cosmos around you as you try to gain this object or fulfill that dream. No energy is lost, and sooner or later the waves based on the false premise will come back to afflict and finally shatter the compound.

If there is no separate individual self, one might ask how Buddhism can talk as it does of reincarnation. What is there to reincarnate?

In one sense, of course, the answer is nothing. But karma also means that you get what you want, or rather continue to be what you think you are. Every cause, including the illusion of being a separate individual self, has an exactly corresponding effect. The illusion then becomes self-perpetuating, life after life.

It might be called a kinetic view of reincarnation. There is nothing solid taken out of one body and put in another, and a deceased person's skandhas are dispersed into the universe. But the karmic waves one has made continue to operate until the precise kind of energy they bear has been appropriately transferred, just as ripples may continue to spread on the face of a pond even after a dropped stone has hit the bottom. The karmic waves will move until they have put together another set of five skandhas having shape, circumstance, and dispositions that are what they are because of the karmic energies left by the previous person. In energy terms, then, if not actual substance, this person can be spoken of as the "reincarnation" of the other person.

THERAVADA BUDDHISM

The Buddhist world is now divided into two great traditions. Theravada ("Path of the Elders") Buddhism[4] is found in the nations of Sri Lanka (formerly Ceylon), Burma, Thailand, Cambodia, and Laos. Mahayana ("Great Vessel") Buddhism has spread throughout China, Korea, Japan, Tibet, Mongolia, Nepal,

---

[4]In some sources this tradition is called Hinayana ("Little Vessel"). That term, however, originated as a derogatory label used by Mahayanists for the other camp in debate, and is not used by Theravadins themselves. It seems more courteous to keep to the word "Theravada."

Bhutan, Vietnam, and corners of India and Soviet Asia.[5] Let us look first at Theravada Buddhism.

If you were to visit one of the Theravada countries, it would not be long before the practical and sociological expressions of Buddhism were evident to you, and through them you would perceive the wide and deep influence of Buddhism in these lands. You would be struck by the great number of temples dotting the cities and lush tropical hills of the countryside. The temples are ornate and elaborate affairs. Curved eaves mount up to pitched roofs. Soaring spires, in the case of those large and lovely edifices like the Shwe Dagon Temple in Rangoon, seem to catch the very soul of the East. Guarding the temple gates are fierce-looking mythological beings; these, like the sculpture and murals one may see of epic heroes such as Rama and Hanuman, are gods borrowed from Hinduism. Shrines to indigenous spirits of nature and weather, *nats* in Burma and *phis* in Thailand, lurk in the temple shadows. Like the borrowed Hindu gods, they are pupils of the Buddha on another plane than the human.

Within the cool temple, however, it is the Buddha who is supreme; his image gleams richly amid lamps and delicate offerings of incense, flowers, fruit, and water. He may be seated, standing, or reclining; these three postures represent respectively the Buddha's enlightment, teaching, and entry into Nirvana. Worshippers come and go doing worshipful acts of merit, which will benefit them in this and coming lives, and prepare them for ultimate release into Nirvana.

On the streets walk monks in their saffron-yellow robes, heads shaved and arms bare in the warm humid air. If it is early morning—Theravada monks do not eat after noon—each may be holding a begging bowl. At the door of a house he will stand silent, head lowered and hands upraised, accepting whatever the indulgent householder deigns to place in his dish.

Most of the monks are young, for in all the Theravada countries except Sri Lanka it is a custom (not always observed today) for every young man, from prince to peasant, to spend a year of his life as a monk. This experience serves to stabilize one's religious life, and is an initiation into manhood. A youth would not marry until after he had served as a monk, and his closest lifelong friends are likely to be those with whom he shared this experience. But the great majority of men, of course, do not remain in the cloister. However, among the morning mendicants will be a few gentle old veterans of the monastic path, and they are afforded great respect.

If you followed one of the monks, you would return after him to a neighborhood temple with its attached monastery. Here the monks would gather after begging to consume the simple meals they had garnered. During the afternoon they will rest, study, and meditate.

---

[5]In the early centuries A.D. Mahayana was strong in the areas of central Asia which are now Kashmir, Afghanistan, Sinkiang, and Soviet Turkestan; from this part of the world it spread to China. But it has been replaced there by Islam. It was also strong in medieval times in much of Southeast Asia, including the Khmer Empire centering in present Cambodia, with its great Buddhist temples of Angkor Wat (originally Hindu later modified to Theravada), and in present Indonesia (where it has been replaced by Islam). But the story of the interaction of Hinduism, Theravada, and Mahayana in Southeast Asia up to early modern times is a very complex one.

The temple may be just a village or town *vihara,* rustic and no tourist attraction, but a center of community life. Here, traditionally, children go to school, festivals public and private are celebrated, and the dead are remembered. For the plain people of the town, monks are counselors, healers, exorcists, and friends.[6]

Or the temple might be one of the popular places of pilgrimage, where the faithful hope to win merit by gilding the Buddha's image, or burning incense before the Buddha's giant footprint—that significant and popular shrine which suggests that the Enlightened One was here, is no longer, but we can follow in the direction he went.

Or the monk you followed might be one of the many who throng the great national temples of the Theravada lands—the Temple of the Emerald Buddha in Bangkok, the Shwe Dagon Temple in Rangoon, the Temple of the Tooth in Kandy, Sri Lanka. The skyward-curved towers of these splendid buildings, their pitched roofs and carved beams, their brilliant gold and color, their inner atmosphere of incense and contemplation, all murmur something of the sense of wonder and glory at the heart of Buddhism—and remind us it is far more than just a philosophy.

In theory, the main task of the monk in the monastery is meditation, for he is to emulate the Buddha himself, and it was through meditation that the Awakened One went thence. That the young novice is emulating the Buddha is shown by the procedure through which he enters the monastery, if only for a few months. He goes to the monastery dressed as a prince, accompanied by a friend who plays the role of the Buddha's charioteer. At the monastery, he will have his head shaved, don his coarse monkish robe, and kneeling before the abbot, take refuge in the Three Jewels.

The monastic initiation of young men in Theravada countries shows evidence of being a continuation of pre-Buddhist initiations like those of primitives: the women weep as the boy departs; his teeth are scraped or blackened suggestive of the ritual knocking out of a tooth of older rites; he is often jostled and ridiculed as he tries to put on his unfamiliar robes.[7]

But the high point is movement in another direction. Upheld by the Three Jewels, the monk knows he is to emulate the silent image of the Buddha in the temple, with its serene and inward gaze. He is to explore and know through meditation the inward realm, and finally to break through it into the Unconditioned—Nirvana. He is to become an arhant, a perfected and enlightened one who has attained Nirvanic consciousness.

First the monk must recognize that there are many worlds besides this one. Except for the animal world, the others are generally invisible, but they are accessi-

---

[6]On the role of the monk, see Jane Bunnag, *Buddhist Monk, Buddhist Layman* (London and New York: Cambridge University Press, 1973); Robert C. Lester, *Theravada Buddhism in Southeast Asia* (Ann Arbor: The University of Michigan Press, 1973), Part II; Richard F. Gombrich, *Precept and Practice: Traditional Buddhism in the Rural Highlands of Ceylon* (London: Oxford University Press, 1971); and Melford E. Spiro, *Buddhism and Society* (New York: Harper and Row Publishers, 1970), Part IV.

[7]A stimulating discussion of monastic initiation is found in Paul Levy, *Buddhism: A 'Mystery Religion'?* (London: The Athlone Press of the University of London, 1957).

ble to inner, mental organs of vision, and are places of possible reincarnation. Like the shaman of old, the monk plunges into their mysterious climes through meditatively altered states of consciousness.

Traditional Buddhism speaks of six *lokas,* possible "locales" or places where one can be reborn. These are, starting with the lowest:[8]

1. The hells. Here demerit or bad karma derived from anger, hatred, and violence is expiated. Demons in the many different Buddhist hells (for different sorts of sin) inflict the most sadistic tortures. But the Buddhist hells are not permanent; one remains in them only as long as necessary to "work off" bad karma through punishment. In this respect they are more like the Roman Catholic purgatory than hell.

2. The Animal World. The life of animals is conceived to be uncomprehending suffering; rebirth as an animal is to expiate bad karma from having thoughts only of food and sex.

3. The Pretas or "Hungry Ghosts." These are pitiful creatures who are always hungry, having huge unsatisfied bellies and tiny mouths. They are clearly the restless spirits of the departed of primitive folk religion who hover around hearth and graveyard. In Buddhism, being born as a preta is in expiation for uncontrolled attachment to family, money, and possessions.

4. The Asuras or Ogres. These are boisterous, passion-ridden giants who are always fighting with each other, rather like the old Germanic gods. Rebirth here is the result of grasping after power. Mara, the tempter of the Buddha at his Enlightenment, was originally said to be from this level.

5. The Human World. A place of mixed joy and sorrow, this sphere is unique in that it is only here one can make meaningful decisions about creating good or bad karma or attaining Nirvana. In the lower worlds previously cited, pain, stupidity, or passion are so great that one is too befogged to do more than endure uncomprehendingly until the evil karma is worked out and one has a human birth again; the realms of the gods are so pleasant that there one does not think of the future. One can stay at the human level life after life, without sinking below it or rising above it, by doing no less and no more than basic human morality through keeping the five precepts: not taking life, not stealing, not engaging in sexual misconduct, not lying, not taking intoxicants. (To do any one of these things makes one an ogre, preta, animal, or hell-slave in principle; the next time one is reborn, then, that's the shape in which one finds oneself.)

6. The Heavens of the Gods. Just as there are many hells, so there are many heavens in Buddhism stacked on top of each other, and presided over by gods taken from Hinduism, such as Indra and Brahma.

The lower six heavens, the "Heavens of the Gods," together with the hells, the animals, the pretas, the ogres, and the humans, all comprise the level of reality

[8]The order of some of the lokas varies in different sources; this presentation follows Lester, *Theravada Buddhism,* pp. 39–41.

called the *Kamadhatu,* or Desire-area, since its inhabitants are all motivated by desire in the sense of kama, the pleasure-principle, and this drives them around and around within it. One is reborn in them through karma; even the Heavens of the Gods, while a reward for good karma, are not a stage on a path to enlightenment. One would not particularly explore the Kamadhatu through meditation, since it is what one wants to flee.

But above the desire-area are higher realms, which correspond to stages of trance entered in meditation, for these levels, while not Nirvana, are also not attained by karmic merit but by meditation. One will be reborn in whichever one attains in meditation exercises. Yet they are not permanent and still have about them light whisps of conditionedness; they are the ultimate extreme of the mental side of our reality, rather than breakthroughs beyond all opposites whatsoever.

The lower sixteen of these spheres above the Heavens of the Gods are called the realms of form (*rupadhatu*). They are transcendent aspects of the four elements and their inhabitants have forms but no desires in the pleasure-principle sense. Their bodies are made of thought; they are immaterial intelligences engaged, the higher up one goes through these ethereal kingdoms, in more and more exalted degrees of meditative joy, concentration, and equanimity.

The upper four of these transcendent spheres are called the realms of nonform (*arupadhatu*). The beings in them are so far evolved beyond matter and desire as not even to have thought-bodies, for even their thoughts no longer have form. Instead, they are just brilliantly aware, on the four levels respectively, of infinity of space, infinity of consciousness, nothingness, and neither perception nor nonperception.

The meditative journeys to these invisible worlds are not paths direct to Nirvana, but are training exercises for that greater leap, and produce many desirable benefits in themselves. For in Theravada Buddhism two basic kinds of meditation obtain: samadhi meditation, which explores these *jhanas,* or higher altered states of consciousness, and the worlds that go with each; and vipassana meditation, which breaks through directly to Nirvana.

The realms above the desire-world then correspond to nine levels of transic meditation, and penetrating into them is the purpose of samadhic meditation. The technique is first to prepare by practicing *sila,* ordinary morality and simplicity, then to begin with "one-pointed" meditation. One starts the control of mind in order to reach transic states just by focusing on one thing: this is an improvement on ordinary consciousness, in which we lazily let the stream-of-consciousness and the rise and fall of appetites, moods, and stimuli "think" for us.

Traditionally, there are forty possible topics for this opening meditation, and they are designed to meet the needs, often by a sort of shock therapy, of the various kinds of rough-hewn personalities who come to the Buddha's way. There are meditations on the Three Jewels, calmness, death, the constituents of the body, the repulsiveness of food. Ten of the topics are grisly cemetery reflections on different kinds of corpses: a corpse gnawed by dogs, a swollen corpse, a blue corpse, a hacked corpse, and so forth. Clearly such meditation would be salutary for one overattached to the lusts of this body, which soon enough will become another molding and crumbling carcass. Or, if one is of irritable temperament and requires cooling rather than shocking images, one can begin with the great qualities of illimitable friendliness, compassion, sympathetic joy, and evenmindedness. Or, one can meditate on an object of one of the four elements, or of the four colors, or light itself; or, at an advanced stage, on one of the four nonform qualities of awareness.

The novice begins by focusing on the object itself, or a mental image of it. When he can retain an "afterimage" of the object a thousand times brighter than the original, he then allows this to expand to fill the entire universe, so that all distractions are swallowed up, and the meditator is left with joy and calm.[9]

Nirvana requires a more direct thrust. The way there is through vipassana, the meditation of analysis. Instead of forty, there are only three hard-hitting topics: the impermanence of all things, that all is "ill" or unsatisfactory, that one is not a real ego or self. Vipassana, then, gets back to the fundamental Buddhist outlook of the Four Noble Truths and anatman.

The vipassana meditator analyzes his own sensations and experiences until he realizes the truth of these three points. Then, as it were in the gaps left by the breakdown of the ordinary ego-centered way of handling experience, flashes of Nirvanic consciousness break through. With the first flash, the meditator becomes a "stream-enterer;" he is on the way and will never fall back, but in a future lifetime will become an arhant. Later, he becomes a "once-returner," with only one more lifetime; or a "never-returner," who may be reborn in one of the transcendent form or nonform heavens and go into Nirvana from there. Last is the arhant stage, that of one in the midst of us who has full Nirvanic realization.

Nirvana is utterly different from even the highest state of transic absorption, beyond even "neither perception nor nonperception." For Nirvana is the opposite of all the conditions and ways of thinking of this world. We experience serial time and multiplicity of objects, so Nirvana is not that. We experience things coming into being and going out of being, so Nirvana is not that. We experience existence, and oppose to it nonexistence, life versus death, so Nirvana is neither. The Buddha is reported to have said (Majjhima I: 167) that Nirvana is "unborn, unrivaled, secure from attachment, undecaying, and unstained . . . deep, difficult to see, difficult to understand, tranquil, excellent, beyond the reach of mere logic, subtle, and to be realized only by the wise." But getting there is essentially just a matter of breaking down self-constructed barriers; this is the task of the vipassana meditation of analysis.[10]

Nirvana, the transformation of consciousness, is the goal of Buddhism. Yet it must not be forgotten that Nirvana, for most, is far away and the life of Buddhism is something quite other than a direct quest for Nirvana or even samadhi meditation. Even among the monks, the great majority are perhaps more interested in passing exams, community affairs, and the daily monastic round than assiduous meditation.

---

[9]The techniques of samadhic meditation are vividly described in B. A. Maitreya, "Buddhism in Theravada Countries," in Kenneth Morgan, ed., *Path of the Buddha* (New York: The Ronald Press Company, 1956), pp. 113–52. Original texts are found in Edward Conze, *Buddhist Meditation* (New York: Harper and Row Publishers, 1969).

[10]For a personal account of the practice of vipassana meditation, see Winston L. King, *A Thousand Lives Away: Buddhism in Contemporary Burma* (Cambridge, Mass.: Harvard University Press, 1964), pp. 225–35.

For the laity, Buddhism in Theravada countries is still other things. Theirs is a Buddhism of the same temples, and shares the same world view governed by the stories of the Buddha's life, the six lokas, and so forth. But it is all seen from a different angle. They do not generally expect to make formal meditations, or to progress in the manner of monks. Rather, for them the tableau of the Buddhist map of the invisible world—its temples, pilgrimage places, and cosmic lore—become ways they can align themselves with streams of good karmic force, those set in motion by the implosion of the Buddha's Great Departure. Buddhism, in other words, comes as a noble instrument for making merit, which will transform destiny to bring good things in this and future lives.

It must not be supposed, however, that the layman's Buddhist orientation toward merit-making means any small or cribbed Buddhist vision. It may well be richer than that of many monks. The splendors of the temples the layman loves offer a glint of the Otherness of Nirvana itself, which illumines his mind on deep levels. The observant visitor often is made aware that popular attitudes toward time, human relations, and good or bad fortune in Theravada cultures show some interiorization of such basic teachings as no self, karma, and the Four Noble Truths. But the layman relates to the Buddhist vision differently: through what he does rather than what he experiences in meditation.

Woman in Burma giving rice to Buddhist monks, an act of merit-making on her part and expression of freedom from possession on theirs.

Wisdom Embarked for the Farther Shore

The layman tries to follow, as well as possible, the five precepts: not to take life, steal, engage in sexual misconduct, lie, or take intoxicants. He tries also to exemplify the four "unlimited" virtues: unlimited friendliness, compassion, sympathetic joy, evenmindedness. Through the four unlimiteds, one can even be reborn in a divine heaven.

Merit can also be made by donations of robes and food to the monks, building pagodas and making monastery improvements, pilgrimages, sponsoring a candidate entering a monastery or a formal scripture-reading, working for community good, giving food to the poor and to animals. The relation of monk and layman is mutually profitable in merit terms: the laity win merit by donations to the monks, the monks by preaching and teaching to the laity and by giving them the opportunity to win merit through gifts. The relation of monks and laity exemplifies one of the deepest Buddhist doctrines, the interdependence of all things.

In Theravada countries, there are services in local temples four times a lunar month, at the four main phases of the moon. The chief annual festival is Wesak in the spring, commemorating the Buddha's birth, enlightenment, and entry into Nirvana. In various places on this day, trees are watered, candles and incense wave in processions, and rockets blaze through the sky—in part all aimed at producing the rain that will be so critical in the coming growing season.

A month later, the rainy period (May through July) begins in Southeast Asia. During this time, following the example of the Buddha himself, the monks remain in retreat in the monasteries. Many of the laity, in this Lentlike season, make a special effort to keep the precepts, or even enter the monastery temporarily themselves, for just the state of being a monk gives merit and benefit.

The monks and monastic life are like a reservoir of merit. The Buddha, the teaching, the order, and the laity are like concentric circles going around the absolute center, Nirvanic consciousness with its ancillary grace of blessed rebirths. Every ring profits through interaction with its neighbors, especially the one next in. [11]

In the twentieth century, Theravada Buddhism has been caught up in the crises of nationalism, modernization, and ideological conflict that have tormented its corner of the world. In Sri Lanka and Burma, some monks played a vigorous role in the movement for independence from Great Britain, and postindependence leaders, especially U Nu in Burma, made much of Buddhism, in part as a symbol of the national non-Western culture. Other Buddhist monks have endeavored to reconcile Buddhism with modern science, democracy, or Marxism. In Thailand, the government has made the rural monasteries centers for official programs in health, agricultural improvement, and anticommunism. In Cambodia and Laos, Buddhist life has been disrupted by war.[12]

Yet despite the incursion of modern problems, visitors to most of the five Theravada countries will still find cultures deeply shaped by centuries of Buddhism. The temples still gleam, and yellow-robed monks still walk the streets.

[11]On the concepts and practices of popular Buddhism in Theravada lands, see Bunnag, *Buddhist Monk, Buddhist Layman;* Lester, *Theravada Buddhism;* Gombrich, *Precept and Practice;* Spiro, *Buddhism and Society;* Maitreya, "Buddhism in Theravada Countries"; and King, *A Thousand Lives Away.*

[12]See Jerrold Schecter, *The New Face of Buddha* (New York: Coward-McCann, 1967).

MAHAYANA BUDDHISM

The northern tier of Buddhist countries, including the great and distinctive Buddhist cultures of Tibet, China, and Japan, are in the Mahayana tradition. The style of being Buddhist and of exploring the meaning of the historical Buddha's experience is different from that of the Theravada Buddhism we have just discussed. It is a tradition almost as old as Theravada, although its mood and interests are not as conservative.

The first appearance of what was to become Mahayana was the school called the Mahasamghika ("Great Monastic Order") within the Buddhist order about a century after the Buddha's death. The points of difference with the Theravadins lay in the Mahasamghika's insistence that students and non-arhants be admitted to monastic meetings, that popular religious practices be reconciled with Buddhism, and that the Buddha was really a supramundane and perfect being who came into our midst as a teacher. These are theoretical points that led directly to Mahayana's universalism, accommodation, and transcendence, although it should be recognized that by the time it became the popular Buddhism of several countries Theravada had made its own adjustments in the same directions.

But through the early centuries of Buddhism a consistently liberal and innovative party was pushing for more flexible forms of the tradition. By the first century A.D. they appeared as a distinctive tradition marked off by the fact that they accepted not only the *tripitaka,* the scriptures in the Pali language dealing with the Buddha's life and teaching and monastic rules accepted by the Theravadins, but also a growing body of Sanskrit scriptures called sutras. Acceptance of the body of sutra literature, rather than any particular doctrine, is the formal test of a Mahayanist.

Nonetheless, a broad consensus of attitude and doctrine runs through the Mahayana sutras, although they were written over several centuries and add up to a hundred times the bulk of the Christian Bible. (In theory, the sutras are put into the mouth of the historical Buddha and ascribed by commentators to various stages of his life; many are said to have been "hidden" for hundreds of years to await times when they would be most needed.)

These scriptures start from a universal rather than a historical perspective, saying there is a universal true reality—the void, Nirvana, Buddha-nature, dharmakaya—everywhere and capable of being realized by anyone. Gautama Buddha realized it at the moment of his enlightenment, and so he in a deeper sense manifests it and comes from it—but there are an infinite number of other Buddhas too, and in a deeper sense everyone is actually an unrealized Buddha. Any means of attaining this realization is acceptable insofar as it works; the gradated practice of Theravada can be dispensed with, and techniques of devotion, chanting, even quasi-magic, brought in from bhakti, tantrism, and folk religion can be employed. In all of this the key figure is the bodhisattva, who becomes for Mahayana the ideal in place of the Theravadin arhant, and in many ways sums up the Mahayana vision. The bodhisattva is on the way to Buddhahood, but holds back at the very threshold by compassion for the countless beings in ignorance and suffering; he dwells both in Nirvana and the phenomenal world, having the power and reality of both; as a borderline figure, he also imparts grace and receives devotion.

All of Buddhism is built on the Buddha's experience of infinite consciousness at the moment of his enlightenment. Buddhism is all various ways of apprehending that the way he saw the universe at that moment is the way it really is, and all other ways partial and so erroneous. It is various ways too of interiorizing the same experience insofar as one can. In Theravada, this means "entering the stream" left by the historical Buddha.

In Mahayana, there is more emphasis that the world perceived by the Buddha at enlightenment is the true reality everywhere present at all times, and so can be apprehended directly by a number of different means and through a number of mediators. The historical Buddha, although respected, is relatively de-emphasized; in the final analysis, all reality is full of Buddhas and is one's teacher of Buddhahood, just as all reality is one's parents—everywhere one can see sages, gods, and Buddhas who are essentially aspects of one's enlightened mind, and the Buddha-nature is in every blade of grass and every grain of sand.

Visiting a Mahayana country, one is immediately struck by a difference in Buddhist tone from Theravada countries. There is still the great splendor and peace of the Buddhist temple. But now, instead of a single, solitary Buddha image on the altar, attended by mere gods and men, one will see radiant Buddha after Buddha, bodhisattva after bodhisattva, all transcendentally aware, but all in different moods and poses, from serene meditation to explosive wrath, and from deep withdrawal to many-armed compassionate activity.

This reflects that Mahayana is a "multimedia" way to Buddhahood. The "turning of the head" needful to see one's true Buddha-nature is not something that must follow only one intellectual or technical structure, for since it relates to the ungraspable it cannot be put into a box. Thus Mahayana has many methods, some very complex and some so simple as to seem insulting until one realizes that the simplicity is the point. Mahayana disdains none of the senses, and no "level" of religion from peasant folk faith to the most recondite metaphysical systems; from different angles of vision, each can be near or far.

Thus Mahayana is Zen monks in Japan in long and immensely calm rows, "sitting quietly doing nothing." It is followers of Pure Land Buddhism chanting "Hail, Amitabha Buddha" and hoping to be brought into the "Pure Land" or Paradise of the Buddha of Infinite Light and Life from where attainment of Nirvana is sure—or perhaps just experiencing the "beingness" of doing the chant. It is Tibetan tantric Buddhists blowing on trumpets of human thighbones and evoking through chanting and intense visualization the form of one's patronal spiritual ideal. Mahayana is finally the great peace of massive temples, the brazen images of supernal figures glowing dimly in incensed air.

Mount Hiei, the site of an ancient Buddhist monastery on the outskirts of Kyoto, in Japan, is a rich example of Mahayana. Here, amid stately moss-bearded old trees and fern-lined crystal streams, the visitor almost as if in a Buddhist cafeteria can wander from temple to temple. The Buddhas of each seem to personify states of consciousness as do Theravada images, but suggest a greater variety of states of mind in relation to the world. Here may be a temple to Amida, the Pure Land Buddha who, in the far remote past, vowed that when he attained supreme enlightenment he would bring all who called upon his name into the western paradise over which he presided, from whence Nirvana is near at hand; this is a Buddhism of egolessness through dependence upon the help of another.

Down the road and past a stony cliff, there is a temple to Kannon, the bodhisattva commonly termed the "goddess of mercy" and often portrayed with many arms to symbolize her countless acts of mercy in answer to prayers in this world. The experience of receiving compassion from a great and enlightened being, even if for a seemingly trivial and worldly matter, can set one on the upward path by shaking out of oneself the conventional mindset; from a Buddha's perspective nothing in the conditioned world is important and nothing is trivial, and no act of compassion is meaningless.

Another temple is dedicated to Dainichi, the "Great Sun Buddha" who personifies the absolute essence of the cosmos itself—Nirvana, reality insofar as it can be personified at all. In these and many other temples the multiplicity of ways to an experience beyond ways or words is expounded; the multiplicity helps defeat the tendency toward grasping by serving to baffle the human tendency to possessiveness over partialities.

This is not all. In Kyoto stands a temple with 3,000 images of Kannon, all different. In the "esoteric" Buddhism of Tibet, Mongolia, and such sects as the Shingon in Japan, paintings (or even sculpture arrangements) called mandalas are popular. They arrange families of Buddhas and bodhisattvas in patterns that bring home both the diversity and unity of the psychocosmic forces they represent. As psychological analysis, they suggest the profound depth at which the human mind is continuous with mental and spiritual realities underlying the whole universe.

Also in Kyoto are famous Zen monasteries where proctors walk with a stick up and down in front of the silent, seated meditators, and incense burns before a tasteful image of the Buddha, most frequently Dainichi. Outside, there is an austere Zen garden, with its seemingly casual bits of rock and moss and raked sand—but as one looks at it, the mind may begin to whirl, and the rocks and moss become ships and islands on an endless sea, or nebulae and galaxies strewn through infinite space—anchorless reality spreading out of the horizonless mind of the Sun Buddha. And there may be a house for the tea ceremony, that typically Zen practice of doing something very ordinary, like serving tea, with a stylized but effortless grace which makes it expressive of the Buddha-nature of that moment.

The ultimate experience of Mahayana then is ineffable, and so can be "turned on" by many different means: meditation, the numinous wonder of a temple that causes one to forget oneself for a moment; the quasi-hypnotic rhythm of chanting; the magical concentration of evocation. The very fact that its view of Nirvanic realization is so tremendous makes it accessible in seemingly easy and multitudinous ways—for it is already here; everyone is already a Buddha.

The Lotus Sutra, one of the most important of all Mahayana texts, tells us that a simple offering of flowers, or of a tiny clay pagoda, presented by a child to a Buddha, is of far more worth than all the proud efforts of an aspiring arhant. For any distance we can advance toward Buddhahood by our own self-centered efforts would be only as an inch to a thousand miles, but if one just forgets oneself in a childlike sense of wonder and giving, one is already there, for in that moment one's high walls of ego have vanished away. True, the temples and gilded images of

Buddhist temples are meaningless from an ultimate point of view, but it is they that can bring us across, for they work with the natural effectiveness of bright baubles.

The Lotus Sutra also tells the parable of a father who, returning home to the house in which his children were waiting, was appalled to see it on fire, and the children apparently unaware of the danger. Thinking quickly, he realized that if he shouted a warning they might panic and be in a worse state. So instead he cried out that he had new toy carts outside for them. Laughing and skipping eagerly, they ran from the house, and were saved. Images, rites, devotion are like toys which draw us from the flames of desire, and begin the process of self-transcendence.

The Buddha acts in a manner consistent with this view. The Lotus Sutra pictures him as like a rain cloud over all the earth, which waters vegetation of all sizes and shapes equally. He is universal, ineffable reality who appears on different levels of reality in different forms, in countless worlds over and over again—as godlike heavenly Buddhas and bodhisattvas, in the human worlds as teachers like Gautama. He is, in the climax of this astounding document, portrayed as descending in a tremendous, bejeweled temple to turn the wheel of his teaching in this universe.[13]

What is the inner story of how these kinds of Buddhist visions emerged? Something of the process can be seen in the Bamian caves in Afghanistan. In a deep green "Shangri-La" of a valley, there was for upward of a thousand years a great Buddhist monastery. This Buddhist center was apparently started during or shortly after the Kushan Empire had its brief period of glory in central Asia, stretching from the Persian frontiers to the Gobi desert and covering much of northern India, under the great Emperor Kanishka (r. (c.) 78–103 A.D.). Kanishka was a vigorous (though tolerant) proponent of Mahayana, and his reign was at the time when the Great Vessel was clearly establishing its separate destiny and traits; he convened the Buddhist Council of Kashmir, which authorized commentaries of Mahayanist tendency. Although Bamian must have been of Mahayana bent from its beginning, one can also feel that here and at monasteries like it the Mahayana vision slowly took richer and richer form.

At Bamian, the deep walls of the canyon are honeycombed with the cavelike cells of the hundreds of monks who lived there in its heyday; the cliffs are dominated by two gigantic statues of the standing Buddha, the greatest 175 feet high, and several smaller images. What is left of the art on the walls of the caves, painted as aids to meditation, is of most interest, however. For over the course of centuries, from the first on, one can see shifts in perspective. The earliest work simply illustrates the Buddha himself; as time goes on there appear great wheels or circles of multifarious Buddhas, universes animated by Buddhas in all directions, of various colors and attributes. What the historic Buddha realized in the moment of his Enlightenment is seen more and more to be actually in everything, in every direction, in every aspect of human awareness, in their pristine form—and all of these are actually Buddhas too, and can be portrayed as such. One can well imagine the profound meditations, the explorations of strange frontiers of consciousness and its symbols, which must have been undertaken in this majestic valley, and out of which the rings of cosmic Buddhas emerged.

[13]A scholarly translation of the Lotus Sutra is Leon Hurvitz, *The Scripture of the Lotus Blossom of the Fine Dharma* (New York: Columbia University Press, 1975).

THE VOID
AND THE BODHISATTVA

The greatest philosophical force in the emergence of Mahayana was the teaching of Nagarjuna (c. A.D. 150–250). His two basic principles are that samsara (the phenomenal world) and Nirvana are not different, and that the most adequate expression for this totality is "void."[14]

That samsara is Nirvana and Nirvana is samsara means that one does not "go" anywhere to "enter" Nirvana. It is here and now; we are all in it all the time, and so we are all Buddhas. Experiencing getting up, walking down the street, or washing dishes as Nirvana rather than as samsara is simply a matter of how it is seen. The way to see it as Nirvana is with complete nonattachment and nonegotism, which means making nothing within the web of our experience more important or more prior than anything else. Neither self, nor any god, nor Buddha, nor the skandhas, nor any concept or idea or principle, are to be made into a basic upon which reality is constructed. None of these exist or persist of their own power. They are all "hollow"—impermanent, part of the flux of entities and ideas out of which the cosmos is constructed. All exist not of "own being" but in their interrelationships only.

The Nirvanic angle of vision, then, is to see all things, including (and this is perhaps the most difficult angle to get) oneself, the observer, equally and as all an endless series of interdependencies and interrelationships. This universe neither starts nor stops anywhere. In it all things are continually rising and falling and moving in and out of each other, and nothing is stable except the totality itself, the "framework" in which this frameless and endless moving picture is situated.

Because the cosmos has no pivot or foundation or point of reference within itself, no starting or ending line, Nagarjuna believed the only adequate word for it is "emptiness" or "void." To say the cosmos is void is not to say that nothing exists. The term "void" is only a metaphor. But emptiness or void are the only appropriate words for Nagarjuna's cosmos, since any other word would imply some standard or "reality" to be grasped in order to understand it, and he taught that there is none. Void or emptiness communicate the nongraspable quality of conditioned reality. Like the inside of a dewdrop or a soap bubble, Mahayana reality is, so to speak, done with mirrors—it is full of light and color, but everything is just a reflection of everything else, and there is nothing to seize. One who tries will be like a man who attempts to lasso a rainbow or bring home a sunset in a bucket.

The secret is the insight-wisdom called *prajna*. It is able to see things as they are without being attached at the same time to any structure of thought or theoretical concept. Theories try to make it possible to see things by interpreting them, but the use of such tools also twists them out of shape.

The importance of prajna came about in this manner: Mahayana began in part in discussion of the six *paramitas,* or areas in which one could attain Buddhist perfection: donation (exchange of gifts), morality, patience, zeal, meditation, and prajna, or wisdom.

[14]On Nagarjuna and his philosophy, see T. R. V. Murti, *The Central Philosophy of Buddhism* (London: Allen and Unwin, 1955), and Frederick J. Streng, *Emptimess: A Study in Religious Meaning* (Nashville: Abingdon Press, 1967).

The supreme *paramita* is *prajnaparamita,* the perfection of wisdom: it must be built on the foundation of perfection in the others. But it is prajna that gives the lightning flash of final insight uniting one firmly, invincibly through every corner of one's subjectivity with the marvelous void itself, and so makes one as secure as it. This is prajnaparamita, the "wisdom which has gone beyond" or the "perfection of wisdom." The earliest distinctive Mahayana literature deals with it. Indeed, in devotional Mahayana, prajnaparamita (like wisdom in the biblical book of proverbs) came to be personified as an initiating maiden greatly to be desired.[15]

The great key figure in Mahayana thought is the bodhisattva ("enlightenment being"). Bodhisattvas, almost endless in name and number, dwell rank on rank in Mahayana heavens and flame out from countless Mahayana altars; there are also numerous of them, known and unknown, at work in this world. Virtually everything that is distinctive and of general interest in Mahayana is related to the bodhisattva and the bodhisattva's path; to understand this class of being, his meaning and methods, is to have the surest key to understanding Mahayana teaching, symbols, and practices.[16]

First, the bodhisattva epitomizes the ideal of samsara and Nirvana being not different, for he lives in both simultaneously. He is in the world, but without attachments, and *therefore* is able to see everything as it really is and to work with all power. He lives on the level of void-consciousness.

Mahayana lore tells us that the bodhisattva is one who has taken a great vow to attain supreme and final enlightenment, however long it takes and at whatever cost, but at the same time to practice unlimited compassion toward all sentient beings, remaining active in this world without passing into absolute Buddhahood until all other beings are brought to enlightenment. The Lotus Sutra portrays the bodhisattva as superior to the Theravada arhant and "private Buddha," who allegedly attain enlightenment for themselves only, falling short of the ideal of universal compassion.

In his work in the world for the liberation of other beings, the bodhisattva is activated by two principles, skill-in-means and compassion. Both of these derive from his unconditioned awareness of the total interrelatedness of all things. Compassion is the ethical consequence of this knowledge; it is merely stating the fundamental Buddhist realization of "dependent cooriginatation" in ethical terms. If one truly realizes that everything in the cosmos is dependent on everything else, and nothing and no one can exist apart from the rest of it, the only logical consequence for behavior is love, which negates all egocentricity, for interdependency shows up the error of centering life around private goals. The bodhisattva—as did the historical Buddha in a previous life—would think nothing of giving his physical body to feed starving tiger cubs, for he knows that body and time are all transitory and mean nothing, whereas compassion is affirming the basic truth of existence, and any holding back would be basing life on a false premise.

[15]On prajnaparamita thought, see two books by Edward Conze: *Buddhist Thought in India* (Ann Arbor: University of Michigan Press, 1967), pp. 198–204, and *The Prajnaparamita Literature* (The Hague, Netherlands: Mouton, 1960). These books contain references to the author's more technical scholarship in this area.

[16]There is no satisfactory general book in English on the bodhisattva. For easily accessible summaries, see Robinson, *Buddhist Religion,* pp. 54–63, and Edward Conze, *Buddhism in Essence and Development* (New York: Harper Brothers Publishers, 1959), pp. 125–30.

The bodhisattva's compassion is not merely a vague, diffuse force, well-intentioned but capable of doing almost as much harm as good because of a lack of knowledge of all factors in a situation, as is the "compassion" of some. The bodhisattva's compassion is instead a sharp, precise instrument, for it is combined with the accurate insight that the bodhisattva's freedom from "thought-coverings" allows. This is what is conveyed in the attribute "skill-in-means." He is able to see all the karmic factors in a life situation, and thus to know just what changes can be wrought to set a person's steps in the right direction.

Moreover, the same deep awareness, undistorted by any egocentricity, gives him a control of appearances in the world, which seems magical but is actually based on unfathomably deeper awareness of subtle forces than the ordinary person has. He is able to take any apparition-body he wants, or rather which compassionate knowledge tells him would be most beneficial in a particular situation. Bodhisattvas have worked in the world, according to Mahayana scriptures and stories, as monks, abbots, orphans, beggars, prostitutes, rich men, and gods.

In his work in the world, the bodhisattva is able to make those small but precise adjustments in a situation that will achieve maximum effect. Even a bodhisattva or Buddha cannot change karma. No power whatsoever can do this. None can change the lot a person has earned by past deeds, or convert the entire world, groaning as it is under the weight of eons of dark karma, at a single stroke. But the bodhisattva can work with subtlety and skill to bring one to make new resolutions through wise teaching, edifying experiences, and a whiff of the wonder of the other side.

Above all, the subtly skilled and compassionate bodhisattvas impart a sense of sublime serenity, save in some of the wrathful manifestations of the Vajrayana tradition. Whether the transcendentally tranquil princes of the Ajanta caves of India, crowned and holding a flower, or the many-armed and enigmatic-eyed Kannon of Japan, they impart a feeling of attainment so perfect as to be effortless, and exuding mercy like the perfume of a lotus. The concept of the bodhisattva, whose beauty has moved hundreds of millions, is the supreme achievement of Mahayana Buddhism. It superbly exemplifies the ultimate meaning of the Middle Way, and the dwelling at once in samsara and Nirvana.

MIND ONLY
AND THE THUNDERBOLT VESSEL

Further developments in Mahayana thought and practice were in store. Some Mahayana thinkers, probably influenced in part by the developing nondualist Vedanta tradition in Hinduism, came to feel that merely to call the fabric of reality a void was inadequate. A new tradition, found in the Avatamsaka and Lankavatara Sutras and the thinkers Asanga and Vasubandhu (c. fourth century A.D.), said that what Nagarjuna had called emptiness is more like mind, like pure consciousness in which particular forms or thoughts rise and fall. This position, called Yogacara or Vijnanavada and best labeled in English "Mind Only" or "Consciousness Only,"

Wisdom Embarked for the Farther Shore

was immensely influential.[17] Most important subsequent schools of Mahayana, including Zen and the Tibetan, are exponents of the Mind Only philosophy and intellectually grounded on it as well as on Nagarjuna's "middle way."

Buddhist Mind Only is comparable to idealistic philosophies of the West, such as that of George Berkeley. Mind Only holds that fundamentally only one clear mind or field of consciousness exists, the Buddha-nature or Nirvana. It is the basis of each person's own existence—we are therefore all Buddhas. But we do not realize this because we each "project" an apparent world of many different things, which we think we see outside of us but which actually is in our heads. It is really like an illusion made by the preconceptions and habitual but false modes of perception in which our individual karmas have bound us up and blinded us.

One can understand this by thinking of a movie projector. The screen is the one mind, the clear universal consciousness, without. The bulb in the projector is the one mind within, which is our own true nature. The reel of film is the "movie" put into the head by karmic forces reaching out of the past through preconception and habit to make us see and experience the kind of world they have made for us. We think we see forms—mountains and trees, cities and people, pleasure and suffering, joy and sadness—marching across the screen and invading our lives. But actually they are moving pictures cast by the reel running through our heads.

One might ask why, if each of us projects an individual "movie," we all seem to see the same world. Actually, this is not strictly the case; the world appears different to a child and to an adult, to people of different language and culture, and in subtle ways even to brothers and sisters. Yet admittedly there is general consensus on the "lay of the land." Mind Only philosophy says that this is because we carry over shared past karmic impressions from collective as well as individual experience. This is called "store consciousness." Perhaps it would not be too much amiss to translate the concept by saying that the way we "see" the world is formed basically by human and community input, such as the common experiences of birth and having parents, language, education, and culture. What is added by individual karma is only like frosting—although it may be very important for individual destiny.

Mind Only, like most Eastern philosophies, is not just a theory. It is also a path to transformation of consciousness. It describes the projections and store consciousness as a prelude to teaching how to get beneath them and live without coverings on the unstained mirror of the one mind.

One method, developed by Zen, is simply through still meditation—"sitting quietly, doing nothing"—to settle down until one lives beneath the coverings and projections. (This will be discussed later.)

Another method is a kind of experiential shock therapy. One experiments with, as it were, taking out one reel and putting in another, until forced to recognize that one can in fact create any universe one wants, and so one knows that no reel is more "real" than any other, and only the one mind is "truly real."

This is the role of the psychic experiments, and the visualizations of Buddhas

[17]There is no adequate book in English on Mind Only. See Conze, *Buddhist Thought in India,* pp. 250–60, and D. T. Suzuki, *Studies in the Lankavatara Sutra* (London: Routledge, 1930).

and bodhisattvas, characteristic of the tantric-influenced "esoteric" tradition in Mahayana. Through sacred and powerful words, gestures, and hard meditation, one creates before onself alternative realities in which unlikely things are as real as rain. One may create a world in which one is a tree, or in which magic works, or where armies of gods battle in the sky, or—and this would be the goal—Buddhas and bodhisattvas appear visibly on one's altar. Then one would "merge" with an evoked Buddha or bodhisattva, and so share his bliss and enlightenment.

To do this, of course, one needed to have a good idea what the universe of innumerable Buddhas and bodhisattvas that Mahayana envisioned—in countless worlds, in aspects of one's mind, in great lineages—was like: what they looked like, how they were organized, how one went about contacting each one. Furthermore, in Mahayana each Buddha and bodhisattva may have his own heaven, a sort of aura around him from which entry into Nirvana through his aid is possible; these are different from the karmic heavens, also accepted by Mahayana, the highest of the six lokas. By devotion to a particular figure, one might enter his Buddha-heaven.[18]

One problem was that the Buddha-reality (reality as seen by the enlightened eye) was encountered in so many different "styles,"—in the void, one mind, Nirvana; in the many transcendent Buddhas and bodhisattvas, which seemed more like gods in heaven than people of this earth; and finally in this world, where the historic Buddha and the bodhisattvas did their works of teaching and mercy. That problem led to yet another development in Mahayana, one which seems to have emerged in Mind Only circles. It is the *trikaya* concept, the idea of three "Buddha bodies," or more to the point, of three ways or levels in which the Buddha-essence is expressed.

First there is the dharmakaya, "truth body," what the universe ultimately is, the one mind through which the atoms and galaxies dance. It is the way the universe looks to a Buddha at the moment of his enlightenment and his entry into Nirvana, when all distinctions disappear and the universe and the Buddha's mind are absolutely one. This absolute nonduality is the Buddha-nature, the unstained mirror of the one mind, the void, Nirvana.

The second form of expression is the samboghakaya, the "bliss body." It is the dharmakaya expressed in paradisal heavens ruled by radiant Buddhas and bodhisattvas, and is represented in art and altar as golden Buddhas surrounded by gilded lotuses. But it must be remembered we are not talking about Buddhas or heavens literally "out there," but of the floating world of Buddhist reality, which is both (and neither) subjective and objective. In a profound sense, the samboghakaya is the absolute Buddha-nature insofar as it can be put into form—so it is now represented by the most luminous, "otherness" kinds of forms possible, those which come out of the realms of dream, vision, and artistic creativity.

The nirmanakaya, "marvelous transformation body," is the Buddha-nature expressed in this world of ordinary, "waking" reality. Because it is a world of seeing people and objects as separate, here the Buddha-nature comes to us as other

---

[18]For an account of most of the Buddhas and bodhisattvas of practical importance in Mahayana art and devotion, see Alice Getty, *The Gods of Northern Buddhism* (Oxford: The Clarendon Press, 1928). See also Walter E. Clark, *Two Lamaist Pantheons* (Cambridge, Mass.: Harvard University Press, 1937).

persons—Gautama the Buddha and all the other Buddha-figures. This is only a development of the mighty concept of the Lotus Sutra that the Buddha-nature is really a universal reality without beginning or end, which comes into the world from time to time in apparent, apparition bodies.

It is evident that these three levels correspond closely to three states of consciousness in the Upanishads. Dharmakaya is the deep sleep without dreams, samboghakaya is the dream state, nirmanakaya is the waking consciousness—with Buddhist imagery applied to them.

The samboghakaya centers around figures called cosmic or meditation Buddhas, as presented in texts such as *The Tibetan Book of the Dead*. These are the images important in esoteric meditation. They are not Buddhas who were at one time historical human beings like Gautama, although sometimes legends about human lives in the remote past were given to them. Essentially, they are subjective-objective aspects of reality, which come into being in meditation and visualization as embodiments of aspects of the mind and the universe in their highest ratios. Each of the five in *The Tibetan Book of the Dead*, for example, corresponds among other things to one of the five skandhas, as though form, feeling, perception, karmic disposition, and consciousness are not merely inside human beings, but reflect universal attributes or potentials that come into a lower level of manifestation in humans and a higher in this realm. Above all, they are forms that give shape to the wonder of the Buddha-nature, and by bringing them into being in meditation one provides bridges toward it.

The form of Mahayana which most developed these kinds of things is Vajrayana—the "Thunderbolt Vessel" or "Diamond Vessel." Today this is the Buddhism of Tibet, Nepal, Bhutan, and Mongolia, and has much affected some schools in China and Japan. But like so much else it originated in old India. It stems from a confluence of Mind Only Buddhism with the same forces that went into Hindu tantrism, and can be thought of as Buddhist tantrism. In the end, Vajrayana produced colorful art, potent devotional techniques, and philosophy no less deep than that of any other Buddhism.

As we have seen, tantrism had its roots in the adaptation of obscure indigenous rites by questing spirits who hoped, in their secret conclaves, to attain greater power than the brahmin and Buddhist "establishments." These practices centered around magic spells, mighty initiations, and usages that sought to generate the power of a kind of shock therapy by deliberately defying ordinary caste, ritual, sexual, and dietary conventions.

Buddhist tantrists took very seriously the dictum that samsara is Nirvana. To them this meant that nothing in the samsaric world is intrinsically evil, and that everything can be used as a means to liberation. Above all this is true of the passions, and the most potent among them is clearly the sexual. Rather than seek to circumvent the passions, which only leaves them lurking behind in one's psyche as potential depth charges, one should wrestle with them, master them, and then deliberately arouse and direct their energy as dynamos of force for the breakthrough to the ultimate goal.

Needless to say, this is a dangerous tack, and the tantric scriptures tell us that what the adept does would cost the ordinary bumbler eons in the hells. But tantrists were nothing if not bold, and prided themselves on their skill at dangerous occultism. Indeed, if samsara is Nirvana, it is necessary to bring all polarities together in the perfected man. The defiance of cultural prohibitions is a way of expressing this.

The dangers meant that secrecy was necessary, and much tantric literature is veiled in a code called "twilight language." It meant also that only the qualified, or those supposed to be, were admitted, and that the student of these techniques had to work under the close supervision of a master or guru. The one absolute in the tantrist's world of inverted values was strict obedience to the master,[19] even if the master command, as some deli-erately did, the most puzzling, repulsive, immoral, or sadistic things—presumably to teach some lesson about the emptiness of the universe.

By the early Middle Ages Buddhist tantra, as Vajrayana, had attained a literature and scholastic exponents. It became the prevailing form of Buddhism in some areas. Inevitably the rough edges were smoothed off; practices that violated conventional Buddhist morality were (since mind is all) translated into subjective meditations, restricted to marriage, or otherwise legitimatized, save in fringe groups. But it never quite lost its wildness either. Tantric adepts have always tended to be fierce, vivid, shamanlike characters, given to heroic spiritual strife deep in mountains or jungles, shunning the more staid academic and religious circles, and leaving behind beguiling tales of wizardry.

In Vajrayana thought, the dharmakaya is made equivalent to prajna (wisdom), and is regarded as feminine, the supreme mistress, the cosmic womb. The adept, from novice to Buddha, is masculine and personifies skill-in-means, seeking to penetrate and unite with prajna. Thus, in Tibetan art, the cosmic Buddhas and bodhisattvas are often shown locked in sexual embrace—as a "father-mother deity"—with their respective personifications of prajna: this represents the supreme enlightenment achievement. The great Vajrayana mantram of Avalokiteshvara, *Om Mani Padma Hum*—The Jewel in the Lotus—expresses all this, the union of Nirvana and samara, of prajna and skill-in-means, and of the male and female principles. In the Vajrayana lands, it is chanted continually by priest and peasant alike, and is the message of a million prayer wheels and prayer flags.

A novice being brought into the Vajrayana path will be given by his guru a particular deity (a Buddha, bodhisattva, or female figure such as Tara representing an aspect of prajna) as his patron, from out of the vast Vajrayana ranks that crowd the mandalas. He will then seek to evoke the patron's presence through concentrated means. He will study the deity's conventional picture, until it appears in his mind even when he is not looking at it. He will seek to unify himself to the deity's lines of spiritual force by repeating his mantra and making his mudra, or gesture, with his hands. Stemming from the Mind Only presuppositions, the practice strives to create for the adept a new universe revolving around his "god." Finally, it is hoped the deity will appear visibly on his altar to accept his client's worship. The student will then pull himself closer and closer to the deity until the ultimate goal is attained, and he becomes one with his deity, shares his intimate embrace of prajna, and his Buddha-enlightenment.

In the process, there is no lack of powers of sorcery the tantrist can wield, generated as by-products of the mantras and supernormal friendship he possesses. But

[19]Fascinating accounts of tantric apprenticeships can be found in Herbert V. Guenther, *The Life and Teaching of Naropa* (London: Oxford University Press, 1963), and W. Y. Evans-Wentz, *Tibet's Great Yogin Milarepa* (London and New York: Oxford University Press, 1969).

Wisdom Embarked for the Farther Shore

the true goal is enlightenment—realizing that all is mind, all gods, bodhisattvas, and Buddhas, and all souls and phenomena, arise out of mind and sink back into it. In this respect, far from being credulous, Vajrayana is psychologically both sophisticated and boldly experimental. It knows that the numerous celestial beings and forces it calls into service exist only in mind. They are projected out of it and then, once isolated and confronted, called back into it to reign over a liberated mind equal to their power. To learn this is to attain the true liberation.

Let us conclude this chapter on Buddhism with a description of one country with an unusual and fascinating Vajrayana Buddhist culture.

TIBET

Tibet, "Land of Snows" and "Roof of the World," has long had a very particular place in the imagination of the other peoples who dwell in lower, more prosaic places. For India, the realm behind the white ramparts of the highest mountains on earth, out of which the sacred Ganges flowed, was the abode of mystic Shiva and of mighty siddhas, wizard-adepts. For China, it was roughly Shangri-La, a paradise where the Queen-Mother of the West presided over a happy nation of Taoist immortals.

For many in Europe and America, Tibet has been no less a land of magic and mystery, a cloudland of abominable snowmen and lost monasteries where occult lore is the specialty and weird psychic phenomena are everyday occurrences. Now, since the Chinese Communist regime closed the curtain on the old Tibet in 1959, the hermit nation of famous spiritual culture has receded into the past, and is locked behind walls of time even more impregnable than ever were the towering guardian mountains. Only in outposts of Tibetan culture such as Sikkim and Bhutan, and among Tibetan exiles in Nepal, India, and the West, can the old religion still be experienced. But it is worth experiencing, if only through reading, for it represents a unique, fascinating, and often profound interpretation of Buddhism and of human experience.

Although many stories about Tibet may be romanticized, there is no doubt that it seemed a very strange place to modern occidentals. It might have appeared a bit more familiar to our medieval ancestors, however. In Tibet as many as a quarter of the male population wore the reddish robes of monks, and the great thick-walled monasteries were centers of trade, finance, and government; there were even monk-soldiers who battled with each other. Other monks concerned themselves with complex meditations calling up the visible presence of strange, colorful deities of fierce or benign countenance, or perhaps with the casting of spells or the writing of histories.

The religion of the common people was equally colorful. Houses as well as the squat, domed temples were decked with bright prayer flags—pennants with brief mantras inscribed on them, flapping in the mountain wind. Prayer wheels—large drums around the outside of a temple, small ones held in the hand, each containing strips of paper written with mantra—turned everywhere sending out auspicious vibrations into the thin, crisp air. On holy days, particularly New Year's Day, brilliant dance pageants were enacted by the local priests and villagers wearing masks of grotesque demons and radiant heroes. Life in old Tibet was hard and doubtless the ordinary people were, from our point of view, backward and exploited by their nobility and monk-rulers. But they were sturdy, immensely proud of their country and its religion, and according to travelers a cheerful, content folk.

The unique Tibetan spiritual culture was essentially a combination of indigenous shamanism with Tantric Vajrayana Buddhism imported from India, and allowed, by the unusual degree of isolation Tibet's geography afforded, to develop in its own way. From shamanism came the fierce desire of the man of power to undergo initiation, demonstrate his courage and vision, explore the infinite new worlds of the psychic plane, and manifest his accomplishments through preternatural talents. From Buddhism came a sophisticated philosophical framework in which to explain these things. One has acquired unlimited full power because one has become one with the universal, invincible void; one travels to strange realms because one is realizing that one creates all one sees out of the karma-twisted mills of one's own mind.

This combination, and something of the wild but profound Tibetan point of view, is made evident in two fascinating institutions, the chod ritual and the well-known *Bardo Thodol,* or *The Tibetan Book of the Dead.* This book cannot review systematically the whole history, teaching, and practice of Tibetan Buddhism. Inevitably, any such concentration on one ritual and one text will give only a partial and one-sided view of an entire culture. But it would be equally inadequate to discuss Buddhism and give no place to the unique Buddhist experience of Tibet. As a Tibetan sampler, then, here are the chod and *The Tibetan Book of the Dead.*

In both cases we see a shamanistic scenario, comparable to the shamanistic initiations and marvelous flights or possessions described in Chapter II, but interpreted with the illumination of Buddhist philosophy. The shaman's altered, ecstatic state of consciousness becomes the unfettered egoless self, omnipotent and fearless because it has smashed its way through every delusion. The shaman's journey through other worlds where he meets and masters strange gods and demons becomes the adept's mastery, in dream, trance, or after death, of all those aspects of his ego structure that he has confused with an external reality.

An important motif of shamanism represents the shaman as the man of courage who goes alone into the wild, not to enjoy any romantic nature mysticism, but to confront the weird, uncanny spirits who dwell there (and in him), conquer, and return with them subject to him. Thus an Eskimo shaman said, "All true wisdom is only found far from men, out in the great solitude, and it can be acquired only through suffering. Privations and sufferings are the only things that can open a man's mind to that which is hidden from others."[20] Moreover, as we have seen, a novice shaman among the Eskimo would be sent from the community to an isolated lodge where he was said to take out all his bones, count them, and wait for the descent of a bright, luminous, empowering spirit which would give him limitless supernatural vision.

Chod, which literally means "cutting," is a rite of comparable effect with a Buddhist rationale. It too is performed in a desolate spot; a monk authorized by his spiritual master to enact it goes to a place like a charnal field, where (in the Tibetan manner) bodies of the deceased had been hacked up and strewn about. Here, the

[20]Andreas Lommel, *Shamanism: The Beginnings of Art* (New York: McGraw-Hill Book Company, 1967), p. 151.

adept performs spiritually the offering of his own body and blood, in a "red and black feast," to a vast host of gods and demons he invites in. Thus he shows his courage, his realization that the body is illusory and the source of dualistic error, and his boundless compassion in feeding even demons with his transitory flesh. Some trained in the chod ritual perform it only once or twice; others, finding it of immense therapeutic value, or perhaps becoming obsessed with it, do the grisly rite many times, often wandering about to enact it in various auspicious settings.

The chod performer first erects a small tent, and takes in hand the macabre instruments of the rite, a trumpet made of a human thighbone, a drum of a human skull, a trident staff, a banner of tiger and leopard hide, the claws of a bird of prey. He stands in front of the tent, and is thus instructed by the text:

> Now visualize thyself as having become, instantaneously,
> The Goddess of the All-Fulfilling Wisdom,
> Possessed of the power of enlarging thyself to the vastness of the Universe,
> And endowed with all the beauties of perfection;
> [Then] blow the human thigh-bone trumpet loudly,
> And dance the Dance which Destroyeth Erroneous Beliefs.

The adept then begins a dance of invitation to the gods, gurus, and demons of the several directions with these words:

> I, the *yogin,* who practices the Dauntless Courage,
> Devoting my thought and energy wholly to the realizing that *Nirvana* and the
>   *Sangsara* are inseparable,

*Tibetan Buddhist temple,
the Kum-Bum in Gyantse.*

Am dancing this measure on [the forms of] spiritual beings who personify the self;
May I [be able to] destroy the *sangsaric* view of duality.[21]

The performer then encourages his eerie and eager guests to gorge themselves on the sacrifice which he spreads of his physical prison, illusory because it is really just a transitory modulation of the interacting cosmos and deceptive because it suggests he is a separate entity. As he makes the sacrifice, he is to think:

Then imagine this body, which is the result of thine own *karmic* propensities,
To be a fat, luscious-looking corpse, huge [enough to embrace the Universe],
Then [saying] *Phat!* visualize the radiant Intellect, which is within thee,
As being the Wrathful Goddess and as standing apart [from thy body],
Having one face and two hands and holding a knife and a skull.
Think that she severeth the head from the corpse,
And setteth it, as a skull [like an enormous cauldron], over three skulls placed like
    legs of a tripod embracing the Three Regions,
And cutteth the corpse into bits and flingeth them inside the skull as offerings to the
    deities.[22]

Significantly, the mystic calls on the wisdom-goddess to perform the killing thrust with her sharp knife—for it is intellect which gets us into trouble, by constructing a world around ego structures, but it is also intellect which can get us out of trouble by that brilliant insight which discriminates between the real and the unreal.

The adept completes the chod ritual with the dedication of the merit of his performance to the salvation of all beings, the manner in which almost all Tibetan rites end, and proceeds back into the world—as one who has again been mystically through becoming one with the universe, self-sacrifice, death, total compassion, and return—as one who has performed a strange holy communion through his own body.

The Tibetan Book of the Dead is a breathtaking panorama of the experience of the individual, or rather the vortex of karmic waves that one has set in motion, after physical death and prior to reincarnation. In this intermediate state one sees divine splendors and terrors undreamed-of by most mortals. In the course of this opening of the portals of immortal reality, one must realize that all in heaven and earth comes out of mind, and that we therefore create our own heaven or hell. If one does not attain this realization, one falls back to be reborn again, to undertake another of one's countless chances to learn the basic lesson of life. In both color and pattern, *The Tibetan Book of the Dead* reminds one of the science fiction movie *2001,* with its initiatory break through the "stargate" to a surrealist realm of brightness and meaning, and the final return of the explorer as an old man or child to this earth in the remote future.

The book is intended to be read into the ear of one who is dying or just deceased. It is based on the premise of the three levels of experienced reality already spoken of as the three Buddha "bodies" or forms of expression: the dharmakaya or absolute essence of the universe; the samboghakaya or heavenly, archetypal, godlike level; and the nirmanakaya or this-worldly, incarnate level. Behind these lies the three

[21] W. Y. Evans-Wentz, *Tibetan Yoga and Secret Doctrines* (London and New York: Oxford University Press, 1967), pp. 301–2. Reprinted with permission.

[22] Ibid, pp. 311–12.

Wisdom Embarked for the Farther Shore

states of consciousness of the Upanishads: the absolute or deep sleep without dreams, the dreaming, and the waking. In *The Tibetan Book of the Dead* these come out as the Chikhai Bardo or "Clear Light of the Void," the Chonyid Bardo with its archetypal visual experiences, and the places of rebirth by passage through a womb-door.

The Tibetan Book of the Dead tells us there are lowly but homey and seductive karma-governed worlds, and there is the bardo state. The bardo state, whether as Clear Light of the Void or resolved into luminous visual images, is the "other" state to us, an obverse, alternative reality to ours.

Contact with this other side is by no means restricted to postmortum experience. *The Tibetan Book of the Dead* tells us that it is also met in the womb, in dreams, and in meditation.[23] It seems to be found, in fact, wherever we are cut off from sensory interaction with an "outer" world and so are brought up against worlds of forms— or formlessness—growing out of our own minds, and must contend with these "inner" beauties and monsters. It is after death, however, that according to this Tibetan book most people confront the bardo state most decisively, for then the response to it sets the conditions of a whole subsequent lifetime.

The after-death adventure starts at the top, as the entity faces the Clear Light of the Void. This is the dharmakaya, the void, the Buddha-nature, itself—the universe in its absolute essence, a stream of interacting vibrations. The book says:

> O nobly-born, when thy body and mind were separating, thou must have experienced a glimpse of the Pure Truth, subtle, sparkling, bright, dazzling, glorious, and radiantly awesome, in appearance like a mirage moving across a landscape in springtime in one continuous stream of vibrations. Be not daunted thereby, nor terrified, nor awed. That is the radiance of thine own true nature. Recognize it.

> From the midst of that radiance, the natural sound of Reality, reverberating like a thousand thunders simultaneously sounding, will come. That is the natural sound of thine own real self. Be not daunted thereby, nor terrified, nor awed.[24]

Here, as always, the "person" is supposed to recognize what is seen— the Clear Light of the Void—as "one's own true nature." One is part of the universe, and so this thunder of cosmic vibration is indeed his, and our, "true nature." But because of ego, we shrink back from accepting this—the light of absolute reality is too bright for our eyes, the joyous laughter of this great dance of atoms, eons, and galaxies seems more threatening than inviting to the ego and its precious notion of separate existence. We would prefer a small womb-born life in some quiet, or even tumultuous, corner of the vast cosmos where we can burrow a hole or build a nest, call it our own, and bare our teeth against others in the dance. We turn our eyes from this vision. So the opportunity of this brief parting of the innermost veil of reality is, for most, lost. A second chance occurs as a paler rendering of the Clear Light appears for a longer time, like an afterimage.

Then, as if shifting gears, the experience drops to a different level—that in

[23]W. Y. Evans-Wentz, *The Tibetan Book of the Dead* (New York: Oxford University Press, 1960), p. 102.

[24]Ibid., p. 104.

which the pilgrim on successive days witnesses the appearance of the five Buddhas of the cosmic mandala. They emerge as radiant apparitions out of the deep blue of heaven, with all the colors, gestures, and symbols that characterize each in Tibetan iconography. This is facing reality on the samboghakaya or "dream" level. Each Buddha is the transcendent essence of one of the skandhas, and each is locked in sexual embrace with his particular wisdom, personified as feminine.

These figures—Vairocana from the Central Realm of the Densely Packed, Ratnasambhava from the yellow Southern Realm, and so forth—represent absolute reality as fully as it can be expressed in terms of form. Why does reality now come in these awesome forms? The pilgrim had rejected it in its clear undifferentiated nature because of clinging to ego—and we always see God basically as we see ourselves. If we can truly think of ourselves as egoless, so will God be known to us, as Clear Light. It we still deep down think of ourselves as a personal ego (regardless of how we may intellectualize about things), so will God be known to us as another personality mirroring us, smiling or frowning as the case may be.

First smiling. These figures represent the splendor of the Clear Light itself lightly channeled into symbol-laden configurations. If the visitor can recognize any of them as his "own true nature"—that is, as a projection on the screen of the void of a high Buddhalike part of himself in touch with reality—through that means he can be liberated from rebirth.

But at the same time there is an "escape hatch," as always, from the self-surrender necessary for liberation. For many the glorious Buddhas also will seem too dazzling to be borne, and their eyes will turn instinctively to a dull light beside each. These are light-paths to the various places of rebirth—white to the place of the gods, green to the world of the titans, yellow to the human place, blue to the animals, reddish to the doleful dominion of the hungry ghosts, smokey to the hells. Many will feel a nearly uncontrollable impulse to follow one of these trails to seek a womb therein, for we have done many karmic works that make one or another seem congenial, more homelike than the brilliant surrealistic sky-world of flashing images. But the book exhorts the pilgrim to reject the dull lights with the dull miseries of stupidity and suffering to which they lead, and to accept against all seeming the glorious truth that it is the Buddhas, not brute or slave or even god, who are one's truest and deepest nature.

On seven consecutive days the bardo-voyager meets the Buddhas of the Center and the Four Directions, then all five together, then the fierce but good "knowledge-holding deities" who accompany them. Then, if the pilgrim is not yet liberated (which most will not be), the mood shifts dramatically.

Now out of sheets of flame lurch a series of forms terrifying as only the lurid Tibetan imagination can paint them: giant three-headed ogres, red and blue and white faces contorted with rage, wearing chains of skulls, holding axe and sword, embracing ghastly "mothers" who offer their consorts skull cups of blood. Yet each bears the "third eye" in the forehead, which tells us these too are aspects of Buddha-wisdom, and so of one's true nature. Here too, then, discriminating wisdom should remove fear. The viewing wanderer is urged to recognize these spectres as coming out of his or her mind like the others, and moreover to see them as the previous peaceful forms in different guise.

Why have they changed? At this stage, the pilgrim who has been sailing on thought-winds through the bardo worlds of confronting the truth about one's ego still is clinging to the illusion of being a separate individual self, or else he would have gone no further than the Clear Light or the peaceful forms, having attained liberation through one of them. But here he is, a karmic self strayed in a level of being keyed to the truth that the essence of reality is indivisible mind. No wonder, then, that the pilgrim finds the bardo realm now *seems* to turn hostile. Finally it gets through that this realm "wants" to take away his separate selfhood. Reality itself appears to change from an accepting to a threatening aspect, although it is not actually reality that changes—it is always just the Clear Light at base—but the aspect of self which projects images on that screen now changes understandably to dread.

But even so, the terrifying images are actually to be recognized as also Vairocana, Ratnasambhava, and so forth, no longer coming as compassionate saviors but as ruthless discriminating intellect, which can also save, though by a harsher means. They come to liberate through the means of shock therapy designed to force the pilgrim to discriminate between illusion and reality. Here too he may find his way out of the wheel of rebirth. One confronts five terrifying deities, then eight wrathful animal-headed figures, then four female doorkeepers—all forms from within one's own head.

If one ask how the Tibetans were so sure just how the Buddha-deities of the bardo state will look, the answer is very simple—this is the way the pilgrim put them there. For we must remember that they all come out of one's own mind, and appear as the way the traveler structures transcendent reality if he cannot accept it in its pure state just as the Clear Light of the Void. If as a Tibetan he has spent many years in the milieu of stylized paintings and images of these same cosmic Buddhas, and perhaps as a monk centered his religious life around their visualization, it is not surprising that he should see the forms on the other side in the same guise as he creates his heaven and hell. Although the book does not say so, one could speculate that it implies a Muslim or Christian or Hindu might see the peaceful and wrathful sides of the divine nature under forms more familiar to him or her. But in any case the one thing one cannot get away from even after death, the book tells us, is oneself, or rather the karmic forces and structures of mind one has set in motion; even the atheist who expects nothing will not escape the bardo level, since it is really within himself, but instead of having the crisp outlines of Vairocana or Ratnasambhava to set against it, presumably he would have to contend with projected painful memories and bright but disturbing chaos.

But the traditional Tibetan was well prepared indeed for the bardo confrontation; his whole spiritual life, grounded on the presupposition that all comes out of mind and that one makes out of mind his whole life here and hereafter, has been directed toward enabling him to populate the bardo with familiar forms. Then in turn he recognizes these forms when he sees them as having been put there by him, and so minimizes the fear and facilitates a successful passage. If it works, there is no room for terror or ignorance. What finally saves most people, in other words, is creating a symbol system to lay against the blankness of primordial reality, and then recognizing that this is what is deliberately being done.

The preparation begins when a novice, after a hard preliminary work of chanting, study, and doing 100,000 prostrations, is finally initiated into the stream of force of one of the cosmic Buddhas by his lama or guru. He is empowered to evoke him by using his mantra, gesture, and mystic rites. He will concentrate on pictures or images of the chosen deity, until he can visualize him. This fleshless companion becomes his *yidam,* or patronal deity, his protector and guide toward liberation.

His task is to make the yidam more and more real and visible, until he identifies himself with him. Alone, the adept performs the rituals of his patron over and over, day after day, week after week, year after year. He prostrates, takes refuge in the three Buddha jewels, generates in his mind Buddha wisdom, presents offerings of rice and butter to his deity, concentrates on his image, throws the rice high into the air as a dedication of grace to all sentient beings. In time, he may begin to see the yidam appear in his sanctuary. At first it may be only as a flash, like a fish leaping out of water. Eventually, the apparition may be "fixed" and come into visibility at will. Then, as the adept faces his deity, he will see a string of letters—the mantra—spin from his mouth and heart to the god's, binding them together—the ritual energy will draw them closer and closer, until in a moment of mystic coalescence the two are one. This sets the stage for recognizing and uniting with the same deity when he is projected into the boundless space of the bardo, and for liberation through him.

In the last part of *The Tibetan Book of the Dead,* the yidam plays another very important role. This is the part dealing with re-entry into a world of rebirth. Assume that, as is the case with most, the pilgrim has not accepted liberation with the Clear Light, the peaceful forms, or the wrathful. He now draws close to the earth again, spiritually speaking, and begins to be aware of what is going on there. The relentless spiritual machinery aimed at his rebirth rumbles louder and louder; his time in the bardo state is growing short. A number of things happen.

Leaving the bright rainbow colors of the transcendent forms, he enters a state of constant gray-white light. He becomes aware for the first time that he is dead, and sees those he left behind mourning for him. He tries to communicate with them, but cannot. At the same time, he has views of possible future existences. He stumbles into a world of huge rocks and mountains, and finds that he has seemingly supernormal powers—he can move right through them. The winds of karma rise; he is blown rapidly hither and yon, and tumbles into pitch darkness filled with shrieks. As he wanders he feels increasingly hopeless, helpless, despairing, longing to have a body again. He has flash visions of judgment, and senses being torn apart in punishment for his sins. Then he sees again the soft colors, seductive and bidding as marshlights, leading to the six worlds of rebirth.

Through all of this, the book tells the pilgrim that he can still be liberated without rebirth if he pays no attention to any of them, and concentrates on the Buddha-nature, his lama, and his patronal deity. Now the long years of evocation and visualization must come into their own, and make it easy in the midst of all these tumults, to focus elsewhere than on the alluring light paths to rebirth—even here, one can make his own state. (Or, if one will, he can as a bodhisattva deliberately choose his own rebirth where he can do the most good, not out of karmic necessity but out of transcendent wisdom and compassion.)

One particularly interesting passage seems to anticipate Sigmund Freud's oedipus complex. The process of conception is described in these words:

> If [about] to be born as a male, the feeling of itself being a male dawneth upon the Knower, and a feeling of intense hatred towards the father and of jealousy and attraction towards the mother is begotten. If [about] to be born as a female, the feeling of itself being a female dawneth upon the Knower, and a feeling of intense hatred towards the mother and of intense attraction and fondness towards the father is begotten. Through this secondary cause—[when] entering upon the path of ether, just at the moment when the sperm and the ovum are about to unite—the Knower experienceth the bliss of the simultaneously-born state, during which state it fainteth away into unconsciousness. [Afterwards] it findeth itself encased in oval form, in the embryonic state . . .[25]

The text tells us that wandering in the samsaric worlds, the world of the suffering-desire syndrome created by partiality, grasping, and false ego-identity concepts, is at root created for the individual by this attraction and repulsion in the womb. Here it is that partiality based on two kinds of feeling is engendered, and the way prepared for constructing an ego walled off from awareness of its true universal connections by passionately held desires and hatreds.

Right at this point, then, the poison ought to be capped and negative rebirth denied. At the moment of conception, we have been told, there is an instant of bliss because father and mother are equal; the two opposites are united in a flash of bliss. This moment is the model for all subsequent high experiences of realization. Thus the way to attain liberation now, and prevent painful rebirth, is to invoke the image of the union of opposites, expressed in the great Tibetan image of the supreme Buddhas locked in sexual embrace with their prajna or wisdom. "Abandon jealousy," the text says, "and meditate upon the *Guru* Father-Mother." Here is another meaning of the resplendant Buddha scenes one has projected upon the bardo, for as stylized union of Buddha and wisdom each is a flash of cosmic sexual and mystical bliss in which all opposites are reconciled, and so all partial passions fulfilled and stilled.

This is really what Buddhism is about, for in the end all of its language, symbols, and practices are expressions of the union of opposites, the reconciliation of all polarities. From the Buddha's proclaimation of a Middle Way, which finds infinite bliss in keeping a breathtakingly delicate balance between indulgence and asceticism, life and death, being and nonbeing, to the Tibetan vision of coupled father-mother gods in the bardo sky, we have met with pointers to an experience of oneness, combined with awareness that it is one's self-made shell of ego encrustations which keeps one from it; out of this egg one has to break with a shout of awakening.

[25]Ibid., p. 179.

FIVE

DRAGON
AND
SUN

Religions of China and Japan

A stele in a Chinese temple portrays Confucius, the Buddha, and Lao-tzu, epitomizing the three great spiritual traditions of China and their harmony.

THE EAST ASIAN SPIRITUAL WORLD

Some years ago, I encountered for the first time a non-Western religion in its homeland. That religion was Shinto in Japan. I saw Japanese Buddhist temples on the same visit, of course, but it was Shinto shrines I saw first and which for some reason buried themselves most deeply in my memory.

I could not forget the *torii,* the gently curved archway that led into the precincts of a shrine, separating the noisy bustle of the street from the quiet shrine with its ancient architecture. The torii was like a mystic portal between one age and another, and even one dimension and another. In the midst of a modern industrial city, these plain but graceful halls of the *kami,* the Shinto gods, are set amidst sacred groves of gnarled old trees, and communicate just a touch of the past, the natural, and the wondrous. In the countryside, where shrines grace mountaintops, clear rushing streams, or inlets of the sea, they lend an aura of the numinous to vistas already beautiful.

I felt strangely stirred by these wooden fanes, simple and rustic in construction with their pitched roofs and heavy doors. The porticos presented such understated but effective symbols of deity as zigzag strips of paper, immense rope lintels, and gleaming eyelike mirrors. I liked the way the shrines seemed never to clash with nature, but only to embellish it. If a divine kami-presence dwelt within the shrine, one felt, he was a deity who knew and respected the old trees in his parish down to their deepest roots, and the insides of the ageless stones, as well as the grandmothers, young people, and babies who lived in the streets around his shrine-home. While musing on dreams of the mythic past, the kami watched with spirit-eyes the frenetic life of a modern nation.

Nor were these kami-presences forgotten. One feature of postwar Japan which has surprised many outside observers is that Shinto, shorn of state control and ultranationalistic overtones but retaining its shrines under local and democratic administration, has not withered away but has prospered as a popular religion. To be sure, few of those frequenting the shrines would call themselves exclusively Shinto.

Most are also Buddhist, at least nominally, or members of one of the "new religions" of Japan. Many would hardly think of themselves as religious at all. Yet they
pause for a moment as they pass a shrine, hardly knowing why.

At shrines of any importance, the visitor will not wait long before seeing a
Japanese individual or family pass through the torii, wash hands and mouth in a
basin, approach the shrine, clap twice, bow, murmur a prayer, and leave a small
offering in a grill.

If the observer is fortunate, he or she may have the opportunity to be at a shrine
festival, or *matsuri*. Then he or she will notice a dramatic change in the atmosphere
of the shrine. Instead of a quiet, shy deity in his leafy refuge, the kami now becomes
a dynamic presence in the midst of his people, calling explosive festivity into being.
First, pure offerings of rice wine (*sake*), vegetables, and seafood are very slowly
presented to the kami by white-robed priests, together with green boughs of the
sacred *sakaki* tree brought forward by leading laymen.

Then, suddenly and startlingly, this mood of classical dignity breaks. Sacred
dance in vivid and fantastic costume is performed. A carnival may be held on the
grounds of the shrine, with everything from cotton candy to *sumo* wrestling. The
kami presence is carried through the streets in a palenquin (*mikoshi*) by running,
sweating young men, who shout "Washo! Washo!" as they zigzag down the ways
and byways of the kami's parish.

Shinto has a highly distinctive personality of its own, yet it also illustrates
several characteristics of the religion of East Asia in general. In Shinto shrines, and
also in Chinese and Japanese Buddhist and other temples, one senses a close
harmony of the human and natural orders. The gods and guides of mankind dwell in
virtual symbiosis with woods, streams, and mountains, suggesting that in a larger
sense society is a part of nature, and kami, immortals, Buddhas, and humans are all
parts of a greater cosmic unity.

Very often, then, the divine is finite and tied to particular places. There may
indeed be an indefinable universal divine principle that underlies all particular
manifestations of the divine, and is infinite. But the individual gods one can know
are limited although impressive, as if no more than glorified human beings. Indeed,
in China for the last two thousand years nearly all deities except Heaven and Earth
themselves were conceived of as having once been humans who acceded to divine
status by exemplary merit. Their ranks and titles were confirmed by the emperor as
though they were simply another class among his subjects—and the emperor alone
was permitted to worship Heaven and Earth directly. In Japan, although only
occasionally entitling gods, the government assigned the status of the various
shrines.

East Asian religion has tended to see a world in which gods and men both have
places, and interact with each other more by agreement and respect than on the
model of master and slave. To be sure, Chinese and Japanese worship is capable of
mystery, awe, and wonder. Buddhism, particularly through the Mahayana
philosophies and techniques described in the previous chapter, has made the
spiritual culture aware of mystical and metaphysical profundities oriented toward
the infinite. Yet it all finally comes down to a human-centered view of mystery and

History of Religion in China and Japan

Dates	CHINA		JAPAN	
	Major Eras	Personalities and Events	Personalities and Events	Major Eras
1500 AD	People's Republic on Mainland (1949—) Republic (1912—) Ch'ing (1644–1911)	Wang-Yang Ming (1472–1529)	New Religions Nationalism Confucianism dominant culturally Hakuin (1685–1768)	Postwar (1945) Modern (1868–1945) Tokugawa (1600–1867)
1000 AD	Ming (1368–1644) Yuan (1280–1368) Sung (960–1127)	Neo-Confucianism dominant Chu Hsi (1130–1200)	Zen dominant Dogen (1200–53) Eisai (1141–1215) Nichiren (1222–82) Shinran (1173–1263) Honen (1133–1212)	Muromachi (1333–1568) Kamakura (1185–1333)
500 AD	T'ang (618–907) Sui (589–618) 6 Dynasties (420–589)	High point of Buddhism Hui-neng (638–713)	Esoteric Buddhism Kobo Daishi (773–835) Kojiki (712) Introduction of Buddhism (early 6th century)	Heian (794–1185) Nara (710–784) Taika (645–710)
1 BC/AD	3 Kingdoms (220–265) Han (206 BC–220 AD)	Beginning of Ch'an and Pure Land Buddhism Ko Hung (283–343)	Clan period; Shamanism very influential	Protohistoric
500 BC	Ch'in (221–206)	Tung Chung-shu (179–104) and Han Confucianism Chuang-tzu (c. 300) Mencius (372–289) Confucius (551–479)		Prehistoric
1000 BC	Chou (1123–221) End of Shang	Lao-tzu(?) Court rituals		

metaphysics—the Chinese and Japanese are rarely forgetful that these things are important to humans insofar as they enrich human life, and help validate its central institutions, the family and the state. Religious style is likely to be more restrained and pragmatic than the ecstatic abandon of the Hindu bhakta or the hard surety of the crusader. Religion is not that kind of commitment; rather, it is part of a ring of relativistic commitments whose real center is inflexible norms of propriety for human and divine relations; these are the true obligation. The value center, in other words, is where propriety finds its home, in one's means of integration into family and community.

The sociological expression is extremely important in understanding religion in East Asia. In particular, "natural" sociological units, family and community, for most East Asians *are* one's link with the infinite. It is through worship of one's particular ancestors that one expresses filial relation to the primordial infinite ancestors of all that breathes—Heaven and Earth. It is through one's particular kami or patronal deity that one integrates oneself into the hierarchy of the divine. It is through reverence to particular Buddhas and bodhisattvas that one acknowledges tacitly the unbounded wisdom a Buddha represents.

All these features come together when one thinks of East Asian faith as being centered in a "one world" concept. There is no god or heaven outside the world system of which we are a part here and now. Gods, heavens, hells, society, nature, family, and individual are all parts of a single unity of which mankind is (at least for humans) the pivot. This means the individual has to be a part of the whole; if there be only one unified system, it is absurd to try to opt out of it. On the other hand, it means that one is under no obligation to emphasize one part of the system more than another—heaven more than this world, a god more than family. All are parts of the same thing, so one's approach is according to one's circumstances or bent. Most would probably agree that a balanced outlook is wisest.

Some commentators have so stressed this supposedly "humanistic" and "this worldly" East Asian attitude as to suggest that religion, life after death, heavens, and supernatural entities are unimportant to the Chinese and Japanese. At least in regard to traditional society, such an assessment is very wide of the mark. Whatever some rationalistic philosophers may have held, popular culture was certainly not behind any other in energy and expense devoted to worship of gods, propitiation of spirits, and assurance of a good fate on the other side of death.

But it is fair to say that this concern, real as it was, is given a special quality by an overarching perception that the visible and invisible realms are parts of one unity, like the obverse and reverse sides of a coin, and that what is really important to mankind is the continuation and well-being of individual, family, and societal human life on both sides. Except for the most mystical of Taoists and Buddhists, this perpetuation of the good life for humans was the supreme good. The apparatus of religion was appreciated by the many who accepted it for the contributions it could make to that objective here and hereafter, as a map of the invisible world which interlocked in cause and effect with this world, but not because of any belief that ordinary religion had absolute, apriori authority.

The interaction of mystery and community was once made very evident to the author in Hawaii, when I visited the annual festival of a large interrelated group which had immigrated in the nineteenth century from a single village in south China. The deity on the brightly-decked altar in the community hall was Kuan Ti, a stern military god who is considered a strong protector against evil forces; he was a famous general back in the third century A.D., so exemplary in his heroism and righteousness that after death the emperor declared him a god. He became well known and worshipped all over China. As members of the community entered the hall, they lit sticks of incense and set them upright before the deity. Spread before Kuan Ti were also food offerings, including a roast pig, paper boxes and houses, and firecrackers.

Then an old Taoist priest vested in a red and green robe put on a peculiar black cap. He stood before the altar, waved incense, and opened a worn liturgical book. Also on the altar were esoteric symbols of the Taoist craft: scissors, a measuring stick, the character for Tao the mystic universal unity.

The *chiao* or Taoist service offered by the priest had nothing directly to do with the community. It was a priestly rite which the officiant did in the community's presence. Through chanting occult formulae he called up a series of high spirits:— the spirits of the eighteen stars of the Big and Little Dipper, the Three Pure Ones— hierarchical rank upon rank, a celestial court like the old imperial bureaucracy. Each level contained fewer but more powerful entities than the one below it. Meditatively, then, the adept brought the cosmos into greater and greater unity, until Yin and Yang, the two ultimate polarities into which all other multiplicity is resolved, alone remained. Then the priest merged them, and stood before the ritually presented great Tao itself, the endless, incomprehensible stream down which all things visible and invisible flow. He did not become Tao, but stood before it in awe.

In a real Taoist temple, such as one can still find on Taiwan, this *chiao* ritual might be preformed in a great ceremony involving several priests and lasting for days at an important festival—and the ritual would be secret, the temple closed to all but the priests participating. Here, however, the members of the community were mostly seated in a big half-circle around priest and altar, many talking and laughing quietly—not out of disrespect, but just because priest, rite, spirits, community, Kuan Ti, the Tao itself, are all part of one big family in which one feels at home. The incoming spirits *wanted* the community to be happy and prosperous, to enjoy the good things of life, good food and good companionship—they were in fact inducing the ripples of merriment and kindly gossip starting to roll around the room as waves in the tide of Tao.

Suddenly the tempo changed. The esoteric part of the mystery was over. The spirits were dispatched by burning the paper offerings outside in a big fire; the firecrackers were set off. The roast pig was quickly cut up ans served. Everyone received a heaping plate of food and truned to enjoy a lavish banquet; a leading community official discreetly handed the priest of Tao the traditional bright red envelop containing payment for his services.

To get a perspective on the specifics of East Asian religion, let us begin with China, and at the beginning. One of the most distinctive features of the Chinese mentality is its feeling that the Chinese people and the soil on which they live are inseparable, and have been together as far back as tradition goes. In most other major societies, a tradition of having come from some other place and conquered the land in which the people now dwell is a feature of incalculable weight in the national image. Consider the significance of the Exodus and the taking of the Promised Land to the Israelites, the journey of Aeneas from Troy to Italy for the Roman mystique, the importance of the Indo-European invasions in both ancient India and Northern Europe, the myth of the conquest of Japan by the first emperor Jimmu for Japanese nationalism, or the immigration and pioneer motifs in America's national consciousness. In China, there is none of this. Instead, the Chinese have felt a quieter but even more secure assurance that they have always been in China, were created there, and belong there as surely as the rivers and mountains and rice fields.

A sense of place, of the cycles of nature, and of lineage were fundamental to the religious outlook of the earliest known Chinese, as they have been ever since. One of the oldest motifs of Chinese religion is the Earth-god. The cultural line that led to Chinese civilization began somewhere around 4000 B.C. in tiny villages in the Yellow River basin where millet, vegetables, and pigs were cultivated. The central sacred feature was often a stone or mound, like a concentration of the forces of the soil into a central focus; these mounds are the ancestors of the city-god temples of today, as well as the great Altar of Heaven in Peking, built like an artificial mountain, where the emperor offered worship at the winter solstice.[1] Worship was also offered very early to the spirits of rivers and of rain, the latter immemorially represented as the dragon, for the rivers and rain bless the fertile earth with moisture.

In burial and ancestrism, continuity of the three identity-giving factors of family, ancestors, and place was emphasized. Burial, the return of the tiller of the earth to its bosom, has always been very important in China. As the peasant works his fields, he may see on the side of an overlooking hill the site he has selected for his tomb. He knows that from there he will in spirit watch his progeny generation after generation work the same fields. At the tomb, at the family shrine with tablets bearing the names of ancestors, and in the home shrine, his descendents will remember him with offerings of food and drink, and with information concerning family events. This reverence may be tinged with awe and dread, for even the humblest of family heads grows mightily in power when he returns to union with the invincible earth itself, and he can reach out from the grave to bless those who keep bright the family honor, or afflict its enemies.

The concern with burial goes as far back as Chinese culture. Neolithic farmers

---

[1]Marcel Granet, *Chinese Civilization* (New York: Meridian Books, 1958), pp. 170–79.

Main Themes of Chinese Thought and Religion

Ideal of the rational, controlled life

Han Confucianism

Confucius

Confucian temples

Imperial worship of
Heaven

                      Yin-yang and five
                        element systems

    Mencius   Monastic
                   Ch'an Buddhism

                            Taoist magic
                            and alchemy

Orientation to Soceity — *Orientation to Nature*

Taoist priesthood

Ancestrism   Lao-tzu

City gods and
  place gods,
  with their temples
  and rites

Pure Land Buddhism

Shamanism   Popular Taoist movements

The emotionally intense, non-rational ideal

Thematic Chart IV. The Chinese tradition is marked by polarities between the Confucian ideal of a rational, virtuous life in a well-ordered society which expresses the Tao; and the Taoist ideal of a life close to the wildness of nature and giving full rein to feeling and fantasy.

buried children in urns under the house, and adults in reserved fields. In the first period of real civilization, the Shang, great pits were dug in the earth for the burial of a king. In what must have been a scene of incredible barbaric horror and splendor, the deceased monarch was interred brilliantly ornamented with jade, together with the richly caparisoned horses who had borne his hearse, hundreds of sacrificed human retainers and prisoners, and a fortune in precious objects.[2]

The Shang dynasty and its successor, the Chou, lasted from about 1750 to 221 B.C. The basic motifs of religion in these eras represent in developing form the fundamental ideas of Chinese religion and philosophy.

The thinkers of those days talked of a supreme ruler or moderator of the universe, Ti or T'ien, usually translated "Heaven," who gave rain, victory, fortune or misfortune, and regulated the moral order. All things ultimately derived from T'ien, but he was more a personification of natural law than a real personality, and was not directly worshipped; he was like the high god of many archaic peoples.

Other gods, lesser but more accessible to worship, were those of sun, moon, stars, rivers, mountains, the four directions, and localities. These were given offerings, some seasonally, some morning and evening. Above all were the ancestral spirits treated to meals and remembrance, and expected to intercede on behalf of the living with T'ien.

The dead, in other words, were made a part of life. They could communicate with the living through the lips of shamanesses and oracles, and unpropitiated ghosts of the dead were much feared. There were also myths of culture heroes who combated floods, built irrigation systems, and taught the people agriculture; if not directly worshipped, such figures as Yu and Hou Chi had marvelous births, precarious and miracle-fraught childhoods, and lives of self-sacrifice and superhuman works comparable to those of divine heroes and saviours elsewhere.

The Shang era is most famous for divination with the "oracle bones." The procedure was that kings would ask their ancestors questions, and the answers would be determined by cracks made in a tortoise shell when it was heated over a fire. Thousands of these bones, with the questions and sometimes the answers inscribed on them in an archaic form of writing, have been preserved.

Archaic Chinese religion is also noteworthy for the importance it gave to ceremonial. Highly stylized and exact rites were performed for each season, for gods and ancestors, and for the major occasions of life. These were done at court, and apparently had their parallels among the common people as well. Court ceremonies were elaborate affairs; as we have seen they sometimes involved grisly but solemn animal and human sacrifices.

Divination, the seasonal cycle, and ceremonialism all suggest one basic principle which has run through Chinese thought from the beginning, that the universe is a unity in which all things fit together. If man aligns himself with it all will fit together for him as it does for nature. On this assumption, traditional Chinese lived with the

[2]See Judith M. Treistman, *The Prehistory of China* (New York: Natural History Press, 1972), pp. 47, 111–16.

turning of the seasons, and in their ceremonies strove to make life into an image of their harmony. Divination is based on the same world view, for it presumes that if the world is a unity each fragment of it—like a tortoise shell—must contain clues of what is or will happen in other parts.

The unity in which all things fit together is called the *Tao*. The word is most often translated "way," and originally meant a road but can also mean "speak." Among philosophers it came to mean the inexpressibly broad track down which all things roll; in philosophical writing, it has been translated by such terms as "way," "nature," "existence," and even "God."

CONFUCIANISM

Tao—how to know it, live it, and construct a society which exemplifies it—is the great theme of Chinese thought and the religious expressions closely related to it. Never was this more the case than in the last two centuries of the Chou dynasty, 403–221 B.C. Called the "Warring States" period, this was an era when, because the emperor had been reduced to a powerless figurehead, rulers of feudal states battled unceasingly with each other. Although it was a time of cultural and material advance, people felt that all sense of restraint and morality had been lost. Even the rough warrior codes no longer held, and society was caught up in a madness of rapacity, intrigue, and violence punctuated by a depraved brutality in which prisoners were routinely killed by slow and horrible means. The peasants, exploited in the best of times, suffered most.

Yet this was a time of creativity for the human spirit. New concepts which could be the foundation of high civilization emerged, if only because thoughtful people were forced to ask themselves questions like, "Where did we go wrong? How can we get society back on the right track and find the Tao? How can a sensitive individual find meaning in the midst of so much crassness?"

In asking how to get back on the track of Tao, three realms were in mind where Tao could be experienced: nature, human society, and one's own inner being. The question was, How are these to be lined up—with what priorities, and with what techniques for ascertaining the "message" of the Tao for man each communicates?

The answers fall into two categories, Confucian and Taoist. (There were other schools that have not survived or did not develop significant religious expression.) The basic difference was that Confucianists thought the Tao was best found by man within human tradition and society, and so was explored through human relationships and rituals and by the use of human reason. The Taoists thought that reason and society perverted the Tao, that it was best found alone in the rapture of confronting infinite nature and the mystical and marvelous.

The difference is comparable to that between rationalists and romantics in the West. Needless to say, Confucianism in China has been mainly associated with moralism, and the ruling "establishment" elite and their education system. Taoism, on the other hand, is linked with indulgence of feelings, with artists and poets, and with all sorts of colorful, bizarre, "nonestablishment" things from fairy tales to unusual sexual techniques, from exorcizing devils to revolutionary secret societies, and esoteric temple rites like that described.

But it is important to recall that relatively few Chinese would think of themselves as exclusively Confucian or Taoist or Buddhist. In the lives of most people features from all sides would have a place. Confucian attitudes would undergird family and work ethics; Buddhism would help to answer questions about what happens after death; a dash of Taoist color would meet esthetic and spiritual needs in family and personal life. (It has been said that Chinese officials were Confucian at work and Taoist on vacation.)

The Confucian tradition is named after the philosopher Confucius (551–479 B.C.) We must distinguish Confucius the man of his time from the almost-deified, impossibly wise and remote figure of the Confucian educational tradition and state cult. But at the same time we must remember why that particular man was selected as the symbolic embodiment of this tradition.

First, we must take into account the winsome, wise, persuasive, and utterly sincere personality of Confucius himself. Born in the feudal state of Lu (modern Shantung) as the son of a minor official or military officer, Kung-fu-tzu (to give Master Kung his Chinese rather than latinized name and title) received an education and sought employment by a prince. He was a member of a class called *ju,* who were specialists in the "six arts"—ceremonial, music, archery, charioteering, history, numbers—and so custodians of what passed in those days for a classical and cultivated tradition. But Confucius had great difficulty in finding a position, apparently because he was too outspoken about proper conduct on the part of rulers and seemed hopelessly to have "his head in the clouds." He had to settle for a role which to him seemed second best, but in the long run proved far more epochal than that of government minister. He became a teacher. Among his students were young men who were successful in attaining practical influence, and who over the years—and through subsequent generations of students over the centuries—reshaped the values and structure of Chinese statecraft, education, and social organization. It was they who understandably added honor upon honor to Confucius' memory, until temples redolent of incense and sacrifice enshrined his name.

Confucius was not revered just for himself, but because he was associated with the classical literature that was the real bedrock of the traditional culture. Five books, which existed in early form by the time of Confucius and which were the basic texts of the ju, are now often called the Confucian classics. These are the *Book of History,* the *Book of Poems,* the *Book of Change* (the famous *I Ching*), the historical *Spring and Autumn Annals,* and the *Book of Rites.* Tradition said, with greater or less exaggeration, that Confucius had written parts of them and edited them all; in any case, he was the symbol of their authority.

Four other books from shortly after the time of Confucius are also canonical and bear the putative seal of the master's authority: the *Analects* (containing the remembered words of Confucius himself), the *Great Learning,* the *Mean,* and the *Book of Mencius.*[3] (Mencius was the next best-known philosopher in Confucian tradition.)

[3]The standard translation of the complete set of nine books is the nineteenth-century work of James Legge (Oxford: The Clarendon Press, various dates), although, of course, its scholarship has now been superseded in various particulars.

These books are important because they reflect basic Chinese values and ways of thinking. Their tradition went back before Confucius and continued after him. Confucius is not a peerless sage because he created this tradition; on the contrary, he is unequalled because the tradition "created" him and he reflected it faithfully.[4]

It was not unfair to Confucius to honor him as the embodiment of a tradition, for the burden of his teaching was above all to maintain this teaching and apply it fully and properly. He was a creative and deeply principled conservative. He believed that the way to get society on the right track again was to go back to the example of ancient sage-emperors. The basic structures of society, he felt, were adequate. The needful thing was to convince people they must act in accordance with the roles society has given them. The father must act like a father, the son like a son; the ruler must be a real ruler like those of old, wise and benevolent; the ministers of state must be true civil servants, loyal and fearless and self-giving.

This change to becoming what one "is" (called "rectification of names") must first of all be within. One must be motivated by virtue, or *jen,* a typically vague but eloquent term suggestive of humanity, love, high principle, and living together in harmony. It is the way of the *chun-tzu,* the superior man, who as the Confucian ideal suggests is a man at once a scholar, a selfless servant of society, and a gentleman steeped in courtesy and tradition; as an official and family head he continually puts philosophy into practice.

Confucius conceded that this noble ideal might be enforced by no outside sanctions except the opinion of good men, for it was based on no belief in divine rewards or punishment after death. Its sincere practice in this life might, as often as not, result in exile and hunger rather than honor from princes. Yet in the end it draws men by the sheer attractiveness of the good, and by the fact that it embodies Tao, and so to follow jen is to align oneself with the way things are.

There follows a fundamental satisfaction from acting in accordance with the real nature of things that the virtueless devotee of passion and gain can never know, and that finally makes such a person's life hollow. For Confucianism has generally believed that at the basic nature of mankind is good. It is only perverted by bad external example or bad social environment, and people will turn naturally to the good when good examples and social conditions are present. To make them present is the weighty responsibility of the ruler, advised by Confucian sages.

External influences, then, can aid in the inner development of jen. This leads to another very important Confucian term, *li.* It indicates rites, proper conduct, ceremonies, courtesy, doing things the right way. Despite a professed lack of concern about ghosts and gods, for Confucius the performance of rituals was extremely important.

It may seem to us excessive that a man at the height of his career, upon the death of his father would go into retirement for three years, wearing sackcloth, wailing through the day and night, eating only tasteless food. It might seem that the government of a nation ought to have better things to do than spend endless hours and money in the preparation and execution of seasonal ceremonies, one after the other.

But li needs to be understood as Confucius understood it, as not cold or mere

---

[4]See Harlee G. Creel, *Sinism* (Chicago: Open Court Publishing Co., 1929).

"formalism" but as a supremely humanizing act. Animals act out of the lust or violent emotion of the moment, but mankind can rise above this in the societies it creates, and li exemplifies this potential. Li expresses a society which becomes a great dance, and so incarnates harmony. In ritual, everyone acts out proper relationships, and has a structured place. Ritual generates order in place of chaos, and nurtures "rectification of names." It can be hoped that if a person acts out, if only ritually, the proper conduct of his or her station in life often enough, in time he or she will interiorize what he or she is doing, and the inner and outer will become one, the ritual father a true father, the ritual prince a true prince. Li, then, is meant to stimulate jen, even as melodious music induces calmness and poetry, heroism.

It is within society that mankind comes to its best, for here the mutual stimuli of jen and li can be operative. Here is the key point of difference with the antisociety Taoists, who contended that society, or at least its regulations and rituals and mandatory relations, obscured the Tao. For Confucius, it was precisely in these social expressions that the Tao became visible and "spoke" to mankind. Society for Confucius was founded on five relationships: ruler and subject, father and son, husband and wife, elder and younger brother, friend and friend. In all of these proper behavior, indeed proper li, was required to give what is simply biological or spontaneous the structure that makes it into human society, calm and enduring for the benefit of all.

The cornerstone relation is the second—father and son. A son was expected to negate his own feelings and individuality in deference to the wishes and pleasure of his father in "filial piety."[5] Here it was, in this relationship which (at least according to Freudian psychoanalysis) is the most feeling-laden and difficult of all, that fundamental attitudes of jen and li and societal orientation were to be learned. It was as though to say: If love and virtue are to be learned truly, they must be learned at home and by making this hard but all-important relation the pivot. Father-son becomes the primal model of an interpersonal relationship, and in Confucianism it is in interpersonal relationships that man is humanized and Tao is manifested. If this relationship can be rectified, then all other relationships will also fall into place.

One might ask, Why is the father-son relation the key, and not mother and child? Perhaps it can be looked at in this way: The mother-child relationship is essentially biological, fraught with deep feelings and instincts which mankind shares with most of the higher animals. The father-son relationship, on the other hand, is more *social* in nature. This is not to say, of course, that the father does not have a biological role, and some instinctual equipment to go with it.

But in many archaic societies the father's biological role does not in itself establish social responsibility for a child. Rather, the crucial factor is the father's taking responsibility for the child *in his social role* as head of the household. The role is defined by his picking up the child, giving him a name, and recognizing him as his ward and heir. In other words, the father-son relationship is the most basic relationship inextricably intertwined with the social as well as biological compo-

---

[5]See the expression of filial piety in the *Hsiao Ching,* the "Classic of Filial Piety": James Legge, *Hsiao King* (Oxford: The Oxford University Press, 1899), and Sister Mary Makra, *The Hsiao Ching* (Annapolis: St. John's University Press, 1961).

nents of human culture, such as language (giving a name), moral responsibility, family as a legal entity, and the combination of privilege and repression that makes learned behavior—all that flows into li and jen—possible.

It is therefore significant that in Confucianism, with its emphasis on human society as the key bearer of the Tao for human beings, the father-son relationship— the primal social, structured relationship—should be central; but that Lao-tzu, whose Taoism emphasized the natural and biological and spontaneous as better than the social for manifesting Tao, should several times use the mother-child relationship as a metaphor for the relation of man with Tao.

Subsequent Confucian philosophers talked about human nature and how society can best be organized to manifest the Tao within it. Mencius (372–289 B.C.), for example, held that human nature is basically good and is only impeded by evil social environment, while Hsun-tzu (fl. 298–238 B.C.) said that man is basically evil in the sense of being self-centered, and needs education and social control to become good.

We must give more attention, however, to the ways in which Confucianism clearly took the three forms of religious expression, presenting a unified structure of teaching, rites, and sociological forms. In a real sense, they have always appeared discretely in the true centers of Confucian values, "natural" units like family and traditional community, since what Confucius was concerned with was to enhance and sanctify *them*. He did not want to establish a center of sacred value elsewhere than in family and community. It was they that his teaching was about, in them his rituals were performed, and they made their own sacred community. The secular was the sacred.

But as Confucianism became a quasi state religion in the Han dynasty (206 B.C. — A. D. 220) and after, it found it needed a quasi theology, a quasi divinity, and a quasi priesthood with their own rites. These it found in Confucius himself, and in the powerful class of Confucian scholars who staffed the bureaucracy of the empire. Confucius, as the peerless infallible sage, was seen as a sort of mystic king, with a true right to rule the inward kingdom of ideas and values upon which the outer realm was based.

This kind of thinking, which may be called the Han synthesis because it generously incorporated Taoist and other traditional motifs into Confucianism, was the work of Tung Chung-shu (c. 179–104 B.C.) more than of any other one man. His thought is like that of cosmic religion in that it is interested in the total interrelationship of all things rather than free, personal ethical and political questioning.

Tung presented a doctrine of correspondences, in which man and nature are parts of an interwoven web. A portent in heaven may be related to a forthcoming event on earth, and the moral decisions of a ruler may affect the prevalence of rain in his nation's fields.

Unlike many moderns, traditional Chinese did not see man and nature as separate, going by different laws. Instead they assumed that man and human history and government cooperate with nature and are governed by the same laws. It is as though we were to say that perpetual motion is as impossible in the history of a nation as in mechanics if it is a true law. To further the comparison, it would be as though we then said that the nation must have a public ritual once a year to counteract the slowing down, and wind the energy up again.

For Tung, the key to the whole web of correspondences of which life is woven is the Yin-Yang concept. This theory had very early origins in occult speculation connected with astrology, alchemy, and *I Ching* divination, but did not emerge fully into the mainstream of Chinese philosophy until the Han synthesis gave it place.

In this view, the Tao—that is, all the ten thousand things—is divisible into two great classifications: Yang things and forces, and Yin. Fundamentally Yang is associated with the masculine, and Yin with the feminine. But their respective meanings goes much beyond gender. Yang is what is male, but also day, sky, spring, and all that is bright, clear, hard, assertive, growing, moving out. Its symbol is the dragon. Yin is female, and also night, earth, moisture, autumn and harvest, spirits of the dead; all that is dark, underneath, recessive, pulling in, connected with the moon, mysterious. Its symbol is the tiger, which must be thought of as like Blake's "Tyger, tyger burning bright/ In the forests of the night"; emblematic of the arcane, inward, unfathomable, yet unescapable in human life.

It must be emphasized that Yin and Yang are by no means "good" or "bad." Neither is "better" than the other. They are both neutral, like gravitation. To keep going, the universe needs both and they need to interact in a balanced way. Too much of either brings disaster, just as rain and sun are both necessary in their places, but too much of either brings flood or draught.

The task of man is to keep these two eternal antagonists and partners, the dragon and the tiger, in proper balance, for the place of man is between them, and he is finally to interiorize them both. An elaborate art called *feng-shui* arose to determine, according to Yin-Yang "bearings," the most auspicious locations for houses and tombs and temples, between, say, a rock considered Yang and a tree determined as Yin. (Much more was involved in the full system of feng-shui and of correspondences too—the values of the five "elements" or modes of natural activity, fire, water, earth, air, and wood, each of which corresponded with seasons, colors, tones, and so forth.) Finally, particularly in esoteric Taoism, one sought through alchemical potions and yogic practices to bring to equilibrium the two forces within oneself, and thus achieve immortality—for it is Yin-Yang imbalance that results in decay and death: one who has them in as perfect harmony as the great Tao itself will be as deathless as the great Tao.

The ritual year, both at the imperial palace and the humblest village, strove to "work" Yin and Yang. The object was to support what the Tao, through the respective force, was doing at that time. The first half of the year, the time of growing and outgoing of nature as it awoke from the sleep of winter, was the time of the dynamic, rain-giving dragon. The Chinese New Year is marked by a parade through the streets of a gigantic, weaving dragon borne by many men. In midsummer, to consummate Yang, dragon boat or horse races are held, and then to inaugurate the Yin months of ingathering and the darkening of days, the lion or tiger dances are held. The traditional harvest festival when (as at Halloween) the dead return is full of Yin symbolism—it is at night, and cakes in the shape of the moon, decorated with moon castles where immortals live, are placed in the courtyards.

In the Han period, this sort of ideology also became political as a part of the new "synthesis" Confucianism. The emperor was Yang, the people Yin, and the ruler was to serve as activator of proper response by the ruled. Moreover, the sovereign was mediator between heaven and earth, the midpoint in a triad of Heaven, Earth, and Human Society. In his lawgiving he was representative of Heaven, the great origin, to man; as chief priest in his worship he represented mankind before heaven. In all this it was his responsibility to promote the proper working of Yin and Yang; if deterioration in nature or society became evident it would be widely said he had lost the Mandate of Heaven, that is, the right to rule as representative of Heaven.

This thinking fitted the needs of the ju, or scholar class, who studied this kind of lore, enacted the rites, and made Confucius the symbol of learning and authority. His cultus grew apace. In A.D. 56 sacrifices to Confucius were ordered in all schools; by the end of the empire in 1912 he had (in 1908) been declared coequal with Heaven and Earth themselves, as though to say the best of human culture was no less a great thing than the matrices of cosmic nature.

The importance of this scholar class in Chinese tradition can hardly be overemphasized. Three things set them apart: they were bearers of the ongoing tradition as dynasties rose and fell; they were unique as a class able to read and write well; in theory they were not a hereditary aristocracy, but an elite of brains who attained their positions in academic competition. As both teachers and administrators, they were indispensable to generations of rulers who found that sooner or later they had to conform to the values and usages of this class since they could not rule without its support.

The role of these Confucian scholars, called mandarins, meant that the real focus of power was not the sword but the pen, and that the vessel of cultural continuity in this society was a class of refined elites who scarcely hid their disdain of the rough soldier, but who made the written language and ability to wield it elegantly the supreme symbol of superiority over the toiling masses. This situation involved no small flourishing of class privilege, yet it also enabled a rudimentary democracy, for the means of entry into the privileged class was through education and the civil service examinations. In nearly all periods there were young men of humble background who managed to succeed in that grueling ordeal.

Dynasties periodically rose and fell, and with the transfer of the Mandate of Heaven a peasant or outlander might well come to the throne. There was no official nobility, and all families experienced years of bad fortune as well as good. The Middle Kingdom, then, did not know the domination of intermarrying noble lines like the Bourbons and Hapsburgs of Europe century after century; what lasted instead was the gray-gowned meritocracy of the learned.

This class naturally developed its own internal traditions and "style." Its members grew fingernails inches long to prove that they did not do manual labor. Anything in writing, however trivial, was treated by them with respect and would be reverently burned rather than thrown out. They would typically be skeptical of beliefs concerning ghosts, spirits, gods, and an afterlife, but would treat such beliefs among the common people (or even the womenfolk in their own households) with a disdainful tolerance. It was better the masses believe in such things than that their discontent with their lot in this life get out of hand. In this spirit, the mandarin scholar appointed governor of a city would conduct the rites of the city-god, even to whipping the image of the deity when that divine protector failed to protect his people from misfortune. He would, however, know that beliefs like this were unworthy of a philosopher.

On a more serious level, the ju would manage the execution of the state ceremonies, culminating in the emperor's worship at the Altar of Heaven in the middle of the night at the winter solstice, and the worship of Earth at the summer solstice. The drama of the midwinter worship of Heaven has been described by many observers prior to 1911. In icy darkness broken only by flaring torches, the sovereign and his ministers, clad in the heaviest furs, would arrange elaborate presentations of food, wine, and cloth on the huge tiered mountain of masonry in Peking called the Altar of Heaven, and the emperor would read an elegant prayer. In principle, only the emperor, as mediator, could worship Heaven and Earth, the greatest ultimates known; others had to be content with ancestral and divine intermediaries. For the Confucianist, these rites were of grave importance as expressions of li; they were contributory to making society into a vast harmony or dance rather than a mere collection of thinking animals.

Another set of rituals were of special meaning to the Confucian elite. These were the major sacrifices to Confucius himself, held at the vernal and autumnal equinoxes, significantly midway between the two great rites of Heaven and Earth. These would be conducted at the temples of Confucius located in the more important cities. Although formerly they contained images of Confucius, since the Middle Ages they gave tribute to the superior worth of writing in the eyes of devotees of the philosopher by presenting only an upright tablet with the inscription "Confucius the Wise and Holy Sage," flanked by similar tablets to the master's disciples. At these rites, the local scholar-rulers would gather, kowtow (kneel deeply so that the forehead touches the floor) before the altar; present offerings of a whole slaughtered bull, pig, and sheep, together with wine and vegetables; offer a tribute; present music and dance supposed to be from the time of Confucius; and feast on the offerings.

Understanding this ritual as enacted by presumably skeptical scholars to one whom no one considered exactly a god creates difficulty for the westerner accustomed to quite different styles of thought. Clearly, it was an act of reverence with sacrifice which was less than divine worship, yet more than western civil ceremonies. It was somewhere between what might be done at the Arlington National Cemetery on Memorial Day and a cathedral service, together with the sort of presenting of animal victims westerners consider barbaric—despite the slaughter of thousands daily with less ceremony in stockyards.

Apart from their value simply as li, the Confucian rites can be thought of best in connection with the ancestral system. The Confucian scholars greatly valued their own family shrines and lineages, yet they were also, as a special called-out class, members of another "family," a spiritual clan of all of their vocation. Of this literati family the supreme scholar Confucius was the putative ancestor.

A word should be said about the Neo-Confucian movement, which began in the eleventh and twelfth centuries during the Sung dynasty, and became the authoritative interpretation of the Confucian intellectual tradition. Partly in response to the issues raised by Taoist and particularly Buddhist thought, Neo-Confucian philosophers greatly enhanced their tradition's metaphysical foundation. It became a comprehensive world view concerned with the nature of mind and the ultimate origin of things, and with simple methods of meditation, as well as a social philosophy, although it never lost the ideal that the philosopher finds joy in the midst of family and social life, not in permanent withdrawal from them. Two leading Neo-Confucianists were Chu Hsi (1130–120) and Wang Yang-ming (or Wang Shou-jen, 1472–1529). Chu Hsi taught that one great ultimate is manifested in the principles of the myriad separate things, as the light of the moon is broken onto many rivers and lakes. Through reflection on particulars, especially human morality, one can know the ultimate. The more idealistic Wang Yang-ming taught sincerity of mind. Through reflections like these, the spiritual and intellectual side of Confucianism was given a transcendence that made the practice of Confucian rites and virtues a more deeply religious way, even a sort of mysticism in the midst of a life of service.

But the most important impact of Confucianism on China was in the area of moral and social values. Although ancestrism, the family system, and the ideal of selfless work for the common good have pre-Confucian roots, Confucianism gave these values ultimate prestige through the civilized centuries. It was of a piece with Confucianism that all important families had ancestral shrines in which the names of parents, grandparents, and great-grandparents were lined up on higher and higher shelves for each generation, and worship was offered them, as it was at the tombs and in the home. Inseparable from ancestrism was the Confucian-based family system, in which loyalty and filial obedience were obligations that gave precedence to no others. Confucianism too underlay the Chinese "work ethic," the high regard for diligence and productivity for the honor and prosperity of one's family name. Without the mental image of the wise and sober sage from the state of Lu, and the words from his and his follower's pens, China would be very different from what we have known it to be for more than twenty centuries.

TAOISM

Confucianism, even in its most expansive forms, does not exhaust the spiritual heritage of China. Few people can be wholly devoted to sober virtues all the time, and the Chinese are not exceptions. There is another side that demands its due. This is the side of human personality that is attracted to what expresses the private fears, fancies, and aspirations of the individual. It is the side that feels for communion with nature, mystic rapture, imaginative works of art and letters, rebellion against social conformity, inward fear of evil, and love for gods. This side affirms the needs of *personal* life against the demands of structured society, and affirms the place of the feeling, symbol-making, nonrational side against the cool, word-oriented rational side. In China, all this side has danced about under the broad umbrella of the Taoist tradition.

Perhaps we can understand the role of Taoism in China by thinking of the cultural situation in America in the 1960s. First, there was the "establishment" and its values: the major institutions of business, government, education, and church making money, waging war, and upholding the usual values in family life, behavior, and the legitimate organization of society. This side corresponds more or less to what Confucianism has undergirded in China.

Then there was what was called the "counterculture." It consisted of people who had to varying degrees "dropped out" of the establishment. They were preoccupied with a gamut of things—living in the woods, writing poetry, painting, chanting before exotic mandalas, new styles of marital and sexual life, trying to reach "altered states of consciousness" by meditation, yoga, and drugs. In some cases they became concerned with strange psychic phenomena and demonic possession. Some discovered new revelations and new gods. Some became involved in revolutionary movements. If there was a unifying idea, it was that a person must above all be true to what he is in the depths of his personal self—he must "get himself together" and "do his own thing."

In China, parallels to all these counterculture features have appeared in connection with the Taoist tradition, most of them as major and recurring themes. As one would expect from this, Taoism has been many things to many different people, and has taken an immense variety of forms over the centuries. It has included hermit poets, temples with lavishly robed priests burning clouds of incense before resplendent gods, and "underground" secret political societies. It has ranged from "nature mysticism" to occult quests for immortality to the rites of spiritualists who call up the dead.

Some commentators have talked about a "pure" philosophical Taoism and a "degenerate," "superstitious" religious Taoism. But as usual such presuppositions get in the way of real understanding. It is more instructive to comprehend how all of Taoism forms a unity of experience around a single pole. After our own experience in the 1960s, this is easier to understand; our "dropouts" also found that once they focused life on the feeling-oriented, nonrational side, it was simple to move rapidly from mysticism to occultism to revolution and back, and from "nature" to the most elaborate religious robes and rites, so long as they expressed something imaginative and personal.

Taoism in China is really a tapestry of countless strands of folk religion, ancient arcana going back to prehistoric shamanism and private vision. But its putative founder is the sage Lao-tzu. Appropriately for such a romantic tradition, he is more legend than fact, and his very name suggests anonymity, for Lao-tzu just means "The Old Man." But stories say that the bearer of this epithet was an older contemporary of Confucius, and indeed that Confucius once met him, found him hard to confront, and said, "Of birds I know that they have wings to fly with, of fish that they have fins to swim with, of wild beasts that they have feet to run with. For feet there are traps, for fins nets, for wings arrows. But who knows how dragons surmount wind and cloud into heaven? This day I have seen Lao-tzu and he is a dragon."

Lao-tzu was also, according to tradition, a "dropout." It is said he was an archive-keeper at the Chou court, and a popular fellow who kept a good table. But he became disgusted with the grasping and hypocrisy of the world, and at the age of eighty left his job, mounted a water buffalo, and wandered off to the west. At the western portals of the empire, the gatekeeper is reported to have detained him as his guest, refusing to let him pass until he had recorded his wisdom. So the Old Man wrote down the book called the *Tao te ching,* and then departed in the direction of Tibet, becoming mysteriously lost to the world.

There are other ways to interpret the emergence of the Taoism of the *Tao te ching*. Some have pointed out that at the time of Confucius there were apparently a number of fairly well educated people around, more than there were government or literary jobs available; Confucius' own difficulty in finding a position may testify to this. Such persons, unable to work at the level of their abilities and too proud to return to the fields, formed a floating intellectual class for whose way of life early Taoism could provide at best an inspiration and at worst a rationalization.[6]

Others have noted that, on the other hand, the *Tao te ching* does contain a political philosophy aimed at rulers as well as reflections for the solitary individual; it must not have been intended only for people without place. Still others have seen in it the veiled but rather technical manual of a yogic school.[7] In sum, the *Tao te ching*'s origin is as mysterious as its meaning; each reader must get from it what he can.

Let us now look at the message of this book ascribed to Lao-tzu, Taoism's traditional founder. It is a book about the Tao, that universal way or track down which all the ten thousand things roll and which is their substratum and the only lasting thing there is; the name *Tao te ching* means something like "The Book of the Tao and How to Apply its Strength."

Although a book about the Tao, it begins with the curious affirmation that nothing can be said about its subject matter:

> Existence [the Tao] is beyond the power of words
> To define:
> Terms may be used
> But are none of them absolute.
> In the beginning of heaven and earth there were no words,
> Words came out of the womb of matter.[8]

There is no word, this means, which is an adequate symbol for the Tao. That is obvious when we consider that all human words come out of finite human experi-

---

[6]Creel, *Sinism*.

[7]Arthur Waley, *The Way and its Power* (London: George Allen and Unwin, 1934), Introduction.

[8]From Witter Bynner, trans., *The Way of Life: According to Lao Tzu* (New York: The John Day Co.). Copyright © 1944 by Witter Bynner (renewed 1972). Reprinted by permission of The John Day Co., publishers.

ence; they do convey something of what really is, but only as human beings with their limited sensory equipment and limited field of experience have know it. When someone says to you the word "tree," certain images pop into your mind. But these images derive only from your own limited experience with trees.

The image you have may be of a tree in your backyard as a child, or which you saw in a picture book when you learned the word; you let this tree represent for you all the trees theoretically covered by the word. The word says little about all the trees you have not seen, or about how trees are experienced by other people or animals, much less about how a tree experiences itself! The word "tree" is really only a very pale thing, calling up a few tentative hints of what "treeness" means to a human being who is alien to a tree's life. It scarcely touches the vast untapped richness contained in the reality of trees "out there"—how they were in ages past before man, what they may be like on other planets, what they seem like to squirrels and birds who live in them, how they "feel" deep down in their own lives.

If this is true of something that is still only a part of creation, how much more must the limitations of language apply to the infinite whole. Add to the limitations of our experience the fact that language by definition cannot really apply a meaningful label to the whole since the purpose of words is to categorize the particular: we use them to distinguish one thing from another; to call something "rice" implies there are other things not rice from which it needs to be distinguished.

Even to use a word ostensibly for the whole, like Tao or existence, does not avoid this limitation. All these words can do is point in a certain direction of comprehension, but they cannot make clear there is really nothing comparable to Tao or existence from which it could be distinguished.

Philosophical discussion like this may begin to open up the kind of realizations which seized the writer of the *Tao te ching*. But for him the book was no mere metaphysical nitpicking—nothing would have more won his contempt.

Rather, these reflections opened up a different, ecstatic mode of being in the world. Once you realize that the Tao which flows in and through everyone and everything cannot be labeled and put in a box, you can respond to it in a different way: with simple wonder, turning to it as an infant turns to its mother. The first chapter ends, "From wonder into wonder Existence [the Tao] opens." Elsewhere we read, "Can you, with the simple stature of a child, breathing nature, become, notwithstanding, a man? . . . Can you, mating with heaven, serve as the female part?" And again, the writer, seeing himself as a misfit in artificial society although marvelously near the Tao that others miss, says, "All these people are making their mark in the world, while I, pigheaded, awkward, different from the rest, am only a glorious infant still nursing at the breast." (We have already noted that, just as the father-son relation was the cornerstone of Confucianism, so the *Tao te ching* makes becoming feminine, or becoming a child in a mother's arms, a basic image for the relation of the individual with the great Tao.)

In the seemingly weak stance of the female or the child is tremendous strength—the strength of water that wears down the hardest rock, or wind and rain that can come and go as they wish. In yielding, bending with the wind like a supple tree and then springing back renewed, is a vital strength that will weave its way subtly through all the permutations of the Tao. But that which is stiff like a man standing on tiptoe will break and fall. We are told the best ruler is he who guides his people unobtrusively, so that they say, "We did this ourselves."

Making comparisons are inimical to this way of life, for they induce partial views and keep one from seeing life and the Tao whole:

> People through finding something beautiful
> Think something else unbeautiful,
> Through finding one man fit
> Judge another unfit . . .
> Take everything that happens as it comes,
> As something to animate, not to appropriate . . .
> If you never assume importance
> You never lose it.[9]

This outlook has political implications, and they are quite contrary to the elitism of "getting the best man for the job" of the Confucianists. There is also an attack on the philosophy of advertising: nothing would be more contrary to Taoist political and economic ideas than our system of choosing leaders through elective competition, and creating prosperity by encouraging consumption.

> It is better not to make merit a matter of reward
> Lest people conspire and contend,
> Not to pile up rich belongings
> Lest they rob,
> Not to excite by display
> Lest they covet.[10]

Elsewhere, we are told in the *Tao te ching* that the ideal community would be a village of simple, hardworking, prosperous farmers, so unsophisticated that they did not even use writing but kept records with knotted cords, and so content that even though they could hear the dogs barking and the cocks crowing in the next village, they never visited it.

Needless to say, this approach was quite at odds with the Confucianists' earnest talk of cultivating virtue and their moral norms such as filial obedience. Lao-tzu instead refers back to a primordial paradise where people lived simply in harmony with the Tao spontaneously. Only when deterioration sets in, he thought, did rules and norms appear, and they were both cause and effect of the deterioration.

> When people lost sight of the way to live
> Came codes of love and honesty,
> Learning came, charity came,
> Hypocrisy took charge;
> When differences weakened family ties
> Came benevolent fathers and dutiful sons;

[9]Ibid., pp. 25–26.

[10]Ibid., pp. 26–27.

And when lands were disrupted and misgoverned
Came ministers commended as loyal.[11]

In other words, what for the Confucianists was the very essence of true civilization, for the Taoists was the token of decay and hypocrisy. To them, true virtue, like that of nature or of a child with eyes full of wonder, could never be forced by bookish ethics. If we got rid of formalized learning and duty, Lao-tzu said, people would be a hundredfold happier, and would do naturally what they now resist just because they are told to do it.

Here we can see clearly the Taoist reaction against ordinary conventions of thought and behavior. It is but a step from this generalized sense of wonder and of the limitations of ordinary words and attitudes to affirmation of the most extraordinary seeming ideas: the possibility of deathlessness, the reality of fabulous secrets, powers, and worlds. In fact, even the *Tao te ching* appears to affirm that one who is in inseparable harmony with the Tao is as immortal as the Tao is, and that through the way of yielding one can find mysterious powers so great as to seem miraculous. But it remained to subsequent Taoist writers to make this potential of Lao-tzu's vision more explicit. The first and greatest is Chuang-tzu (died c. 300 B.C.).[12]

Little is known of Chuang-tzu apart from his book, but it is enough. Written in a vivid, fanciful, and humorous style, it immediately brings the reader into a world of expanding horizons. One is first told of strange marvels, as though from tales of Sinbad—of an immense fish thousands of miles long, which changes into a bird just as large, and flies to a celestial lake in the south. The writer then juxtaposes these examples of the fabulously large with mention of the tiny motes in the air which make the sky blue, and tells us that to a mustard seed a teacup is an ocean. As the reader's imagination is swung violently from the microscopically small to the immensely huge, from the fairy tale antipodes of the mind to the homey, he or she gets a sense of mental vertigo. One feels that one is spinning and things around one are coming unfastened.

That is just what Chuang-tzu wants one to feel, for he wants to shake the reader loose from the ordinary way of seeing things. Chuang-tzu wanted persons to be free—above all, free from oneself, one's own prejudices, partial views, categories, and from judging everything in terms of oneself. To this Taoist, man is *not* the measure of all things. The way the universe happens to appear to a biped six feet tall is no more the way it is than the way it appears to a fish, a mote, an eagle, or a star. Only the Tao itself is the measure.

In the same way, the ordinary rational waking consciousness is no more the measure of all things than the world of dreams and fancy and of the improbable. Chuang-tzu tells us he once dreamed he was a butterfly, and when he awoke he did not know whether he was Chuang-tzu who had dreamed he was a butterfly, or a butterfly dreaming he was Chuang-tzu. The dream world, in other words, is just as real as any other.

[11]Ibid., p. 35.

[12]See Burton Watson, *Chuang Tzu: Basic Writings* (New York: Columbia University Press, 1964).

Unlike the sober Confucianist, Chuang-tzu delights in the world of fantasy rocs and leviathans, wizards who can fly over the clouds, and islands of immortals. The world of the unconscious and the imagination, he is saying, is just as much a manifestation of the Tao as the rational—and may indeed better lead us to comprehending the Tao. At least it opens us to that sense of wonder and infinity beyond all limits which is necessary to comprehend the Tao—for the Tao is precisely the unbounded.

This was the direction in which Taoism went. A later Taoist thinker, Ko Hung (A.D. 283–c. 343), put it even more clearly, both in his life and his writing. He lived during the three and a half centuries (221–589 A.D.) of division and political confusion that disturbed China between the fall of the Han dynasty and the relatively stable and unified Sui (589–618) and T'ang (618–907) dynasties. Extensive but ephemeral conquests in the north by various nomadic peoples, and Chinese cultural expansion in the south, combined with the inability of the nation to come together under a single leadership, shaped the uncertain social background of the periods between 221 and 589—a time which nonetheless was culturally quite creative. Buddhism spread extensively, Taoism revived, and brilliant new forms in art and literature emerged to express the visions of these new, and newly personal, spiritual visions.

Confucianism was still accepted as normative, but the collapse of the social order based on its Han synthesis version discredited it for many: in any case, a view of life oriented toward the communication of value through social usages and interpersonal obligations simply cannot "work" well in a time of social confusion. Many will be driven to look for more personal paths which promise inner meaning in spite of what is going on around one.

For some the answer was Buddhism, flowing into China from India via central Asia. For others—skeptical perhaps as the Chinese tend to be of imported gifts—it was some form of the Taoist heritage. They turned back to the books of Lao-tzu and Chuang-tzu, which by then already formed part of a counterculture constellation that included the heritage of various late Han "revivalistic" movements promising healing and magic on the popular level, and a complex pattern of occult learning on the more sophisticated. Some of it, such as the Yin-Yang and "correspondences" thought, was also part of the Han synthesis. But the last was now more personalized; what had been a key to imperial rites was now the privilege of the informed individual striving to solve personal problems. (In the same way, in the West the astrology that was once the recourse of princes now "belongs" to everyone who reads a newspaper.)

To this effect it is interesting that Ko Hung's book, the *Pao-p'u-tzu,* contains what are called Outer and Inner parts. The Outer presents conventional Confucian teaching; the Inner offers Taoist material centering on the achievement of personal immortality through alchemy and yogic techniques. It is as though to say that while Confucianism may still be adequate for social ideology, a new self-consciousness and sense of social failure has made Confucianism hollow without something for the individual as well.

This quest for personal immortality was a basic theme of the new Taoism, and with it came interest in the worlds of miracles and of immortal supernatural beings the quest implied and almost predicated. It had, as we have noted, philosophical roots in Lao-tzu's implication that harmony with the Tao is immortality, and in Chuang-tzu's that truth is found in unfettered openness to all levels of consciousness and all possibilities, however fantastic.

The consequent distinction between Confucian and Taoist styles of thinking is very clear in a fictional debate that Ko Hung composed between a Confucianist and a Taoist on the possibility of immortality. The Confucianist argues that every living thing anyone has ever heard of dies, and that therefore belief in immortality is untenable nonsense. Pao-p'u-tzu, the Taoist, responds that there are exceptions to every rule, and that just because most things of which we know die, we cannot say that everything in this universe of which we really know so little *must* die. In effect, the Confucianist says, "You can't prove immortality," and the Taoist says, "You can't prove there isn't immortality." Perhaps little is proved in this particular argument except that, for Confucianists, the instinctive response to a query is the safe, rational, commonsense answer, and for Taoists, the romantic, speculative approach open to nonrational, "mind-blowing" possibilities. The cleavage is temperamental and comparable to the gulf between Enlightenment rationalism and the Romanticism that followed it in the West.

Other Taoists of the "interim" period followed lifestyles that seemed almost to repudiate the importance of personal immortality (as did earlier Chuang-tzu), so much did they emphasize spontaneity. To them, living with the Tao meant a *feng-liu* ("wind and stream") life, acting according to the movement of "what was happening" day by day. Many were artists and poets, or at least esthetes, and the unplanned life, which savored the beauty of each event and the richness of each impulse, well suited the temperament of their callings. Philosophical works which went with this Taoist stance, such as *Kuo-Hsiang's* Commentary on the *Chuang-tzu,* and the *Lieh-tzu,* made much of Tao as being *wu-wei,* nonbeing or not doing, in the rather technical sense that the Tao is not a "thing" or a "cause" and does not produce by plan or through work. Instead, all things just flow out of it freely or spontaneously in an endless stream of flux and change; the person who is attuned to Tao lives his life in this way.[13]

It was religious Taoism, however, with its popular gods and quest for immortality, that took lasting institutional form. Its roots are complex, reach far back into the murky past, and are far from having been adequately traced.[14] We have noted that magical techniques to attain deathlessness, and yogic practices to control breath and

---

[13]Fung Yu-lan, *A Short History of Chinese Philosophy* (New York: The Macmillan Company, 1960), Chapters 19 and 20. A good brief summary of the Taoism of this period.

[14]The best introduction to religious Taoism, as well as to other aspects of Taoism, is Holmes Welch, *Taoism: The Parting of the Way* (Boston: Beacon Press,1965). See also Michael R. Saso, *Taoism and the Rite of Cosmic Renewal* (Pullman: Washington State University Press, 1972), which provides a striking description of modern religious Taoism, together with useful and informed comments on the history and meaning of religious Taoism; Peter Goulart, *The Monastery of Jade Mountain (London: John Murray,* Ltd., 1961), which offers a vivid if uncritical picture of Taoist life in mainland China in the decades before the Communist revolution; the same can be said of John Blofeld, *The Secret and Sublime: Taoist Mysteries and Magic* (London: George Allen and Unwin, 1973). Two older multivolumed works, J. J. M. de Groot, *The Religious Systems of China,* 6 vols. (Leiden: E. J. Brill, 1892–1910; reprinted Taipei: Literature House, 1964), and Henri M. Doré, *Researches into Chinese Supersititions,* 13 vols., in English (Shanghai: Tusewei Press, 1914–38; reprinted Taipei: Ch'eng-wen Publishing Co., 1968) provide an immense wealth of material on the Taoist pantheon and related rites and beliefs, as well as on other matters, although the scholarship and attitudes are dated.

induce joy, may be reflected in the *Tao te ching* and are very ancient. We have also mentioned that in the Han period, popular religious movements emphasizing healing and revolution were attached to the *Tao te ching* tradition. For example, Chang Ling in the second century A.D. started a revivalistic healing movement which established itself as a state within a state in mountainous areas. Chang Ling said that Lao-tzu had appeared to him from the realm of spirits and given him a sword and other apparatus by which he was able to exercise control over the spiritual world. Chang was called Heavenly Teacher, and his direct descendents (sometimes misleadingly called the "Taoist Pope") have continued the title to the present. They dwelt on a Dragon and Tiger Mountain in central China, exercised a tenuous spiritual authority over Taoist priests in the south, and sold mysterious charms which were distributed far and wide.

The popular Taoist religious system, which embraces the "Taoist Pope," and his charms and priests, presents a rich and colorful face. Perhaps no religion in the world has had a more vast pantheon of gods—many said to have been once human beings who became immortal and finally reached divine status. Some gods are ancient, although many were "appointed" to divinity by T'ang and especially Ming (1368–1644) emperors.

This recalls the extensive interaction between Confucian and Taoist, as well as Buddhist, systems in China. Not only did the emperor, in designating approved worship, act out the role of mediator between heaven and earth assigned by Confucian thought, but the pantheon itself exemplified a heavenly reflection of the earthly bureaucracy manned by Confucian officials. Many of the deities, like Kuan Ti, were originally earthly officials immortalized in the heavenly court.

Supreme deity in religious Taoism was the Jade Emperor, a personal high god for the masses ineligible to worship Heaven directly; he was enthroned in the Pole Star. Around him was his court: the Three Pure Ones—Lao-tzu, the Yellow Emperor (mythical first sovereign of China), and Pan-ku (the primal man); the Eight Immortals, very popular in art and folk tales; gods of literature, medicine, war, weather, and so forth. The gods and immortals lived in numerous heavenly grottos, in Islands of the Blessed to the East, and the Shangri-La of the Mother Goddess to the West, deep in the mountains.

The priests of this faith were a varied lot, affiliated with several different sectarian strands with differing specialities. Some were celibate and monastic, others married. Some were contemplative, concerned above all else with perfecting in themselves the seeds of immortality. Some were custodians of lavish temples with huge and ornate images of the Jade Emperor and other worthies; to these temples believers would come to receive divination, have memorial services performed on behalf of their departed, and worship at important festivals which were also occasions for carnival and feasting. Other Taoist clergy were mediums, male and female, who would deliver messages from the Other Side; some were sellers of charms, perhaps issued by the "Taoist Pope"; some were exorcists who performed dramatic rites of driving demons out of possessed persons and places.

Behind all of this lay the affirmation of immortality and of immortal entities; the panorama of religious Taoism made visible the invisible but deathless realm of gods and sages who had won the priceless secret. Those who would reveal the secret were not lacking, however. Religious Taoism pointed to three main highways to immortality: alchemy, yoga, and merit.

Alchemy referred to the preparation of elixirs supposed, in combination with spiritual preparation, to circumvent death through manipulation of Yin and Yang and the five elements. Most were based on cinnebar or mercury ore (HgS); some seven Chinese emperors are said to have died of mercury poisoning as a result of taking this medicine of immortality! Yet, as scholars like C.G. Jung and Mircea Eliade have pointed out, both Chinese and Western alchemy contains very important spiritual and proto-scientific insights that cannot be neglected by the serious historian of ideas.[15]

Taoist yoga is equally complex. Its central motif, however, seems to have been the holding of the breath to circulate it throughout the body inwardly, awakening the gods of various physical centers, and finally to unite breath and semen to produce an immortal "spiritual embryo" who emerges as new life within the self. As it flourishes, the old mortal shell can fall away like the chrysalis of a butterfly. Diet and sometimes sexual practices of the tantric sort were important supports of this process.

More available to the masses who were not adepts was the hope of attaining immortality by merit. The idea was approached with typical Chinese concreteness. Some popular temples even had a large abacus or calculating machine in full view to recall to the faithful the reckoning of good and bad deeds that will be required. Various texts cite the number and kinds of good deeds—building roads, acts of charity, compassion to living things—which would win immortality at various grades; even one demerit, however, would require the aspirant to start at the beginning of his labors again.

Taoism is usually presented as but one of the spiritual traditions of China, and was not the most prestigious in the eyes of traditional scholars. But the attitudes of religious Taoism came closest to the spiritual world of the vast majority of ordinary people. Even Buddhism and Confucianism became "Taoicized" in cultus though not in doctrine and morals; whatever their origin, most plain people thought of the Buddhas, bodhisattvas, and even Confucius himself as immortalized humans now become spirits, and able to send down blessings from above. Taoist and Buddhist priests served interchangeably in many localities, but their major functions such as funerals and exorcisms and village festivals were Taoist (that is to say, popular Chinese) in style. To be sure, popular Taoism may have borrowed much from Buddhism—the use of images, clerical organization—and the bureaucratic model of its pantheon from Confucianism—but those are historical matters, not all readily apparent to the man on the street.

Taoism, as the pervasive tone setter of the "nonestablishment" side of Chinese life, has contributed that undying element of cheerful fancy, fairy tales, colorful festivals, bright pictures, and striking spiritual practices which is as much a part of Chinese life as Confucian common sense.

---

[15]See Mircea Eliade, *The Forge and the Crucible* (New York: Harper and Brothers, Publishers, 1962), Chapter 11.

BUDDHISM IN CHINA

Buddhism first entered China in the Han period, but did not spread widely until the three centuries of disruption which followed the fall of that dynasty, and reached its peak of maturity and creativity during the T'ang era.[16] It was chiefly brought in the caravans of traders, not directly from India but from central Asia. As one would expect, the new faith first took root in the major cities and among the aristocrats. In the late Han and post-Han times, as we have seen, many of this class were searching among occult, mystical, aesthetic possibilities for a richer inner life than a decaying social order and its tired Confucian rationale could offer. The wilder side of Taoism naturally appealed to some of them, but the profound mysteries of Buddhism, brought by exotic blue-eyed foreigners and bearing a whiff of the mystic perfume of India, as well as a more substantial philosophical and ethical base, was to many even more appealing. It speaks both of the power of Buddhism and the dissatisfaction of those times, that until the modern Western influence and subsequent Marxist triumph, no outside cultural force other than Buddhism has succeeded in making a major impact on China.

In the period when Buddhism was taking root in China, it was quite fashionable. Aristocrats entertained visiting Buddhist savants, commissioned the translation of scriptures, and built temples in the mountains to which they would retire for genteel retreats. They also built hospitals and orphanages in the cities in accordance with the dictates of Buddhist compassion.

Buddhism opened up a new world of artistic possibilities with its demand for massive sculpture, mystic painting, and temple architecture. Buddhism also broadened ethical horizons more than many were prepared to accept with its very new (and very controversial) notions of universal compassion, monasticism, and the relative independence of religion from the state cultus. These emphases, although adumbrated in Taoism, went strongly against the Confucian grain, with its feeling that the arts are more frivolous than civil service, and that obligation to family and sovereign is primary. In particular, the ideal of the celibate Buddhist monk stood contrary to Confucianism, which put family life and the subordination of self to society at the center of value.

But Buddhism also made its adjustments to China. Indeed, for a long time the Indian religion was considered a variant of Taoism—an illusion promoted by some Taoists, who even claimed that Lao-tzu, after disappearing into the West, had gone to India and become the Buddha. In the translation of Buddhist texts from Sanskrit to Chinese, Taoist and Confucian terms were used, with inevitable shifts in connotation. Thus, dharma became Tao, arhant became immortal, and Buddhist morality was couched in the terms of submission and obedience hallowed by Confucian usage.[17]

---

[16]The best general book on Chinese Buddhism is Kenneth Ch'en, *Buddhism in China* (Princeton University Press, 1964). Also useful is Arthur F. Wright, *Buddhism in Chinese History* (Stanford, Calif.: Stanford University Press, 1959). For the actual life of Chinese Buddhist monasteries and popular devotion, see Holmes Welch, *The Practice of Chinese Buddhism, 1900–1950* (Cambridge, Mass.: Harvard University Press, 1967), and J. Prip-Møller, *Chinese Buddhist Monasteries* (New York: Oxford University Press, 1937, 1967).

[17]See Wright, *Buddhism in Chinese History,* pp. 36–37.

Even the monastic system was modified in the direction of supporting rather than challenging the Chinese family unit. Young monks acquired a filial relation to their teachers, in imitation of obedience to father, and moreover were expected to assist dutifully their natural families by devoting much attention to prayer on behalf of relatives living and dead. Sometimes boys were dedicated to the monastery by their families for this reason, or in fulfillment of a vow made in prayer, it being considered beneficial for a family to number a monk among its members.

Finally, monasteries were brought under the control of the throne, which licensed them and regulated the number of ordinations they could perform.

On the level of popular religion, Buddhism accommodated itself to China even more thoroughly. As already mentioned, popular Buddhas and bodhisattvas came to be regarded as blessing-giving deities little different from indigenous gods, except perhaps more broadly compassionate. The bodhisattva Avalokiteshvara became Kwan-yin, the so-called Goddess of Mercy who answered prayers for healing, women in childbirth, and wanderers. Maitreya, the Buddha of the future who would bring to pass a new paradisal era, was transformed from the lean, elegant, poised contemplative of Indian art to the immensely fat, laughing Mi-lo of China, who suggests a heartier, earthier vision of the joys of the new age. He has also been associated with revolutionary religio-political movements. In fact, even the Indian origin of Mi-lo, as of other Buddhist figures, came to be forgotten: folklore identified him with a popular wandering wise-fool monk of the tenth century.

Probably the most important contribution of Buddhism to popular religion was in concepts of life after death. Previously, the Chinese had known belief in survival as ancestral spirits, as ghosts, or as Taoist immortals in blissful hermitages. To this Buddhism added the novel ideas of reincarnation and of elaborately gradated heavens and hells. Both these notions, however inconsistent with each other and with indigenous belief, were widely received, even by many who understood little else of Buddhism.

Reincarnation appears as a popular theme in literature. The hells were described in religious tracts, temple paintings, and sculpture displays (such as the well-known Tiger Balm Garden in Hong Kong) with a blood-splattered realism that could not escape even the dullest countryman. The officials of hell, presided over by Yen-lo (originally the Indic Yama, whom we previously encountered in the Katha Upanishad), were Confucian bureaucrats. As a reward for years of conscientious service, they were allowed to continue in the same metier on the other side, where they saw to it that demons administered horrendous (but not eternal) punishments for infractions of both Confucian and Buddhist moralities.[18]

On the intellectual level, a number of different traditions of Buddhist thought and practice were introduced into China. Only the broad, tolerant, and variegated Mahayana had any success, however. But within it, the Void school, Yogacara or Mind Only, and esoteric Buddhism or Vajrayana all had early followings at various monastic centers. On Mount T'ien T'ai, the syncretistic T'ien T'ai school endeavored to reconcile all styles of Buddhist thought into a system which made the Lotus

---

[18]This area is well portrayed in Wolfram Eberhard, *Guilt and Sin in Traditional China* (Berkeley: University of California Press, 1967).

Sutra the summit of many planes of accommodation in the Buddha's teaching; T'ien T'ai, and with it the Lotus Sutra, became immensely important in Japan.

When the dust settled, however, two strands of Buddhism emerged as by far the most important in China—Ch'an and Pure Land. The concept of clearly defined denominations, like those of Christianity or even of Japanese Buddhism, is alien to China except for minority sectarian movements. But it has ended up that most monasteries in China proper followed largely Ch'an teaching and practice, and Pure Land Buddhism was most popular among lay followers. Significantly, both (while having ultimate Indian roots) are highly Sinicized styles of Buddhism, owing much to different sorts of Taoist belief. Both are variants of an apprehension, emergent early in Chinese Buddhism's independent development, that true enlightenment is a sudden, spontaneous happening rather than a laborious process.

Ch'an, the tradition better known under its Japanese name of Zen, means the school of *dhyana,* Sanskrit for "meditation."[19] For it, enlightenment arises unexpectedly, often suddenly, in the course of "sitting quietly, doing nothing" in meditation, or perhaps in response to an unconventional teaching gesture by a master. Ch'an enlightenment is really like following the Taoist concept of Wu-wei, notdoing, and so letting anything happen spontaneously. The assumption is that what is truly spontaneous is the Tao at work—or in this case one's true Buddha-nature—while what is planned is of human egoistic contrivance, artificial and inauthentic.

Ch'an teaching and practice is a "therapeutic" means of bringing people to inward realization of the basic ideas of Mahayana, especially the void teaching of Nagarjuna and the Mind Only insight of Yogacara. What is distinctive about Ch'an is the fierce and direct means used to shake aspirants into inward realization of basic Mahayana truth. That was the truth of nondualism, that getting entangled in making distinctions keeps us from realizing that we and all else are the indivisible Buddhanature now and forever. Ch'an masters claimed that their tradition was one of getting at the truth by "direct pointing," and that it was transmitted "outside the scriptures" in that it did not depend on words and letters, but on immediate experience passed from master to disciple.

The experience, tradition said, began long ago when the Buddha silently handed a flower to a disciple named Kashyapa, and smiled. The disciple smiled back and *knew*—the flower and smile conveyed a universe of wisdom indefinable by any words or books.

After Kashyapa, the secret of the smile was passed down through a lineage of "patriarchs" in India, until the twenty-eighth, a sage from India called Bodhidharma, brought the tradition to China, where it became Ch'an, in A.D. 520. To exemplify it, Bodhidharma spent years meditating in front of a brick wall, and did not hesitate to tell an emperor to his face that all the temples he had built, scriptures he had ordered copied, and monks and nuns he had supported, had won him no merit whatsoever.

In several ways this account is fictitious and misleading. The line of patriarchs in India is undoubtedly an invention, and Ch'an was well on the way to formation in

---

[19]The best treatment is Heinrich Dumoulin, S. J., *A History of Zen Buddhism* (New York: McGraw-Hill Paperbacks, 1965).

China even before the time of Bodhidharma. The claim of Ch'an to be "outside the scriptures" requires qualification, for the Heart Sutra and others are chanted and expounded in its monasteries, and Ch'an is nothing more than a means toward realization of the central Mahayana concepts that these sutras proclaim. But Bodhidharma does dramatize that Ch'an is interested not in learning for its own sake, but in hard, sharp, direct realization—and that colorful stories and exaggerated making-of-points are among its armory of techniques.

So it is that the idea of emptiness or void, and of the Buddha being found only in one's own consciousness (for all sentient beings are Buddhas, and need only to be awakened to realize it) is shown in Ch'an disparagement of conventional Buddhist piety. In some places Buddha-images were chopped up periodically. In the earlier days of Ch'an, monks worked in the fields like peasants. A disciple once went up to his master, who was apparently weighing out a harvest of flax, and asked him, "What is the Buddha?" The master, continuing with his work, answered, "Three pounds of flax."

Another master had a habit of remaining silent and merely pointing up his thumb when asked a question like this. A disciple, seeing this and thinking cleverly to himself that there was some occult significance to this gesture, began to imitate his mentor by holding up his thumb in the same way. One day the master saw the boy do this, and quick as a flash he whipped out a knife and cut the thumb off. When the disciple had recovered himself, he approached the master once more and brought himself to ask again the question, "What is the Buddha?" As though nothing had happened, the master held up his thumb. At that, the disciple attained enlightenment.

Perhaps this anecdote is related to the Ch'an saying, "When a finger is pointing at the moon, do not look at the finger." Scriptures, practices, and a good master may indeed point to the moon (a Buddhist symbol of Nirvana). But the idea is not to look at them, but at where they are pointing. For the reality to which Ch'an points, like the Tao of the *Tao te ching,* is prior to words and cannot be reduced to them. A Ch'an master was once asked what the "First Principle" is. He replied, "If I told you, it would become the Second Principle!"

Once again, the truth prior to words, which Ch'an and Zen radiate, is that one *is* the Buddha and in Nirvana now, in the "unborn mind" before thought, and that this realization is attained not by effort but by "doing nothing" and seeing who one is when one is not oriented toward doing anything. That "empty-handed" truth is well presented in a story of Hui-neng (638–713), called the Sixth Patriarch of Ch'an in China, author of the Platform Scripture, and the man most responsible for the development of the Ch'an tradition.

Hui-neng came as a youth to the monastery of the Fifth Patriarch, Hung-jen. Only a poor and obscure novice from the far south, then considered on the fringes of civilization, Hui-neng was set to such menial tasks as pounding rice.

One day the Fifth Patriarch called the monks together and announced that he would make the Sixth Patriarch whichever of them could write a poem evidencing deep understanding and true enlightenment.

One promising monk, Shen-hsiu (who became patriarch of the later extinct "Northern School" of Ch'an), wrote:

Our body is the tree of Perfect Wisdom
And our mind is a bright mirror.
At all times diligently wipe them,
So that they will be free from dust.

The Fifth Patriarch said that these lines showed understanding. But he perceived that this rather pedestrian and moralistic approach did not come near the great breakthrough possible in Ch'an.

The next night, an anonymous verse appeared on the bulletin board. It read:

The tree of Perfect Wisdom is originally no tree.
Nor has the bright mirror any frame.
Buddha-nature is forever clear and pure.
Where is there any dust?

Here was the insight Hung-jen had been looking for. True enlightenment cannot consist of obsessively trying to wipe away symbolic dust particles, but is the marvelous freedom of realizing that one's mind, one's self, and the dust are all equally "empty" and so unbounded. The Fifth Patriarch grasped that Hui-neng had written this poem, secretly called him in from the rice pounding room, and made him his successor as Sixth Patriarch.

How was the realization of one's true nature to be attained? By not striving to attain it. How does one reach a state of not-striving? Ch'an masters used several means. The most important is meditation: just sitting, doing nothing, striving for nothing, attaining nothing. However, Ch'an sitting does mean a definite posture and long hours. It produces a situation of nonstriving in which something can happen.

Many masters found that other techniques could hurry along the process of reaching nonstriving in their pupils. Some would fiercely scold, strike, and beat the disciples when they showed signs of trying too hard while missing the point, like the pupil who got his thumb cut off. All this was intended as shock therapy to knock the novice out of the rut his thinking was in to a different perspective.

Many masters used the enigmatic Ch'an anecdotes, riddles, and sayings (known in the West by the Japanese names *mondo* and *koan*), such as "What is the sound of one hand clapping?" or "Where was your face before you were born?" While these puzzles can be answered in terms of the void and Mind Only philosophies, the real point is that such conundrums bring the ordinary, rational "monkey mind" to a stop. They stop its perpetual chatter by feeding it something it cannot handle in its usual way. Perhaps, Ch'an says, if the relentless mental process can be quashed for just a moment, the mind will have a chance to see what it is when it is not chattering and chewing.

But liberating what is genuinely free and spontaneous within is not easy. Unlike some shallow romantics, Ch'an does not confuse true spontaneity with mere self-indulgence. Liberation is not doing what you want to do, for the tradition is well aware that what the ordinary, unenlightened person thinks he wants to do is merely the operation of those attachment-rooted desires which, fullfilled or not, can only enslave one in the bitter syndrome of craving, anxiety, and despair. The life of a well-ordered Ch'an monastery was very much the reverse of a hedonistic life; through the deprivation techniques of celibacy, scanty food and sleep, hard work, long meditation in freezing halls, and on top of that sometimes physical and verbal abuse, it was hoped that the monk would find out who he is apart from the desire-wrought illusion of being a separate person.

When success comes, then the seeker is truly free—for he lives on the level of spontaneous enlightenment and Buddhahood everywhere, even in the most trivial aspects of life. One master, Hui-hai, when asked if he did anything special to live in the Tao, replied, "Yes; when hungry I eat, when tired, I sleep." When asked how this way differed from what ordinary people did, he replied in effect that ordinary people do not just eat when they eat, but use eating as an occasion to let the desire-stimulated imagination run wild, thinking of what food one would like, or having conceits of how the food one is eating symbolizes one's prosperity, lifestyle, and the like; similarly, ordinary people do not just sleep when they sleep, but lie on their beds awash with waves of restless worries, fancies, and lusts. The goal of Ch'an, however, is just to eat when you are hungry and sleep when you are tired, and nothing more.

In the same vein, another master, Ch'ing-yuan, said that before he studied Ch'an for thirty years, he saw mountains as mountains and waters as waters. When he had made some progress, he no longer saw mountains as mountains and waters as waters. But when he got to the very heart of Ch'an, he again saw mountains as mountains and waters as waters.

The other important style of Chinese Buddhism, Pure Land, likewise evokes the freedom of nonstriving and nondependence on one's ego-self. A highly seminal early Chinese Buddhist philosopher, Tao-sheng (d. 434), spoke for both Ch'an and Pure Land when he argued that enlightenment has to be a sudden leap. Since it is a leap into the indivisible, he said, one can no more go through gradual stages of partial enlightenment than one can jump across a chasm in several steps.

But in Pure Land the structure is different; one has freedom from gradualism, striving, and self by dependence on the marvelous help of another, Amitabha Buddha, who can instantaneously and effortlessly give, out of his endless store of merit and grace, assurance to all who call upon his name that they will be reborn in his Pure Land where full enlightenment is easily available.

Amitabha, called O-mi-to in Chinese and Amida in Japanese, is the Buddha in the West of the esoteric mandala and *The Tibetan Book of the Dead,* and his Pure Land is also called the Western Paradise. It was said that countless ages ago he was an aspirant who, in setting foot on the path, vowed (the "Original Vow") that if he attained full and perfect enlightenment, out of compassion he would bring all who called upon his name into his Buddha-paradise (an enlightenment world which surrounds a Buddha like an aura, in which his devotees can dwell; not to be confused with the desire-heavens among the six lokas). Amitabha's paradise is described in marvelous, virtually psychedelic terms. There are jeweled trees linked by gold threads, fields of lapis lazuli, and perfumed rivers that give off music.

While the scriptures which describe the Pure Land and Amitabha's Original Vow derive from India, it was only in China and Japan that Pure Land became an important and distinct form of Buddhism. This was partly because, like Ch'an, it could easily be related to Taoist ideas—in this case, not only effortless and spontaneous wu-wei release, but also popular belief in paradisal realms to the West where immortals dwelt amid fairy-tale loveliness.

In China and Japan, Amitabha became, for vast numbers of worshippers, virtually the only Buddha (assisted by Kwan-yin, who as mercy-working bodhisattva has generally been closely linked to Pure Land Buddhism). Amitabha came to be in effect the universal Buddha-nature, and placing trust in him an act of release negating the individual ego in favor of harmonizing it with Nirvana or the universal. The Pure Land experience, then, ideally is not really different in character from the enlightenment experiences described in quite different words by other Buddhists.

These two doctrinal traditions, usually working closely together and not seen as inconsistent, formed the basis of Chinese Buddhism in recent centuries. The nation boasted scores of large monasteries. They followed a Ch'an regimen for the most part, modified by concessions to Pure Land, esoteric practices, and the economic necessity that Buddhist monks perform funeral and memorial rites—for many these last were quite time-consuming, but kept them in touch with the lay public.

Monastic novices were ordained by a rite which included burning incense in several spots on the candidate's shaved head, a painful practice leaving scars intended to exemplify the bodhisattva vow to work and suffer at whatever cost for the salvation of all beings. The monasteries were headed by an elected abbot, and were flourishing economic units busy with administering lands and dealing with pilgrims; the monks would often devote themselves to meditation and work on half-year shifts. Four monasteries on mountains in the four directions were especially important as pilgrimage centers. The roads to them would be lined with colorful shrines and hermitages; travel to these places for the sake of a vacation, enjoyment of natural beauty, and spiritual renewal all together was very popular. Many monks traveled frequently from one monastery to another in a manner akin to the wandering students of medieval Europe. Others might become hermits.

The majority of those who were students in a major monastery, however, would be receiving training like a seminarian, and would sooner or later become priests in village temples. There the priest would live a fairly easy life, unless he were given to much study or spiritual practice, keeping his temple in order as a place for prayer and performing funerals, memorial rites, and other services as his parishioners required and could pay for them. Although the priest probably had Ch'an training, the temple would doubtless give principal encouragement to the Pure Land and Kwan-yin devotions as being more suitable for the laity. However, among more sophisticated urban lay Buddhists, especially of more recent times, many took one or another of the monastic vows, such as celibacy or vegetarianism, as a lay associate of a major temple, and received advanced training in meditation or other practices from a distinguished master.

RELIGION
IN TRADITIONAL CHINA

We began by observing that East Asian religion is generally religion of the particular place and social unit, deeply rooted in soil and family. We have, however, devoted much attention to exploring historical tracks made by the Confucian, Taoist, and Buddhist traditions; this has necessitated portraying them as three major traditions extending through time as though they were great independent causes. It is not possible to understand religious China fully without this historical and philosophical background, but it must be understood that it is not in such terms that the traditions would have impacted the lives of ordinary people in traditional China. It is now time to refocus on the particular to see how they are combined in practice.

Consider a single family in old China, the Changs. They live in a home in the countryside; the setting and ornamentation of the house itself reflects some ideas we have discussed, for when it was built its location was carefully determined so it would be at the meeting point of Yin and Yang forces in the environment, and would be spiritually protected. Open places and straight lines dissipated the benevolent breath of nature and encouraged invisible evil forces; for this reason the house was situated between a sunken pond and a bamboo grove, and the road up to it was curved.

The Changs took very seriously the veneration of their ancestors. In three places were they memorialized: in the home at a small shrine to tablets bearing their names; in the chapel of the Chang clan or extended family where large tablets would be set up, rank on rank rising on higher and higher tiers the further back up the generations one went; and at the cemetary. A bit of water, incense, and food would be presented daily at the household shrine. Several times a year, the clan shrine and cemetery would be visited, cleaned, and given larger offerings and a report on family events. Ancestrism, combining very old spiritualist beliefs with Confucian filial piety toward departed parents and grandparents, was most important.

The biggest annual holiday was New Year's. At the end of the year, debts would be settled and the house cleaned. On New Year's Eve, the picture of the protective "kitchen-god," which had been hanging in the house all year, would have its mouth smeared with honey, to put it in a good mood, and be burned—for it was believed that this deity would then ascend to the court of the Jade Emperor to give his report on the merits and demerits of the family for the past year. On New Year's Day itself, members of the Chang family being gathered from far and wide, extensive offerings of food and drink—plus a plate of soup set outside for lonely spirits without family to care for them—would be placed with bows and prayers before the family shrine, full of ancestors and protective gods. Then the family would join in a feast. Outside, they would hear firecrackers and doubtless see a Yang dragon parading down the road, animated by the feet of many men.

The Harvest Festival in the autumn would have a different, Yin sort of atmosphere, being oriented toward the moon, night, and returning spirits. Round cakes would be made, and tables set up in the courtyard of the house, both showing the fabulous palaces of the moon where Taoist immortals dwelt.

In the Chang household, sober Confucianism would have its due as well as Taoist fancy. The sons would bow to their father, and if educated, they would study first and foremost the Confucian Classics. When the elder Chang died, the sons would mourn for him according to Confucian ritual—although somewhat modified and shortened—kneeling before the father's portrait or tablet, wearing a gown of rough sackcloth, and eating coarse and tasteless food.

For the funeral and subsequent memorial rites, Buddhist or Taoist priests would be called in. They would chant sutras or prayers, and burn elaborate paper houses and imitation money offerings to be used by the deceased on the Other Side. They would pray the protecting city-god to serve as his advocate before the dread court of Yen-lo. The family might discuss the possibilities before the deceased amid the many hells, heavens, and paths back to reincarnation in this world. They might well consult a medium, of Taoist ties, who would contact the departed spirit to find out what the disposition of his case had been, and how he fared, and what the living could do to help him. There were even shamanistic Taoist priests who cut themselves with knives in order to take on themselves the after-death suffering of their clients.

For answers to problems in this life, the Changs might consult a diviner who would use the ancient *I Ching*. He would throw coins or sticks to determine which of the sixty-four "hexagrams," or sets of six lines (some unbroken Yang lines; some broken Yin lines) unfolded the meaning of the situation in question. The text in the *I Ching* for that hexagram would suggest, in fairly cryptic language, whether favorable or unfavorable lines of force were in operation, whether it was a time for action or waiting, and the like. This book, now popular in the West, is perhaps the oldest extant Chinese book in its most ancient parts; it is one of the Confucian classics, yet also expresses a Taoistic philosophy. In its own way it epitomizes a Chinese world view that underlies both traditions based on a profound sense of the continual, rhythmic interaction of visible and invisible forces within a unfied world process to which mankind must gently and wisely accommodate itself.[20]

From time to time a representative of the Chang family would go to a temple in the locality. The temples may vary from a tiny edifice with an image the size of a doll, to huge structures with giant, superhuman gods of awesome countenance. Some would be Taoist, some Buddhist, some mixed. But it should be realized that they are homes of the gods, not generally places of congregational worship. When Mr. Chang or another of the family visited the temple, it was generally to ask a favor or pay respects as one would to a powerful neighbor. Most frequently the visit would be to ask advice of the deity, done by throwing two woodblocks, drawing a printed oracle, or perhaps consulting a medium retained by the temple. Sometimes the family representative would make an offering of incense or paper temple money

[20]The most useful translations are John Blofeld, *I Ching* (New York: Dutton, 1968), and Richard Wilhelm, *I Ching, or Book of Changes* (New York: Pantheon Books, 1950).

Dance with dragon, the yang symbol, at the Buddhist temple to the bodhisattva Kannon in Asakusa, Tokyo, Japan. Note the influence of China tradition on both Buddhism and Japan.

in thanksgiving for a favor, or in response to a vow. This worship would be done especially at earth-god shrines, humble but ubiquitous temples to deities of the soil older and closer to the people than any of the major faiths, in the spring for the crops, and in the fall in thanksgiving for the harvest. Food might be presented to the deity, but would be brought back home for a feast.

At irregular intervals, depending on local custom, the temple would hold a great festival. Brilliant red candles would be burned around the divine image, priests would perform elaborate rituals such as a secret Taoist *chiao,* and villagers and visitors alike would throng the temple with offerings and divinations. The temple courtyard would be set up like a fair, with booths and amusements and colorful pageantry. There would be ranks of offerings, particularly pigs, presented by families and businesses. Here the Chang family might well be represented, and the family members (except women in a traditional middle and upper class family) would delightedly attend.

If Mr. Chang were of the mandarin class, he would also go to the nearest Confucian temple at the two equinoxes to join with his peers in the old dances and offerings presented to the Wise and Holy Sage by his latter-day disciples. He would probably also take part in the rites of the city god, the protector of the town, honoring him with thanks and perhaps punishing him when misfortune struck, for his cultus was part of the official religion.

Then again one day Mr. Chang, or someone else in the family, might become pious, or at least acquire a wanderlust, and go on a pilgrimage to some Buddhist or Taoist monastery on a cloud-wrapped mountaintop or an isolated island. There he would break his routine by living with the monks for a spell, sharing their meals and conversation, and renewing his spirit in a setting of exalted beauty.

The Chang family, then, would be touched by the attitudes and institutional life of all three of the great traditions, and by ancestrism and the earth-gods as well. This combined experience is nowhere better expressed than in the first part of the old Chinese fantasy novel *Monkey*.[21] In it, the Buddha and the Jade Emperor visit and consult with one another; dragon kings, bodhisattvas, and sages with the secret of immortality move in and out of the narrative—yet the monkey-hero, like the sturdy peasant farmers of China, when needful employs both wiles and wonders to combat monolithic authority, even the hosts of heaven itself, to preserve the autonomy of himself and his household.

Today, this tradition is broken irrevocably. It still survives in Taiwan, Hong Kong, Singapore, and other Chinese outposts outside the People's Republic of China, but on the mainland the situation is very different. Fully accurate information about religion in mainland China is not easy to come by, but it appears that although some Buddhist temples are still maintained, and some popular religious customs may not be entirely dead, by and large the hold of religion is shattered. Confucius and the values he represents have been fervently attacked, although a few Buddhist thinkers have seen Buddhist thought as not incompatible with Marxism. But while the revolution itself and its symbols have had overtones of religious experience in China, for the great majority the old religion apparently seems irrelevant in the new society.

SHINTO IN JAPAN

Let us return now to the Shinto shrine in the grove. Like the Chinese city-god and ancestral chapels, it expresses Japanese religion's rootedness in place and family. But typically the Shinto shrine will have a light, clean construction contrasting with the heavy and ornate quality of Chinese temples. Shinto shrines, and the Shinto religious complex, have distinctive attitudes and practices to go with the unique architecture. If we were to remain around a Shinto shrine and observe its activity, we would see things happen that would bring out four basic

---

[21]Arthur Waley, trans., *Monkey: Folk Novel of China by Wu Ch'eng-En* (New York: Grove Press, Inc., 1958).

Main Themes of Japanese Religion

Individual experience

Seicho-no-Ie

Esoteric Shingon and
Tendai

Shinran

Omoto New Religions

Japanese *miko* or shamans

Yamabushi

Nichiren Buddhism

Pure Land Buddhist sects

Konkokyo

Tenrikyo

Imported ───────────────────────────────── *Indigenous*

Zen

Shinto sects

Soka Gakkai

Shinto shrines

Shinto *matsuri* or
festivals

State Shinto

Popular Shingon and
Tendai

Community religion

Thematic Chart V.   Not only has Japanese religion and culture long been sharply aware of the distinction between traditions indigenous to Japan and those motifs imported from the Asian mainland or (more recently) the West, it has also long been riven by two modes of experiencing the gods, rites, and religious personalities of both: as sanctifiers of stable community life, and as shamanistic conveyors of intensity and new revelation.

affirmations which implicitly undergird Shinto: affirmation of tradition, of life in this world, of purity, and of festival.

Virtually every Shinto shrine has its unique set of traditions: what festivals are celebrated, what rituals are performed. Some are ancient and some less so, but all strongly affirm the links of the present with the past; they appear in the midst of modern Japan like time capsules from earlier centuries. The traditions of some shrines present brilliant spectacles drawing vast throngs of tourists; others are of only local interest. But in any case, the observer will note that while Shintoists may have little idea exactly why a rite is performed in a certain manner, or what it means theologically or philosophically, the action will be done in the precisely prescribed way. The fire to cook the offerings may be started with a traditional fire drill, a ring of evergreen may be set up in the same way each year for people to walk through to remove pollution. What is really being affirmed is not so much the importance of this or that particular custom, as the importance of having tradition itself, of living in the presence of visible carryovers from ages gone by, with all their color and evocative power. For millions of modern Japanese, living in a rapidly changing and technilogical world, this role of embodying a traditional past they do not want entirely to lose is the most important function of Shinto, and one very precious to them.

The affirmation of tradition is clearly related to the motif of affirmation of life in this world. Shinto, the religion of clans and their communal spirit, of joyous festivals and bountiful harvests, affirms the good things of this world and the natural relationships. Its land of the dead is shadowy and its mystical and intellectual life relatively undeveloped. But in the exuberant festivals of harvest, or the stately splendor of ancient dance and ritual, Shinto comes into its own. Most Japanese tend to think of Shinto as religion concerned with the high and happy moments of this life, and Buddhism with somber and profound things, such as suffering and death. People are married and babies are blessed in Shinto shrines; funerals and memorial services are held in Buddhist temples.

This affirmation is related to another important Shinto motif: the distinction between purity and pollution. Shinto shrines, demarcated off by their torii, represent pure spaces in the midst of a polluted world. One entering the shrine precincts washes oneself, and rituals begin with the sweeping away of impurity by a green branch. What is fresh, lively, and bright is pure; what is stagnant, decaying, sick, or dying is impure. Blood, disease, and death are the most impure things. A dead body would not be brought into a shrine; on the rare occasion of a Shinto funeral, the rite is held at another place. Through its avoidance of impurity, Shinto affirms the persistence and superiority of life and joy.

The fourth motif is festival. As we have seen, the quiet, inactive shrine in its wood or beside its stream may have an air of still purity, but it is not until the kami is stirred to vigorous life by the drums of a matsuri, or Shinto festival, that the full color and dynamism of the divine side of reality is manifested. For one who has been at a matsuri, the sylvan quietude of the shrine on ordinary days, when only individual worshippers approach it to clap twice and pray, has a feel of expectant waiting about it. The still drum plainly visible on the open porch at the front of the shrine, and the dance pavillion, remind one of another mood.

Fully to understand Shinto worship and festival, it is necessary to have a mental picture of the structure of a shrine. After the visitor has entered under the crossbeams of the torii and passed the purificatory font, he or she approaches the porch with its drum, *gohei* or zigzag paper streamers, and other accountrements; this is the *haiden,* or hall of worship, where the laity pray and sacred dance is offered. Behind it, but visible from the front, is a second segment with a curious eight-legged table for offerings; this is the *heiden,* or hall of offerings. Behind the table, the observer will note a set of extremely steep steps leading up to a massive, richly ornamented door. It leads to the *honden,* an enclosed room much higher than the rest of the shrine, and the symbolic dwelling place of the kami himself. In this room will be a heavily wrapped object called the *shintai,* "body" of the god—an old sword, mirror, inscription, or something else—which from ancient times has been the sacred presence of divinity in this shrine, in a manner somewhat analogous to the reserved sacrament in a Roman Catholic church.

Formal Shinto worship occurs at varying intervals, depending on the importance of the shrine. Some small shrines without a resident priest will enjoy offerings only two or three times a year; others will have service monthly, or every ten days, or daily in a few major shrines. Special rites commissioned on behalf of families and groups are common at larger shrines too. The spring and fall festivals will usually be the most important matsuri. However, many shrines also have very colorful and dramatic midsummer rites directed against evil influences. New Year's is a time of considerable shrine activity too, especially for private visits.

All full Shinto worship follows a basic structure. It can be remembered by a series of four words beginning with the letter *P:* purification, presentation, prayer, and participation.

First, a priest, dressed in white or perhaps lightly colored garments and a high black hat (derived from ancient court costumes), may, according to local usage, wave a branch or stick with paper or sprinkle salt water over the heads of the people gathered in the courtyard.

Then the priest will enter the shrine, and present the offerings, very neatly arranged, before the kami-presence on the eight-legged table—or on very important occasions, he will open the great doors and lay them on the floor of the honden. The presentation is accompanied by dramatically accelerating drumbeats and perhaps the eerie tones of reed flutes. The offerings, mostly fruit, vegetables, rice, seafood, salt, water, and rice wine, are borne up and arranged with reverent care.

Then, all in order on the altar, the priest reads a formal prayer, either silently or in a high chanting voice.

Next follows one of several possibilities, depending on the elaborateness of the occasion and the resources of the shrine. While the offerings are still on the altar, formal dance may be presented as part of the offering and as a representation of the divine presence to the worshippers. At the close of the service, individuals may present as an offering a small branch, as though to show their participation, and as a kind of holy communion partake of a tiny bit of the wine and perhaps other offerings. (Prior to this, the offerings had been solemnly removed from the altar.)

Particularly at the main annual matsuri, vivid local activities affording everyone participation in the festival spirit occur. These will be as exuberant as the offering

Young men carrying a portable shrine during a Shinto matsuri, *or festival.*

and prayer were solemn, suggesting a dramatic, divine change of pace as the kami-spirit animates his people. The kami may be borne through the streets in a palenquin by young men zigzagging and shouting. All over the shrine grounds, booths are set up as for a carnival, with cotton candy sold and sumo wrestling exhibitions. As soon as the offerings are removed, it is understood that the solemn part is over, the booths are opened, and crowds throng onto the carnival grounds with laughter and squealing children.

In some great shrines, splendid parades, historical pageants, folk dances, medieval horse racing or archery performances, fireworks, indeed an almost endless variety of traditional activities, may be parts of the "participation" aspect of the matsuri. Some are rustic fairs little known outside the locality; some take months of professional preparation and draw spectators from around the world.

So far we have described only Shinto shrines and worship, saying nothing about the particular deities who are the recipients of this worship. This is not inappropriate, for to most Japanese the name and story of a particular kami means little; it is the shrine, worship, and festival itself that counts. A partial exception is the familiar Inari shrines, distinguished by their red torii and stone foxes, to which people go to pray for prosperity. But Shintoists are far from having the kind of relation to their kami as Hindu bhaktas with Shiva or Krishna; Japanese religion, like the Japanese temperament, is much more reserved and formal.

Nonetheless, the kami do have names and myths. In many cases they are only local. But there is also a national myth in which some of the shrine kami appear, recorded in two of the oldest books in Japanese, the *Kojiki* (A.D. 712) and the *Nihonshoki* (A.D. 720), compiled by order of the imperial court to present its divine descent and commission.[22] Not all important shrine kami have major roles in this myth. But it is important for two reasons: it illustrates many of the basic Shinto motifs, and it explicates the relation between Shinto and sovereignty.

The *Kojiki* and *Nihonshoki,* although written around the sixth century, often reflect the world of prehistoric religion. In those days, the Japanese were divided into *uji,* or clans. Each had a kami who was the spiritual guard and guide of his people. The clan chieftain was the priest who presented offerings and prayer to this deity, usually at an outdoor altar by a stream or on a hilltop, for this was even before the day of shrine buildings. It appears that a woman, probably wife or relative of the chief, served as official shamaness, and would go into trance and deliver messages from the clan deity regarding matters of state.

One clan, ancestors of the present imperial family of Japan, seems to have long had an ill-defined paramountcy among the clans out of which the Japanese state emerged. The earliest emperors themselves had a consort or princess who served as oracle. Indeed, if reports of Chinese travelers and mythical histories are to be believed, on one or two occasions the shamaness herself ruled as a sort of sorceress-queen.

Although each clan had its own divine patron, people were aware that he was but one, although the one they knew best, of a more vast pantheon. Early Shinto prayers speak of "the gods of heaven and the gods of earth." The religious world view centered on feeling that there were two classes of gods, of sky and soil, and that the world advances through dynamic interaction between the two. The fundamental pattern in Japanese myth is for male gods to descend from heaven, marry female kami of the earth, and produce children who, as sons of both earth and heaven, have great and versatile power; the greatest heroes and clan kami are of this type.

This pattern fitted well the religious outlook of farmers after the introduction of rice agriculture between 300 B.C. and A.D. 300. It was believed that the heavenly kami descended on top of mountains in the spring, and villagers would ascend to greet them with festivity. They would be brought into the fields to mate with the female kami of the soil and rice, work to bring in the crop-child, and then be thanked and sent off at the harvest festival.

The national myth in the *Kojiki* and *Nihonshoki* tells us that in the beginning the High Kami in heaven sent the primal parents, the male Izanagi and the female Izanami, down from the High Plain of Heaven. They indulged in a virtual orgy of procreation, giving birth to islands and gods, until Izanami was burned to death upon the birth of the fire-god. Izanagi tried to bring his wife out of the underworld, but was unable to do so because she had already eaten of its food. Izanagi then exchanged boasts with Izanami about the greater power of life than death. He bathed

---

[22]The best translations are Donald M. Philippi, *Kojiki* (Tokyo: University of Tokyo Press, 1968), and W. G. Aston, *Nihongi* (London: George Allen and Unwin, 1896, 1956).

in the ocean to cleanse himself of the pollution of the underworld; from his washings were born several great gods, above all Amaterasu, the lovely goddess associated with the sun and ancestress of the imperial house. Here we see two Shinto themes: the affirmation of life, the importance of purification.

In heaven, Amaterasu once hid herself in a cave when her brother greatly offended her at the harvest festival; she was drawn out when a goddess did a ribald dance and another kami held up a mirror to her emerging face; this story suggests the Shinto affirmation of festivity, and reminds us ancient mirrors are often symbols of deity.

Later, Amaterasu gave the same mirror (now said by tradition to be enshrined as sacred object in the Grand Shrine of Ise) to her grandson, who was sent down from heaven to establish the line of sovereigns on earth. This brings us to another aspect of Shinto, its relationship to the Japanese state.

During the period of modern nationalism in Japan up to 1945, this mythical divine descent of the imperial house, and the accompanying ancient belief that the emperor is himself in a mysterious sense "manifest deity," was used (often in a rather cynical way) to focus extreme loyalty and to justify militaristic policy. The ancient role of the emperor, however, was one of sacred kingship in the priestly sense; in most periods of Japanese history, he has exercised very little real power. He has a special role toward the kami, however, which is well expressed in the Daijo-sai, the harvest festival as celebrated by the emperor after his accession, described in Chapter II.[23]

Before ending a discussion of Shinto, a word must be said about the Grand Shrine of Ise, a site that beautifully combines all the motifs of this religion. The Grand Shrine, located on the east coast south of Nagoya, is really two major shrines about five miles apart, one dedicated to Amaterasu and said to enshrine the mirror she gave to Prince Ninigi; the other is dedicated to Toyouke, goddess of food. The shrines are set amid splendid old trees not far from clear streams in which pilgrims purify themselves. In the vicinity are a number of lesser shrines, and places where the offerings of food and cloth are prepared by ancient means. As the shrine of the chief imperial ancestress, Ise has long had a special relation to the imperial household; emperors report important events to the goddess, and offerings from the imperial household are presented by envoys in ancient court dress on important festivals. In a very interesting rite of renewal, every twenty years the shrines are taken down after new shrines, exactly identical to the old, have been erected with many traditional ceremonies in lots adjacent to the old sites; at the Harvest Festival, the sacred objects are moved with impressive solemnity from the old to the new shrines.[24]

[23]See Daniel C. Holtom, *The Japanese Enthronement Ceremonies* (Tokyo: Kyo Bun Kwan, 1928; Sophia University, 1972), and Robert S. Ellwood, Jr., *The Feast of Kingship* (Tokyo: Sophia University, 1973).

[24]See Kenzo Tange and Noboru Kawazoe, *Ise: Prototype of Japanese Architecture* (Cambridge, Mass.: MIT Press, 1965); Felicia G. Bock, "The Rites of Renewal at Ise," *Monumenta Nipponica,* XXIX, No. 1 (Spring 1974), 55–68; and Robert S. Ellwood, Jr., "Harvest and Renewal at the Grand Shrine of Ise," *Numen,* XV, no. 3 (November 1968), 165–90.

The word "Shinto" actually means "The Way of the Gods," and the *to,* "way," is the Chinese Tao. Shinto is a broad path offering a pattern of rites, attitudes, and subtle experiences, which harmonize mankind with the many faces of its spiritual environment in the context of an ancient culture.

Shrine Shinto is just one part of a complex Japanese religious synthesis related to Shinto. From the beginning of historical times until the late nineteenth century, Shinto and Buddhism coexisted in a sort of symbiosis. Shinto and Buddhist places of worship would be put together, a pagoda in the courtyard of a shrine or a small shrine in the precincts of a temple. The kami was considered a protector, pupil, or form of manifestation of the Buddha; one school made it the other way around. In any case, Buddha and kami were a unified display of the sacred for the average worshipper, and not in competition. Only in 1868 did a new, modernizing government require the separation of Shinto and Buddhism, in its eagerness to make Shinto a vehicle for nationalistic expression, and the present absolute distinctiveness of Shinto and Buddhist places of worship dates only from that time.

Confucianism and Taoism, early imported from China, have also been important factors in general Japanese spirituality. Both were influences shaping the earliest rationalizations of Japanese polity on the continental model; in the Heian period, formal education as well as the formal organization of the bureaucracy was Confucian in pattern. Taoist-related directional taboos and calendric gods appear in Heian literature; by early modern times these beliefs and much else of religious Taoism had worked their way down to affect Japanese folk religion, as can be seen in the account of the Japanese shamanness in Chapter II.

Neo-Confucianism, introduced through Zen, was important in Japan particularly in the Tokugawa period (1600–1867), when it was virtually a state ideology, although it rarely took explicitly religious expression in Japan. Japanese Neo-Confucian thinkers greatly emphasized obligation and loyalty to one's feudal lord, as in *bushido* or the samurai knightly code, to the emperor, as well as to parents; their importance in forming general Japanese values is great. In the modern nationalistic period, the Japanese Confucian concept of high loyalty to the sovereign combined well with the Shinto myths of imperial divine descent to give nationalism a moral and sacred aura.

These themes come together in Japanese ancestrism. Ancestral memorial tablets are most often on home Buddhist altars, just as funerals are usually conducted out of Buddhist temples. Yet ancestrism is related to Shinto since (although whether this was originally the case is debatable) the kami have come to be widely regarded as ancestors or relatives to the families of which they are patrons, on the model of Amaterasu and the imperial family itself. Confucian teachings of loyalty and filial piety gave great impetus to ancestrism in Japan as well.

Mention should also be made of Christianity in Japan. Catholicism was brought in by Francis Xavier and his Jesuit missionaries in 1549; they were later supplemented by Franciscans. For several decades, times of immense social disorder in Japan, they were remarkably successful. But around the turn of the century, and especially after the accession of Tokugawa power in 1600, Christians suffered horrible persecution and finally seemed to be stamped out. But when the first modern Catholic missionaries came to Japan in 1868, they were surprised to be met in some towns and villages by people called *kakure Kirishitan,* "hidden Christians," who had kept a garbled "underground" version of the earlier missionary faith alive for two and a half centuries.

BUDDHISM IN JAPAN

Nearly as common as Shinto shrines, and also of graceful wooden architecture but without the torii, are the Buddhist temples of Japan. However, the Buddhist edifices are likely to be larger than the shrines, with room for throngs of worshippers within. And the temple will be dominated by imposing Buddhist images, some perhaps large and of a deeply glowing gold. These images personify a spiritual force which is not as old in Japan as the kami, who go back to misty prehistory, but is as old as history itself. For with the coming of Buddhism to Japan came writing, new models for art and governmental organization, many material boons of continental civilization, the keeping of records, and consciousness of history.

Buddhism arrived in Japan from Korea in the early sixth century.[25] This island nation had long closer ties with the the Korean peninsula than with China proper, even to the extent of maintaining military and trading settlements there. In the sixth century, Buddhism had recently come to Korea from T'ang China, and in China itself had only been a strong influence for some three centuries. It still was a young and dynamic enthusiasm in that part of the world, and the *Ninonshoki* says a Korean king, anxious to cement an alliance, sent the Japanese emperor a Buddhist image and scriptures.

But we must remember that as new as Buddhism seemed then, that faith already had behind it nearly a thousand years of development. Mahayana, tantrism, temple architecture, sutras, images, mandalas, schools such as Ch'an and Pure Land—all these had reached mature forms before Buddhism touched the then shamanistic and nearly unlettered people of old Japan.

Buddhism came, therefore, as a powerfully more sophisticated culture, with splendors of art and subtleties of concept undreamed of before. It was far from well understood, but it was a force and a presence that could hardly be avoided. As they have repeatedly since, the Japanese responded initially with debate between the desire to keep their culture intact and the desire to be open to everything foreign that seemed advanced and advantageous; then as later, they swung between extremes on each hand. But from then on, Buddhism was an increasingly deeply rooted part of Japanese culture.

The first great Buddhist era was the Nara period (710–84), named after the first permanent Japanese capital, established in that ancient and beautiful city in order to provide a court in the continental model. The government, immensely proud of its new Buddhist culture, lavishly endowed temples and monasteries. The lovely Nara park, with its shrine and pagoda and tame deer, is a momento of this era, as is the

---

[25]Aston, *Nihongi,* Part II, pp. 65–67.

magnificent Giant Buddha in the Todaiji temple. The latter is really the Sun Buddha, Vairocana, and indicates that from the beginning Japanese Buddhism was shaped by the more expansive and mystic forms of Mahayana. This temple belongs to the Kegon denomination, which emphasizes the presence of the Buddha-nature in all things, every blade of grass and every grain of sand; the Giant Buddha Vairocana is really the dharmakaya, and behind him is sculpted a great array of smaller Buddhas, to indicate that the Sun Buddha is reflected as in countless mirrors in the Buddhas of innumerable worlds.

The artistic and mystical splendors of Nara were not without price, however. The temples claimed great holdings of tax-free land, and received valuable gifts from wealthy patrons. True, they were not only strictly religious centers, but orphanages, alms houses, hospitals, and purveyors of the new "modernizing" education and culture being brought in from the continent. The government sent a series of priests to China, who returned years later with much learning and shiploads of cultural goods, even as in the late nineteenth century it sent students to Europe and America to bring Japan up-to-date on what the outside world had attained by then. But the cost at first (and this was little different in the nineteenth century) was an increased gulf between the elite and the peasants, and more efficiently thorough exploitation of the latter.

Nonetheless, the countryside also had some glimmer of the power of the new Buddhism. Although the official "six sects" of Nara Buddhism with their sophisticated glories were one with the world of the aristocrats, the country people had their own version of the Buddha's path. It was a Buddhism in continuity with the old religion of shamans and Shinto mountain gods, a shamanistic Buddhism comparable to that of Tibet: rustic magicians, healers, and diviners under nominal Buddhist influence, called *ubasoku,* ranged the countryside. They acquired occult powers through great austerities and initiations in the mountains, and then returned to wander among the hard-pressed peasants teaching and healing. Their teaching was a rough-and-ready doctrine which mainly made the Buddha a great healer and wizard, their medicine a medley of shamanism and folk magic. But they were at least close to the people and their needs—many also led in practical enterprises such as building bridges, roads, and irrigation ditches, and did not hesitate to criticize sharply the ecclesiastical establishment, which was on the side of the state and paid little attention to the spiritual needs of the masses. The ubasoku called their way the Bosatsu-do, the bodhisattva's way.[26]

Down through the centuries, two kinds of Buddhism, the official-orthodox and the popular-shamanistic, have existed as poles in Japan. The shamanistic side has most recently emerged in some of the new religions of today. But there has also been continual movements toward rapprochement between the two poles. Even in the Nara period, the Emperor Shomu, when he wished to raise support for the building of the Giant Buddha as a sort of national cathedral, was forced to call on the great popular ubasoku leader Gyogi (670–749) for assistance and make him chief Buddhist priest of the nation.

[26]See Joseph M. Kitagawa, *Religion in Japanese History* (New York: Columbia University Press, 1966), pp. 38–45.

The Buddhist denominations that flourished in the next period, the Heian, advanced the reconciliation, for they combined power at the highest levels of society with ancient mountain and shamanistic themes. The capital was moved from Nara in 781, and established in the new city of Heian (modern Kyoto) ten years later. The basic reason for the move was the excessive political role of the priesthood in the former site, which culminated in an ambitious court chaplain's becoming romantically involved with an empress. Perhaps, lay authorities thought, if Nara teeming with monks is left behind, a new and better start can be made elsewhere.

But on Mount Hiei, the northeast guardian of the valley where the new capital was situated, there dwelt a hermit named Saicho, known posthumously as Dengyo Daishi (762–822). His enthusiasm was the Lotus Sutra as interpreted by the T'ien-t'ai school in China, which made it the final and culminating expression of the Buddha's teaching, a comprehensive umbrella in which all sorts of practices from Pure Land to esotericism could be seen as ways to realize the eternal Buddhahood in all things, and eternal Buddhahood also makes all things absolutely real just as they are.

Saicho gathered about him a group of disciples. When the capital moved to Heian the emperor made it possible for him to go to China to study at the great T'ien-t'ai monastery. When he returned in 805, he established the monastery on Mount Hiei called the Enryaku-ji, the home monastery of the Tendai denomination in Japan. For many centuries Mount Hiei was the most influential of all religious centers in Japan, for its nearness to the capital made it politically influential, and its influence on the future spiritual history of Japan is incomparable. Not seldom did the monks of Mount Hiei sweep down to demonstrate before the palace until their demands were met, and future independent Buddhist movements—Pure Land, Nichiren, and even Zen—had roots in the comprehensive Tendai system, and leaders trained on Mount Hiei. On this spectacular mountaintop, with its magnificent old mossy trees, clear streams, and isolated temples scattered deep in the woods, meditations were made which shaped the future.

A contemporary of Saicho, Kukai, posthumously called Kobo Daishi (773–835), founder of the Shingon denomination, was an even more remarkable personality. Many legends testify to his brilliance and charismatic power.[27] Kukai was at first trained for government service, but had a change of heart and turned to religion. Many stories suggest that he then spent long years in mental and psychophysical training in the tradition of the shamanistic Buddhists. Above all, however, he was interested in synthesis, in attaining the most comprehensive truth. In 797 Saicho wrote a book trying to synthesize Taoism, Confucianism, and Buddhism.

His remarkable intellect attracted imperial attention, and Kukai like Saicho was sent to China, where he stayed from 804 to 806. His bent led him to the study of tantric Buddhism. Above all he was attracted to the Great Sun Sutra (*Mahavairocana Sutra*), with its teaching of esoteric practices by which an adept could become one with the essence of the universe. When he returned to Japan,

---

[27]See Joseph M. Kitagawa, "Master and Saviour" [on Kobo Daishi] in *Studies of Esoteric Buddhism and Tantrism* (Koyasan, Japan: Koyasan University, 1965), pp. 1–26.

Kukai established a great monastery on Mount Koya, some sixty mountainous miles south of Kyoto, and still a fabulous treasury of art, history, and spiritual practice.

Shingon considers the Great Sun Buddha to be the central deity, for Vairocana personifies the dharmakaya, the cosmic unitary essence. The heavenly and earthly Buddha-bodies are lesser, relativized expressions of the pure dharmakaya. The important thing, then, is not to refer back to Gautama Buddha, but to become a Buddha now through direct access to the dharmakaya as he did then. Kobo Daishi taught that one can become a Buddha in this body, in this lifetime, through the esoteric "three secrets" he taught: mudras (hand gestures), dharani (mystic chants), and yoga (meditation, including evocations).

Shingon uses rich symbols, rituals, and art. They are sacred because they manifest the Buddha-nature latent in all things—to make an image of the Buddha out of a piece of wood brings out the Buddha-nature of the wood, and in the process is a kind of meditation for the artist. Above all, Shingon makes use of great mandalas, which manifest the hidden realities and lines of force in the universe.[28]

For all its recondite inner doctrines, Shingon and Kobo Daishi did much to popularize Buddhism and reconcile the shamanistic countryside with both the court and the Buddhist intellectual tradition. Kobo Daishi was able to mount spectacular rituals immensely pleasing to the court, and the brilliant, mystical images and paintings his tradition fostered brought the numinous wonder of Buddhism home to the masses innocent of books or philosophy. Esoteric Buddhas and bodhisattvas stepped out of his mandalas, so to speak, to become the folk deities of wayside shrines and household altars—like Kannon (Kwan-yin, Avaloketishvara); Fudo (the "Invincible Buddha" with sword and rope and fire); and Jizo "earth-womb"), a bodhisattva said to help women, children, and wanderers—way stations were dedicated to him, and he was reported to lead dead children to the netherworld. At Mount Koya there is a long line of Jizo images wearing bibs like babies; pilgrims pour ladles of water over them as acts of devotion.

The emphasis in Shingon, and soon enough in Tendai as well, on rapid attainment by mystic, magic-appearing tantric means made easy contact with the world of shamanistic Buddhists and of archaic Shinto. The chief monasteries of Shingon and Tendai were themselves on wild mountains rather than flat city streets. Orders of mountain priests called *yamabushi* came to be affiliated with both Hiei and Koya; the relationship was rather tenuous, however, and for the most part the yamabushi continued the ubasoku life of receiving fierce initiations in their sacred mountainous precincts, like Dewa in the north and Ontake in the south, and serving as healers, deviners, and pilgrim-guides in their communities. Yamabushi initiations, in which candidates would run their way out of a cave hung with red and white streamers to represent the womb, and leap over fires, and be suspended by the heels from cliffs for a "peek into eternity," were unforgettable. Until the last century, the yamabushi way, called Shugendo, had immense impact on popular religion in Japan.[29]

[28]See Yoshito S. Hakeda, trans., *Kukai: Major Works* (New York: Columbia University Press, 1972).

[29]See H. Byron Earhart, *A Religious Study of the Mount Haguro Sect of Shugendo* (Tokyo: Sophia University, 1970).

Buddhism in the Heian period (794–1185) was above all directed at comprehensiveness. It had priestly, aristocratic, and popular faces; it was concerned to fit all known kinds of Buddhist practice and experience into larger wholes, which made each one of many paths to the summit. Kobo Daishi, in fact, developed a scheme that showed how all world religions of which he knew, and all forms of Buddhism, are equivalent to stages through which one passes to reach the supreme realization achieved in the Sun Buddha. Both Tendai and Shingon developed systems through which Shinto too was reconciled to Buddhism; the kami were made guardians, or manifestations, of the Buddhist mysteries and powers.[30]

THE KAMAKURA BUDDHIST REFORMATION

The next period, the Kamakura (1185–1333), was a different kind of age with different values. The Heian order broke down in the Middle Ages basically for economic reasons, in which the wealthy, nonproductive monasteries played their part. Military leaders of clans in outlying regions rose up, and one house, the Minamoto, became supreme. While preserving the imperial institution in Kyoto, the new overlords established the political capital far away in Kamakura, on modern Tokyo Bay, under a shogun, as the ruler was called, who administered the nation in the emperor's name.

If Heian was dominated by the elegant refined courtier and the esoteric monk, Kamakura was characterized by the simple, direct warrior. Moreover, times were troubled, and pessimism was in the air. People talked of the Buddhist idea of the *mappo,* the last age, when doctrine and morality would deteriorate so much that one could be saved only by faith, if at all. To meet the new age, three new forms of Buddhism arose in Japan—Pure Land, Nichiren, and Zen.

Each in its own way represented a popularization of Buddhism as a path to liberation for the masses. Each also represented a radical Buddhist simplification. Kamakura Buddhism was a soldier's reaction against the deep metaphysics and ostentatious rituals of Heian. The soldier, in a time of disorder and death, wanted assurance of salvation, but his straightforward and manly nature was not attracted by monasticism or beautiful but impersonal rites or subtle philosophy. He insisted on some simple and sure key to salvation, as dependable on the battlefield as in the monastic temple.

Hence synthesis and mystery gave way to simple faith, popular preachers, and practical techniques. An age can be understood as well or better through the questions it asks, as through the answers it gives; if the Heian period (like medieval Europe) asked, "How can all knowledge and spiritual experience be brought into a great inclusive system?" then Kamakura Japan (like Reformation Europe) was asking instead, "How can I know that I am saved?" It was eager to shuck the brain-splitting mysteries of the cosmic mandala and the three Buddha-bodies and the rest, for a sure answer to this desperate question that anyone could understand.

[30]See Alicia Masunaga, *The Buddhist Philosophy of Assimilation* (Tokyo and Rutland, Vt.: Sophia University and Charles E. Tuttle Company, 1969).

The Kamakura movements met this question in different ways. Pure Land, as in China but now with a typically Japanese more extreme and exclusive thrust, expressed the new radical simplicity through popular evangelism and mass movements, which said that just invoking Amida Buddha even once was enough. Nichiren taught that an equally simple and direct faith in the Lotus Sutra was sufficient; his character, in some ways more that of a warrior than a priest, epitomized the era.

Zen as a Kamakura expression is a somewhat different case, although less so when considered historically in Japan. While Pure Land and Nichiren were mass movements, Zen tended to be the favored path of the Kamakura military aristocracy when it was introduced from China, although continental Ch'an was far removed from the world of the sword. But in Japan, Zen's unpretentious simplicity, its lack of obscurantism, ritual, and metaphysical verbiage, appealed to the new warlords. Whenever the cares of battle and state became too great, one could find a few hours of relaxing calm by going to his favorite Zen monastery for tea, and meditation on rocks and moss and naturalistic paintings. Moreover, the virtues Zen taught— perfect self-control, indifference to fear or death, ability to live in rigorous simplicity—were just those that the warriors most valued in themselves and their sons. They were the virtues a statesman or a fighting man needs. There grew up a tacit alliance between Zen and the warrior or samurai class, and such skills as the Zen art of archery or the Zen art of swordsmanship. While Zen, like Ch'an, as an expression of Buddhism certainly has nothing to do with militarism, this unlikely but understandable relationship between rough soldiers acquiring culture and an austere contemplative sect helps to explain the many-faceted cultural influence of Zen in Japan.

Another characteristic of the Kamakura denominations is that they are evangelistic—concerned with spreading the faith and making converts—in a way the older Buddhism was not. The older Buddhism took hold in its own more archaic ways, by working through the feudal structures, by assimilating itself subtly to folk religion. But the new groups made, and still make, a more modern kind of direct appeal to individuals to accept their proffered simple and sure keys. For evidence, we need only to consider that during the Kamakura period over half of Japanese Buddhists entered one of the new denominations, the phenomenal postwar growth of Nichiren Buddhism in Japan, and the fact that the only forms of Buddhism, Pure Land, Zen and Nichiren, which have had anything approaching widespread appeal in the Occident are actually Japanese Kamakura forms. The majority of Japanese-Americans who are Buddhist belong to Pure Land, partly because this denomination was exceptionally efficient in organizing overseas work. Some 200,000 Americans, largely of Occidental descent, have taken up Nichiren Buddhism since 1960. Zen has spread in its own way; while Zen organizations may not claim such a large number of actual "joiners," its cultural influence in the modern West has been inestimable, much greater than that of any other style of Buddhism.

This evangelistic orientation seems to be a part of the makeup of the Kamakura denominations, as it is of many faiths throughout the world with a simple, sure way. When one has found a simple way, a sure key, which like simple faith or simple chanting requires only a partial dislocation of natural life—and so frees one to "be saved" while continuing life as a householder or farmer or shopkeeper, and to talk among one's brethren—one tends to devote much new energy into bringing others into this way. It is the nature of a simple faith that it wants to spread, partly for reinforcement of believers, partly because it has not tapped off the energy and time that the priest or monk of an esoteric and complex way must put into his own salvation.

Let us look first at Pure Land Buddhism in Kamakura Japan. It has taken the form of two great denominations, Jodo (Pure Land) founded by Honen (1133–1212), and Jodo Shinshu (True Pure Land) founded by his disciple Shinran (1173–1263).

Amidism or Pure Land, and chanting *"Namu Amida Butsu"* ("Glory to Amida Buddha," the conventional expression of the faith which brings one to the western paradise), had been known in Japan prior to the Kamakura period, both as a part of the Tendai synthesis and as a growing folk religion movement. But it was Honen who was the real founder of denominational Amidism in Japan.[31] He studied at Hiei, became a priest, and retired to a hermitage to meditate. He said that he read all the Buddhist scriptures five times, but was not satisfied with religion as he had learned it. It gave him no peace in those troubled times. Then he achieved enlightenment by reading a book on Amida's vow. Salvation in accordance with Amida's vow was the peace he was seeking, for it depended not on one's own strength, but on the strength of another.

This he began to teach. Honen divided religious practice into two ways—Shodo, or the Holy Path, the way of a saintly ascetic or mighty adept who reaches Buddhahood through his own prodigious efforts; and Jodo, the Pure Land path of reliance on the help of Amida. Hope for mankind, he taught, lay in the latter. Indeed, in a deep sense it may even be more profoundly Buddhist than the Holy Path, for Pure Land's humility, confidence in outside help, and lack of assertion of mystical powers may be a better affirmation in practice of no self and dependent coinherence. But Honen did not criticize the Holy Path as a way for the few who could master it.

On the Pure Land path, only the recitation of the Nembutsu (the *"Namu Amida Butsu"*) with faith is necessary; the power of grace it releases is always and immediately available; even sinners are pardoned if they call on Amida in sincerity. Traditional Buddhist belief in karma and reincarnation does play a part, however, for good merit from preceeding existences can prepare one to believe in and long for rebirth in Amida's Pure Land.

Honen lived a long and successful life. Despite some reverses and persecutions, he was able to lay a firm foundation for Amidism in Japan. But he was a mild and quiet man, however saintly. It took another to make of this new faith a dynamic movement. That was Shinran, one of the most colorful and important of all figures in Japanese religion.[32] Sometimes called the Martin Luther of Japan, Shinran taught

---

[31]Harper Havelock Coates and Ryugaku Ishizuka, *Honen the Buddhist Saint* (Kyoto: Choin-in, 1925).

[32]Alfred Bloom, *Shinran's Gospel of Pure Grace* (Tucson: University of Arizona Press, 1965).

*The Great Buddha, Kamak-
ura, Japan. This is Amida,
the Buddha of the Pure
Land or Western Paradise.*

an even more radical salvation by faith alone than Honen, and implemented it thoroughly—he demanded married clergy, the removal of all figures in temples except Amida, and a new "secular" Buddhist way of life, for if salvation is by Nembutsu faith and that alone, all the rest of the vast baggage of Buddhist rites and rules collapses into superfluity.

Shinran was only eight years old when he was sent to the Tendai monastery at Mount Hiei, and he stayed there twenty years. He became a follower of Honen and, as he would put it, decided to risk his whole existence on Amida's saving power.

Shinran much appreciated what Honen meant by entitling one of his books *Senchaku Hongan Nembutsu-shu,* "Writings on Choosing the 'Original Vow' and the Nembutsu." *Senchaku,* "choosing," was for Shinran the clue to the unique appeal of Amidism. It does not mean merely "shopping around" for the best way to be saved, but implies a willingness to take a risk in faith. It means what we might call making an existential decision on faith. In this context, Honen's Pure Land option was not just another path among many, but was qualitatively different both from earlier Pure Land ideas and from other kinds of Buddhism.

Shinran seized on this difference, which so much answered his own spiritual anxiety. He stated he did not know, and did not care, whether the Nembutsu was really the means to rebirth in the Pure Land or the road to hell. "Even though," he said, "having been persuaded by Honen, I should go to hell through the Nembutsu I should not regret it." This sort of extreme statement, typical of Shinran, came out of a profound soul-searching in which he realized the ultimate utter helplessness of the human being, and that uncertainty and self-deception dog the attempt to try to save oneself through one's own efforts. Meditation, spiritual techniques, and philosophies only feed the ego they mean to kill. Outwardly people pretend to speak truth, but inwardly their hearts are filled with greed, anger, and deceitfulness— above all self-deceit. Shinran could not overcome his sense of human depravity. After testing all other paths, there was nothing left for him but the mercy of Amida, and this punctiliar meeting of unconditioned faith and grace he grasped with a happy zeal.

Shinran believed it is not even man who "chooses" Amida. Rather Amida's original vow chose all other beings to be saved. Even our faith is really the gift of Amida's "other power." "Shameless though I be and having no truth in my soul," he said, "yet the virtue of the Holy Name, the gift of him that is enlightened, is spread through the world through my words, although I am as I am."

Thus Amida's grace reaches for the sinner; moral qualifications are transcended. Honen had taught that "even a bad man will be saved, how much more a good man." Shinran reversed this to say, "Even a good man will be received, how much more a bad man!" Neither good nor bad counts, only the saving vow of Amida. Even the Nembutsu should not be said in order to be saved, but as an expression of gratitude toward the one who has chosen to redeem us, whatever we are.

Shinran was the most radical Amidist—a man with a single overwhelming experience and the temperament of a joyful warrior of faith. He lived ninety vigorous years, which included much travel, exile, leaving his monastic garb to marry and have children, and controversy—especially against those who would water down his faith, only even the slightest. He insisted that even one Nembutsu is enough, that no qualitative test can be made of faith, although he granted that good morality and good karma are not to be deprecated.

The Jodo Shinshu denomination he created became the largest in Japan, and was particularly popular among peasants and Japan's growing class of merchants and craftsmen. It soon enough lost its radical tone to inculcate conventional morality, and became instead the faith of a stable middle class, family centered and given to impressive temples and rites. But its clergy and married (indeed, commonly hereditary), its altars bear images only of Amida and Shinran, and its rites center on chanting the Nembutsu.

The militant Kamakura spirit in religion is supremely manifested in Nichiren (1222–82).[33] The son of a poor fisherman, Nichiren as an intelligent and perceptive youth was haunted by two questions. He wondered why, in the struggle between the old Heian regime and the rebellious warlords, the imperial armies had been defeated despite the countless incantations offered on their behalf by the Tendai and Shingon clerics. And he asked, like so many in his day, how one could experience the certainty of salvation. Both of these are serious themes, which were to become

[33]Masaharu Anesaki, *Nichiren the Buddhist Prophet* (Cambridge, Mass.: Harvard University Press, 1916).

pillars of the faith he finally offered the world: the religious interpretation of historical event, and the quest for absolute self-integration.

In 1242 Nichiren went to study at Mount Hiei, where he stayed until 1253.
Under the influence of Tendai, he became convinced the answer to his problems
lay in the Lotus Sutra. Not only in its teachings, although they are the supreme
expression of Buddhist truth, but in the gesture of accepting the Lotus Sutra as the
sole bearer of Buddhist faith and authority. In 1253 he began a prophetic mission,
urging the whole nation to return to the Lotus Sutra. The calamities plaguing the
nation, tokens that the last age had come, could only be reversed by such an act of
corporate faith in the Lotus Sutra. Further, Nichiren said, foreign invasions would
strike Japan because of its false faith—and when the Mongols invaded in 1274 and
1281 he claimed to be vindicated.

Nichiren emphasized that the Lotus Sutra taught the oneness of the three
Buddha-bodies—the essential, heavenly, and earthly. He bitterly attacked Shingon,
Pure Land, and Zen for, as he saw it, stressing one and neglecting the others. The
point was more than merely an obscure quibble, for it set the tone in Buddhist
theological language for a basic Nichiren religious experience—knowing the presence and unity of all planes of existence in the here and now. Essence, heaven, and
earth, plus the gods, titans, and hells and all the other places of rebirth, are here and
now—a person can go through them all in a half hour. Matter and spirit are not
separate realms, but one—a spiritual cause, like the chant, can produce a material
result, and one's environment affects one's life. This unifying, here-and-now-
centered insight, so much stressed by modern Nichiren people, has its roots in
Nichiren's insistence on the unity of the three forms of Buddha-expression, which
he saw in the Lotus Sutra. It makes him a prophet of a faith for the modern world,
which tends to forget heaven.

He was modern in other ways too. He made much of national corporate life and
destiny, and was aware of the religious meaning of historical transitions—both
kinds of awareness far less developed in the medieval Orient than today. Nichiren
saw Japan as a unity that should accept the Lotus Sutra as a unity, which would
suffer reward or punishment as a unity depending on its faith and which had a
special destiny in the world as a nation. He believed that his day was a turning point
in history, when the mappo, or last age, was entering in, and in this day only the
Lotus Sutra was effective. But this was no cause for pessimism, for a new world
could be built on this faith. It would start from Japan and spread throughout the
earth.

The "practical" expression of Nichiren's Buddhism was said by him to center
on three points: the chanting of the daimoku, the chant *"Nam Myoho Renge Kyo"*
("Glory to the Marvelous Teaching of the Lotus Sutra"—although Nichiren people
give it a deeper meaning of referring to the unity of the absolute and the phenomenal
world through sound); the·*Gohonzon,* a scroll originally made by Nichiren containing names of the main figures in the Lotus Sutra set up as an object of concentration
while chanting; and the *kaidan,* the "ordination platform." The last derives from
Nichiren's insistence that his movement should have the right to ordain its own
priestly succession; it can be taken to typify the movement's tendency to be a

dynamic, exclusive, closely knit group. Another characteristic is veneration of Nichiren himself, for the prophet identified himself with a suffering bodhisattva in the Lotus Sutra, and most of his followers today believe him to be the bodhisattva or Buddha for this age, superseding Gautama, and refer to no other authority than him and the Lotus Sutra.

From the beginning Nichiren Buddhism had a rigorist quality; his disciples did not shrink from using contentious and disruptive means to spread the faith. While for several centuries his faith then settled down to become a fairly ordinary denomination, Nichiren's thought was not without its effect on Japanese nationalism and modernization. Since World War II, a new Nichiren movement, the Soka Gakkai (actually a layman's organization within Nichiren Shoshu, the largest of the Nichiren sects), founded by persons who suffered persecution from the wartime nationalist regime, has grown remarkably. Placing special emphasis on the power of chanting to achieve results in this life, after the this-worldly promises of Nichiren faith to augur a new age of human fulfillment, this tightly organized order has shown the force of Nichiren as a prophet for the modern world. Thanks largely to the work of Soka Gakkai ("Value-creation Society"), about a third of the Japanese people are now related to Nichiren faith.[34]

Since the basic principles of Zen have already been presented in connection with its sources in Chinese Ch'an, it will be sufficient here just to make a few comments on its Japanese development. Ch'an was transmitted to Japan by two men, Eisai (1141–1215) and Dogen (1200–53). Both were priests educated at Mount Hiei, and both like many others were looking for something more. Each went to China, and each came in contact with one of two major traditions of Ch'an. Eisai brought back the Lin-chi school, which became Rinzai in Japan; Dogen returned with the Ts'ao-tung, Soto in Japan.

The two men differed in more than sect. Eisai had an inclusive mentality; he brought back from China with Ch'an Neo-Confucianism and various cultural expressions of Ch'an, such as tea and simple naturalistic paintings. He was willing to compromise with the military rulers of Japan and the other Buddhists in order to assure the success of his monastery, and indeed it did become fashionable among the new elite.

Dogen, on the other hand, was a purist and interested only in Zen. When he returned from China to Japan, he came with "empty hands," bearing no sutras, pictures, or images. He founded his own "pure Zen" monastery, which refused compromise with either temple or state, and emphasized simply *zazen,* or Zen meditation, avoiding intellectualism or cultural flourishes. Instead Dogen was impressed with the fact that Ch'an monks did their own manual labor and lived a genuinely simple life, both materially and spiritually.

Besides being a denomination that administers temples not remarkably different from any others, Zen in Japan is two things: a way of monastic life and spiritual practice, and a distinctive esthetic and cultural influence.

As a spiritual method, Japanese Zen like Chinese Ch'an emphasizes spontane-

---

[34]See James W. White, *The Sokagakkai and Mass Society* (Stanford, Calif.: Stanford University Press, 1970).

Dragon and Sun

ous enlightenment welling up in meditation, or sparked by encounters with a master. Rinzai emphasized the use of *koans,* the Zen puzzles such as "What is the sound of one hand clapping?" (Hakuin (1685–1768), who revitalized Rinzai Zen in the eighteenth century and preached to monks and peasants alike, elaborately systematized the koans.

Dogen, on the other hand, mistrusted koans, for he felt the sudden enlightenment they were meant to incite indicated overpreoccupation with momentary experience. Rather, his monks sat meditating facing a bare wall (Rinzai monks sit facing each other across the meditation hall), just "sitting quietly, doing nothing." They focus on posture and breathing, counting breaths or just being "mindful" of breathing, as quiet devices for stilling the "monkey mind."

In both cases, the idea is to discover one's true, spontaneous nature beneath the level of impulse, ideation, and self-consciousness that beclouds our ordinary lives. Zen life, meditation, and puzzles are designed to stop this swirling surface. This means a highly disciplined life. Some may confuse spontaneity and living in the immediacy of the void with living according to every whim and appetite, but the life of a Zen monastery is certainly the opposite of that. One meditates for hours absolutely still, while a proctor goes up and down with a stick to strike one at any sign of restlessness or sleep.

Zen is not giving free rein to natural impulse, but rather freeing the truly natural *from* impulse. It cuts out, at the cost of tremendous discipline, all that is not truly natural. The ordinary man has too much—the natural is there, but lost among the excess, which must be pruned away by control and discipline to allow the natural to stand alone.

It is in this light that the Zen cultural contributions can be understood, for they are attempts to demonstrate the same thing. In one medium or another, they strive to create beauty by pruning away, by allowing a single simple core of exquisite, perhaps momentary, naturalness and beauty (ultimately the same thing) to stand alone, free of entanglements. Meditation on such an object may of itself give *satori,* or sudden, spontaneous enlightenment, beyond words.

Zen painting, for example, is often mostly white spaces; the point is to convey just the bare essential "feel" of a branch, or a face with character, in a few strokes—but precisely the right ones, splashed on with a control so perfect as to seem spontaneous. The Zen art of swordsmanship tells us that the perfect swordsman does not have to strike a blow at all; his opponent is defeated, and retires in disarray, just by seeing the utterly controlled poise and mien of the master. And if the Zen swordsman does have to strike, a single thrust as sure as a painter's hand will be sufficient.

The Zen-related form of poetry, the seventeen-syllable *haiku* verse, seeks in the same manner to encapsulate a perfect and significant but understated image in a minimum of words. Perhaps the best known of all is this one by the wandering Zen poet Basho (1644–94):

> An ancient pond,
> A frog jumps in—
> The sound of water.

These lines have been said to sum up the whole of Buddhism in a few words. (Think of the pond as Nirvana, and compare the poem to the "implosion" image of the Buddha's entry into Nirvana in the last chapter.)

The same approach obtains in the tea ceremony, a fixture of traditional Japanese culture developed by a Zen priest. The tea ceremony is a formal ritual designed to suggest the Zen experience of the absolute in the ordinary, and the natural in that perfect simplicity which comes out of perfect control. Here, one does nothing but make and serve thick, whipped green tea in a plain, gardenlike environment. But if the gestures are correct, the act is suffused with a grace that makes it an inseparable part of the universe, and so of the Buddha nature.

Finally, there is the Zen garden. A Zen monastery has a garden around it, a garden with raked gravel and moss and gnarled trees. The objects will not be spaced in the geometric patterns of a European formal garden, as at Versailles, but in a seemingly natural and irregular way, which nonetheless enchants and satisfies. Like all the other Zen arts, it manifests the truly natural by pruning and control.

Early one mild spring morning, I sat overlooking the world famous stone garden of the Ryoanji Zen temple in Kyoto. This garden is simply a large rectangle of raked white gravel in which are set five rough boulders, "islands" of rock, with bits of moss around them. The big stones are in a seemingly random pattern, yet one cannot quite leave them alone. For long periods I gazed at them, torn between the intellect's insatiable desire to make everything into meaningful relationships, and the inherent meaninglessness of this, which was yet a work of art. Over and over again, I felt I had almost but not quite seen the meaning of the rocks' relationship, that I knew it but could not quite say it. Finally, like a koan, the rocks and their relationship brought me up against the futility of the pattern-making mind in dealing with certain ultimates. In gazing at the garden, I saw now random bits of moss and stone, now a cluster of galaxies in the trackless void of space.

THE JAPANESE NEW RELIGIONS

One of the most fascinating of all contemporary religious phenomena is a set of groups called *Shinko Shukyo,* "newly-arisen religions," in Japan. While most of them have earlier roots, they grew and flourished tremendously in the postwar years of disillusionment with traditional life, including conventional Shinto and Buddhism. The "Golden Age" of these religions was the 1950s, when many were growing at fantastic rates and in some the original charismatic leader was still alive. But in the last quarter of the century they are still very much a part of the Japanese scene, and (if new Nichiren groups, like Soka Gakkai, be counted as new religions as they usually are) one in three Japanese have some relationship to one of them.

The new religions present a vividly diverse panorama of doctrines and practices. Tenrikyo ("Religion of Heavenly Wisdom") members perform sacred dances with gestures of sweeping movement to symbolize clearing away spiritual dust. Members of Perfect Liberty, believing that "Life is art" and that all aspects of life need to be integrated into a total work of art, emphasize sports and when possible have a golf course by their church. The Church of World Messianity offers johrei, in which the "Divine Light of God" is "channeled" through the cupped hand of one who administers it to a recipient.

Nonetheless, they have significant common characteristics as well. They are founded by strong, shamanistic figures. In this they represent a very old Japanese pattern repeated in such men as Kobo Daishi, Shinran, and Nichiren, and more recently in figures like Miki Nakayama (1798–1887), foundress of Tenrikyo, one of the oldest and most prototypical of the new religions.

Miki was of prosperous farmer stock, but she and her husband became increasingly poor amid the economic decline and social trouble of Japan during the first half of the nineteenth century, before its remarkable modernization set in. Times of change and upheaval, of course, are generally productive of new religious movements. Then, when she was forty-one, in 1838, Miki's oldest son suffered a severe pain in the leg while working. An exorcist, probably a yamabushi, was called; he gave a series of treatments. In this ritual, it was customary for a female assistant, really a medium, to go into trance. She would then be possessed by a deity who would reveal the cause of the illness and to whom prayers would be addressed for healing. On one occasion the regular medium was unable to be present, and Miki took her place.

The deity who spoke through Miki's lips said that he was the True and Original God, and that he wished to use Miki's body as a shrine to save the world. From then on, she lived wholly as the vessel of this holy one, known to Tenrikyo as the Father-Mother God. Through her came the sacred scriptures of the religion, the lovely divine dances, and the site of its great temple, located where it is believed the creation of the world began and divine dew will fall from heaven to mark the inception of the paradisal age. There is a shrine to Miki herself in this temple, as in all Tenrikyo churches.

Tenrikyo shows roots in old shamanistic motifs, but also emphasizes belief in one God. This belief contrasts with Shinto polytheism; minority withdrawal religious movements have always tended to be more monotheistic than folk religions.

In all the new religions we see evidence of syncretism. Ideas from East and West are combined into new mixes; Jesus is quoted in their literature along with the Buddha. Seicho-no-Ie, for example, a group teaching that "All is perfect," draws both from the Western "New Thought," positive thinking tradition, and from Mahayana belief in the universal unstained One Mind.

Modernity is particularly apparent in belief in a coming paradisal new age. Far removed from traditional pessimism, the new religions have an intense optimism about the human future. Soon, by divine action, this weary world will be transformed into a paradise. Mankind has a glorious future, not in some distant heaven, but here in this world, and all will partake in it through reincarnation. Indeed, the new age is foreshadowed in the life of the founder and the communal experience of the group.

Communal life is especially represented in the Sacred Center. Like Tenri City of Tenrikyo, Soka Gakkai's new glorious temple on the slopes of Mount Fuji, and the headquarters of Perfect Liberty with its super golf course near Osaka, the new religions tend to have gorgeous centers, often large communities, which are places of pilgrimage and show what the world will be like when the new age comes in.

The new religions have closely knit organizations. Everyone is taken seriously and given a part. This makes them appealing to the dislocated millions moved far from ancestral shrines to impersonal industrial cities by modernization.

The new religions emphasize that an individual makes his or her own world, health, and prosperity, through the attitude of his or her own mind. Like the "positive thinking" philosophy in the West, and partly influenced by it, they tend to place full responsibility for one's condition in the individual—a ramification of the modern isolation of the individual, in contrast to archaic village or tribal society and religion. Part of this is expressed in their concern for healing, but it goes further than that.

It is not possible here to discuss individual new religions in detail. Some perspective may be provided, however, by noting that they fall into three main groups.[35]

First, there are the "old" new religions, which go back to the early nineteenth century, to the time of the breakdown of old social patterns before modernization. Two from this era are important today: Tenrikyo, already discussed, and Konkokyo. The founder of Konkokyo, Bunjiro Kawate, called Konko Daijin, also had a shamanistic vision in which a folk religion deity revealed himself to be actually a monotheistic high god. The major distinctive rite of this religion is a practice of personal spiritual guidance somewhat comparable to Roman Catholic confession.

Second, there are the Nichiren groups: Soka Gakkai, already discussed, affiliated with the old Nichiren Shoshu denomination; and two new groups, which also venerate the Lotus Sutra—Reiyukai and Rissho Kosei Kai.

Third, there are the Omoto groups. Omoto, meaning "great source," was the name of a group founded by a peasant woman, Nao Deguchi, and her son-in-law and adoptive son, Onisaburo Deguchi (1871–1948). The latter was a colorful spiritualist, mystic, organizer, and social commentator, with a remarkable genius for religious creativity. Omoto emphasizes the existence of a spiritual world (Onisaburo and Nao delivered much information about it in trance), the coming of a new age and a new messiah, healing, mental powers, the creation of paradise on earth, the religious importance of art. The three most important new religions in the Omoto tradition are World Messianity, Seicho-no-Ie, and Perfect Liberty.

The founders of the first two were at one time associates of Onisaburo Deguchi. The Church of World Messianity has emphasized the Omoto teaching about the coming of a new age marked by increase in the divine light (channeled through johrei) and has carried over modifications of certain Omoto techniques. Seicho-no-Ie has emphasized the mind-is-all philosophy and meditation techniques of Omoto,

[35]This division is based on that in Harry Thomsen, *The New Religions of Japan* (Tokyo and Rutland, Vt.: Charles E. Tuttle Co., 1963), which is the most readable general introduction to the subject. See also Robert S. Ellwood, Jr., *The Eagle and the Rising Sun: Americans and the New Religions of Japan* (Philadelphia: The Westminster Press, 1974).

as well as borrowing from Buddhism and Western "New Thought." Perfect Liberty, while apparently not directly influenced by Omoto, shares its emphasis on art, wholeness, and personal spiritual guidance; this is the religion that makes much of sports and says "Life is art," but it also has a procedure for members to receive individual written answers to spiritual or personal problems, and a special prayer technique with symbolic gestures.

This is the story of Japanese religion: a long pilgrimage from ancient clan kami to modern philosophies of health and success, but preserving profoundly shamanistic and charismatic themes all the way through.

SIX

GODS, KINGS, AND MYSTERIES

Religions of the Ancient Near East and Europe

The Parthenon, ancient temple on the Acropolis of Athens to Athena, patroness of the city.

INTRODUCTION

Now we will look at some cultures that lie directly in the stream of history which leads up to modern Europe and America. Some impressions of these cultures are familiar to most people: almost everyone has seen pictures of pyramids and Greek temples, and has heard of gods named Zeus, Mercury, and Wotan. But actual information about the religious life behind them is apt to be spotty. In this chapter we will provide contexts in which what everyone knows about ancient religion can be placed.

The cultures discussed here cannot be lumped together, but certain motifs do run through them. Broadly speaking, they are at a stage when cosmic religion is making the long, slow transition into literate, historically conscious civilization. They have strong ties to both sides. The temple with its holy precincts and rituals, the agricultural cycle, and sacred sovereigns point back to cosmic religion. The increasing writing of philosophy and history, and the growth of desire for individual salvation, point ahead.

All these religious cultures except Zoroastrianism have polytheism, belief in many gods, in common. It is therefore necessary to have an empathetic understanding of what polytheism means as a religious experience. Polytheism is more than just acknowledging a plural number of gods; it suggests a different *kind* of religious world view than monotheism. To the monotheist, or believer in one God, the universe is united under a single intelligence and is pointed toward a single purpose. This means that strong demands and unconditional choices are presented to the individual, for some things accord to the single will and purpose, and some do not.

The polytheist instead detects multiple forces, values, and directions in the world. This is not to say he or she does not know strong behavior imperatives and strong loyalties; these will be there, enforced by community, ruler, and a high god. Yet at the same time the experience of divinity is of a different tone from monotheism—it is complex, shifting, open to subtle variations.

The polytheist's universe is a complex of spirits corresponding to the many inconsistent moods of nature and the human psyche, and of different peoples and places. As in Shinto, every glade and waterfall may have its little spirit who should be respected by the passerby; every human preoccupation—the frenzy of war, the ecstasy of love, the diligence of work—is the seizure of a kind of divinity, absolute in its own time. The wheeling of the seasons, important places of the home like threshold and hearth, the activities of seedtime and harvest, are all apertures to something beyond the merely human, and so are also parts of the map of the invisible world.

It must be realized, however, that ancient polytheism did not appear as the result of someone's attempt to categorize everything systematically as some god or other. System-making appeared much later, after the plural gods were already there. Instead, the developed polytheisms of these ancient civilizations were a result of the coming together of many smaller tribes and towns, each with its own patron deity, local spirits, and myths. Trade and the formation of empires created elaborate polytheism, not deliberate theologizing.

Imperial rulers in the ancient Mediterranean as in China and Japan often bolstered polytheistic religions. They found that a heavenly court and bureaucracy paralleling the hub of the earthly empire, and the unity-in-diversity of a polytheistic system, were great ideological aids to imperial control of vast territories. The sovereign was the religion's chief patron and priest, if not himself divine.

A second frequent feature, in fact, of some of these religious cultures is sacred kingship. Details differed, but often it was held that the ruler was aligned with the structures of reality in a very special way, which meant that his accession, rituals, and decrees were divine mysteries which brought life and renewal to the society, and even hope of immortality.

A third common theme moves in a different direction from polytheism and sacred kingship. It is increasing interest, as most of these systems changed over the centuries, in individual devotion and initiatory experience. As time went on, mystery rites offering personal immortality and relationship to gods, once the preserve of priests and kings, were more and more open to all who felt drawn to them, and desired a mystic passage through death to rebirth.

EGYPTIAN RELIGION

Ancient Egypt has seemed to observers ancient and modern a land possessed by powerful but baffling religion. The wealth of its priesthood and the monumental splendor of its temples with their bizarre animal-headed gods; the divinity of the pharoah who was at once Horus, the sun, the falcon, and after death Osiris the resurrected judge of all souls; the magnificently engineered pyramids with their testimony to a consuming hope of immortality—all this suggests religion of remarkable complexity and richness. Indeed, the further one explores this world the more baffling it becomes. In the texts, gods seem to be identified with a kaleidoscope of symbols, roles, and theological systems, all inconsistent and yet all applied simultaneously with equanimity. As one scholar has put it, "The impression made on the modern mind is that of a people searching in the dark for a key to truth and, having found not one but many keys resembling the pattern of the lock, retaining all lest perchance the appropriate one should be discarded."[1]

This was the outlook of the land of the Nile, where the floodwaters rose year after year to fertilize the fields, and the divine pharaoh ruled a generally calm and well-tuned state. To attempt to describe this religion in an overly systematic way would do violence to its own nature; one can only jump into the middle and splash in several directions, until some of the main currents begin to show themselves.

As one might expect in a warm and nearly cloudless land, the sun was of major importance. The day-orb was identified with most of the main masculine deities— Amon-Re, Aton, Horus, Atum—and was apparently an original principle object of worship. Venerated outdoors before an obelisk, the sun was also the pharaoh, falcon, and sacred scarab beetle pushing his ball of mud.

Animals were much venerated by the Egyptians; they were sacred to various gods and identified with them in a symbolic way. Many gods were pictured as animal-headed. Thoth was a baboon, Anubis a jackel, Sekhmet a lion. Many temples kept pampered animals belonging to a god; upon death the animal might be mummified.

For example, Apis, the sacred bull at a temple of the god Ptah, was believed to be the "living soul" of Osiris—Osiris who was also vegetation, the god brought back to life, judge of the dead, the deceased pharaoh, and an ancient giver of civilization. The bull was attended by a large retinue of priests, and his movements, choice of place to stand, and appetite were considered divine oracles. After twenty-five years he was secretly killed by the priests, but the people were told he had thrown himself into the river; a new bull was inaugurated with great festival.

The oldest and most important deities of all were the sun gods—really the same under different names—connected with creation. The priests of different centers, however, had varying myths or theologies about the beginning.

At Heliopolis, they said Atum was the creator who appeared on or as the first hillock, which emerged, like land out of the Nile floods, from the original chaos. He generated the first gods mating with himself, and they produced further generations in pairs: Shu and Tefnet as air and moisture, Geb and Nut as earth and sky, and so on.

At Memphis this account was rationalized by making Ptah, the craftsman-god, the central figure who appeared on the primal hill. He created the other gods intellectually—Horus was his heart or thought, Thoth his tongue or word.

Amon was perhaps the most profound of the Egyptian gods, although relatively late in achieving prominence. He was the sun, symbolized by rays said to reach to the ends of the earth. He was also a "breath" which infused all things, and was of course pharaoh, the visible ruler and all-pervader. At Thebes and Hermopolis, Amon-Re (Amon-Ra), two fused solar deities of great antiquity, was worshipped.

A few other important deities may be named. Thoth, a scribe with the head of an ibis or baboon and connected with the moon, was god of wisdom, science, and reconciliation. Sobek, crocodile-headed, was god of the Nile, water, and fertility.

---

[1] I. E. S. Edwards, *The Pyramids of Egypt* (West Drayton, England: Penguin Books, 1947), pp. 27–28.

The ancient Egyptian temple at Karnak.

The jackel-headed Anubis was god of death and the mortuary sciences. There was Bastet the cat-god; Min, a goddess of fertility; and Hathor, the cow and mother, a goddess sometimes fierce and sometimes beautiful.

Best known of all Egyptian gods is the triad of Osiris, Isis, and Horus. They became increasingly important in Egypt and were the basis of a famous cult all over the Mediterranean world in the days of the Roman Empire.

It was said that Osiris, the life of plants and giver of culture to humanity, was killed and cut into pieces by his jealous brother, Set. But Isis, the "throne" of pharaoh and wife of Osiris, gathered up the pieces and with the help of Thoth brought him magically back to life. Then Horus, Osiris' son, defeated Set in vengeance, in the process losing his left eye (the moon); it was restored by Thoth.

This battle was ritually re-enacted with pharaoh taking the role of Horus; the restored eye was a powerful amulet and a byword for something magical, powerful, and precious, which was lost and found again. After his resuscitation, Osiris became judge and lord in the underworld; through identification with him in mystery rites believers could be brought to life after death.

Turning to the "practical" side of Egyptian religion, let us look at how the gods of Egypt were worshipped. The fundamental intent of temple ritual was to strengthen the life of the god, who in turn would sustain the life of the people. Ritual was a redoing of the primordial coming-into-being of the gods from the original ocean of chaos. As the shrine was opened and the deity took on fullness of life through consuming a banquet, he was treated as one would that other divinity, pharaoh. Like modern Hindu gods in their temples, his image was a king in the midst of his court.

Before a new statue of a deity was used, a ceremony called the "Opening of the Mouth" was employed to transmit life to it. The image was purified with water, natron, and incense; then sacrificial animals were slaughtered and presented before it, presumably in a transference of life from the victims to the new image. Then the statue was dressed with robes and jewels, anointed and given royal emblems, and finally presented with incense and a banquet.

Daily rituals followed the pattern of the latter part of this rite. The temple was not a place of public worship, but the dwelling place of the god; one intruded on his privacy no more than one would that of anyone else in his home. Only the priests, his servants, were admitted to the innermost chamber where the deity lived. Their job was to sustain the world order by vitalizing the gods with food and hymns. This was done three times a day, the most important worship being at sunrise.

The priest began the morning ritual by purifying himself in a sacred pool. At the temple he would light a fire and burn incense, then he opened the door of the small, richly painted box in which the divine image itself resided. Upon facing his divine lord, the priest would immediately cast himself upon the ground. He presented hymns and incense and circumambulations. Next the image was anointed with unguents, dressed, and bejewelled. The eyelids were painted anew with green and black. A meal was slowly and reverently presented, each course being raised before the presence. Thus, if as was most likely the image was of one of the modes of the sun-god, he had been reborn mystically within the temple even as he was rising physically without, and the world was renewed for another day on both inner and outer planes. The food offering was called the Eye of Horus—it represented a precious thing lost and restored.

Significantly, before the enactment of a ritual at which the pharaoh served as chief priest, the divine king was prepared—that is, his divine nature was strengthened—in a similar manner. In the great rituals in which pharaoh was chief officiant Egyptian religion most of all came to life.

At the accession of a new pharaoh, a mystery play was enacted of the death of Osiris, emphasizing his rising again in the Other World, and in this world as Osiris' son Horus, the new pharaoh. Thoth says, "Horus has grown up and takes possession of his Eye," and this was the motif of the drama. A big pillar was raised symbolizing the resurrection of the new pharaoh's predecessor in the Other World. A mock battle was fought between the "Children of Set" and the "Children of Horus," the latter played by members of the pharaoh's family. Food, called the Eye of Horus as in temple worship, was offered the new sovereign, and the double crown was bestowed upon him. Finally, scenes represented the transfiguration of the new monarch's predecessor into the Lord of the Dead.[2]

After thirty years of reign, the pharaohs often performed what was called the Sed festival. In a sense it was a re-enactment of the accession rites to celebrate and renew the pharaoh's divine strength. The sovereign sat on two thrones successively and was again crowned as King of Upper and Lower Egypt. A great pillar representing the raising of Osiris was erected by the Nile. The pharaoh did a peculiar sort of dance four times through a field, dressed only in a short skirt with an animal tail hanging behind. He then visited temples of the gods. The Sed would thereafter be repeated every three or four years.

At harvest time, the pharaoh celebrated the Min festival. He would enter a temporary shrine in a field white with harvest with his queen and a procession. There the queen walked around the pharaoh as one would circumambulate a shirne, and the sovereign cut the first sheaf of grain. At the great shrine of Osiris at Abydos, an image of the god was made of earth and barley seed, and the statue was made to "live" by letting the barley sprout and grow until it became a man of green representing Osiris at once vegetation and the lord risen from the dead.

Egyptian religion had countless variations; the preceeding should give some impression of the flavor of its gods and rites. It gives a feeling of incredible diversity and seeming inconsistency. Osiris "is" at once a bull, a green man of barley, a upraised pillar, a dead pharaoh, and much more. But this is not because the Egyptians were incapable of straight thinking. To the contrary, they were a most perceptive and intelligent people, and in a real sense the confusing religious variety reflects their perceptivity and intelligence, not naivete. They could see that the great forces in the universe manifest themselves in a tremendous diversity of ways, that nothing is simple—yet there are basic forces which can only be called divine. All the above forms of Osiris, for example, involve the profound themes of fertility and life returning after it seemed dead, in ritual symbol, plant, animal, and human life after death.

To the Egyptians the gods and rites were complex and jumbled because that is the way the universe is—yet through the universe ran forces for the supremacy of light, life, and order over darkness and chaos. The former, represented by Amon, Osiris, the Nile, and the pharaoh, are augmented and strengthened by all the signs and symbols on the side of life.

The victory of light and life is the motif of the mortuary cult and the belief in immortality, the most famous aspects of Egyptian religion. As with everything else, there is inconsistency about the exact nature of the afterlife, but most typically it is the Field of Reeds to the West, a land of perpetual spring and fertility, where life continues much as here but happier. It was also said that a deceased pharaoh rides in the boat of the sun, especially in its nocturnal passage under the earth. At first only the pharaoh was thought to be immortal, then his nobles were believed to accom-

[2]Henri Frankfort, *Kingship and the Gods* (Chicago: University of Chicago Press, 1948), pp. 126–30.

pany him "like stars," then his servants to assist him, and finally everyone was said able to have immortality in Osiris.

Mummification was a preparation for immortality. The process was to extract the brain and entrails, then apply a mixture of resin, natron, and animal fat to the body. The corpse was wrapped, covered with amulets, and placed in a mummy case. The rituals that accompanied the procedure served to identify the dead king with Osiris. A long procession took it to the tomb—a pyramid in the greatest days—by way of Busiris and Abydos, cities sacred to Osiris. The tomb was always on the opposite side of the Nile from where the deceased had lived. Before being put in the burial chamber, the mummy was set upright and the "Opening of the Mouth" ceremony enacted on its behalf.

The first *Pyramid Texts* (c. 2345 B.C. and the earliest written sources) suggest that the king's entry to the fields of immortality was based more on temerity than merit. In one it says he hunts, lassos, and devours various gods in order to acquire their immortality. In another he is represented as having to convince by various deceits the ferryman who transports voyagers across the "Lily Lake" to the "Fields where the gods were begotten, over which the gods rejoice on their New Years Day" that he is entitled to enter that land.[3] Very different is the mood of the later *Book of the Dead,* describing the judgment of all souls by Osiris when immortality to extended to everyone. Then, in the courts of the other side, the heart is weighed against a feather symbolizing truth. Thoth did the weighing, while Osiris presided.[4]

It should not be thought that the ancient Egyptians were preoccupied with religion and the life after death in a somber way, or exclusive of joy in the life of this world. It is true they had countless gods and temples, great mortuary pyramids, and a wealthy priesthood. But Egypt was rich. There was enough for this and a good life in the present world. The Egyptians knew how to enjoy the latter, just as one gets the impression they enjoyed their colorful religion.

By ancient standards Egypt was a prosperous and fortunate society. The floods of the Nile were steady, the government was stronger and stabler than most, for millenia the Land of the Nile was usually out of the way of enemies. There was enough wealth for all to have enough to eat most of the time, and for the middle and upper classes to enjoy lovely homes, gay parties, and sports.

The priesthood, to be sure, was rich in land and privileges, and became more so as time went on—however, the temples were not only places where the gods dwelt, but also centers of cultural tradition and education. Slavery was certainly part of the social system. But as ancient societies go, Egypt—far from being the god-ridden tyranny sometimes pictured in older books—was a relatively relaxed, humane, and worldly wise land with bulging granaries, whose many gods were affirmers of the good life here and now, and whose afterlife was but a perpetuation of it. Even the pyramids, we are now told, may not have been built by slaves groaning under the lash, but by small groups of skilled peasants recruited in the off-season, who went home full of bread and drunk with beer at the pharaoh's expense.[5]

[3]Edwards, *The Pyramids of Egypt,* pp. 30–32.

[4]E. A. Wallis Budge, *The Book of the Dead* (New York: University Books, 1960).

[5]Lionel Carson, *Ancient Egypt* (New York: Time-Life Books, 1965), pp. 92–115, 134.

One puzzling, anomalous figure appears amid the broad, tolerant stream of Egyptian culture. That is Akhenaton, who was pharaoh 1379–62 B.C. He opposed the prevailing worship of Amon and the other gods, and their priesthoods. Abetted by his beautiful and strong-willed wife Nefertiti, Akhenaton sought to introduce in their place the worship of Aton, the solar disc. To introduce another god would have been no great thing in Egypt, but Akhenaton took the unprecedented step of ordering the temples of the other gods (especially Amon, whom he hated) closed and defaced, and the name of Amon wiped out wherever it appeared. Akhenaton thought of Aton as his father, and offered beautiful hymns in his praise. He constructed a new capital city, centered around a temple of the great Aton symbolized by sunbeams ending in hands of help and blessing. But the priests of Amon whom he persecuted apparently succeeded in intrigue against Akhenaton. Nothing is known of the manner of his death, but when he was succeeded by his son-in-law Tutankamon, the Atonic reforms were suppressed and then forgotten.[6]

Akhenaton, original, narrow-minded yet seized by a lofty purpose, is controversial even after nearly thirty-five centuries. Some have interpreted him as a great spiritual figure, a royal prophet of universal ethical monotheism and repudiator of superstition and priestcraft. Others see him as a proto-fascist, an intolerant fanatic seeking to centralize his state around an imposed, lockstep ideology. Two things are certain: the new Aton ideology impelled a cultural outburst which produced a brilliant new naturalism in art and a simple sincerity in verse; and the easygoing Egyptians soon tired of Atonism and its propagator, and wanted no more of such zealotry from the throne.

This fascinating episode was only a moment, however, in the long chronicle of Egypt's multiform religion, which like the River Nile itself was broad and deep, changing with the seasons yet always the same, branching into a delta of substreams, and touching with nourishment every patch of the ancient land.

MESOPOTAMIAN RELIGION

Superficially, the ancient civilization of the Valley of the Two Rivers, modern Iraq, seems comparable to ancient Egypt. Both were agrarian cultures in dry areas watered by the floods of mighty rivers. Both embraced a rich polytheism of which the king was the chief ritualist. But the further one looks, the more differences appear.

First, the rivers were different. Whereas the Nile is superbly constant in its rise and fall, suggesting a stable, reliable, abundant universe, the Tigris and Euphrates are fickle. They suggest divinities whose hands are prone to quaver, sending forth drought or destructive flood as often as abundant harvests, and violent storm as impartially as sun or food.

Second, Mesopotamia is much more exposed than Egypt to war. Egypt was remarkably isolated from possible invaders; for long centuries at a time, its people

---

[6]On Akhenaton, see Barbara Mertz, *Temples, Tombs, and Hieroglyphs* (New York: Coward-McCann, Inc., 1964), Chapter VIII.

were able to live preoccupied mostly with their own affairs. But Mesopotamia was an arena of continuing internal and external wars.

The ancient Mesopotamians were a powerful and creative people. Yet their culture gives a feel of an unstable and uncertain civilization compared to Egypt. It is the civilization of a people wracked by anxiety and emotional peaks and abysses, who viewed the cosmos and its gods as often cruel, and who too often reflected these gods in their own behavior. They were also people capable of great skepticism, and just beneath its surface was pessimism.

The ancient Mesopotamians were not one but three peoples. The earliest were the Sumerians, who flourished in the lower part of the Mesopotamian basin approximately 4000–2000 B.C. The Sumerians are a rather mysterious people; it is not known just where they came from or to what other peoples they were related, for their language is not similar to any other known tongue.[7] Apparently they derived from the more mountainous areas to the north of Iraq and succeeded in pushing out others to establish the site of their civilization.

Eventually Semitic peoples (that is, peoples related to the Hebrews and Arabs) managed to press the Sumerians south and finally absorbed them and their culture. This took place around 2050 B.C. For the next 1,500 years the valley was ruled more or less alternatively by two closely related but rivalrous Semitic peoples, the Babylonians and Assyrians. Each spoke dialects of the Akkadian tongue, written with signs called cuneiform, made by wedge-shaped instruments in clay. Finally, after conquest by the Persian emperor Cyrus in 538 B.C., ancient Assyria and Babylonia came to an end as independent nations and cultures.

The Assyrians and Babylonians, although mighty at war, borrowed much of their culture and particularly their religion from the conquered Sumerians. Indeed, the Sumerian language was used for religious rites and texts all through the Babylonian-Assyrian period, just as Latin was in the Roman Catholic world up to modern times. In this brief account distinctions will not be made between Sumerian, Babylonian, or Assyrian usages, but Akkadain names and Babylonian rites will generally be presented, since they represent the culminating point of ancient civilization in the Valley of the Two Rivers. This was the stage at which Mesopotamian religion was most influential, notably on the Hebrews just to the west who produced the Old Testament.

Mesopotamian religion was dominated by the worship of several major deities, by rites and beliefs concerning kingship and the seasons, and by great emphasis on magic and divination. On the other hand, it has a literature that searchingly analyzes the human condition, in which black despair often seems near to breaking through—borne not on doubts of the gods' existence, but of their justice and concern for humankind.

Each of the great cities boasted a temple to its patron deity, and the mythologies strove to fit together these different gods of different places. Ur had Sin, the moon-god; Nippur worshipped Enlil, the storm-god; Babylon served Marduk; Ashur hon-

[7]See Samuel Noah Kramer, *Sumerian Mythology* (New York: Harper Torchbooks, 1961), and *The Sumerians: Their History, Culture, and Character* (Chicago: University of Chicago Press, 1963).

Gods, Kings, and Mysteries

ored Ashur who took the role of Enlil and Marduk for the Assyrians; Ninevah was sacred to Ishtar, goddess of love.

The god in the temple was thought of as the actual owner or landlord of the town and its farmlands; the king was in the uncomfortable position of being agent of this exacting master. The people of the community were likewise the possession of the god, having been created for his pleasure and service. In turn, the god gave his people life and order. But although gods and people gave service to each other, in Mesopotamia the unequal nature of this exchange was not forgotten. The gods might (or might not) be pleased by man's offerings; mankind depended on them unconditionally.

Let us examine a Babylonian temple. In its courtyards would be the residences of the priests, and also facilities for special private services for those sick or otherwise in special need.[8] At the rear of the central courtyard was a small room opening off it containing the actual statue of the god. This statue, having gone through a rite like the Egyptian "Opening of the Mouth," was considered to contain the life of the deity in a limited but actual manner. Every day the priests ministered to him with washing, dressing, and feeding the image, fumigating and purifying the shrine with incense and pure water. Offerings of food included bread, cakes, and a wide variety of flesh: the killing of the animal victims was carried out ritually. During the day, and particularly on festivals, throngs of worshippers filed through the courtyard, each leaving an offering before the image.

Many temples also had sacred prostitutes; union with them by male worshippers was considered a sort of sacrament, arousing the fertility-giving power of the god or goddess, and giving the worshipper a sense of ecstatic union with divinity. To serve as a sacred prostitute was an honorable occupation, one which girls of good family would often follow for a time as a divine offerering on their own part, giving the fees to the god or goddess. Sacred prostitution was particularly connected with temples of Ishtar (in Syria, Astarte), goddess of love and fertility, who was pictured as riding a leopard, carrying bow and arrow, and wearing an indented crown topped with the planet Venus.

Although each city was particularly sacred to one deity, either the original patron or a supplanter imported by some conquest or another, some high gods were recognized almost everywhere. They form themselves into sets of three—triads reminiscent of the Christian Trinity.

The supreme triad consisted of Anu, Enlil, and Ea. Anu was king of the gods, rather remote, and not particularly friendly to mankind, although later sources make him the husband of the great Ishtar. Enlil was a storm-god also often angry at mankind. It was mainly he who brought about the flood that nearly destroyed humankind. Yet Enlil could also be helpful if one gained his favor, and it was he who fixed the destiny of all species at the time of creation, in an act analoguous to Adan's naming the animals in the Genesis account. Ea, on the other hand, was friendly to humans and sometimes reversed the destructive work of Enlil.

[8]S. H. Hooke, *Babylonian and Assyrian Religion* (Norman: University of Oklahoma Press, 1963), pp. 100 ff.

A secondary triad was composed of Sin, the moon-god; Shamash, the sun-god; and Hadad, the storm-god. Closely associated with this group was Ishtar, the most loved and worshipped of all the goddesses. Her brother and spouse was Tammuz, a vegetation-god. In a myth similar to that of Isis and Osiris, Tammuz was said to die and go to the underworld in the fall. Ishtar wept for him, descended into the realm of shades, and triumphantly brought him back in the spring with vibrant rejoicing. This myth had great worship expression among the common people, as well as reflection in the state worship; probably the farmers who made up the bulk of the population found the sorrow and joy of Ishtar and Tammuz more congenial than the narratives of more aristocratic gods. Rituals of weeping for Tammuz and rejoicing in his yearly return in the spring spread to the adjacent areas of Syria and Palestine. We read of it in the Old Testament (Ezek. 8:14) as among the practices the prophets condemned.

More interaction between the religion of Babylon and the Old Testament can be seen in the great epic of Gilgamesh.[9] The basic theme is the quest of the hero Gilgamesh for immortality after the death of his friend Enkidu. After many trials, Gilgamesh sought out the aged Utnapishtim, who may be called the Mesopotamian Noah. He was also survivor of a universal flood, and as a reward he and his wife were the only humans to be granted immortality by the gods.

Utnapishtim related to Gilgamesh the story of the flood. At Enlil's instigation long ago, the gods determined to destroy mankind by a flood. But Ea, friendly to man, secretly warned Utnapishtim and instructed him how to build a ship in which he, his family, and specimens of all animals could be preserved. When the waters receded, the ship settled on Mount Nisir. After seven days, Utnapishtim sent out a dove, a swallow, and a raven. When the raven did not come back, he opened the ship and offered sacrifices, which much pleased the deities above. But there was a stormy scene in the divine assembly shortly thereafter, for Ishtar was enraged at Enlil for the destruction of so many people, and Enlil angrily accused Ea of having betrayed the secrets of the gods. Eventually these squabbles among the immortals were patched up.

Utnapishtim was not able to offer Gilgamesh much hope in the quest for immortality; the ancient navigator's own gift was unique. Finally he told Gilgamesh where he could find a plant at the bottom of the sea which could at least make the old young again. Gilgamesh found it and brought it ashore. But on his way home he stopped to swim in a pool, and a snake came up from the water and stole the precious herb. The serpent shed its skin and crawled off, and Gilgamesh could only lament the loss; the snake could now become young again whenever it aged, but not he.

For the Mesopotamians accepted no immortality except in a shadowy sort of underworld which was the same for all. The only rewards or punishments, justice or injustice the gods granted was in this life. At one point in the epic Gilgamesh talked with an old woman he met in an inn, who seemed to be really a form of Ishtar. She

---

[9]See Hooke, *Babylonian and Assyrian Religion,* pp. 63–68, and N. K. Sandars, *The Epic of Gilgamesh* (Baltimore: Penguin Books, 1964).

Gods, Kings, and Mysteries

said, "The life thou persuest thou shalt not find. When the gods created mankind, death for mankind they set aside, life in their own hands retaining."

Two very important deities not of Sumerian origin were Marduk and Ashur, patrons of Babylon and Ashur in the days of the two empires respectively. Marduk was the son of Ea, and had special place in the great state rituals. According to the Akkadian creation epic, the *Enuma Elish,* the primordial gods were Apsu, the rain, and his wife Tiamat, the sea. Their children, the older gods, were so obstreperous that Apsu determined to kill them, but Ea, learning of this plan, killed his father first. Then Tiamat married the evil deity Kingu and with his help and that of monsters set out to kill the children. But one god, Marduk son of Ea, arose to challenge his chaos-grandmother. He succeeded in slaying her and Kingu. Then, helped by the other liberated gods, Marduk fashioned the world out of Tiamat's body. He placed into it mankind, made from the blood of Kingu.

The Babylonian New Years festival presented a recitation of this battle, and also enacted the Tammuz story. After the recitation, the king entered the temple of Marduk. A priest took away all the king's regalia, and then sharply struck him and forced him to kneel. The monarch made a sort of negative confession, saying, "I have not sinned, O Lord of the Lands, I have not been unregardful for thy godhead . . ." The priest struck the king again; if tears came to the royal eyes, it was a good omen.[10] Again we see that the Babylonian and Assyrian sovereign's lot, however exalted, was an anxious one. Not only was the succession often chancy, but he was merely a quasi-divine caretaker for proud and capricious landlords of full deity.

While this was going on in the temple at New Years, the city was in ritual mourning, for it was said that Marduk had been imprisoned in the mountains. But then Marduk's son, Nebo, was reported coming to rescue him. The barges arrived bearing the deities of many towns, and among them was Nebo, who was hailed triumphantly into the city in a joyous procession, sometimes with the king himself playing the role of Nebo. The visiting gods then all met in a great "determination of destiny" assembly to decide the happenings of the coming year.[11]

A most important aspect of Mesopotamian religion was this belief in destiny. The people of the Two Rivers saw the universe as a tightly knit web, in which every event had ramifications in every other, and therefore the course of the future could be seen in signs. Astrology and numerology were elaborately developed by them—and thereby first steps were taken in astronomy and mathematics. Each of the gods had his number and his sector of the sky. Reading the liver of a sacrificial victim, or the patterns of oil poured on water, or casting lots, were among other methods used by trained divining priests. Some seers, more often than not women, would go into trance and deliver mediumistic oracles in the words of a god.

That the Babylonians were basically a practical, this-worldly people is indicated by the fact that most divinations concerned economic, healing, and political mat-

[10]C. J. Gadd, "Babylonian Myth and Ritual," in S. H. Hooke, *Myth and Ritual* (London: Oxford University Press, 1933), p. 53.

[11]Frankfort, *Kingship and the Gods,* pp. 295–96.

ters. They had little belief in heaven or postmortem judgment, and little faith that the gods' concern for mankind was likely to run very deep. Yet the gods were sources of power here and now, and this power could be experienced vibrantly in the moments when biology and the psyche came together: wailing for Tammuz or Marduk in the desolation of midwinter, or the ecstatic moment of sexual union.

Divine power could also be tapped by magical substitutionary rites. A healing rite for a sick man involved burying a slain kid or perhaps a clay image of Tammuz, and then it was said the sick man would be healed even as Tammuz would arise from death. Countless charms and amulets from Babylon exist too, for while the Mesopotamians did not believe that death itself could be reversed, in the present interlocking universe it was always thought possible to coerce divine power as well as stand in fear of it, for things below are interrelated with those above.

The remains of a Sumerian temple dating back to 4000 B.C. near Eridu, the most ancient Sumerian city of all.

ZOROASTRIANISM

Between Mesopotamia and India lies the vast expanse of the land called Persia or Iran. It is a land of paradoxes: nearly empty, yet the homeland of an ancient and immensely creative civilization; forbidding, with its endless deserts and stony mountain ranges, yet a country incomparably important as the transmitter of goods and ideas between East and West. From Alexander to Marco Polo, Persia was the portal of the East for intrepid westerners; in China, foreigners of Persian or cognate race were the chief importers of ideas from the West. Perhaps astrology, of Babylonian origin, was introduced to Indians and Chinese by Persians. Even

Buddhism came from India to China largely by way of central Asia, and its chief envoys to the Middle Kingdom included "blue eyes" like Kumarajiva and Bodhidharma.

Persia had, and Iran still has, a distinctive and splendid culture of its own too. It has given its own gift of the magi to the religious world in Zoroastrianism, a faith now much diminished in numbers, but one which has had immense influence both East and West. Even after Persia formally submitted to the Muslim crescent, its ancient faith made rich contributions to the art, literature, and thought of Islam.

Wherever Persian spiritual influence has been felt, Zoroastrianism has given or reinforced three basic motifs: a battle between light and darkness as respectively good and evil; eschatology, or emphasis on an end to history, a divine judgment, and the making of a new purified earth; and the concept of paradise (a Persian word), an ideal heavenly realm with a divine court and abode of the blessed. In turn, these ideas have impelled religion in Persia and elsewhere toward monotheism, ethics, and a sense of the religious meaning of history. These Iranian contributions have done much to take religion out of mystical identification with the forces of nature and with states of consciousness.

Indeed, while the ancient Hebrews believed in one God who judged and punished those with whom he was angry in this life, it was not until after they had had some contact with Persia that such ideas as resurrection of the dead at the end of the world, a final judgment, the making of a new heaven and earth, and heaven and hell, became important in the Old Testament. These ideas, all part and parcel of Zoroastrianism, entered the biblical tradition after the exile of the Hebrews to Babylon, from which they were rescued by the great Persian king Cyrus; thereafter contact between Jew and Zoroastrian was frequent. Today ideas like final judgment and heaven and hell are important to traditional Judaism, Christianity, and Islam. (The exact nature and extent of Iranian influence on Judaeo-Christian eschatology is a matter of scholarly dispute, and other factors such as Greek and Egyptian influence and indigenous development play a part too. But nowhere in the ancient world, prior to late Judaism, Christianity, and Islam, is there an eschatological scenario with the grandeur of the Persian; one cannot doubt its vision would be stimulative to the further thought of those who came to know it.)

A visitor to modern Iran soon comes to grasp something of why this country was a homeland of eschatology. An immense, rugged, dry terrain not unlike the American southwest under infinite blue sky suggests the contingency of human life in a world alien to it, and the inescapable sovereignty of heaven. Here and there, like oases breaking the inhospitable contours of nature, the Persians have created islands of paradise in the midst of the desert: the Persian garden with its pool and ornamental trees, the cool mosque with its arabesques, even the Persian carpet and exquisite miniature painting or illuminated book. All suggest the theme of radical opposition between present environment and the visionary's hope; they suggest that set like jewels in this wearisome world are a few foretastes of a new paradise.

The greatest son of Persia to perceive this vision, according to tradition, was the prophet Zoroaster (or Zarathustra; probably 660–583 B.C.). The ancient Iranians were cousins to the Aryan peoples who invaded India. Prior to the time of Zoroaster their religion was similar to that of the Vedas. They worshipped gods like Varuna and Mithra with sacrifice, chiefly of cattle, in the open air. They had a sacred drink, *haoma,* comparable to the Indic soma. The magi were probably a priestly class similar to the Brahmins in Vedic times. Probably (although Herodotus seems to deny this) fire, *asha,* was of sacred importance in the rites in a way similar to the role of Agni in India. It is not clear to what extent eschatology, judgment, and paradise motifs were widespread before Zoroaster; no doubt they had some importance.

About Zoroaster too we have little reliable information, for all the influence he had.[12] He came, according to tradition, from the east, was of prominent family, and probably was a priest. His wife was a daughter of a noble in the court of King Vishtaspa of Bactria or Balkh, a Persian area in what is now western Afghanistan.

Zoroaster had one of the most remarkably independent minds known to history, and he was less than satisfied with the customary rites. He was repelled by the sacrifice of cattle, and the ecstatic intoxication of men who drank haoma. In his sight, the innocent, suffering eyes of cattle falling under the knife represented the affronts the good always suffer from evil: they are like the cattle of God. The ritual, irresponsible bliss of haoma, too, had in this prophet's eyes little to do with the serious matters between God and man. But his criticisms made him unpopular and he was forced to flee.

Zoroaster wandered the mighty plains and towering mountains of his homeland striving to resolve his spiritual discomfit. Some say he spent ten years in this solitary quest. Finally, atop a great peak, he experienced a transcendent vision. He saw Ahura Mazda, as he named the high god, in all his splendor and glory above and beyond the old gods.

Zoroaster understood then that religion is not just religion, but reflects an ongoing universal battle. Ahura Mazda and his forces of light are in combat against the legions of Ahriman or Angra Mainyu, the evil spirit also called the Lie, and the *daevas* who are in his following. Boldly, Zoroaster gave the dark army the name "daeva," meaning deva or god in the old polytheistic sense—from daeva comes our word "devil."

The great battle was a battle of Truth versus the Lie. Ahura Mazda was accompanied by six Amesha Spentas, Holy Immortals or Good Spirits, angels or perhaps aspects of God himself. Of the other gods, Varuna probably gave his name to Ahura Mazda; Mithra and a few others became aides in the courts of light. But the underlying monotheism of the vision of Zoroaster himself comes through strongly, together with a second level dualism or belief in two polarized forces. Ahura is a god of goodness and morality, Ahriman is the Lie; men must choose, out of free will, which side they are going to be on.

The battle of good and evil was the most satisfactory way Zoroaster could explain the ill he saw around him. Ahura Mazda, he believed, is only good; therefore he could create only good things and do only good deeds. Like all who wrestle with the problem of evil and find it very hard to explain its coexistence with an

---

[12]See R. C. Zaehner, *The Dawn and Twilight of Zoroastrianism* (London: Weidenfelt and Nicolson, 1961).

all-powerful good God, Zoroaster and his followers had difficulty explaining theologically the relation between Ahura Mazda and Ahriman—whether they are both eternal realities, meaning that Ahura's power is limited; or whether, as many thought, Ahriman is an offspring of Ahura who rebelled against him. But there is no question of the moral force of what Zoroaster was trying to say: that we are combatants in a war of ultimate significance and cosmic dimension, that no one can be just neutral in it, but that in every area of life, day by day, everyone must decide which lord he will side with, the Lord of Light or the Lord of the Lie.

Each person, then, is under judgment. Here the eschatology of Zoroastrianism comes in. While Zoroaster himself undoubtedly had strong eschatological ideas, they have been preserved in a later form. That form centers on reward and punishment (although, in contrast to the Judaeo-Christian tradition, punishment in hell is not eternal), and on the making of a new world.

Zoroastrians said that on the fourth day after death, a deceased person had to cross the bridge called Chinvat, which connects with the unseen world. The righteous will find it broad as a highway, and they will take it to enter the House of Song, where they will await the Last Day. Yet to the wicked the bridge will seen narrow as a razor, and they will fall off it into hell.

But on the Last Day, Ahura Mazda will defeat evil. He will purify the entire world and reign over it. All persons will be raised in a general resurrection; the souls of the wicked, having been purified along with the earth, will be brought out of hell with their sentences terminated. All together will enter a new age in a new world free from all evil, ever young and rejoicing.

Just before the Last Day, it was said, Zoroaster would return in the form of a prophet conceived of a virgin by his own seed, stored in a mountain lake. A prophet would in fact appear in this way at thousand-year intervals during the three thousand years between Zoroaster and the renovation of the world.

Ahura Mazda, we are told, made this present world as a trap in order that his masterpiece, mankind, might ensnare the enemy. Humans are the bait—by drawing Ahriman, eager to tempt and win over mankind, into Ahura Mazda's world and by then freely choosing the good when tempted, mankind weakens Ahriman's force and wears him down so that he can eventually be destroyed.[13] This is the game being played over the three thousand years.

Zoroaster was finally successful in converting the court of King Vishtaspa to his faith. The new religion was launched at about the same time as the great Persian Empire. Although the power of the Medes and Persians was growing at the time of Zoroaster, it was Cyrus the Great (r. 559–30 B.C., probably born about the time of Zoroaster's death), who incorporated Mesopotamia into his realm, sent the Jewish captives home, helped them rebuild the temple in Jerusalem, and effectively unified Asia from India to the Mediterranean into an empire. It is not evident that Cyrus himself was much influenced by Zoroaster's teaching; the first Persian emperor is best known instead for his enlightened policy of tolerance and support of the faiths of all his diverse subjects. But the Zoroastrian teaching spread rapidly; his succes-

[13]See R. C. Zaehner, *The Teachings of the Magi: A Compendium of Zoroastrian Beliefs* (London: George Allen and Unwin, 1956; New York: The Macmillan Company, 1956), pp. 53–55.

sors, such as Darius and Xerxes, worshipped Ahura Mazda and claimed his protection.

How widespread or exclusive a religion Zoroastrianism was in this period is disputed. Its heyday as an official, organized religion was the Sasanian Empire (A.D. 224–651). By this time Zoroastrianism had reincorporated haoma, sacrifices, and polytheistic elements—probably never lost in popular religion—and was fraught with priestly regulations concerning purifications, expulsions of demons, and the minute division of animals, insects, and so forth into the ranks of light and darkness. During this period the Zend Avesta, the Zoroastrian scriptures, were compiled; although they contain the Gathas, hymns ascribed to Zoroaster himself,[14] there is much material of a later and more sacerdotal character.

The Zoroastrian priests, or *mobeds* (derived from magi), were great practicioners of magic as well as profound philosophers. In the days of the Roman Empire (as the account of the visit of several of them to Bethlehem in the New Testament bears witness), they were a byword for astrologers and wizards. Zoroaster himself was accounted a great magician. However, many of those called magi around the ancient Mediterranean were probably only from Mesopotamia where the occult arts flourished mightily. The Parthian Empire, Rome's great rival, ruled the Persian and Mesopotamian regions from 250 B.C. to A.D. 224; it was a melting pot of polytheism, Zoroastrianism, Hellenism, Babylonian religion, and teachings from East and West, out of which mystical and esoteric movements bubbled continually. Among them were the influential Mithraism, worship of Mithra transformed into an initiatory mystery popular among Roman soldiers; and Manichaeism, an ascetic and syncretistic faith to be discussed later.

After the fall of the Sasanian Empire, Persia was converted to Islam, and the minority of Persians who wished to remain faithful to the old religion were under pressure. Some—about 14,000—remain in Iran to this day. Others moved to the more tolerant atmosphere of India. Zoroastrians there, now called Parsees ("Persians") and living mostly around Bombay, number perhaps 150,000.

The Parsees in India have greatly prospered and are now one of the wealthiest classes in that nation. In large part this owes to their "work ethic," strong moral code, and philanthropy. They are well-known for their fire temples and Towers of Silence.

Their Zoroastrianism is life-affirming. It says that the world, having been made good by Ahura Mazda, is to be accepted with thanks. One's basic duties are to confess the religion, take a wife and procreate offspring, and to treat livestock justly; asceticism and world negation are not approved. The main places of worship are the clean, attractive fire temples, where a perpetual flame is kept burning as a symbol of the purity of God, being fed five times a day with prayers; here the scriptures are chanted and other rituals performed.[15]

The Towers of Silence are unique structures on which the bodies of Parsee dead

---

[14]Jacques Duschesne-Guillaume, *The Hymns of Zarathustra* (Boston: Beacon Press, 1963) is a good translation of the Gathas. The bulk of the Zend Avesta is translated in *The Sacred Books of the East*.

[15]Rustom Masani, *The Religion of the Good Life* (New York: Collier Books, 1962), gives an account by a Parsee of their present-day beliefs and practices.

are placed to be devoured by vultures. This custom reflects some basic Zoroastrian attitudes and some adjustments it has made.

Because the world is made by God and is good, and death is a pollution, a corpse cannot be consigned to any of the four elements—it can be neither exposed to the air, buried, given to the sea, nor cremated. The ingenious solution was to give the body to carnivorous birds. In Iran, bodies were apparently left for them on high mountains. In the flatlands of India the Parsees instead built the remarkable Towers of Silence, over which vultures are always slowly wheeling; a corpse placed there will be completely stripped of flesh within an hour or two.

After death, the body is washed and clothed in white. It is shown to a so-called four-eyed dog (because he has two spots just above his eyes); this dog is believed able to detect whether life is extinct. After the body has been reverently taken to the Tower of Silence and left there, services are held to pray for the deceased as he crosses the Chinvat Bridge, and donations are made in his name to charity.

Purity is important to Parsees; elaborate rituals are prescribed for the expiation of pollution. Initiations of boys and girls into the faith of Zoroaster are occasions of colorful and joyful parties, processions, and rites. Even more elaborate is initiation into the hereditary office of *dastur,* or priest.

The faith of cosmic battle and renewal given us by Zoroaster, and once the religion of a powerful empire, is now much diminished in numbers. But no decline can erase its immense influence on the history of religions, an influence that has touched the spiritual lives of countless millions past and present.

GREEK RELIGION

"The glory that was Greece"—this familiar phrase calls up images of white temples atop gentle hills, which honor immortals carrying out their loves and spats on lofty Olympus. Below, democratic assemblies debate while robed philosophers discourse on goodness, truth, and beauty. It is an appealing picture of a tiny land which, together with that of the Hebrews, has affected Western civilization more than any other.

Yet this picture of Olympian gods, democracy, and philosophy does not reflect the whole of ancient Greece or its religion. Spiritual life in Athens, Sparta, and the other Hellenic cities was, as everywhere, a complex of many strands and levels. Aristotle said that the origin of human ideas of the divine is twofold: the phenomena of the sky and the phenomena of the soul. Greek religion certainly reflects both, in the Zeus who sends down lightning bolts from above and the Dionysus who gives ecstasy of spirit. Moreover, it reflects the extremes of both sky and soul—the rage of a thunderstorm and the peace of a sunny harvest; the frenzy of the god-possessed soul and the calm of contemplation.

To understand the full range of Greek religion a historical framework is helpful.

Greek-speaking Indo-Europeans started coming into the Greek peninsula about 2000 B.C., the same time their Aryan kinsmen may have started entering India. They easily supplanted a primitive culture on the Greek mainland, but found a civilization on Crete, the Minoan, much in advance of their own. The culture that the Greeks, under Minoan influence, developed is called the Mycenaean, from the city of Mycenae, where the palace of Agamemnon was located. This is the era reflected in the celebrated *Iliad* and *Odyssey* of Homer, in which heroic armies from Greece proper under King Agamemnon fought and destroyed the city of Troy in Asia Minor (culturally also Mycenaean Greek) ruled by King Priam, and the hero Ulysses (Odysseus) wended his adventurous way home. The sack of Troy reflected in the epic took place about 1150 B.C.; shortly afterward Mycenaean civilization itself crumbled in the wake of new invasions from the north.

After a period of relative decline, the classical Greece of city-states, of which Athens was the most important commercially and the most splendid in culture, emerged. The classical history of this era was climaxed by the wars in which invading Persia was defeated (490–79 B.C.), and the subsequent Athenian "Golden Age" in the fifth century B.C. under Pericles and Alcibiades. These were the days of the dramatists Aeschylus, Sophocles, and Euripides, the building of the Parthenon, and the philosophy of Socrates and the young Plato.

But the long-drawn-out Peloponnesian War between Athens and Sparta in the closing decades of the century drained strength from this impressive culture. The fourth century B.C. began with Socrates drinking the hemlock (399 B.C.). Plato (427–347 B.C.) was entering his maturity, and Aristotle (384–22 B.C.) was soon to follow. Nevertheless, the fourth century was a time of trouble and of relative decline from the brilliant standards of the previous era.

But the century culminated with Greek political triumph so sudden and unexpected as to seem beyond belief: the brief empire of Alexander the Great (356–23 B.C.). Alexander spread Greek rule from the Adriatic to the Indus, from Egypt to the Oxus. He brought Greek culture to these far-flung realms, and opened up Greek civilization to the influence of the East. Because of Alexander, Buddhist art bears something of the stamp of Hellas, and subsequent Greek philosophy perhaps something of a taste of Buddhism.

Alexander's empire broke up after his death, but left oriental states under Greek kings in Egypt, the Near East, and even India; they were breeding grounds for striking and influential new movements in philosophy, religion, and culture. The period and culture of this post-Alexandrian mix of Greek, Egyptian, Babylonian, Zoroastrian, and Indic motifs is called the Hellenistic. The Hellenistic period is often dated from 323 to 32 B.C., the latter being the date that the eastern Mediterranean fell under Roman rule, although typically Hellenistic thought and religion continued unabated in the Roman world until Christianity replaced ancient civilization in the fourth century A.D.

During the fifteen centuries from the Trojan War to the victory of the cross, Greek religion underwent immense changes. It transited from vigorous gods of sky, war, and agriculture, who aided according to their fancy one side or the other in battle, through the dignified civic rituals of the classic period, to the philosophic pessimism, mysticism, and syncretism of the Hellenistic and Roman periods.[16] All the way through, moreover, there were persistent countercurrents: fertility cults of

[16]See Gilbert Murray, *Five Stages of Greek Religion* (Oxford: The Clarendon Press, 1925).

planting and harvest, gods of place and soil, emotional rites of frenzy or mystery, oracles and shamans, folk religion beliefs in witchcraft and magic.[17]

Homeric religion can be compared with that of Vedic India. A basic principle of sovereignty located in the sky is combined with a picture of energetic, competing gods associated with different natural phenomena and different tribes. Zeus was sky-father and guardian of the moral order, although he also played a fertility-giving role celebrating the marriage of heaven and earth to perpetuate life. (The latter role, superficially, seemed sometimes to put him in positions at variance with that of upholding the moral law, as in the myth of his taking the form of a swan to rape Leda and thereby beget Helen of Troy.)

Another Homeric god was Apollo. Originally fearsome and unpredictible yet a wise master of healing like Rudra, Apollo became a beautiful god of music and harmony, healing and atonement. His most important place of worship was Delphi, where he spoke through the famous oracle. At Delphi, a priestess called the Pythia sat on a tripod at a spot considered the center of the earth, went into trance, and uttered often enigmatic sentences considered infallible—if they could be understood. Many of the greatest figures in ancient history consulted the wisdom of Apollo expressed through this medium at critical points in their careers.

Hermes was another very ancient god. His realms were those of mystery; he was called "the god who is met unexpectedly." He was psychopomp or guide of souls to the underworld. He ruled sleep and dreams, invented the shepherd's pipe, guarded honest travelers and thieves alike. He was also a fertility deity, symbolized by "herms" or phallic pillars placed in crossroads, city squares, and public buildings everywhere.

Other gods can only be named here: Poseidon, of the sea; Ares, of strength and war; Aphrodite, comparable to Ishtar, of love and beauty; Artemis, the virginal huntress; Hades, of the underworld.

Homeric man felt a kinship with the gods, for he believed his family to be descended from one or more of them. His relationship with them was a combination of awe and familiarity. It would be oriented toward the joys and business of this life, for Homeric man had no belief in moral judgment or heaven after death—except for a few heroes who might go to the Western Isles, all alike would descend to a shadowy life in the underworld of Hades, of which Achilles in the *Odyssey* said that he would rather be a servant to a poor man above ground, than ruler of all the dead. The gods were celebrated by feasts and great offerings of cattle, and were petitioned for victory in war and fruitful harvests in peace, rather than for other-worldly desires. Yet they were certainly possessed of an uncanny, numinous, mysterious side, which could speak through the rustling of leaves in a sacred grove and was at work whenever something beyond human ken occurred.[18]

During the "Golden Age" of the fifth century, the same gods were the major deities of the city-states. They were joined by Athena, patron of the city of

[17]See Jane Harrison, *Prolegomena to the Study of Greek Religion* (New York: Meridian Books, 1957).

[18]Martin P. Nilsson, *A History of Greek Religion* (Oxford: The Clarendon Press, 1949), pp. 137–38.

Athens—she was said to have sprung in full armor from the head of Zeus, and to combine muscular warlike energy with patronage of science, reason, and art.

The civic gods were worshipped with sacrifices at their altars; the victim would be led up to the altar by the priest, barley would be sprinkled on the floor or ground, and the animal's throat would be cut as the women present raised a high-pitched yell. The entrails were wrapped in fat and burned, while the good cuts of meat were used for a sacred feast. Lesser offerings, which the poor might give, were cereal, drink, or incense. The great festivals, basically agricultural, would include spectacular processions to the temple with flowers and offerings; musical, gymnastic, and dramatic performances; and the bestowing of rich new garments on the image of the deity. Greece had no powerful priesthood as did Egypt or Babylon; the head of the household was priest for his family. A rotating priesthood, or the chief magistrate, offered the sacrifices and maintained the temples of the state rites; sometimes the civic priesthood was even offered to the highest bidder.[19] While there was vague belief in ghosts, and in Hades, the realm of the dead to which the deceased were ferried by Charon, the afterlife was still of no great importance in official religion.

Some signs in the classic period, however, pointed to a coming new stage in religion, one marked by the increasing interest in personal immortality which usually goes with the greater individualizing of spiritual experience in advancing culture. The earliest instance appears to be the cult of Dionysus, which came to Greece from Thrace around 600 B.C. The frenzied worshippers of this ecstatic god rampaged through the countryside in hordes with wild music and dance, throwing themselves upon bulls (considered gods) and eating them alive. In time this cult of savage rapture was softened to a rural agricultural festival of drinking, masquerade, and wild release at harvest; the focus of religion on felt subjectivity rather than civic solidarity remained or was transmuted into other cults.

The Orphic cult, perhaps influenced by Pythagorean philosophy, is the major example. According to the cult myth, the god Orpheus, son of Apollo, sang and played the lyre so beautifully that even the animals were enchanted. He married a nymph called Eurydice; when she died Orpheus followed her to the underworld and charmed its god into freeing her, but he lost her because he did not obey the injunction not to look back to see if she were following. Finally maddened women of the Dionysian cult tore Orpheus to pieces, but his severed head continued to sing. Orpheus then went to the Other World, and was able to bring his followers into immortality.

These devotees of Orpheus believed themselves strayed citizens of a better world. They were part earthly and part divine; through asceticism and the Orphic initiations the divine part could be purified out and led home again. On arrival in the Other World the redeemed devotee would say, "I am son of earth and starry heaven . . . by good fortune I have escaped the circle of burdensome care, and to the crown of yearning have I come with swift foot; I bury myself in the lap of the Lady who rules in Hades . . ." The lady is apparently Eurydice. Orphists believed in reincarnation; it might take many lifetimes for a soul to be purified. A body was

<hr />

[19]Nilsson, *Greek Religion,* pp. 242–43, and H. J. Rose, *Religion in Greece and Rome* (New York: Harper Torchbooks, 1959), pp. 38–39, 44–45.

considered a tomb in which the divine spirit was entrapped; this was a theme quite different from the earlier Greek approach, but one which was to resound more and more in the philosophy and religion of the Hellenistic and Roman periods. Plato and the Neoplatonists were much influenced by Orphism, and so indirectly was theological Christianity.[20]

Another "mystery cult" that influenced Plato was Eleusis. ("Mystery" is from the Greek word for a secret initiatory religion, originally from a word meaning to close eyes and mouth.) This small city near Athens was the site of a temple specializing in the enactment of mystery rites into which individuals from near and far could be initiated. Thousands came, paid, and "experienced" (although what they experienced they could not relate, being vowed to silence), whether called by curiosity, fashion, or desire for a better lot in this life and the next.

The myth on which the rites of Eleusis were based was this: Pluto or Hades, god of the underworld, abducted Persephone or Kore (sowing or grain), daughter of Demeter (Earth-mother, Mother Earth herself). Demeter fell into despair and all growth stopped. Searching everywhere for her child, she came to Eleusis as an old woman, served as nursemaid to the king's son, and sought to give the infant immortality by anointing him with ambrosia, blowing on him, and putting him in the fire. (However the Queen interrupted her and the child remained mortal.) When Demeter's identity was revealed, a great temple to her was built at Eleusis. Finally Hades permitted the return of Persephone provided the maiden spend one third of the year with him as his queen.

This myth, with its immortality-granting themes such as the return of Persephone as the spring and the child who might have been made magically deathless, was enacted at Eleusis linked to seedtime and harvest rites. But how it was climaxed and applied to the individual is not known—there are suggestions that, in flickering torchlight, a sheaf of grain or a newborn child was held up before the initiates in a dramatic gesture. A sacred thick drink of unknown composition was given to initiates—there is circumstantial evidence it may have contained hallucinogens.

We have seen that these mystery cults influenced Plato. A word must be said about Greek philosophy, which so much influenced everything that came after in Western religion. While formal Greek religion was focusing on the separate gods of each tribe and function, and the initiatory cults on the ecstasy and salvation of each individual, philosophers and proto-scientists (much the same thing) began to ask what all things have in common. Is everything fire or water? Is it static, or in perpetual flux? Even more important, what is mankind? Plaything of the gods or measure of all things?

Socrates (469–399 B.C.) was most insistent in asking questions. He demanded, as he taught his young disciples to cut through conventional assumptions—and conventional skepticisms—with searching queries, that they realize one cannot even ask questions meaningfully unless one has some standard of integrity, some sincere purpose of following an inner spirit, or *daimon*. But the upholders of convention did not appreciate the challenge. Socrates was arraigned and charged

[20]See Harrison, *Prolegomena,* Chapters IX–XII and Appendix.

with corrupting the young and with atheism, because he had omitted to worship the gods of the city. This was not because the Athenians were bigots about religion; quite the reverse. Worshipping the city gods was regarded as something any normal, loyal citizen ought to do as a token of patriotism just because it was so routine. Socrates claimed that, although he may have forgotten some such obligations, his inner loyalty to God as the source of value—whether Zeus or the spirit within—was unimpaired. Condemned to die by a small majority of the voting citizens, Socrates drank a cup of poison hemlock and died with great dignity.

His greatest disciple, Plato, accepted the same idea of divine oneness reflected in the mind of man. Plato added that the spirit or consciousness-principle is prior to matter (here he was probably influenced by Orphism), for matter is given form by ideas. By expanding awareness through the arousal of a sense of wonder, we can perceive the divine and transcendent realities which underlie the ordinary. (He may have here been influenced by initiatory experiences such as those of Eleusis). Plato's expression of the idea of the origin of the world in universal mind, and of an immortal soul, had an incalculable impact on later philosophical exposition of Jewish, Christian, and Muslim thought.

Aristotle, with more of a logical, scientific mind than Plato and less mystical or intuitive, observed nature and worked backward by inductive logic to an "Unmoved Mover" who started and sustains the universe by pure thought. Aristotle also greatly influenced Muslim, Jewish, and Christian philosophy, especially medieval and modern scholasticism.

RELIGIONS OF ROME
AND THE ROMAN EMPIRE

Most visitors to Rome have been to the Forum. This area, several blocks long and near the grim Coliseum, was the heart of ancient Rome, and is full of monuments at least to the official side of its spiritual life. One of the oldest buildings is the broad-stepped and columned Temple of Saturn. Not far away is the Temple of Castor and Pollux, the twin helping gods who parallel the Vedic Nasatyas and remind us that the religions of the widely scattered Indo-European peoples tend to converge at their oldest levels. Next is the Temple of Vesta, goddess of the hearth and the ongoing life of the community; here dwelt the Vestal Virgins, women of good family chosen for thirty years of service to keep alive the sacred flame in the temple—they had many privileges, but unchastity on the part of a Vestal Virgin was punishable by entombment alive.[21] Alongside the temples, and the Curia where the Senate met, are monuments to the glorious moments of Roman history, such as the triumphal arches of the emperors Septimus Severus and Titus.

The Forum suggests a religious expression with deep roots in the past, closely tied to civic life and to history, but perhaps more a formal veneration than fervent. All this is true; right up to the end of the empire, when it was only the palest specter

[21]Rose, *Religion in Greece and Rome,* p. 201 ff.

of its former glory, patricians felt deeply the solemn meaning of performing rites as they had been done for twelve centuries. But most Romans, if they were not simply skeptics, turned to other faiths for individual salvation and subjective religious feeling. Indeed, the Roman gods themselves turned elsewhere, chiefly to Greek mythology, for their stories and sometimes even their names.

The early Romans were a singularly practical, unimaginative people who had little feeling for gods except as unavoidable forces best dealt with on a businesslike basis. Their gods possessed little personality and less myth; they were simply *numen,* powerful presences that conveyed a sense of mystery and awe. The world was alive with them. In the home, Vesta at the hearth was most important; there were also the *penates* who watched the storeroom, the *lares* at the boundaries and threshold. Invisible but ever-present, the manes or spirits of the family dead, and the *lemures* or angry ghosts, worked their influences for blessing or bane. The gods of the home were served by the head of the household, the *paterfamilias,* who was accompanied by the *genius* or family spirit which passed from one family head to the next.

Just as each household had its spirits, so did the community as a whole. The most important were the triad of Jupiter, Mars, and Quirinus. Jupiter was Zeus; Mars was originally a wild Rudralike god of forests and mountains, who later became the warlike but faithful protector of the Roman people; little is known of Quirinus. Other old Roman deities included Vesta, Juno, Minerva the goddess of crafts, Venus who was identified with the Greek Aphrodite, Saturn god of seedtime and harvest and later of time, Neptune identified with Poseidon, Janus guardian of the city gates who was worshipped on the first of the month by the chief priest.

The several classes of priests were public officials. The *flamen* lit the altar fires; the *sacerdos* handled the animal sacrifices, the chief act in public temples; the *pontifex maximus* appointed other priests. Performing the sacrifices in precisely the correct manner was important. The basic idea was exchange with the gods: *do ut des,* "I give this to you, now you give that to us." Divination was also important. A board of augurs foretold the future by reading omens in the sky and in the movement of birds and animals; later, divination from reading the livers of animals, like that of Babylon, became important.

Much consulted also was the Delphi-like oracle at the Greek colony of Cumae, near Naples, where a priestess of Apollo called the Sibyl had given out messages transcribed in documents called the Sybilline Books. These were early purchased and brought to Rome; when they were burned in 82 B.C. new oracular lines were assembled from various places to make new Sybilline Books. At a motion in the Senate, these books would be consulted by a board of fifteen through some unknown process of selecting a passage at random, and then applying its seeming advice to a critical matter of state.[22]

Even during the republican period, before Rome became an empire, new gods and ideas were pouring into the city on the Tiber, mostly from Greece and points farther east. First the Roman gods were equated with those from Greece, and picked

[22]R. M. Ogilvie, *The Romans and their Gods in the Age of Augustus* (New York: W. W. Norton, 1969), pp. 62–63.

up distinctive mythologies from their counterparts. But Roman intellectuals like Cicero and Marcus Aurelius were influenced by Greek philosophies to interpret the traditional gods as symbols of nature and human moods, or even as ridiculous fabrications.

As the republic became an empire, Hellenistic ideas of sacred kingship from the East affected it, and ideas of grandeur and destiny became deeply rooted in the Roman psyche. The Roman spiritual vision is nowhere better displayed than in the verse of Virgil (70-19 B.C.). Poet of the Augustan era when the mighty Roman Empire was shaped and consolidated, he was late enough to see the true dimensions of its destiny. Yet the spirit of his Rome had as yet been only lightly touched by the East. The *Aeneid,* Virgil's masterpiece, tells of the legendary founding of Rome by a junior branch of the house of Troy and makes the tale into a legitimation of Rome and its gods. Aeneas, devotedly following the call of the gods to found a new city, forsook the passionate love of Dido in Africa to proceed to Italy, where he consulted the Sibyl at Cumae and even descended to Avernus, the underworld. The whole poem is pervaded by a deep sense of the unrolling of destiny, leading up to the greatness of Rome under Caesar Augustus; elsewhere Virgil prophesied a forthcoming golden age under a son of Augustus—a prophecy not realized, for Augustus had no son. Yet for all that, the tone of Virgil's work is a very Roman sense of dignified melancholy amid all the triumphs; Virgil is saddened by the carnage of the battles upon which the predestined ascendancy of Rome was

The Forum at Rome, site of several temples of the official Roman religion, including the shrine of the Vestal Virgins.

won; all that is mortal is touched by tears and falls in the end to the gloom of Avernus. Even the gods, he says, though themselves deathless, cannot prevent this end.

Such long thoughts, however, did not suit the spiritual appetites of all in this teeming new world. As the Roman Empire unified the Mediterranean, ancient cultures were shattered, leaving countless individuals desolate, wanting something they could believe in and experience for themselves. Beliefs based on individual faith and initiation, promising individual security and immortality, would clearly best fill this need. At the same time, the caesars unified the ancient world, enabling cults to spread rapidly from one port to another, so that Rome became virtually a second Orient, or as an ancient writer said, the Orontes flowed into the Tiber.

The mysteries of Greece, such as Orphism and Eleusis, were popular, and several Roman emperors were initiated at Eleusis. Other imports from Asia and Africa included the worship of the Great Mother Cybele and her consort Attis, the cult of Isis and Osiris, the faith of Mithra from Persia, Christianity, Gnosticism, and Manichaeism. All these diverse and colorful faiths had two things in common: a personal salvation experience, and a trend toward monotheism, the unifying of all divine power in a single god or goddess.

The intellectual spine of the world of these religions was Middle Platonism and Neoplatonism, more mystical developments of Plato's thought which made the universe a series of emanations from the One. Humans may return to union with the One through mystical experiences in which the limitations of matter are transcended. It is easy to see how thinking of this sort could be fitted into initiatory and salvation religions.

One of the most popular of the new movements was the religion of the Magna Mater, or Great Mother. She went by many names, but was basically similar to the Syro-Babylian Astarte or Ishtar, though in Rome she went commonly by the Phrygian name of Cybele. Her dying-rising consort was Attis, who castrated himself rather than be unfaithful to the goddess, died, was violently bewailed by Cybele, and was brought back to life. This cult was notable for the frenzy it produced among its devotees, particularly the eunuch priests, who would perform fanatical dances, slashing themselves with knives to show their devotion as children and lovers of the Great Mother.

The religion of Isis was more decorous, but equally a cult of the Great Mother, Isis, and the dying-rising god, Osiris. Isaism was a well-organized church, with shaven-headed celibate priests, temples with morning and evening devotions, impressive initiations, and the annual great holy season of wailing for the lost Osiris, then uniting with the joy of Isis in welcoming him back as he returns to life each year. The Isaic liturgies were lovely. Each spring the white-stoled priests, carrying bells and sacred water from the Nile and a model of a ship, would process to the ocean shore. The mother of the stars, Isis, would be honored with torches, incense, music or flute and pipe, and the scattering of flowers as the procession wended its way. At the beach, the ship would be consecrated and set asail with prayers for travelers and sailors on the deep. Most important, though, was the experience of transformation in the mysteries of Isis. The Roman novelist Apuleius, in

Metamorphoses, describes his hero's tremendous vision of Isis on the nocturnal oceanside, and his subsequent Isaic initiation; in that rite, he "drew near to the confines of death . . . at the dead of night, saw the sun shining brightly . . . approached the gods above and the gods below."[23]

A religion particularly popular among soldiers was the cult of Mithra, the Persian god mentioned in connection with Zoroastrianism, who broke loose to form a faith of his own in the Roman world. Mithraism projected a masculine image and inculcated manly virtues, while offering immortality through a kind of baptism. Mithra, god of light, was presented as the invincible one who created the world by sacrificing a bull; he was often pictured in this act.

Judaism was also an important part of this religious flux; Jews lived not only in Palestine but in most major cities of the empire. Despite its cultural distinctiveness, Judaism with its one God and individual moral choice struck many as being highly relevant to the spiritual quest of the times; not a few Greeks and others seemed to live spiritually on its fringes. This was the situation that led naturally to mediating movements on the borderline between the Jewish and Gentile worlds. The most important of these was Christianity, which provided opportunity for non-Jews to feel "grafted into" the Jewish experience of one God through the mediating personality of Jesus Christ.

But there were others. The set of ideas and attitudes called Gnosticism flourished in the matrix of Judaism, Christianity, Platonism, and influences from Babylon and Persia. The basic beliefs of the many Gnostic groups tell us the following. There is an unknown and transcendent true God, and distinct from him a lower, imperfect "demiurge," who created this imperfect world. Man is a stranger is this world, for in his true nature he is akin to the unknown true God; man is a spark of heavenly light imprisoned in a material body and so subject to the demiurge and his cruel powers. A myth of a fall before the creation of the world accounts for man's present state and his yearning for deliverance. The means of deliverance is through *gnosis,* saving knowledge or wisdom, by which man is awakened to his true nature.[24]

Much Gnosticism was Christian in that it identified Jesus Christ as its saviour figure who brought the true gnosis. But at the same time it typically rejected the Old Testament God, believing at best he was the demiurge, a lesser and more fallible force, who could only create such a world of matter and suffering as this one.

A similar movement of great interest and importance is Manichaeism, already mentioned in connection with Zoroastrianism. This new religion was deliberately founded to convert the world and was made up artificially of elements of several faiths. Manichaeism lasted some eleven centuries, and spread from Britain to China, but its followers were generally a minority wherever they lived, and as often as not they were severely persecuted. Indeed, despite the fact that the vegetarian and pacifist Manichaeans were outwardly harmless, few groups except the Jews have been as insanely hated and persecuted as they, whether in the Albigensian Crusade

[23]Frederick C. Grant, *Hellenistic Religions* (New York: The Liberal Arts Press, 1953), pp. 108–09. The passage is from *Metamorphoses,* XI, 23.

[24]Based on R. M. J. Wilson, *Gnosis and the New Testament* (Oxford: Basil Blackwell, Ltd., 1968), p. 4.

in medieval Europe or the parallel suppression of Manichaeism as a cult of sorcerers in Ming China. Owing to these unnatural fates the movement has not survived.

Its founder was Mani (A.D. 216–77), a native of Mesopotamia. After two visions from the angel who was his heavenly self, Mani began to preach his faith; at first he had official support and traveled widely. But the third Sasanian emperor, Bahram I, incited by the magi and by fear of Mani's ties with the Parthian royal house that the Sasanids had supplanted, had him put to death, and began the sect's long history of suffering.

Mani's teaching was a straightforward dualism. It said there are "two roots"— holy spiritual light, and the darkness which includes matter.[25] The nature of darkness is strife. In its tempestuousness, according to the basic Manichaean myth, the darkness invaded the realms of light and became attracted to them. In order to defeat the darkness, God allowed sparks of the light to be entrapped by darkness and matter that they might eventually purify it. When they forgot their origin and purpose, Christ came down to recall them to it and awaken them from illusion; the Prophet Mani, although not strictly divine, was sent for the same purpose.

The religion of Mani was ascetic. It believed that by denying all carnal pleasures (though Mani did say that music and perfume were spiritual enough sensuous pleasures to be allowed even the highest of the elect), one liberated one's soul from the toils of flesh, and worked toward the defeat of the dark forces. The faith was divided into several grades. Monklike elect followed celibate and ascetic lives, owning nothing but a single black robe, and living on offerings. The lay people, who might marry and have jobs, but who lived lives of self-denial according to their situations, were called Hearers.

Manichaeism, like other mystery and Gnostic groups, was popular in the Roman Empire in the third and fourth centuries A.D. The religious life of Greece and Rome, then, with its increasing exposure to the heavy weight of imperial history, moved over the centuries from the simple gods of hearth and grove, to bearing the anguish and lostness of a dark, enslaved universe from which all natural innocence had fled.

CELTIC RELIGION

In the days when Roman legions were first marching west, vast reaches of what fell under their dominion, together with areas such as Ireland and Scotland where the Roman eagles never flew, were inhabited by people called Celts. Their lands were the British Isles, Gaul (modern France), much of Iberia (modern Spain and Portugal), central Europe, and even a corner of Asia Minor—the Galatia to which St. Paul wrote one of his epistles. Today, distinguishable Celtic stock, culture, and language survive, sometimes tenuously, only in the so-called Celtic fringe of Western Europe—Scotland, Wales, Ireland, Cornwall, and Brittany.

But the Celtic world, with its gods, heroes, and Druidic rites, lies over Europe at the dawn of its history like a gossamar mist, pierced only here and there by flashes

[25]See Duncan Greenless, *The Gospel of the Prophet Mani* (Adyar, Madras, India: Theosophical Publishing House, 1956).

of sunlight. It is a background presence felt everywhere, and indeed it lives on in folk beliefs about fairies and charms still found in rural Ireland and Brittany. But so early did most of the Celtic lands fall under Roman and then Christian influence, and so late were their own traditions recorded, that there are great gaps in our knowledge of Celtic society in its heyday. Julius Caesar in his *Gallic Wars* and other classical writers give us some accounts, and other clues come from archaeology and folklore, but much is tantalizingly vague.

One difficulty is that the Celts themselves were far from being a single nation. They were a collection of unlettered tribes, warring with each other as often as not. Yet some spiritual attitudes were widespread in the Celtic world. Most Celts had a "horizontal" or "terrestial" cosmology—emphasis on the coming and going of gods, spirits of the departed, or heroes east or west over the sea or in and out of the ground, rather than divine descent from above. The major deities are associated with earth and sea, and there is a vivid concept of the Other World, located either on paradisal islands or underground. Among most Celts a priesthood wise in magical lore—the famous Druids—is reported. Most had a sacred calendar centering around four seasonal festivals. Most had forms of worship emphasizing sacrifice, and on occasion grisly human sacrifice. Some specific motifs, like three-faced or threefold deities and a cauldron of immortality, seem general in the Celtic world.

The Romans liked to equate the Celtic gods with their own, and so we often know them best by Latin names. According to Caesar, the Gauls believed themselves descended from Dispater, "Earth-father," Lord of the Underworld; a myth is suggested, such as that found in many parts of the world, of the first people pushing their way up through the soil. The Romans also spoke of a Celtic Apollo, also called Bormo, "Warm," in Gaul; like Apollo he was associated with hot springs and healing. Equivalents to Mars were widespread among people so prone to fighting. The name Jupiter was given numerous mountain and thunder spirits, but it is uncertain whether they were sky-gods. Another set of Celtic gods, such as the Irish Lug, were called Mercury, for they governed speech, roads, and boundaries; the Celtic peoples have ever been lovers of words and rhyme, and of travel. Minerva was equated by the Romans with Celtic goddesses of industry and crafts, such as the Irish culture-goddess Brigit, whose name later appeared as that of the Christian St. Brigit. Very intriguing is the horned god Cernunnos, who often is shown squatting in a Buddhalike posture; he has been compared to figures as diverse as the paleolithic reindeer-horned shaman of cave paintings, the yogic Shivalike master of animals of the Indus Valley seal, and the later "god of the witches."

The outlook of the insular Celts (those of Great Britain and Ireland) is better known that that of the mainland Celts because of the survival of some ancient literature in the islands. Those people believed themselves descended from a mother-goddess called Dana or Don. Her progeny were called the Tuath De Danann, "Tribesmen of Dana." Her divine sons include Goibniu, a Vulcanlike god of the forge who also brewed a beer of immortality; Nudd, Lludd, or Nodons, a kingly giver of wealth who had a silver hand; Amaethon, of agriculture; and (in Wales) Gwydion, of art and civilization.

Llyr or Ler, originally a sea-god, sometimes has a parent-of-the-gods role like

Gods, Kings, and Mysteries

that of Dana. (Ler is also the original of Shakespeare's King Lear; he had a daughter whose name became Cordelia. He was one of several Celtic gods who, after the conversion of the islands to Christianity, was remembered just as a human king of ancient Britain back in a legendary past.)

Ler's sons were mighty figures in their own right, and many stories were woven of them. Bran was a giant and hero who had a magic cauldron by which the dead could be brought back to life; after he was killed, his severed head continued to talk for the eighty-seven years it took to convey it to London for burial. The Irish variant, Bron, was a legendary sailor who, enticed by a goddess, pressed to reach even the paradisal world of the immortals in the Uttermost West. Later, the Christian St. Brendan (c. 484–577), according to accounts popular in the Middle Ages, made Atlantic voyages as a monk-explorer to various Atlantic islands of wonder, among which perhaps the American coast was his continental "Promised Land of the Saints." He is apparently the pagan god's emulator and namesake.[26]

Another son of Ler was Manannan, a great magician with three legs; the Isle of Man was named after him, and retains to this day his three legs on its coat-of-arms, set in a pinwheel formation.

The chief Irish god was called the Dagda, "the Good God." He was skillful at everything; he had a magic cauldron which could feed the world, a magic club one end of which would kill the living and the other would revive the dead; and a harp by which he summoned the seasons in turn. As a fertility figure and earth-god, he may have been similar to the Gallic "Dispater."

The Irish national epic is recorded in the *Leabhar Gabhala*. The present version of the story has been much influenced by classical and Christian writings, but it nonetheless reflects something of the old Celtic world view. Briefly, we are told that between 2640 and 2400 B.C. several races from Europe landed in Ireland; they each had to fight indigenous monsters called the Fomors, and in time the first races united.

Then came quite a different group, the Tuatha De Danann, the magical and divine children of Dana, led by Nudd. They came from the west and brought their magic cauldrons and wondrous arts of healing and culture. Defeating the Fomors and the peoples already there, they established a splendid kingdom. But in time they were overthrown by intrigues between men, the Fomors, and the spirits of the dead. The Tuatha De Danann then withdrew into the Fairy Mounds still respected in Ireland, through which they would return to the Plain of Joy and the Land of Youth, asking only to be remembered in worship by those whom they left behind, who would miss them and rue their own ingratitude once the marvelous folk had left. Once simply gods and ancestors, the Tuatha De Danann in this late narration have become a fairy-folk, in a strange position between human and divine.

A somewhat similar state is perhaps that of King Arthur in Britain, celebrated in song and story down to the musical *Camelot,* and of the Holy Grail. Arthur may have some historical background as a British (that is, Celtic) king who tried to fend

[26]See Geoffrey Ashe, *Land to the West: St. Brendan's Voyage to America* (New York: Viking Press, 1962).

off the invading Anglo-Saxons in the fourth or fifth century, just after the collapse of Roman rule. But many elements of his stories, including his ultimate passing to the Uttermost West, are clearly drawn from Celtic myths. Some have suggested that the Holy Grail, now regarded as the cup of Christ's Last Supper, is also related to the magic cauldrons of plenty and immortality so popular in pagan Celtic stories, and which mortals and other gods alike were always trying to steal.[27]

Through all that has been presented so far about Celtic belief, a bright thread has run—the luminous concept of the Other World. The Celtic Other World is not the shadowy and unappealing afterlife of most of the ancients (except the Egyptians), and was perhaps the Celtic idea that the Romans found most surprising and interesting.

Whether underground and reached through Fairy Mounds, or off beyond the Western Sea, a land wondrous and desirable awaited the intrepid or foolhardy. It was filled with shimmering trees and pure song, was undisturbed by storm or sickness, and its inhabitants lived forever. Mortals might be lured to this world— but the summoning gods or fairies, though marvelous, might not always put the interests of men ahead of their own. Many are the tales told of countrymen who followed a lady of beauty not meant for mortal eyes, or who fell asleep on a Fairy Mound, and disappeared for long years into the Other World, finally returning with fairy gold that turned to dry leaves under our sun.[28]

In the Christian-influenced times for which we have extensive record, the Other World was a fairyland parallel to this world, but not officially the abode of the dead. It seems probable, however, that fairyland is more or less continuous with the pagan realms of both the gods and the departed spirits. For the old Celtic land of the deceased was also a bright and cheerful place. Presumably, like man's place of ultimate origin, it was also underground, for the dead were buried and the grave was considered an entry to this land.

Archaeology reveals that nobles were provided with chariots and elaborate gear, including drinking goblets and hunks of meat for feasting on the other side. Over there, all conceivable perfection was actualized, all food and delight was at hand, and all those wounded or slain in war would arise the next day healed. It was a land of magic, ruled by gods. This strong belief in a happy immortality made the Celts fearless in battle, for death was no enemy. (Belief in reincarnation has also been attributed to the Celts, but this probably comes from a misunderstanding by ancient Greek and Roman writers of the Celtic concept of a vigorous afterlife in a better world.)

Those accounted learned in these matters, and in all other important lore, were

---

[27]Among the many books on the Arthurian and grail legends, Roger Sherman Loomis, *The Grail: From Celtic Myth to Christian Symbol* (New York: Columbia University Press, 1963) is a careful study emphasizing Celtic origins. An attractive popular book on Arthur, which includes reference to Celtic myths, is Helen Hill Miller, *The Realms of Arthur* (New York: Charles Scribner's, 1969).

[28]A fascinating collection of data on the belief in the "Little People," although to be used with some caution, is W. Y. Evans-Wentz, *The Fairy-Faith in Celtic Countries* (New York: University Books, 1966; first published 1911.)

the Druids. The title is thought to be related to the Greek *drus,* "oak," and the Indo-European root *vid,* "to see or know," common to such diverse words as wit, witch, video, and Veda.

The Druids have been much romanticized, both in ancient and modern times. The idea of an esoteric body of wise men, which one joins only through long training and strenuous initiation, is fascinating. There is an appeal for the city-pent in altars in oak groves, and such simple rites as the cutting of a branch of mistletoe with a gold sickle on the sixth day of the moon. But the Romans tried to stamp out the Druids because of their connection with the Celtic human sacrifices, which (despite the Romans' own brutalities) they found uncivilized and horrifying.

The facts seem to be that the Druids were a body within much of Celtic society who served as priests, professors, and judges. They preserved in oral tradition the rituals, poetry, history, and customary law of the tribes, and were referred to for expert advice on these matters. They read omens, made up the calendar, and predicted lucky and unlucky days. They presided at the great festivals, and could exclude those who did not respect them from participation, in effect outcasting recalcitrants. There is some evidence that many Druids, at least, constituted a wandering and intertribal class who met across tribal lines and could even stop battles. To become a full Druid took study (from memory and without books) for up to twenty years; lower orders of bards and seers seem related to Druidism. The blessings of Druids were full of magical potency, and their maledictions were feared; a terrible curse was dispatched by a Druid standing on one foot, pointing with one finger at the accursed one, and staring at him with one eye while the other was shut.

Sacrifice was the major business of the great rites at which the Druids presided. Part of the catch in a hunt and of the booty in war seems to have been set aside as sacred and could not be touched. At festivals, sacrificed animals were eaten for a feast.

Human sacrifice was widespread, but seems to have been related chiefly to occasions of crisis or triumph. At times of epidemic, or before a battle, it was common to offer human victims as propitiation; after a great victory, such sacrifices might be presented to the gods in thanksgiving. Not only prisoners of war or criminals, but even one's own women and children, might be the oblations. Humans were also offered as first-fruits to promote fertility. We read of huge wicker baskets being filled with humans as gifts to the gods and set on fire, of victims shot with arrows or impaled in temples, or drowned in vats, to appease these fierce deities. The shocked Roman and Greek authors, whose pride in their own gentility led them to spare the reader little, tell us also of the backs of Celtic human victims being opened in order to divine the future from the entrails, or of being stabbed with daggers in order to read the future from the way they fell, or from how their limbs twitched, or their blood flowed.

It is not clear, however, to what extent the great sacrifices actively involved only the ruling warrior and priestly classes. Some have suggested that most of the gods, mythologies, and rites so far cited were just those of the aristocracy, but if so, we know little about the worship of the Celtic common folk. One classical text refers to a sorceress, Mongfhinn, to whom "the women and common people addressed their prayers."[29]

All classes must have had some part in the four great seasonal festivals, even though they were basically celebrations of the courts and have a pastoral rather than planter background. They were Samhain on November 1, Imbolc on February 1, Beltane on May 1, and Lugnasad on August 1. These festivals, corresponding roughly to the equinoxes and solstices, have been perpetuated in the living non-Christian folk holidays of Halloween, Groundhog Day, May Day, and Midsummer's Night.[30]

The holiday celebrations were fundamentally to promote fertility. At Samhain and Beltane, bonfires were lit to "catch" the increase-giving power of the sun, and people danced around them in a sunwise direction. Cattle were driven between the fires that they might gain fertility. Other aspects of Samhain and Beltane (some post-Celtic) have been discussed in Chapter II.

This is a taste of Celtic religion: an ancient world of beautiful and imaginative myth, bright hopes of an Other World, and the wheel of seasonal festivals, amid the swords and blood of a harsh society.

THE RELIGION
OF THE GERMANIC PEOPLES

The Celts shared northern and central Europe with another people, a folk who spoke languages upon which modern German, Dutch, the Scandinavian tongues, and English are based. They were the Teutonic or Germanic people who came to populate much of northern Europe in the early centuries A.D.; the Viking raiders and the Anglo-Saxon settlers in England were among them. Theirs was the religion of the pre-Christian ancestors of a large number of Americans.

The Germanic peoples shared some religious patterns with their Celtic neighbors, cousins, and foemen. But they had their own gods, mythology, and spirit; their spiritual world is another realm.

Most people have a few mental images, if only from Richard Wagner's operas, to go with this realm. Heroes picked for death in battle by fair but grave Valkyrie maidens fight and feast in Valhalla until the end of this world. Wotan presides over those festivities with a brooding dignity. He is one-eyed and dark-cloaked; two ravens perch on his shoulders and bring him news of the world, two dogs wait before him to eat his meals, for Wotan subsists on mead alone. Other images arise too: horn-helmeted warriors filled with berserk battle-frenzy grappling to the death; the "Twilight of the Gods," and the final overpoweringly dramatic end of this world

[29]John X. W. P. Corcoran, "Celtic Mythology," in *Larousse Encyclopedia of Mythology* (New York: Prometheus Press, 1960), p. 250.

[30]On the meaning of the Celtic calendar and festivals, see Alwyn Rees and Brinley Rees, *Celtic Heritage* (New York: Grove Press, 1961), Chapter II.

in cosmic flame. On a lesser scale, one envisions delightful troupes of fairy-tale elves, dwarfs, trolls, and giants tumbling out of old Germanic lore.

These pictures are one-sided; Valhalla and its gods were chiefly worshipped by the aristocratic warrior class. But they do convey something of the atmosphere of northern religion, or at least its literary myths. Here is a world where the gods themselves are mortal, linked for the most part to a particular age. Moreover the gods battle with each other, and their conflicts cause deterioration in the state of humans. If the gods themselves are mostly mortal, certainly humans have no escape from death. Even Valhalla, where those slain in a day's sport-fighting are returned to life the next morning, will come to an end in the final conflagration. Those less than heroes have little more to look forward to after death than becoming a restless ghost haunting a burial mound. In this hard world, a man's destiny is shaped by the unconquerable fate that leads to death in the end, but one can face it with honor and heroic courage, and hope to be remembered when tales of immortal deeds are told around the fires of future generations.

The Germanic mythology reflects this view of human life, although it also suggests hope beyond the end. The versions of the German mythology we have are late literary redactions put down after the coming of Christian and classical influences; this needs to be taken into account, as does the world of the aristocratic warrior which it reflects. It may be that the less-well-understood popular and agricultural religion of the humbler classes would have revealed a more relaxed relation to the world and a greater affirmation of life and its eternal renewal.

Nonetheless, Germanic mythology deserves attention, for it is in itself a powerful and important component of the world's spiritual heritage. The major sources are the *Younger* or *Prose Edda,* written down in Iceland in the thirteenth century by Snorri Sturluson, and the *Elder* or *Poetic Edda,* a verse narrative put to paper in Iceland about the same time, though containing some very old material.[31]

In the myth, we are told that at the beginning there was only a vast emptiness. Then Niflheim, a world of fog and half-light, appeared in the north, and Muspellheim, a land of fire, in the south. Niflheim, dark, cold, and snowy, guarded by the nightmarish dog Garm, in time became also the dismal underworld of the dead ruled by the goddess Hel. But the mixing together of forces from Niflheim and Muspellheim produced between them water and earth, and eventually the body of Ymir, the first giant, and the world where humans and their gods live. From Ymir (compare the Indic Yama) and the cow Audhumla, giants, humankind, and the gods descended.

In a somewhat incompatible account, it was also said that the world was a giant tree called Yggdrasil. This marvelous tree had roots which extended deep into the hidden wellsprings of being; at its base was the fountain of Mimir in which all wisdom lay, and from it Wotan himself drank, even though the price was the loss of an eye. At the very top of Yggdrasil an eagle and a gold rooster scanned the world on behalf of the gods, in its foliage animals fed, at its base the grim serpent or

---

[31]Jean I. Young, trans., *The Prose Edda of Snorri Sturluson: Tales from Norse Mythology* (Berkeley and Los Angeles: University of California Press, 1971), and Henry Adams Bellows, *The Poetic Edda* (Princeton: Princeton University Press, 1923).

dragon Nidhoggr gnawed, indifferent that his appetite would bring an end to all that is fair. Indeed, the cosmic tree would quickly die, were it not continually watered from the icy springs of Niflheim and from Mimir's fountain by the Norns who control the future.

While the tree stood, Wotan and the other gods led a vigorous life. The Germanic deities are a numerous family and cannot all be named here. Basically they fall into two classes, the Aesir and the Vanir. The aristocratic Aesir include Wotan and Thor, best-known of gods.

Wotan (Odin) is the priest-king. He deeply sought knowledge of the runes, the old northern form of writing used mainly for charms and spells, even as he had sought Mimir's wisdom. He presented himself as a sacrifice to win them. An old poem tells that he hung himself for nine nights on the tree Yggdrasil to gain this runic initiation.

> I ween that I hung on the windy tree,
> Hung there for nights full nine:
> With the spear I was wounded, and offered I was
> To Odin, myself to myself.
> On the tree that none may ever know
> What root beneath it runs.
> They gave me neither food nor drink,
> I bent and looked down below . . .[32]

After this ordeal, Wotan was allowed to drink again from the well of Mimir, and this restored him to full vigor and the mastery of all arcane lore. As a magician, he could take many shapes, and was something of an ominous, mysterious figure. He often wandered the earth on strange missions wearing a low hat, a dark cloak, and a black patch over one eye, or else riding his incredibly fast eight-legged horse Sleipnir. He was a mystical warrior who in every conflict picked a side to favor. Through his magic he saw that they had victory, and the Valkyries brought the slain home to him in Valhalla to join his band. Wotan's battle-joy was best seen in the Berserkers, bands of crazed fighting men who actually existed in the ancient North. Considered Wotan's special devotees, they would rush into battle seized by a trance-like frenzy, indifferent to fear, pain, or death, and it was said that few could withstand their terrible fury. Sometimes this wizard-warrior would even call out the dead to join his rampaging band, for when it thundered on a wild stormy night people would say the Wild Hunt—Wotan accompanied by spirits of the dead he had summoned out of burial mounds—was in furious course. The name Wotan itself is connected with the German word *wüten,* the frenzy and fury of battle.

Less enigmatic is Thor (Donar). If Wotan was priest-king, Thor was simply the ordinary warrior, the common good fellow, writ large. He had no wizard craft and could be bamboozled by magic, but he was immensely strong and fundamentally reliable. Thor the red-bearded always had with him a short hammer with which he

---

[32]From Hans-Joachim Schoeps, *The Religions of Mankind,* trans. Richard and Clara Winston. Copyright © 1966 by Doubleday and Company, Inc., Garden City, New York, p. 109. Reprinted by permission of the publisher, and of Victor Gallancz, Ltd., London.

pounded enemies and obstacles; numerous small models of it used as charms have been found in northern Europe.

The other set of gods beside the Aesir were the Vanir. They were especially connected with wealth and fertility; unlike the tumultous Aesir, the Vanir were peaceful and benevolent in mood, bringing sunlight and life-giving rain rather than battle and storm. The most important of these givers of plenty were Njord who lived in the sea and controlled its wealth, Freyr god of peace, and Freyja goddess of love.

Long ago the Aesir and Vanir engaged in war. The Vanir entered the land of the gods where the Aesir were already located, and forced the Aesir to allow them to dwell there also. Possibly this is a mythic way of saying that the Aesir, as gods of war and the hunt, were known to the Germanic peoples first, but that later with the introduction of agriculture another set of deities was discovered. In any case, by the time of the recorded mythologies both groups were well known, and the drama of their interrelationship was underway. Indeed, Freyja (Frigg), sister of Freyr, was already reckoned wife of Wotan, although admittedly the marriage was a tempestuous one.

But that was nothing compared to the tragedies that were later to result from the conflict of Aesir and Vanir. When the Aesir tortured the Vanir goddess Gollweig in order to extort gold, events moved headlong into the end of the age of Aesir and Vanir, to the Twilight of the Gods.

There were other roots of disaster too. The most significant involves Loki, originally a fire-demon, a god mischievous and unpredictible, who on more than one occasion tactlessly denounced all the other gods, and whose heartless tricks often prevented the establishment of the happiness and harmony the other gods desired, if they did not deserve.

The most grievous offense of Loki was in connection with the death of Balder. Balder, full of light, son of Wotan and Freyja, was a beautiful, innocent god beloved of all and who held no malice against anyone. All the gods and all the creatures of earth vowed to do him no harm. But they failed to take into account two exceptions: the mistletoe plant, which was not asked to swear because it seemed too obscure, and the irrascible Loki, who resented the claims of Balder to invulnerability. When the gods sought to tempt fate and test Balder's invincibility by throwing stones and drawing swords at him, Loki persuaded a blind god, Hoder, to throw a sprig of mistletoe at Balder. The beautiful god was killed.

Even as he went to the underworld ruled by Hel (Balder did not go to Valhalla since he did not die in battle), there was a chance he might be saved. Freyja, his sorrowful mother, persuaded Hel to agree to allow him to return if all creatures on earth mourned for Balder. All did—with one exception. The cruel Loki transformed himself into a giantess, who said, "Neither in his life nor after his death did Balder render me the least service. Let Hel keep what she has." She refused to shed a single tear. Balder remained below, and the realms of both the gods and of men experienced no more pristine happiness, beauty, or righteousness.

Things then rushed on toward Ragnorok, the End of the Age. As it approaches the giants are to grow strong and shake the great tree Yggdrasil, causing the earth to tremble, and then the giants will attack the gods. Old scores are settled, and all the great deities—Wotan, Thor, Loki, and the rest—will be slain. The universe itself will be shattered, and dissolved in tremendous cataclysms of fire and flood. The abyss will open and even sun and stars will disappear into it.

This will not be the final end, however. After the total destruction of the old world, beyond all hope or expectation a new world will emerge from the chaos. Pure, beautiful, and fresh, it will give life a new chance. All the gods of this coming world will be new, save that those who had no part in the crimes of the old world will arise in this one. At their head will be Balder, now resurrected as sovereign of a new and better earth where his peaceful ways will be law.

Let us now glance briefly at the practices of old Northern religion. Kings were sacred and the chief priests of their people. Emulating the role of Wotan, they were the mystical consorts, perhaps, of fertility goddesses, and the chief sacrificers at offerings. Royal regalia pointed to myth and rite; the king's arm-ring was a sign of royal power and was sacred, his wand was a branch of mistletoe.

The *blót,* or blood-sacrifices, the king or chief performed were to increase his own life and that of his people. These elaborate public rites took place out-of-doors, for despite some earlier belief to the contrary it now seems the northmen had few if any large temples or impressive images.[33] There is some evidence that the king by sacrificing his sons prolonged his own life and power, until finally when he became decrepit he offered himself at the arrangement of the queen, perhaps in imitation of Wotan's self-sacrifice and renewal on the tree.[34]

In any case, sacrificial religion was bloody. At major festivals, such as the one to Freyr for fertility every nine years at Uppsala, Sweden, prisoners of war and animal victims were hung on a tree. After sacrifices, the blood would be scattered on the sacred altar or mound, and everyone would feast.

Agricultural religion was equally important. In Sweden, a wagon with an image of Freyr as the sun was drawn from village to village during the spring with great celebration to restore life and fertility to the fields. A maiden, playing the role of the god's consort, rode in it.[35] Great fertility festivals, often including orgy, marked the short northern Summer.

Among the ordinary people, the practice of Germanic religion seems also to have been an individualistic thing. A man might devote most of his attention to a particular god who became his patron. His worship might be an occasional sacrifice at an elf mound at the back of his farm, or carrying a hammer of Thor when he put out to sea to fish or raid.

Death was an important matter, for funeral customs were elaborate. Funeral pyres or burial mounds were sometimes embellished with ships placed in the grave.

---

[33]H. R. E. Davidson, "Progress on the Northern Front," *Religion: A Journal of Religion and Religions,* IV, part 2 (Autumn 1974), p. 153.

[34]A. V. Ström, "The King God and his Connection with Sacrifice in Old Norse Religion," in *Sacral Kingship/Regalità Sacra* (Leiden: E. J. Brill, 1959), pp. 702–15.

[35]E. O. G. Turville-Petre, *Myth and Religion of the North* (London: Weidenfeld and Nicolson, 1964), pp. 172–75; 256–57.

Burials of those who could afford it were rich with gold, swords, and food left for the departed. Sometimes a wife, mistress, or retainer would be killed and buried with a great man to give him companionship.

But, unless he was a warrior going to Valhalla, he might enjoy this wealth in no better world than the grave itself. The soul was thought to be separable from the body, and could even leave the body during sleep, but after death was linked to the body in the burial mound—although it might venture forth as a ghost or barrow-wight into the vicinity to work grisly havoc, or dash frenzied through stormy skies with Wotan on the Wild Hunt.

SEVEN

ONE GOD, MANY WORDS AND WONDERS

Three Great Monotheistic Religions

Rabbi blowing a shofar or ram's horn before an opened ark containing scrolls of the Torah under richly-ornamented covers.

THE NATURE
OF MONOTHEISTIC RELIGION

Monotheistic religions are those professing belief in one all-powerful and personal God, and in no other gods. The largest and most influential of these faiths today are Judaism, Christianity, and Islam. These three are a family, for they all explicitly go back to one source, the experience of one God of the ancient Israelites recorded in the Old Testament. The God of Judaism, Christianity, and Islam is the God of Abraham and Moses and the prophets; these fathers in faith are venerated by all three.

As we have seen, there are other monotheisms too: Zoroastrianism, Sikhism, and in a sense bhaktic Hinduism and Amidist Buddhism. There are overtones of monotheism in the primitive high god, and nondualist Hinduism and Buddhism. But for all that, these three monotheisms are a family—though Zoroastrianism may have had no small impact on their development—and are uniquely bound together in origin and history. Even their quarrels—and never have religious hatreds and persecutions matched those among and within these three—have the special bitterness of family fights, when an ancient kinship one does not want to honor makes rage all the worse.

Yet these three religions, for all their shared past and common beliefs, should not be thought of as in a separate category from all other faiths. To do so would be to overemphasize the first of the three forms of religious expression, the theoretical—that is, the myths, doctrines, and ideologies, which usually include what historical awareness there is among believers—and neglect the message of the other two: the practical or worship and cultus; and the sociological, or types of groups formed. For in the last two we find divergences both between and within the three faiths every bit as great as between one of them and, say, what is found in Hinduism or Shinto.

Thus, the following discussion of the characteristics of the monotheistic traditions may appear full of qualifications, exceptions, and statements that this or that trait is shared by other traditions too. That is because religious life simply is that

One God, Many Words and Wonders

way. A distinctive belief, such as belief in one personal God, does not necessarily make the religion different in practice all the way through—and different people may experience the same religion in different ways. There is certainly a distinctively monotheistic style of relation to God, a relation of interpersonal awe, love, and obedience unshared by polytheism or mystical monism. But not everyone in a monotheistic tradition is really concerned with that sort of relationship to God, or feels he ought to be. For many the "temple" aspects of a monotheistic religion— worship, law, customs, society, mysticism—are what is important.

What is more, we find striking parallels in patterns of worship and styles of religious groups which seem to pay little heed to whether the faith is theoretically monotheistic or polytheistic. Religious activity throughout the world could be classified according to way of worship—that is, whether images are used or not, whether pilgrimages are important or not, and so forth. Or, it could be classified according to types of groups formed—whether monasticism is normative, whether there are "services" with a congregation—instead of in the usual way, according to formal "beliefs." By these classifications, the lines would be quite different from what we are used to, and would cut across some of what are termed "religions," to link parts of one with parts of another in a far different corner of the world. For most people, style of worship and group have a deep, half-conscious impact on attitudes which may well exceed that of formal belief.

Within the monotheistic family itself, the messages communicated by the practical and social forms, including art and architecture, could hardly be more contrasting. Compare the Muslim mosque in the Alhambra in Granada with a Spanish Roman Catholic church. The mosque is of clean lines, devoid of pictures or images, the worshippers who prayed in it having been oriented only by a bare niche in the wall to the direction of Mecca. Yet far from giving an impression of mere bareness, the cool, still arabesqued interior of the mosque is in an almost indescribable way fullness and light. It turns thoughts to God, for all that is not God is expunged; nonrepresentational designs of arabesque fantasy line the walls and dome, raising the mind beyond image to dimensions of meditation which lead to God as pure spirit.

The traditional Spanish Catholic church also evokes feelings of wonder and awe, but in a very different way. Here one typically is confronted with richness and diversity of forms to rival a jewel box. The altar is a gleaming shape of gold and brocade, and behind it the reredos reaches to the ceiling, an ornate waterfall of gilt, lights, and statues of saints. Indeed, images are not exhausted at the altar, but continue around the church, each in its own little chapel—of sorrowful and bleeding Christs; of the Blessed Virgin Mary, Queen of the Universe in imperial crown and robe; St. James of Compostela on his horse, and so on. Apostles, monks, nuns, bishops, kings, each unique yet each part of a larger mosaic, suggest that in this church the power of the beam of monotheistic light is shown by the many different colors and forms into which it breaks as it interacts with the world. This faith appears close to polytheism, though it is not that. Yet neither is it the clear, austere monotheism of Islam, whose simplicity, oddly enough, is matched by the rustic grace of many shrines of that most polytheistic of religions, Shinto.

History of the Three Main Western Monotheistic Faiths

Dates	General Influences	Judaism	Christianity	Islam
1500 AD	Marxism French & Amer. revolutions European pre-eminence	State of Israel (1948) Holocaust Conservative Reform Hasidism	American Christianity John Wesley (1703–91) Radical Reformers English Ref. (1534) Calvin (1509–64) Luther (1483–1546)	Nationalism Growth of Islam in Africa Sufi orders and devotion prominent
1000 AD	Renaissance Feudalism	Kabbalah Zohar (1275) Maimonides (1135–1204)	Medieval "heretics" Medieval Catholicism Aquinas (1225–1274) St. Francis (1181–1226)	Rise of Ottoman Empire Islam spreads to India, Malaysia, Indonesia Al-Arabi (d. 1290)
500 AD	Byzantine Empire	Jewish dispersion throughout Europe, Asia & N. Africa	Separation of Eastern Orthodox and Roman Catholic churches (1056) Monasticism Rise of medieval papacy Conversion of Europe	Al-Ghazali (d. 1111) Avicenna (980–1037) Baghdad Caliphate (750–1258) Rise of Sufism Muslim conquests Muhammad (570–652)

History of the Three Main Western Monotheistic Faiths

Dates	General Influences	Judaism	Christianity	Islam
1 AD/BC	Roman Empire	Talmud Temple destroyed (80)	Augustine (354–430) Council of Nicaea (323) Constantine (r. 312–37) Gospels (60–100) Paul (c. 50) Jesus (c. 30)	
500 BC	Hellenistic Culture Alexander Persian Empire	John the Baptizer Maccabees (204) Apocalyptic literature Most Wisdom literature Return from captivity in Babylon (538)	*Jewish Religion Before the Christian and Islamic Eras*	
1000 BC	Cyrus Zoroaster Trojan War	Exile (586) Early prophets: Amos Elijah Solomon (r. 961–22) David (c. 100)		
1500 BC	Egypt and Mesopotamia dominant in Near East	Judges Exodus (c. 1290) Moses		
2000 BC	Sumerians decline Pyramid Texts	Abraham		

On the other hand, if one were to compare a Quaker meetinghouse or a New England village church with the mosque, one would feel one was, at least, in the same world. Orders of monks and nuns bring Roman Catholic and Eastern Orthodox Christianity closer to Buddhism, in this particular sociological respect, than to most of their Protestant, Jewish, and Muslim neighbors. Many different grids can be laid over the religious world to produce different configurations of similarity and difference.

Nonetheless, the three monotheistic faiths have common features, both historically and practically. All have their roots in what Karl Jaspers has called the "axial age." The impact of this period, covering centuries and capable of flexible definition, yet in retrospect a distinctive historical "moment," is marked in certain fundamental ways. (It has been discussed in Chapter I.) Human consciousness emerged from cosmic religion into a state in which it was apparent that things change and do not change back, that human history is a process in which the new and more complex is always unfolding. This increasing consciousness of history suggests a force, greater than seasonal natural forces, which governs this larger process. Awareness of history also makes possible monotheism's central pivot in history—the distinctive revelation, prophet, and scripture—which can give meaning to the new and more complicated historical world.

Each monotheistic religion, then, traces itself back to a historical founder, such as Moses, Jesus, Muhammad, or, further east, Zoroaster and Nanak. Monotheism is never a simple continuation of something growing out of a timeless past, even though it may embrace important elements of cosmic religion. The idea of a special revelation through a known historical figure, who at a known point in time gave an authoritative word from the one personal God which the monotheistic faith proclaims, seems to be inseparable from monotheistic expression.

Thus monotheism generally has strong roots in the "prophet" as well as the "temple" stance, with intense individual commitment and emphasis on verbal expression. This means that the written word, scripture, is of great importance in monotheistic religion. While other religions also have constantly studied and chanted scriptures, in the monotheistic religions scriptures (characteristically short and clear-cut compared to Vedas or Sutras) are especially decisive statements of general law and belief as well as mystical hymns, monastic rules, and philosophy. They are to be universally proclaimed, and are given through the founder, or at least are fruits of a process started by him, at the pivotal moment. These scriptures are written; significantly in the axial age writing also emerged.

In keeping with its linkage to the discovery of history, monotheism is inevitably tied to what we have spoken of as a linear concept of time. While the idea has played different roles in different times and places, Zoroastrianism and the three monotheisms now under discussion have taught that the world was created by God at the beginning of time, and is moving toward a climax at an equally definite end: the coming of the Messiah, the final judgment, the making of a new heaven and earth. Monotheisms are, in other words, eschatological.

Finally, it can be noted that monotheisms arise or become socially important in periods of rapid cultural change; that is, in conjunction with the emergence of national cultures and political institutions—ancient Israel, the Arabs at the time of Muhammad, Christianity in the flux of the Roman world and subsequently providing a cultural focus for the dying Roman Empire and the new European nations. (Of course, other axial age religions such as Buddhism and Confucianism have done this too.) Monotheism, with its idea of a universal God who can legitimatize one sovereign and one law below, helps greatly in a transition from tribalism to nationhood.

But monotheism also, by its own intrinsic logic, is universalist, for if there is but one God with one message, it must be for all people everywhere. This is modified considerably in Judaism, with its idea of the "chosen people" with a special calling by the one God, but even so, the chosen people are to mediate a blessing to all the families of the earth. In Islam and Christianity, monotheism and belief in one revelation have at various times served as an ideological undergirding for the creation of empires uniting many cultures and peoples—even though as we have seen, systematic polytheism can also serve this function. But an international, universal gospel serves especially well as a dynamic for the vigorous missionary expansion of culture. It is usually personal monotheism, then, or a psychologically similar form of Buddhism, such as those of Kamakura Japan, which strongly missionizes and spreads cross-culturally.

Monotheism is like a river running through religious history. The obscure springs where it arose are located very far back indeed, doubtless with the primordial high god of archaic hunters. The river flows through the fertile lowlands of the inevitable polytheism of archaic agricultural religion, with its emphasis on the marriage of heaven and earth to produce the divine child, and of the ancient empires uniting the local gods of many tribes and towns into an organized composite. Even then, however, monotheism glimmered faintly in the usual concept of a controlling universal principle, associated with an often vague but sovereign deity: T'ien, Varuna, Amon, Zeus. In the ancient Judaism of Abraham, Moses, and the prophets, the river first emerges as a distinct current: it is then fed by tributaries such as Zoroastrianism and Greek philosophy, and at the same time spreads out like a delta to form its three main branches. Sometimes these branches flow torrentially; more often they become slow, amiable, domesticated streams and millponds, which coexist comfortably with diverse forests of cosmic religion, folk religion, and local culture. But the river never quite stops moving toward a destination.

Judaism

JEWISH UNIQUENESS

Every religion is unique in its own way. But none perhaps is as distinctive or has as remarkable a history as that of the Jews. It seems always to be the exception to every rule of history, just as Jewish thought or even the mere presence of the Jewish community has so often pointed up the limitations of whatever "universal" truth and practice someone else has tried to lay out. Toward the ancient empires and polytheisms, toward Eastern mysticism and Christian salvationism, toward modern nationalism, dictatorship, communism, mass culture, and disbelief, Judaism—or at least some Jews—have always said "Yes, but. . . ."

They have not opposed all of these things: Judaism, for example, has had mystical thinkers worthy of compare with those of India, and also its share of skeptics, and has been and is today expressed in nationhood. But it has always been wary of making an "ism" out of them, and then saying that mysticism, or skepticism, or nationalism is the end of meaning and truth, that when you have that, "you've arrived." Jews have always had a tendency, fired by centuries of living as a minority "different" from the majority culture of whatever nation they happen to be inhabiting, and honed by centuries of hard study of the bristly legal texts of their law, to say, "Yes, but perhaps there's another side—maybe there's more than just this one thing."

The questions have not always even been put verbally. The mere presence of the Jewish community as an all-too-visible exception to a nation's spiritual and cultural homogeneity has stated them more eloquently than words. Needless to say, such questions, whether verbal or implicit, are not always welcome to those who prefer to leave the waters of mystical or cultural unity unruffled. Jewish "differentness" and the awkward queries it implies for others have given Jews much suffering. But they have persisted in making the question felt, and have thereby also pressed human society not to settle for partial truths.

Jews have been exceptions from the beginning of the tradition among the Israelites of the Old Testament (as Christians call that part of their Bible which is the

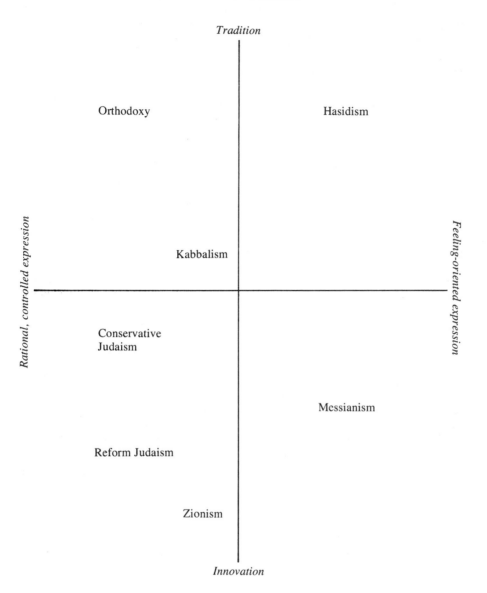

Main Themes of Judaism

Tradition

Orthodoxy   Hasidism

Rational, controlled expression   *Feeling-oriented expression*

Kabbalism

Conservative
Judaism

Messianism

Reform Judaism

Zionism

Innovation

Thematic Chart VI. In Judaism, polarity between intellectual and emotional modes of religious expression has been particularly marked, modified by the fact that both have been used as conveyors of both traditionalist and innovative visions and Judaism, and by the fact that both come together in actual Jewish community and family life.

Jewish Scriptures). They had developed toward monotheism of a personal God as polytheism became richer and richer among their neighbors.

Why this exclusive reliance on one God, and finally belief that he is the only God and sole king of the universe, developed uniquely among the Israelites is hard to say. It may have arisen in part out of the climatic situation of pastoral peoples wandering over the face of the hard desert. The fact that humans are like aliens in these lands caring for flocks who would die were they not taken to pasture and well by shepherds, suggests that God in the infinite desert sky above is as "other" from earth as man from desert, yet guides his people like a shepherd his flock. That the shepherd, like Abraham, sets up an altar and worships the same God in many different places, wherever his wanderings take him, implies that his God is universal, not tied to place or nature like an agricultural deity. (Yet, although the early monotheists were pastoralists, many pastoralists did not become monotheists.)

The traditional Jewish interpretation was simply that God, for reasons of his own, himself selected this people and made himself known to them. This did not mean that he meant to make life smooth and easy for them; the call involved heavy responsibilities and frequent suffering. He established a covenant or agreement with them, that they would worship him, follow his law, and be faithful to him; on his part God would preserve them throughout history, even to a consummation at the end of history when the meaning of this procedure would be made known. A core, at least, of Jews have maintained this trust; no people so dispersed as they have been for two thousand years, so much a minority and so persecuted, has ever kept a faith intact for so long.

This faith has not been *centered* on belief in an afterlife, or an experience of salvation in personal or mystical terms, or a philosophy, or a technique of meditation, or even a set of doctrines. It has been centered on awareness of this unique relationship with God, but has taken different forms at different times. It was first God who called Abraham from Mesopotamia, and the Israelite people from Egypt, as they viewed it. Then the relationship was one of God helping them win their wars and establish their nation. Next the relationship was expressed chiefly through following an elaborate law they believed God had given them to show the differentness, with unusual stipulations regarding food, work, worship, and much else. In modern times still other views of the special relationship have been put forward. But in any case, what has made Jews stand apart has not been any special elaborate beliefs or exotic spiritual attainments, but something harder to pin down—varying ways in which a sense of being different has been expressed, which in turn have helped to create the difference and so the sense of it—but together with a belief, at least traditionally, that it is the one God who initiated and sustains the process.

THE ANCIENT STORY
OF JUDAISM

The ancient religion of Syria and Palestine itself, and no doubt of the earliest Hebrews, was related to that of the major Semitic civilization, in the Valley of the Two Rivers, which we have surveyed. These peoples were all Semitic (except the Sumerians) and knew in common deities like the Great Mother Ashtoreth (Ishtar) and the dying-rising vegetation god Tammuz or Baal. The account in the Book of Genesis tells us that Abraham, father of the Hebrews, came out of Ur in the Valley of the Two Rivers, affirming still more strongly the common cultural background. This is reinforced by many passages in the Old Testament, from the obvious parallels between the flood story featuring Noah in Genesis and that of Ut-Napishtim in Babylon (though the monotheism of the former and the polytheism of the latter afford quite a difference in tone), to the reference in Ezekiel to the practice in Israel of "wailing for Tammuz"—of which the prophet much disapproved. The difference was that the Hebrews were originally herdsmen Semites, like the Arab bedouins of today, in contrast to the more numerous and prosperous sedentary agriculturalist Semites of Mesopotamia and the fertile regions of Syria and Palestine who worshipped fertility-giving lords of the land such as Baal.

But the Hebrews, wandering herdsmen originally on the fringes of the great Semitic civilizations, had their own God. They were familiar with the Baals and Ashtoreths and Marduks, for from time to time they must have come into the cities to trade and could not help but notice the massive temples, the powerful priests, the sacred prostitutes. But for themselves, at sacred stones and mountaintops deep in the desert they knew better than anyone else, they worshipped their own God, Yahweh, who was not tied to one place but could be served wherever the tribe wandered.[1] Moreover, he was not pleased with the offerings from the cultivated field, but preferred instead the odor of roasting flesh from the herds of his own poor but free people, as the story of Cain and Abel tells us (Gen. 4:3–5).

It was not until most of the Hebrews themselves became agriculturalists after settling in the land of Canaan (Palestine) that the issue of the Baals and Ashtoreths became acute. Should the tribes stay with a god of the desert after they had become people of the soil, or go to the Baals and their kin, whose province seemed to be the agricultural way of life? Many understandably took the latter option.

But there were always those, led by the prophets, who contended that the Hebrews should continue to worship Yahweh even in the new way of life. This was because Yahweh was particularly connected with the basic rules of the nation, the Law of Moses, and with inspiration (originally more or less shamanistic in type) which seized the nonpriestly spiritual leaders called prophets. Because they harked back to the nomadic period with its simpler ways, the parties favoring continuing loyalty to Yahweh had a rigid, conservative appearance, and the other side doubtless a suggestion of judicious flexibility.

Ironically, the faith in Yahweh had far more future to it and apparently far more potential for adjusting to various cultural levels, from planting to modern industrial; the desert god of the Hebrews lives today, while the Semitic agricultural religion, which seemed the height of sophistication in 800 B.C., did not outlive the cultural level it served.

A statement like this is, of course, only one side of the situation. A deity can

[1]In Hebrew the name of God is always, out of reverence, written just with the consonants and without the marks that indicate vowels. Transliterated into Roman letters, the divine name, called the tetragrammaton, is YHVH. The pronunciation must have been something like Yahweh or Yahveh. The name "Jehovah" of the King James Bible is an older attempt at pronouncing the same name by supplying the vowels of the title Adonai, "The Lord." Devout Jews, of course, would not make the attempt to pronounce the name; as in the Bible, God is spoken of not by name but by terms like Adonai.

keep the same name and become different, or change names and remain the same. The "wailing for Husain," which is a part of Islam in some sections of Iraq, India, and even Trinidad today, seems in direct continuity with the ancient near eastern wailing for Tammuz. Although the name of Yahweh was kept among the agricultural Hebrews in the end, his worship evolved to include farming feasts and offerings, and these were retained among Jews long after they became urban.

It is no mark against Yahweh if his worship undergoes development, regardless of what the case may be with other gods. For a fundamental feature of the Old Testament is what we have spoken of as a historical or linear concept of time. A picture steadily emerges of the relation between God and the Children of Abraham as like a dialogue, in which God's faithfulness is always constant, but as his people are more or less loyal to their pledge the situation takes different forms, reward for obedience and punishment for disobedience. The Books of Deuteronomy and Chronicles in particular interpret the history of Israel in these terms, as do the prophets regarding the events of their day. One can think of it as a graph, with the high peaks representing the moments when Israel was seen as close to God, and the low points the periods of apostasy.

The story begins with a very high point, the creation of the world and the placing of Adam and Eve in the Garden of Eden. But suddenly the graph falls to near the bottom as the primal couple disobey God in the matter of eating the forbidden fruit, and are expelled from the original paradise. From then on, the dealings of God with the people of Israel are really a part of his plan to bring mankind back to the original high level of relationship.

The story of Noah, the ark, and the flood tells us that the process began as God retained enough concern to save one righteous family, and specimens of the animals, in the destruction of the wicked. But the plan did not really get underway until Abraham and his family were called to leave Ur of the Chaldees, in order to go to a new land which God promised to give Abraham, and where he would make of him a mighty nation. This was not for Abraham's sake alone, but was part of a plan for the good of the whole earth, for God said "by you all the families of the earth will bless themselves" (Gen. 12:1–3). The ancient city of Ur has been excavated, and it has been verified that there were people there called Hapiru (Hebrews) in Ur, a Sumerian capital, before around 2000 B.C., when it appears Abraham and his people left for the Promised Land by way of Haran, a city in northern Mesopotamia which was a center of the cult of Sin, the moon god.

This Covenant of God with Abraham was ratified by Abraham's sacrificing to God, and confirmed by God's giving Abraham a son, Isaac, in his old age. The promise then passed to Isaac, and to his son Jacob, also called Israel, the name by which the Hebrew people became known. Under Abraham, Isaac and Jacob, the line on the graph clearly moved upward; for all their human failings, a new relationship was being established between God and mankind in the patriarchs. Indeed, the sharp difference between Hebrew religion and some others could scarcely be more evident than in the personality of the father of faith, Abraham, and his son and grandson. They are not mystics or meditators, magicians or philosophers, but shrewd, barely literate, sometimes coarse, obscure wanderers on the edge of civilization, who fought and made love and drove hard bargains and (at least in the case of the young Jacob) were not above trickery to get their ends. In the Bible, however, it is not the self-purification or spiritual achievements of a yogin or an adept or a Buddha which makes one available to God to advance his work. It is rather that the one God, with true omnipotence, is able to reach to the "bottom of the barrel" if he wishes and select whomever he wants, however unpromising.

There were very hard times in the latter days of Jacob, and he went down to Egypt (where Jacob's son Joseph had been taken earlier and risen to power) to try to buy food. But in time the Children of Israel ended up in bondage there, and this was a low point on the graph, for the God of the patriarchs and his worship were nearly forgotten.

After 400 years, we are told, this situation was reversed through the labors of Moses, the most outstanding figure in the Old Testament. Moses appears as a member of the oppressed Hebrew class in Egypt who nonetheless advanced high in the service of pharaoh. But he killed an Egyptian he saw beating a Hebrew, and was forced to flee to the deserts of Midian (now northwest Saudi Arabia) where he kept the flocks of distant kinsmen. There God spoke to him in a vision of a burning bush, and Moses returned to Egypt to lead the Hebrew people out of bondage. He succeeded, and the event was fraught with great drama. Moses and his brother Aaron brought ghastly plagues to pass to force pharaoh's hand, culminating in the death of the firstborn, save those of the Hebrews who marked their homes with sacrificial blood. That night, too, they ate a meal standing up in preparation for the flight from Egypt; this is commemorated in the Passover.

The Exodus probably occurred about 1300 B.C., although some date it a couple centuries or so earlier. The narratives of the parting of the Red Sea, so that the escaping slaves could thwart their last pursuers, and of the forty years of wandering in the desert, are well known. At Mount Sinai, in the midst of this trek, the final definition of the covenant or agreement between God and Israel was made. Amid the thunder and lightning of a great storm, Moses received the Ten Commandments on the mountain, and the rest of the law recorded in the Torah, or first five books of the Bible. At this point, the line on the graph moves sharply up.

Moses himself died before he could lead Israel into the Promised Land; this difficult and warlike task was undertaken by his successor Joshua. Gradually a nation was put together from an assortment of restless herding and raiding tribes, who were at best a rough democracy under emergent leaders called "judges." (It might be pointed out here that many scholars believe the Book of Judges contains the oldest material in the Bible which can be accepted as history in the ordinary sense, some of it having been written virtually on the scene. The accounts of the patriarchs, Moses, and the Exodus are of inestimable importance for the Judaeo-Christian-Islamic religious outlook, and certainly reflect real events, but these scholars would say they reach us in the form of tradition rather than of strictly historical documents.) As the Hebrews adapted to the agricultural way of life indigenous to Palestine, sedentary institutions like kingship came to seem more and more appealing. Finally, it is written that God consented to the anointing of the first king, Saul, though Yahweh expressed only reluctant approval through the prophet Samuel for this development, indicating the conservative nature of the Yahwist and prophetic faith.

Saul, however, proved unworthy of the kingship; he failed to liquidate completely the people and flocks of the Amalek folk, as Samuel said Israel was commanded to do by the Lord. Saul was replaced by David, and David was succeeded by one of his sons, Solomon.

Under Solomon a great temple to Yahweh was built in which all the ritual prescriptions of the Law of Moses for temple worship could be carried out; from the time of Moses until then Yahweh had been worshipped in a movable shrine called the tabernacle. After Solomon the kingdom divided, into Israel in the north and Judah around Jerusalem, and the glory of the people relatively declined.

During these times the line on the graph, as read by devout later historians, wavered up and down like a fever chart. In the time of Joshua and the judges, it was presumed that whenever Israel won, the Lord was pleased with them; when Israel lost, it was because there had been sin. But then came figures such as Samuel, Elijah, Elisha, and Nathan, and after them writing prophets like Amos, Isaiah, Jeremiah, and the rest, who argued this was not necessarily the case. The prophets were apparently originally members of a class of seers who entered into some sort of visionary, divinatory trance not wholly unlike a shaman's, and there gave out the direct word of God for a situation. As in the case of Samuel reproving Saul even as the king stood victorious over the Amalekites, or Nathan reproving David at the height of his glory for having taken Bathsheba, another man's wife, the word of the Lord that came through these envoys could well indicate God was displeased even when his people seemed successful. It could still happen that they were forgetting the fullness of God's commandments. Even in prosperity, they might, as Amos said, be too much "at ease in Zion," and sell the needy for a pair of shoes.

The low point in this period came in 586 B.C. when the Babylonians took Jerusalem, destroyed the temple, and carried off leading citizens to Babylon for a life of exile and servitude. Prophets like Jeremiah blamed this on the failings of the king and nation. When, seventy years later, Cyrus of Persia defeated Assyria and allowed the exiles to return and the temple to be rebuilt (an event celebrated in Isaiah chapters 40 to 66, and described in Nehemiah and Ezra), it seemed a marvel beyond hope or belief, a victory of God when all was darkest, and is so sung in Isaiah 58:8 and many passages of similar power:

> Then shall your light break forth like the dawn,
> and your healing shall spring up speedily;
> your righteousness shall go before you,
> and the glory of the Lord shall be your rear guard.

Or in a psalm like 126:

> When the Lord restored the fortunes of Zion,
> we were like those who dream.
> Then our mouth was filled with laughter,
> and our tongue with shouts of joy.

One God, Many Words and Wonders

Yet for all that, the religious experience of Israel was not fully satisfied with the return, for it was also a return, like all such, to the ambiguities of ordinary life in history. There were new sins within, and new external dangers, now from the Greeks under Alexander and his Hellenistic successors, and finally from the Romans. These produced two responses, the development of a literature of wisdom, and a growth of belief in a Last Day and a Messiah.

The books of Job, Psalms, Proverbs, Ecclesiastes, and the Song of Solomon in the Old Testament are designated the Wisdom Books, in contrast to law and history (Genesis through Esther) and the Prophetic Books (Isaiah through Malachi). They are called Wisdom Books because they are primarily concerned with presenting timeless words of devotion, reflection, moral advice, and philosophy. They are remarkably diverse; to one whose view of the Bible is chiefly shaped by those parts concerned with God's law, judgment on sin or calls to faith, substantial passages of the Wisdom Books may seem amazingly skeptical or easygoing.

MEDIEVAL
AND MODERN JUDAISM

Just as one sees changes in Judaism from the desert wanderers' religion of Abraham or Moses to the temple of Solomon, spiritual center of a kingdom and of a largely farming society, so has it continually adjusted to new situations through its long subsequent history. There was the destruction of the first temple and the exile to Babylon, but the temple was rebuilt, as we have seen. It was destroyed again by the Romans in A.D. 80, and from then on Judaism made a transition to a way based on the home-centered ethical and ceremonial precepts of the law, without the temple with its bleating animals, its heavy smells of blood and incense, its richly vested priests. The transition was not as difficult as might seem, for it had already been made in effect everywhere in the widely dispersed Jewish community except Jerusalem. Worship outside the city was held in synagogues, "gathering places," and consisted of prayer and study of the Scriptures, without sacrifice. Jewish scholars, especially in Babylon where a large community had remained even after the return from the Exile, prepared out of close argumentation the vast commentaries on the law called the Talmud, which made it both precise and flexible enough to be applicable to the new times in which Jews were more likely to be an urban minority than rural farmers and herders. Pilgrimage to the temple had once been the main bond of worldwide Jewry; now cohesion lay in the "Fence of the Torah," following the law as interpreted by the Talmud, which gave them inwardly and in the eyes of others a separate identity in a world of change and confusion. There were other kinds of flexibility, too; Philo of Alexandria (first century), for example, interpreted the scriptures allegorically in terms of Platonic philosophy.

The "Fence of the Torah" style of Judaism persisted through the Middle Ages and into modern times, as Jews dwindled to very small numbers in their homeland, first ruled by Christians and then by Muslims, but became important minorities in

European and near eastern cities, and spread as far as India and China. When they did not suffer persecution, they generally flourished and many Jews rose to prominence in Christian or Muslim societies. Their education and diligence, fruits of the careful study that the law required, were frequently superior to that of their neighbors.

Several new developments colored medieval Judaism. The form of Jewish mysticism called the kabbala had its supreme expression in the *Zohar,* or Book of Splendor, probably composed within a developing tradition by Moses de León in Spain about 1275.[2] Based on finding deeper, allegorical meanings in the words and letters of the Hebrew Torah which point to metaphysical realities, it held that God in himself is infinite and incomprehensible, but that his attributes provide windows of insight into God as he relates to mankind. As topics of meditation, certain basic attributes of God drawn from the Scriptures are arranged into a pattern of male-female polarities and on different levels in the hierarchy of spiritual things called the "kabbalistic tree." Meditation on their dynamic interaction provides a subtle and often profound spiritual path.

Kabbalism had many areas of influence, from magic to messianic movements. The most important was the more popular form of Jewish mysticism called Hasidism. This was a pietistic movement that started in eastern Europe in the eighteenth century through the teaching of Ba'al Shem Tov (1700–60). Hasidism was a feeling-oriented reaction against rabbinic emphasis on learning and legalism, and against stifling social conditions; it taught Jews to follow the law, but to make it an expression of fervent love for God. The colorful stories and doctrines with which its venerated *tzaddiqim* explained the meaning of love for God and the symbolism of ritual law were deeply dyed with kabbalistic lore, and emphasize pious love and the wisdom of the person of simple devotion as of greater importance than scholarly learning. Music, dancing, and even uncontrolled ecstatic behavior were frequently part of Hasidic worship. Small but vigorous groups of Hasidic background, such as the Lubovitcher movement, which has done much to encourage a return to orthodox practice, are still active in Israel and America.[3]

Another strand of modern Judaism, the liberal and rationalistic, has roots both in certain ancient schools and in the thought of the medieval philosopher Moses Maimonides (1135–1204), whose commentaries on the Talmud and law codification made use of Greek philosophy and presented a smooth, logical face to the faith. It was not until the eighteenth century Enlightenment, however, that this lineage exercised its full influence on Jewish life. Particularly in Germany, Jewish leaders and thinkers like Moses Mendelssohn (1729–86) emphasized acculturation to non-Jewish European life and the critique and defense of Judaism through philosophy. In the end—although this was not Mendelssohn's intention—many Jews in Western Europe became more or less secularized, like countless Christians of the same period, more interested in the mainstream of European culture than the law and the synagogue.

[2]See Gershom G. Scholem, *Major Trends in Jewish Mysticism* (New York: Schocken Books, 1961), pp. 156–204.

[3]Colorful accounts of Hasidim can be found in the writings of Martin Buber and in Herbert Weiner, *9½ Mystics* (New York: Holt, Rinehart, Winston, 1969).

Modern Jewish life is a conflux of several forces. It has been touched by traditional orthodoxy, Hasidism, and Enlightenment secularization and liberalism. It is influenced also by the bitter effects of persecution, especially in Russia in the late nineteenth and early twentieth centuries, and by a milder but ugly antisemitism which was widespread in Europe and America (and still exists to some extent), restricting Jewish participation in many areas of life. Most horrible of all, of course, was the "holocaust" under Nazism, in which some six million Jews perished before and during World War II, and traditional Jewish life in Europe was devastated. Against this, Jewish immigration to America provided a reservoir of strength there; American Jewish population is about six million.[4]

One of these forces is the movement known as Zionism, which led to the establishment of the state of Israel. Zionism, the effort of Jews to make a national homeland of their own, preferably in Palestine, began late in the nineteenth century as a response to the frustrations of confinement and prejudice in Europe. Palestine had been mainly Muslim for a thousand years and was then part of the Turkish Empire, but Jews began settling there in the 1890s, often forging out new lifestyles like that of the agricultural communes, the kibbutzim. Against all probability, the global vicissitudes of the twentieth century led to the birth of the state of Israel in 1948. Its population includes Jews of all types from the most secular to the extremely orthodox and Hasidic; Israel is also a center of Jewish learning. Israel is today important as a cultural and religious focal point for world Jewry; it is important to many Jews also to be able to know there is one small place in the world that is free and definitely Jewish.

American Judaism is not homogeneous, but is divided into three major traditions. Orthodox synagogues teach the full following of the law, or Torah, and are quite traditional in Talmudic scholarship, theology, and forms of festival and worship. Reform Judaism, which calls its places of worship temples rather than synagogues, has roots in the German Enlightenment experience. It is liberal in attitude, oriented more to the prophets than the law, and believes the essence of Judaism does not involve following the law legalistically. Most Reform Jews follow it hardly at all save for major festivals. Between the Reform and Orthodox camps is Conservative Judaism, which takes the law seriously as a guide to life, but believes that its provisions can and should be adjusted to suit the conditions of modern living.

JEWISH LIFE

Let us examine some of the specifics of Jewish life. It should be remembered always that there are various degrees of observance, and various attitudes toward the importance of, for example, the dietary laws and strictness of Sabbath-keeping. The differences are not only between the serious and the lax; Jews of equal inner commitment, insofar as this can be gauged, may place the

---

[4]See Howard Sacher, *The Course of Modern Jewish History* (New York: World Publishing Co., 1958).

emphasis on different strands of the tradition. (Differences of these kinds are, of course, found between the various traditions of all major religions.)

But throughout all of Jewish life a special chord reverberates. It is made up of a tradition of respect for education, awareness of history, and a sense of being an often persecuted minority group, as well as the specific festivals, customs, and religious rites of Judaism. The close family and community life of Judaism reflects this tone, through whichever of several possible styles of Jewish life it is expressed. There is always some sense of Jewish identity, too; it has often been commented that every Jew, however nonpracticing and secularized, knows that he or she is a Jew.

The sociological bedrock of Jewish life is the family. With only very few possible exceptions, such as the prophet Jeremiah and perhaps the Essene communities of Hellenistic times, religious celibacy has had no place in Judaism. One of the most consistent themes of all Jewish history, after the theme of being a special called-out covenant people, is marriage and the procreation of children: a fundamental religious duty for the wisest and holiest rabbi as well as any other Jew. It is not a concession to the weakness of the flesh, but a sacred as well as a joyful way of life and a part of the covenant:

> The whole world depends on the holiness of the union between man and woman, for the world was created for the sake of God's glory and the essential revelation of His glory comes through the increase of mankind. Man must therefore sanctify himself in order to bring to the world holy people through whom God's glory will be increased. . . .[5]

It is in the family, then, that religious observances begin. The Sabbath, festivals, and the dietary rules all involve, especially in Orthodox tradition, much more that is done at home than in the synagogue with the community as a whole—the Sabbath meal and prayers, holiday blessings and customs like Hanuka lights and the Passover meal in which the head of the family is the religious leader, the hours spent preparing food according to religious regulation. Beside this, the synagogue is not where religion "happens" so much as where one receives instruction and inspiration to make it happen in its true locus. But under the changed conditions of modern life the tendency, especially in the more liberal traditions, is to express Jewish identity more through synagogue, temple, or community participation and less through the complicated and time-consuming home actions in their traditional forms. Even so, it must be emphasized that the home can still be a place where Jewish identity in its moral and cultural meaning is learned and deeply felt.

The cornerstone of Jewish practice is the observance of the Sabbath. This period of twenty-four hours from sunset Friday to sunset Saturday commemorates the Lord's day of rest after the work of creation, and is intended for the rest and refreshment of both body and soul. On it no work is done, and there is feast and celebration and nourishment for the body and mind and soul at the table and the

---

[5]Rabbi Nahman of Bratslav (1772–1811), cited in Arthur Hertzberg, ed., *Judaism* (New York: George Braziller, Inc., 1961), pp. 91–92. Reprinted with the permission of the publisher. Copyright © 1961 by Arthur Hertzberg.

One God, Many Words and Wonders

synagogue. Far from being an onerous burden or a time of negative prohibition, the classical Jewish literature sees the Sabbath as a bountiful gift to God's people, as a lovely bride to be welcomed with eager love.[6]

Traditional Sabbath observance begins with concluding one's ordinary business, bathing, and putting on fresh garments reserved for that festive day on Friday afternoon. After sundown, the previously prepared Sabbath meal is eaten, with traditional Sabbath dishes, and prayers and blessings over the food, and the full cup of wine.

On the next day there is public worship in the morning and late afternoon. Synagogue or temple worship consists basically of reading from the Torah and the other Scriptures, prayers, and chants. But the atmosphere of the worship will vary considerably from one tradition to another. In Orthodox synagogues, men and women will be on separate sides; the liturgy will be in Hebrew; and the preservation of many ornate ritual customs, as well as in some cases a certain Hasidic exuberance expressed, perhaps, in swaying or dancing to the music, will suggest that this is the Judaism most in continuity with that of old world Europe. In Reform temples, the service will be plain and dignified, with more emphasis on the sermon. Conservative synagogues will follow a middle course. However, Reform and Conservative worship, like that of some once-staid Christian churches, is today in a new way discovering the heritage of lively music, dance, and chant, especially in services for young people.

The most important object in any Jewish place of worship is the Torah, the scroll of the law, in its large ornamented box at the front of the hall. A lamp continually burns before it. Opening the door and curtains in front of the Torah, and finally removing it from the case for reverent reading, are major actions in the drama of the service.

FESTIVALS

Besides the regular Sabbath worship, the Jewish year is marked by several festivals. Although not really as important as the weekly celebration of the Sabbath—only the Sabbath is mentioned in the Ten Commandments—many Jews today observe something of the "High Holy Days" (Rosh Hashana and Yom Kippur) and the Passover if nothing else. The holidays can be divided into three groups. Because they follow the Jewish lunar calendar, the dates (like that of the Christian Easter) vary from year to year.

First are the "High Holy Days" or "Days of Awe," which come in the autumn. Rosh Hashana, literally "Head of the Year" is kept as the anniversary of the creation and is the Jewish New Year's Day. Then, after a sacred season of ten days for repentance, is Yom Kippur, the Day of Atonement. It is said to be the day when God reckons up the sins of each person for the previous year and accordingly sets his or her fate for the coming year; this is only a metaphor, of course, but it sets the

---

[6]The meaning of the Sabbath is vividly described in Herman Wouk, *This is my God* (Garden City, N.Y.: Doubleday & Co., 1959), pp. 55–66.

tone of Yom Kippur, a day when each person in his or her heart assesses guilt and determines how to amend his or her life. The customs of the day create a backdrop for this inward strife and turning; fasting for twenty-four hours and a daylong synagogue service full of haunting, dirgelike music and corporate confession.

Three happier festivals are basically grounded in the agricultural society of ancient Israel, and fit the seasonal cycle of all archaic agricultural religion, yet also have meaning as commemorating the mighty acts of God for Israel recorded in the Bible; they orient the believer to God's work both in nature and in history. These are the Passover in the spring, Shavuot in late spring or early summer, and Sukkot in autumn.

The Passover, or Pesah, recalls the hurried meal that the Israelites enslaved in Egypt ate before leaving for the great events of the Exodus, the parting of the Red Sea and the receiving of the law at Sinai, and the entry into the Promised Land. An impressive family rite, the Passover meal, with its traditional foods (the paschal lamb, which is not actually eaten but is like a sacrifice, unleavened bread, roasted egg, vegetable, bitter herbs, wine, and so forth) and the question and answers between the youngest son and the father concerning the meaning of the symbols, is deeply loved in Jewish homes, and is the Jewish holiday best known to Christians because of its association with the death of Jesus.

Shavuot, or Pentecost, seven weeks after Passover, was anciently a harvest festival for grain, and is also commemorated as the anniversary of the giving of the law on Mount Sinai. Traditional Jews mark it by all-night study of the Torah, and it is a customary time for religious confirmation and graduation exercises.

Bright and colorful Sukkot is the autumn harvest festival for fruit and vegetables. When possible, "booths" are set up on lawns and in temples, gaily decorated with apples, pomegranates, gourds, corn, and the like. The booths are covered with straw, boughs, or palm fronds, but with spaces so one can see the stars. People eat, study, and sometimes sleep in them; like so much of Judaism, it is the sort of religious rite that children find exciting and unforgettable.

Finally, there are several minor holy days. Only two of the best known will be cited, Purim and Hanuka.

Purim, in February or March, commemorates the story recounted in the Book of Esther: how the Jews were saved from the wicked designs of Haman, chief minister of the Persian king, by Esther the queen and her father Mordecai. Like Mardi Gras or carnival in Latin countries, which comes at approximately the same time, Purim is the time when religion gives sanction to the role of comedy, buffoonery, and "letting go" in human life. Tradition says one may drink until one cannot tell the difference between "Blessed be Mordecai" and "Cursed be Haman." During the reading of the story in the synagogue, children gleefully make a tremendous racket with noisemakers whenever the name Haman is spoken. Strolling players and schoolchildren perform farces in which solemn rabbis and elders might be spoofed most of all.[7]

Hanuka comes at about the time of the Christian Christmas and has become popular in America partly as a result of this association. It commemorates the

[7]Wouk, *This is my God* also contains a particularly colorful account of Purim, pp. 96–99.

One God, Many Words and Wonders

Candles for Hanuka, the Jewish festival commemorating the rededication of the temple in 165 B.C.

rededication of the temple in Jerusalem in 165 B.C. after rebels led by the House of Maccabee had defeated the Seleucid Greek rulers (placed by Alexander the Great nearly two centuries earlier), who had lately tried to convert the Jewish people and the temple to pagan worship. The event is too late even to have been included in the Jewish Bible, although the Books of Maccabees do appear in the Roman Catholic Bible and the "Apocrypha" of some Protestant versions. The celebration is simple and is carried out in the home. An eight-branch Hanuka menorah, or candlestick, is lit, and a Hanuka song sung, over an eight-day period. On the first night cakes and gifts are presented to the children.

Jewish boys undergo certain rites of passage: circumcision, performed as a religious act, at eight days; Bar Mitzvah, when the boy reads from the Hebrew Scriptures and begins the entry into manhood. In America, the Bar Mitzvah has often become the occasion for gala celebrations; in the Reform tradition, and to some extent in the Conservative tradition, a parallel festival for girls has been introduced. Reform Judaism also has a confirmation rite for young people of high school age, when commitment to the faith is expressed.

The Jewish dietary laws have had an immense role over the centuries in keeping the faith alive and its people together, for rules of food preparation so exacting make it almost a practical necessity that if they are to be kept one must eat with, and therefore live in and marry within, his or her own community. Today, however, their observance varies; some follow them minutely, some give them only token honor such as refusal to eat pork, some feel they are entirely irrelevant to the modern world and observe them not at all.

No restrictions govern food from plants; the law deals only with killing and eating conscious life. The basic rules are that animals eaten must have a split hoof and chew the cud; this includes cattle and sheep but excludes a vast swarm: swine, reptiles, elephants, monkeys, horses, and all carnivorous beasts, among others. Of sea creatures, only those with fins and scales may be taken; of aerial creatures, birds of prey and insects are forbidden. Furthermore, meat must be slaughtered and prepared in special ways to be "kosher," or edible by those keeping the dietary rules. The rules also forbid the eating of meat and dairy products together, and even expects that separate pots and plates will be used for them; the keeping of two sets of dishes (and a third for Passover) is a sure sign of a quite traditional Jewish home.

The tradition requires men to pray morning and evening and to give time to Torah study, although it never puts obligations on women that must be met at particular times save the purifications connected with the female cycle. Two styles of life in relation to God, the male dealing with word and schedule, the female with food preparation and home, are encompassed in Judaism. Perhaps this gives a clue to the fundamental experience of Judaism. This ancient faith is not primarily oriented toward doctrine as its basis; one finds that ideas about God and such matters as the afterlife vary immensely, and that even many fairly orthodox observants profess to be skeptical or uninterested in such matters. Yet Judaism continues to be intensely felt as a way of life here and now.

The reason may be that it is oriented toward time and history, rather than eternal ideas, as the source of human meaning and obligation. The law is important because it comes out of past history and now controls present time and makes it holy through demands on how it is spent and how biological events in time are sanctified. In turn the Jewish hope of salvation is chiefly oriented toward future time. The tradition affirms that God will, in his time, send the Messiah, a hero heir to the greatest kings and prophets of old but greater than they, and in his day and through his work all evils on the earth will be rectified and an era of joy will be initiated. Some interpret this hope literally, others figuratively, in terms of a "Messianic Age." For some, Zionism and the building up of the nation of Israel had messianic overtones.

But overall, Judaism is a religion whose centers of value are in time: tradition out of the past and hope for the future. We are beings in time and history, and are to look in these directions first, rather than up and down, to find what we need most to know and believe to live this human life as it is meant to be lived.

Christianity

THE SCOPE OF CHRISTIANITY

For the majority of Americans, Christianity is the most familiar form of religious expression. In fact, it will probably shape unconscious attitudes about what religion "ought" to be like.

In a sense this reaction is appropriate today, for in the twentieth century no country has more influenced the world's religious history than the United States, except in a very different way the Marxist countries. Apart from countless indirect American influences on world culture and hence on religion, America has served in this century as chief bastion, financial resource, and exporter of its various forms of Christianity, from Roman Catholicism to Pentecostalism, the latter originating here in its present form in this century and now becoming a Christian "third force" worldwide.

But Christianity is also an ancient faith with a long history, the greater part of it before America was settled by Europeans, and set in cultural environments immensely remote from ours. Most of the other major faiths, except Islam, are closer to 2,500 than 2,000 years old, the age of Christianity. But Christianity is scarcely behind any of them in the sense of antiquity breathed by its oldest shrines in the old world. The comparatively new brick, glass, or wood churches that dot Christian America in their tens of thousands may give this religion an almost modern facade, but that is not the impression it gives in other places. In Europe the church buildings are often the oldest structures in an old city, giving a feel of the remote past.

The hymns and worship style *we* call the "old-time religion" largely date only from the nineteenth century American frontier. Before that are eighteen other centuries of Christianity. Some of the forms it took in them would seem almost as exotic as Tibet to us, and much of this history is relatively little understood or known by most American Christians.

In the waning days of the Roman Empire, Christians not only worshipped in underground burial tunnels called catacombs and met lions in the coliseum, but wrote, argued, and took the faith to barbarian tribes who built churches on wagons to follow them on their wanderings. While western Europe was in the Dark Ages, worship in Constantinople with its opulently robed priests, clouds of incense, and sonorous music reached a splendor that visiting Russians reportedly said was closer to heaven than earth. In the tenth century, the "Nestorian" Church of the East, following the caravan routes, was planted from Mesopotamia to the imperial city of T'ang China. A Christian church of Eastern Orthodox type has existed in South India since the fourth century at least. At the other end of the world, Irish monks let God guide their flimsy coracles to remote islands and promontories, inhabited only by sea gulls, to build rough monasteries.

Then there are somewhat more familiar but no less colorful Christian images: medieval popes in monarchical splendor, crusaders, and manuscript copying monks; Canterbury pilgrims, Protestant reformers, visionaries of the Blessed Virgin Mary at Lourdes or Fatima, missionaries on cannibal-inhabited islands. Christianity embraces worshippers at high masses and at silent Quaker meetings, people for whom the faith is a liberal charter and those for whom it demands the most rigorous conservatism on both social and theological issues.

JESUS

Like all major religions, Christianity has integrated into itself meanings and practices from many places where it has dwelt; the process begins with the Greek vocabulary of the New Testament itself. But there is only one focal point which brings together all this diversity: the last two or three years in the earthly life of Jesus of Nazareth, called the Messiah or Christ, in the first century A.D.

He appeared publicly in Roman-occupied Palestine around the year A.D. 30. Jesus was first visible as an associate of a man called John the Baptizer, an ascetic who had lived in the desert and then had come into the Jordan valley to preach fiery outdoor sermons calling on people to repent and change their ways, for God was about to judge the world and punish the wicked. Such apocalyptic expectation was rife at this time, all the more since the heavy hand of Roman tyranny seemed to block all nonsupernatural hope for the Jewish nation, and for individuals except those who curried favor with Rome.[8] The repentance John called for was marked by a ritual washing, or baptism, which he administered to his converts in the Jordan River.

Among those who received this baptism was a young man from Nazareth called Jesus (Joshua). Not much is definitely known about his background; the stories later told about his descent from David, miraculous conception, birth in Bethlehem, and childhood, are hard to corroborate historically and are generally accepted or not on the basis of one's religious outlook; for Christians, they embody important religious truths about Jesus.

Shortly after Jesus' baptism by John, the latter was arrested and then executed.

[8]See Robert M. Grant, *A Historical Introduction to the New Testament* (New York: Harper & Row Publishers, 1963).

One God, Many Words and Wonders

Main Themes of Christianity after Constantine

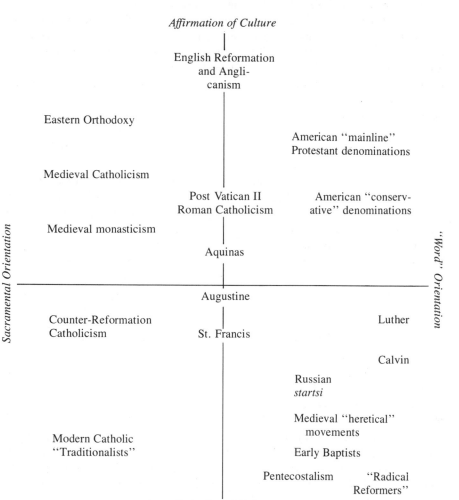

Affirmation of Culture

English Reformation and Angli- canism

Eastern Orthodoxy

American "mainline" Protestant denominations

Medieval Catholicism

Post Vatican II Roman Catholicism

American "conserv- ative" denominations

Medieval monasticism

Aquinas

Sacramental Orientation

"Word" Orientation

Augustine

Counter-Reformation Catholicism

Luther

St. Francis

Calvin

Russian *startsi*

Medieval "heretical" movements

Modern Catholic "Traditionalists"

Early Baptists

Pentecostalism "Radical Reformers"

Rejection of Culture

Thematic Chart VII. Throughout history, some Christians have emphasized the importance of the "Word"—preaching and studying the Bible—in Christian life, and others the impor- tance of Christianity's sacramental institutions—baptism, Holy Communion, priesthood, etc.—as mediums of the grace God gave to mankind in Jesus Christ. On both sides of this polarity have been those who have emphasized that Christians can and should accept while sanctifying from within the surrounding culture in which they find themselves, and others who have emphasized that Christians should see themselves as a "called out" people who have as little to do with it as they can. (On the chart, "culture" means the values, attitudes, and norms of the surrounding, comtemporary society, not classical or "high" culture.)

This arrest did not give Jesus the leadership of John's movement directly, but did partly inspire him to gather his own disciples and start a ministry of his own, which was in some ways parallel but came to develop distinctive characteristics.

Like John, Jesus began by proclaiming in his preaching that the Kingdom of God was at hand. The "kingdom" meant the paradisal rule of God which would follow the apocalyptic distress and judgment. The Kingdom as a concept was intimately tied up with the work of the Messiah, which would inaugurate it.[9] Jesus also taught that people should repent of their former ways and live now as though in the kingdom, in preparation for it. The principles for this way of life are assembled in the Sermon on the Mount in chapters 5, 6, and 7 of Matthew's Gospel; the essence is to practice forbearing love and nonresistance of evil because God will shortly be dealing with it in judgment, and to be perfect even as the God who is to rule is perfect. By comparison, John's moral message was merely repentance and following justice.

Unlike John, Jesus did not baptize, although his followers did. It was his work of healing, however, which like the earlier baptism of John was the major sign in his ministry of the power of the coming kingdom. His miracles upon the sick, the insane, the blind and the paralyzed, and his other miracles such as feeding the 5,000 with two loaves and five small fish, are presented as signs of the kingdom's arrival. Healing was often understood as the exorcism of evil spirits from the disturbed; Jesus said "If it is by the finger of God that I cast out demons, then the kingdom of God has come upon you" (Luke 11:20).

The nature miracles and healings bring to light another special feature of Jesus' ministry, his aura of authority and his mingling with both sexes and with all classes of society. Jesus taught everywhere, not only in synagogues but also by the lakeshore and in open fields. Instead of using close argument or extensive scriptural authority, he used stories—parables—and simple but acute aphorisms to make his points; or, better, to catch up the hearer in the luminous web of his vision of the kingdom's nearness, so near its power is already breaking through and is within reach of those who see its rising light.

Just as the kingdom was for everyone, but in a special sense for the poor who had so little now, so did Jesus bring its message to everyone. He numbered among his associates fishermen, prostitutes, the revolutionary zealots, the despised tax collectors, and (though he also harshly upbraided them) members of the strict religious party, the Pharisees. He did not inculcate extreme asceticism, but rather was known as the teacher who came eating and drinking, and his illustrations show a sympathetic awareness of the ways and problems of ordinary life with its sorrows, joys, and innocent festivities.

After only a short year or two of this life, however, the young wandering preacher and charismatic wonder-worker of the kingdom left Galilee, his homeland, and went down to Jerusalem shortly before the Passover. He clearly intended this journey, which God had laid upon him, to be a climactic appeal to Israel to accept the incoming kingdom and reject perversions of religion. To this end he made certain dramatic gestures: he entered the pilgrim-thronged holy city in a sort of

[9]See John Bright, *The Kingdom of God* (Nashville: The Abingdon Press, 1953).

procession, and he caused a disturbance overturning the tables of the currency exchangers, and the chairs of the sellers of birds and animals for sacrifice, in the temple courtyard. He and his disciples then withdrew for a few days to live in suburban Bethany and teach in the temple precincts.

But in the edgy political situation, these gestures combined with news of Jesus' popular appeal in Galilee understandably came to the concerned attention of Roman and Jewish authorities alike. They perceived revolutionary political overtones in the young prophet's activities and appeal—how far this perception was justified is much disputed by historians, but there is no doubt there were those among both supporters and opponents of Jesus who expected him to be at least the figurehead in an uprising against Rome, and perhaps against the collaborating Jewish elite as well.[10] This was an upshot neither the Romans nor the Jewish elite wished. Before the end of the week the decision had been taken and carried out to dispose of him.

Jesus was arrested with the help of a disgruntled radical among his disciples, hastily tried by the various authorities concerned but decisively before the harsh Pontius Pilate, the Roman governor who throughout his tenure had shown no pity to protesters against Roman rule. (Indeed, Rome finally recalled him for excessive cruelty.) On Friday in Passover week Jesus was executed by being nailed to a structure made of two crossed beams and set upright, the slow and agonizing death that Rome awarded to rebels. But the story did not end there.

THE EARLY CHRISTIAN COMMUNITY

The drama of this tragic death of one so young, beloved, and appealing to many inevitably worked deeply into the minds of those who had been committed to his movement and caught up in his vision of the kingdom. They tried to find ways to understand the man and the event in categories familiar to them. Some thought of the tradition of a coming Messiah, "Anointed One" or King (the title "Christ" is the literal Greek translation of "Messiah"), and wondered if, as some of Jesus' words and deeds suggested, he were this figure. In particular, they now conjoined the Messiah image with the poignant passages in Isaiah about the "suffering servant"—the hero who saves his people not by military victory but by underoing excruciating pain, baring his back to the smiters, his cheek to those who plucked out the hairs.

Some thought of the words "Son of Man," which he had often used, words which his hearers would have recognized as referring to the mysterious judge who would descend on clouds at the Last Day in the current apocalyptic expectations; it was frequently ambiguous whether Jesus meant the title to refer to himself or another coming one, or if he meant both at the same time. Others, closer to the Greek religious tradition, thought of the titles "Lord" and "Son of God" used of Hellenistic kings and deities alike, or even of philosophical concepts like *Logos*

---

[10]Two popular books by Hugh J. Schonfield have presented rather extreme views of the revolutionary political nature of Jesus' work. They are *The Passover Plot* (New York: Bantam Books, 1971), and *The Jesus Party* (New York: The Macmillan Company, 1974).

("Word" or "Principle") or *Sophia* ("Wisdom"), used to describe the creative power of God at work in the world, in connection with the enigmatic and unforgettable man from Nazareth. As to exactly how he thought of himself and his mission, in his own subjectivity, who can say? Almost all we know of him, including the words he is reported to have spoken, comes to us through the hands of those who saw him in light of categories such as the above. Beyond all the words, however, there is mystery—the mystery of one whose charm and sternness, magic and endurance of torture, empathy and remoteness, combined to make him both unknown and unforgettable. He had the combination of mystery and clarification of all great religious images and symbols.

Soon enough he was a supreme symbol of the ineffable mysteries of life, death, and God, all of which he somehow seemed to focus, and his form and the instrument of his suffering were reproduced in gold and silver and gems around the world.

This kind of thinking took hold in the community of Jesus' disciples and followers. Historical Christianity has never been a purely individual religion. Even before the crucifixion, it was communal; the disciples, leaving job and family, formed a new social group around Jesus, and it was in the context of this group especially formed in expectation of the kingdom that the teaching about the kingdom and the wonders which foreshadowed it were imparted. The disciples were always at hand for Jesus' preaching and miracles, and it was they who were told the inner meaning of parables and signs. The disciples were a called-out group who knew the kingdom of heaven was at hand, and lived for that reality.

On the Friday Jesus died on the cross, this community was dispirited and scattered; Peter went back to his fishing. But on the first day of the next week, word of a new event brought the community together again. It was reported by Mary Magdalene, a former prostitute who was close to Jesus and the disciples, and then by Peter himself, that the tomb was empty and Jesus was walking in the garden where he had been interred. More such accounts were quickly bruited about: he had joined two disciples walking to Emmaus, and when they broke bread together he was known to them; the disciples were in a room with the doors shut, and he appeared in their midst; they were in a boat, and he appeared on the shore and cooked breakfast for them. He seemed the same and yet different in these postdeath appearances, as though partly in a different dimension. He ate. "Doubting Thomas" was able to touch his wounds to assure himself he was really the crucified one and not a ghost or imposter. Yet this Jesus was able to pass through shut doors and appeared or disappeared unexpectedly and by no pattern discernible to mortals. Finally, forty days after the first appearance in the garden, the resurrected Jesus appeared to them, we are told, in familiar Bethany. There as they talked he took them out to a nearby hill, blessed them, and was taken up into heaven.

By now, the nascent Christian community—the disciples, certain women such as Mary Magdalene and Mary the mother of Jesus, and peripheral followers—was vitalized and enthusiastic. The series of mysterious resurrection appearances, which came only to members of the community, greatly reinforced its thinking about who Jesus was along the lines of the categories mentioned above. The supreme event came when, during Pentecost shortly after the last appearance of the sequence, they

One God, Many Words and Wonders

were gathered in an upstairs room. Suddenly they felt shaken tremendously by a spiritual force they were certain was the Holy Spirit of God mentioned in the Old Testament, and whose coming was remembered to have been promised by Jesus.

After receiving the Holy Spirit, the apostles, as the inner core of the group were now called, began preaching in the streets to the many peoples who crowded into the holy city. They preached basically that Jesus who had died was risen from the dead, that this event confirmed that he was and is both Lord and Messiah, and so all the scriptural prophecies about both the Jewish and universal roles of the Messiah and the Last Days were fulfilled or will be in him.

Many heard and believed. Most were Jews, but some of the earliest converts to the truth and significance of this new happening in Judaism were Greeks, probably of a class called proselytes who, without undertaking the whole of the law, admired Judaism, worshipped its God, and accepted as much of its teaching and practice as possible. The incipient universalism of the Christian sect, with its proclamation of a new age when the reign of the Jewish God would be evident everywhere, and was now already present in Christ, eased the spiritual plight of such half-and-half people greatly—it was the breakthrough in Judaism for which many must have yearned.

PAUL

This role of Christianity in presenting Jesus as a manifestation of God who welcomed Jew and Greek alike was given preliminary definition by the council of the Apostles described in Acts 15, where only a minimal adherence to the Jewish law was required of non-Jews. But it was in the work of Paul, the most notable convert and missionary in the days of the early fellowship, that this universalism in Christ fully came through.[11]

Paul was originally called Saul. He was a strict follower of the law and a persecutor of the new Christian sect. But while traveling from Jerusalem to Damascus in his anti-Christian efforts, at one place in the road he unexpectedly fell to the ground in a violent rapture; he experienced a vision of Jesus the Christ appearing to him and saying "Saul, Saul, why do you persecute me?"

Although he waited some fourteen years before beginning public work, Paul was a great if controversial advocate of the new faith between about A.D. 45 and 65. His labors on its behalf took him through Asia Minor, Greece, and finally to Rome. More and more he saw himself as the apostle to the Gentiles (non-Jews), whose calling was to show that, in these days after Jesus, the Gentiles had been "grafted" into Israel an alien branch onto an old tree, and so when they prayed in the name of Jesus they had all the privileges and responsibilities of being God's people which had formerly been Israel's alone. But this did not mean, for Paul, that they had to follow the Law of Moses. They had only to believe the Gospel, or "Good News,"

[11]See Gunther Bornkamm, *Paul,* trans. D. B. G. Stalker (New York: Harper & Row, Publishers, 1971), John Knox, *Chapters in a Life of Paul* (London: Adam and Charles Black, 1954); and Richard Longenecker, *Paul: Apostle of Liberty* (New York: Harper & Row, Publishers, 1964).

about Jesus and have trust in him, and they would be brought into his Kingdom of God not on their own merits, but as a free gift of God transmitted even as they were grafted into old Israel through Jesus Christ. His death on the cross, Paul said, broke the sway of sin and death in the world, and his rising again brought new life. By joining oneself to Christ by faith (not only belief, but a commitment of one's whole self) and the acceptance of baptism (the ritual immersion in water representing initiatory rebirth), one died and rose with Christ, was no longer of this world which is passing away, but entered the everlasting reign of God.

CHRISTIANITY
IN THE ROMAN WORLD

By now clearly a number of interpretations of the Christian message and community had become articulated. Some still thought of Jesus primarily as the Jewish Messiah who would soon return to vindicate Israel. Some thought of Christianity as a continuation—one might say an "export version"—of Judaism making its promises available freely to all apart from the social and dietary law. (One can compare the relation of Buddhism to Hinduism.) Others doubtless experienced Christianity as something closer to the well-known Greek "mystery religions," the purveyor of a belief and an experience that would give a blissful state after death to one who received it; the death and resurrection of Christ provided for them the pattern of such a deliverance, which one needed only to appropriate for oneself. All of these, and other philosophical and religious themes as well, found their way into the letters of Paul to his churches, and into an emerging Christian world view.

All these ideas were stirring in groups that Paul and the other apostles established throughout the Roman world. They were usually fringe groups to the Jewish community, but embraced many others as well, rich and poor, slave and free, but more of the humble than of the mighty or highly educated in the polyglot, spiritually mobile Mediterranean world.

As the first century advanced, the life of the new Christian church naturally became more stabilized. One sign of this was the writing down and circulating of "standard" lives of Jesus. Four became accepted; there were others, more fanciful and tendentious, which were not. The first three of the Gospels or lives of Jesus are called the Synoptic Gospels; they obviously go together because long passages are virtually identical. The shortest, Mark, was evidently written first, probably between A.D. 65 and 70; Matthew (c. 70–80) and Luke (c. 80) borrowed much from him and added much of their own. The fourth gospel, John (its date is uncertain, but is probably late first century) is evidently written from a different point of view. Concerned to present Jesus as the light and life of the world, the eternal Logos or principle of God's activity revealed to the eye of faith, it contains much that is religiously beautiful and profound, yet is perhaps less close to the historical facts about Jesus than the other three—though matters like this are the subject of continuing scholarly discussion beyond the scope of this book.[12]

Added to this growing corpus of Christian literature were the letters of Paul, written only 20 to 30 years after the crucifixion, much treasured in the churches he had founded; the Acts of the Apostles by Luke (probably written A.D. 85–90); and other writings of varying caliber, some of which finally became part of the Christian Bible and some of which did not.

Another sign of stabilization was the emergence of normative Christian beliefs, rites, and church organization. This stage, called sometimes "early Catholicism" because it obviously represents the beginning of the course of Christian development which led to the structure of the medieval church, can be found as far back as the New Testament "Pastoral Epistles" (I and II Timothy, Titus) and the epistles of Peter. There were formulas of belief slowly becoming standardized into creeds (for example, II Timothy 2:11-13), attacks on heretics (such as Titus 1:10-16), and a quieter, more sober and conventionally moralistic way of life. With the hope of many in the Christian community for an early appearance of the Lord in glory disappointed, the virtues of soundness and self-control were urged, being needed for a long-term sojourn as the children of light in the midst of a dark (but not yet passing away) world. The brilliant apocalyptic colors of the Gospels and the halcyon early days of Acts fade; concern turns to sorting out true from false doctrine and the proper qualifications and prerogatives of church officers and various classes of members, such as young men and widows.

Yet the church of those days has an appeal of its own. Each local church came to be headed by an *episcopos* ("overseer"—our "bishop" is derived from this Greek word), assisted by a council of *presbyteroi* ("elders"—"priests" or "presbyters" in English), and by deacons ("servers" whose special duty was caring for the needy). The churches apparently had many other categories of roles as well, from readers and healers to widows, each with special duties in worship and otherwise, and perhaps special places to stand during service. Everyone was to have a definite and important part. The church did extensive welfare work among its membership; like most such organizations in the Roman world, it was a mutual aid society as well as a religious fellowship.

The church met for worship early in the morning on Sunday (of course, just another ordinary workday then), the day commemorating the resurrection, and perhaps on other days as well. To avoid legal problems, Christians often gathered quietly and, until late in the third century when churches began to be built, in private homes or catacombs. Worship combined scripture, prayer, and instruction with the sacred communal meal representing the Last Supper which, as the Mass or Holy Communion, remains the principal act of worship of Roman Catholic, Eastern Orthodox, and some Protestant churches.

The evidence suggests that a typical service in those days would have been as follows. At the back of the room, behind a table, sat the bishop, with his presbyters

[12]See John Marsh, *The Gospel of St. John* (Harmondsworth, England: Penguin Books, 1968).

seated on either side. In front of the table would stand the deacons, probably two in number. The service would begin with readings from the scriptures the Old Testament, with emphasis on the passages believed to prophesy the coming of Christ, and the psalms, used as hymns of praise. Many people might take part in these readings. The bishop, and possibly others, would discourse on their meaning. Perhaps letters of the apostles and accounts from the life of Christ would be read too; gradually these came to be more and more a formal part of Christian worship until they evolved into the normative collection known as the New Testament. The bishop would then pray at some length, and the Kiss of Peace be exchanged. After this, everyone would bring up to the table a gift of bread or wine. The bishop, standing behind the table with the elders, would raise his eyes to heaven and offer thanks for this food. Then the people would come forward to receive a piece of bread from the bishop and a bit of wine offered in a chalice held by a deacon, believing this to be a sacred meal in which Jesus Christ is mystically known and his grace imparted.[13] Not to be confused with the communion was the *agape,* or lovefeast, held afterward as a social communal meal.

The other great service was baptism. This initiation into the Christian life was generally held on Easter Eve. Only those who had received baptism would take part in the communion just described; catechumens, or those receiving instruction, and also penitents going through a process of readmission after confessing a major sin, would remain at the service only through the first part. Instruction would be very long and careful, perhaps for two full years, and would be followed by careful intellectual and moral examination. Then during the week before Easter the candidates would be given a final exam by the bishop on Wednesday, would bathe on Thursday, fast on Friday, be blessed and exorcised by the bishop on Saturday, keep an all-night vigil, and finally early on Easter morning would be baptized in a font or by having water poured over them, and would immediately afterward receive Holy Communion.[14]

During this period, Christian intellectual life continued to increase the philosophical sophistication with which the faith was presented. Christian thinkers such as Clement of Rome, Clement of Alexandria, Origen, Justin Martyr, Irenaeus, Tertullian, and others moved the emphasis from showing the continuity of Christianity with Judaism to showing its compatibility with Greek and Roman philosophy, and its points of difference from it. This is natural, since the non-Jewish classical atmosphere became increasingly the milieu of Christianity.

The tone of various Christian thinkers ranges from the fiery Tertullian (c. 155–225), a former lawyer who thought that everything pagan was alien to Christianity and who deemed faith alone and a very strict moral life the only proper Christian way, to the mild Clement of Alexandria who, with his fellow Alexandrian Origen emphasized that all truth leads to Christ, who is the Word or creative principle known to philosophy. Some Christians went much further; the Gnostics, already mentioned, combined Christianity with more esoteric and mythical elements of

---

[13]See Dom Gregory Dix, *The Shape of the Liturgy* (London: Dacre Press, 1945), pp. 36–45.

[14]J. W. C. Wand, *A History of the Early Church* (London: Methuen & Co., 1937), p. 97.

One God, Many Words and Wonders

Greek and Asian thought. They were countered by the bishop of Lyons, Irenaeus, who emphasized the importance for Christians of following the traditions passed down from the apostles, particularly the truth of God's taking human flesh in Christ in order to undo the tangled knot of evil wrought in Adam, and thus to bring the creation back to himself by one who is flesh of our flesh. This was in conscious opposition to Gnostic ideas that, the flesh being evil or virtually worthless, the taking of flesh by God is only illusory or allegorical, and salvation means escape from the world.

During the same period, and largely in reaction to the same doctrinal disputes, the canon of authoritative New Testament scriptures was established. It was not finalized until the council of bishops at Carthage in 419. The final codification of scripture thus was fairly late, and came after much of the development of Christian teaching, worship, and social organization. On the other hand, the selection was influenced by the fact that most of those books to be considered canonical were already accepted as authoritative; the last disputes were chiefly over the pastoral epistles, Jude, and the Book of Revelation, and whether the Epistle to the Hebrews was actually by Paul. Many then as now were dubious about its Pauline authorship, but accepted it anyway as part of the New Testament.[15]

Everyone has heard of the persecutions of Christians under the Roman Empire: of martyrs hung upside down on crosses, or burned at the stake, or thrown to the lions in the coliseum. Indeed there were ghastly persecutions, although they were highly sporadic and local until the third century. For the most part Christians in the empire lived undisturbed lives, and while they were not officially a recognized religion, the general policy was to tolerate all groups, however bizarre, which did not present a clear threat to the government. The authorities generally had other things to do than worry about this obscure sect. Tradition has it that the Emperor Nero (r. 54–68) did instigate a persecution (which caught up the apostles Peter and Paul) to deflect blame from himself for the disastrous fire at Rome; this may have happened, but if so it was limited to Rome.

In the third century, however, there were persecutions ordered for the entire empire under Decius (r. 249–51), Valerian (r. 253–60), and Diocletian (r. 284–305). By this time the numbers of Christians had grown quite visible, and troubles were increasing in the Roman state requiring both solidarity and a scapegoat. In the face of external invasion and internal dissension, these emperors desperately wanted unity, and did not yet realize that the empire and Christianity could converge and be mutually supportive, as they were to do within a century. Ironically, it was generally those emperors otherwise most just and conscientious who persecuted Christianity, for they took most seriously their responsibility for unifying and strengthening their realm.

Usually the persecution was in the context of a drive for all subjects of the empire to express loyalty to the sovereign, who was nominally regarded as divine. Few took this seriously, but it was expected that patriotism would be expressed by

---

[15]See Robert M. Grant, *The Formation of the New Testament* (New York: Harper & Row, Publishers, 1965).

burning a bit of incense before a portrait or image of the emperor, an act regarded as offering divine honor. At the times of persecution, Christians might be summoned by the authorities and required to make this and comparable gestures, or suffer imprisonment and possibly death. Christians, regarding the token gesture as idolatry, frequently refused it; this was taken as proof that they were subversive, and they suffered the consequences.

Greatest havoc was wrought by Diocletian, a dedicated man striving desperately to save through extensive reform a rapidly disintegrating state, and who suffered many problems and bad advice. By his time the Christians had many churches, costly possessions, and large numbers. He shrank at first from shedding blood, but ordered all Christian buildings, artifacts, and books destroyed, seeking thereby to vitiate the obstreperous movement. That did not work, and before long his agents were working torture and death among the faithful.

It must be noted that among the Christians a certain cult of martyrdom flourished. Those who died violently under the various persecutions were afforded heroic status, and the bones and graves of many became relics and shrines. Here began the veneration of saints. There were those who, though not explicitly seeking martyrdom, looked to the example of Jesus Christ and the earlier martyrs, and were fully prepared for death. Thus Ignatius, bishop of Antioch, was taken to Rome in the days of Trajan (r. 98–117) where he met his death at the jaws of wild beasts in the amphitheatre. Thinking no doubt of the Holy Communion, he wrote to the church at Rome while on his journey to death:

> I am God's wheat; I am ground by the teeth of the wild beasts that I may end as the pure bread of Christ. If anything, coax the beasts on to become my sepulchre and to leave nothing of my body undevoured so that, when I am dead, I may be no bother to anyone. I shall be really a disciple of Jesus Christ if and when the world can no longer see so much as my body. Make petition, then, to the Lord for me, so that by these means I may be made a sacrifice to God.

In this vein, he also said:

> The pangs of new birth are upon me. Forgive me, brethren, do nothing to prevent this new life.[16]

THE CHRISTIAN TRIUMPH

Not long in terms of world history was Christianity to dwell in this smell of beasts and blood, save in memory. In the early decades of the fourth century, Christianity emerged from its place as merely one of the competitors in the lavish spiritual marketplace, to become first the dominant and then the sole official religion of the empire, and in time of all Europe. This reversal happened with surprising speed. True, the church had done well during the long years of comparative peace

---

[16]From the Epistle of St. Ignatius of Antioch to the Romans, vv. 4 and 6. Francis X. Glimm and others, *The Apostolic Fathers* (New York: Christian Heritage, Inc., 1947.), pp. 109–10.

since the end of the Decian persecution in 251. In some places, especially Asia Minor, Christianity was the majority faith, and nearby Armenia had become the first officially Christian nation around 300. In many cities, including Nicomedia in Asia Minor (modern Turkey), to which Diocletian had moved his capital, there stood impressive churches, and members of the emperor's family as well as the lowly supported them.

The reasons for the triumph of Christianity around 312 are not all immediately apparent. The faith of Christ had no greater prestige than the Neoplatonic mysticism favored by philosophers, or the Mithraism popular in the army, or the ancient polytheisms nostalgically upheld by patrician traditionalists. Indeed, it had been only a few years earlier (303) that, at the instigation of his son-in-law Galerius, the aging Diocletian imposed his persecution.

But one of Diocletian's commanders, Constantine, who emerged in western Europe after the former's death as an Augustus or "co-emperor," favored the Christian cause. Another co-emperor, the sadistic Maximin Daza, who continued persecution in the East, was deposed by a rival, Licinius. The latter met with Constantine in 313 to issue a decree of toleration, the so-called Edict of Milan, although no such document actually exists. Thereafter Constantine and Licinius ruled together.

Deep psychological currents favorable to Christianity apparently ran through the complex mind of Constantine; his mother Helena was Christian, and at the famous battle of the Milvian Bridge, where he defeated a rival in 312, it is said he saw a cross and the letters IHS—the Greek beginning of the name Jesus, or the Latin initials for "In Hoc Signo," "By this sign," in the sky.[17]

After 323 Constantine was emperor alone. He established his capital at Byzantium (modern Constantinople or Istanbul) and pursued policies favorable to Christianity, although was not himself baptized until on his deathbed. In 323 he sponsored a council of bishops at Nicaea, which made most of what is now the Nicene Creed the standard of doctrine. But Christianity did not become the official religion, the only one whose open practice was possible, until the reign of Theodosius I (379–95).

While the great pagan temples were turned into churches or public buildings, and the centers of pagan learning dispersed, paganism lingered a long time in the countryside. In the course of becoming the dominant religion of society and subsuming all the roles and drives which had animated the former faiths, from folk religion to the mysteries to Neoplatonist philosophy, Christianity naturally underwent development. In church organization, the bishops remained in the cities where the faith had long held sway, becoming more and more the spiritual parallels of governors and magistrate. Successors of the *presbyteroi* of old, parish priests, ordinarily one to a church, strove to Christianize the archaic agricultural religion of the countryside. Festivals like Christmas and Easter became colorful public holidays; pagan shrines and temples changed names. Moreover, the new faith spread rapidly among the restless Germanic tribes and Viking raiders, who were replacing Roman provinces with their rude kingdoms and dukedoms.

[17]See Hermann Dörres, *Constantine the Great,* trans. Roland Bainton (New York: Harper & Row, Publishers, 1972).

THE FOUNDATIONS
OF MEDIEVAL CHRISTIANITY

Let us look more explicitly at the changes Christianity underwent in terms of the forms of religious expression.

Theoretical expression became more and more solidified, particularly in regard to understanding of the incarnation, or how God became man in Christ. This articulation took place by means of general councils, meetings to which all bishops were invited. They sought to condemn heresy or false teaching and define correct or orthodox teaching. The councils had political overtones as well, for they were all held in the area of Byzantium, and the theological issues were often identified with parties or nationalities of political significance within the empire. In particular, issues were frequently polarized between Egypt and the northern part of the Eastern Empire. The Bishop of Rome, being an outsider to Eastern squabbles, often could mediate these problems. This increased his authority and helped in the development of his office into the medieval and modern papacy.

The four first and most important general councils were these. Nicaea in 325 affirmed, in the Nicene Creed, that Christ is of one substance or essence with God the Father; this definition opposed the Arians who held that at best Christ was only "like" God and a lower being sent as his envoy. Constantinople reaffirmed this position in 381. Ephesus in 431 affirmed Christ was always God, from his mother's womb (and so it called Mary his mother "theotokos," "God-bearer"), not a man who had been made Son of God. Chalcedon, in 451, affirmed that Christ is both True God and True Man, two natures conjoined in one person.

A similar matter theologically refined at about the same time, although never the subject of a general council, was the trinity. Christians had experienced God in three basic ways: as God the Heavenly Father, as the Son of God in Jesus Christ, and as the Holy Spirit who was promised by Christ and who filled the community in the upper room on Pentecost. Now it was written that these are three persons bound together in infinite love, who nonetheless are but one God.

In the West, Christians were less involved in the general councils than in the East, but theological work continued there too. The greatest western figure was Augustine, an African bishop who taught about the trinity and about grace, God's gift or help, among other topics. Concerning grace Augustine emphasized that God takes the initiative in relations between himself and us; all begins with grace, for we cannot seek God or do things pleasing to him unless he first enables us, since each of us naturally is self-centered and does not truly seek God or do selfless acts on his own. In such terms as these Augustine explained "original sin" and "prevenient grace."

It is too easy, however, to stress the history of ideas in the church and forget that changes were going on in worship and social organization of just as immense consequence. As the church moved out of the spiritual underground of the great cities and into spacious buildings, typically modeled on the basilica or Roman court of law, or into the rural world of peasant and lord, the liturgy or pattern of worship also changed. It became expressive and ornate. The clergy wore symbolically colored garments and moved with slow ritual, accompanied by music and incense, to present and bless the bread and wine. In the West the language of the service was Latin, in the East Greek. These tongues, especially Latin, quickly became "sacred" languages like Sanskrit in India, as the vernacular changed and as numerous new peoples came into the orbit of the faith.

For the Christian population was rapidly growing and changing. During the fourth century virtually all the peoples of the old Roman Empire were at least superficially Christianized, even those of areas no longer Chrisitan today such as North Africa, Egypt, Syria, Palestine, and Asia Minor. In the East missionaries won converts in Ethiopia, Mesopotamia, Persia, and even India. In the West, as hosts of heathen invaders out for plunder and new land—Visigoths, Saxons, Vikings, Franks, and the like—swept across lands only barely brought under the cross in the waning days of the imperial order, the situation was often chaotic; this is the era known as the Dark Ages. By the year 1000, however, all but a few corners of Europe had been converted, and the rambunctious tribes had begun slow progress toward becoming nations. We cannot trace here the full course of this missionary effort, although its annals contain many fascinating and adventurous tales.

A couple of examples, however: England and Ireland. Christianity came to Roman Britain in the third century. Apparently it was brought by unknown soldiers and merchants, although stories were told in the Middle Ages that Paul himself had visited Britain, or that Joseph of Arimathea (he who claimed the body of Jesus) had come there and planted the sacred tree known as the Glastonbury Thorn, a favorite place of pilgrimage. These legends are significant because they typify the romantic world of medieval Christianity. The Celtic and Roman settler population had become widely Christian after Britain was cut off from Rome early in the fifth century.

Shortly afterward, massive invasions of Danes, Angles, and Saxons, still adherents of the old Germanic religion of Wotan and Thor, had pushed the Christianized Celts back to the far West, to what is now Wales and Cornwall and their vicinity. There they held out; the tales of King Arthur reflect in part the days of these beleaguered Celts, who still remembered something of Rome and Christ, as well as old Celtic religious motifs. But in 597 a missionary named Augustine (not the same as the North African) was sent out from Rome to Kent, the Saxon kingdom in the extreme southeast corner of England. Its king and people, through the agency of the king's Christian wife, were converted, and not long afterward all the Anglo-Saxon kingdoms—Wessex, Sussex, Mercia, and the rest—had submitted to the faith of Christ.

Ireland's conversion was worked by the famous Patrick, who died in 461. The population was still tribal, and such organization as the church had followed tribal lines. It was full of zeal and its monks full of wanderlust. Missionaries from Ireland traveled to many parts of Europe. Ireland was Christian while England and much of the continent was not; in those confused times Ireland was a preeminent center of Christian learning and effort in the West.

The classical pattern of bishops, who governed the church in geographical areas called dioceses, and parish priests in each community, was perpetuated wherever the church acquired a foothold. Moreover, the bishops of major cities became known as archbishops. The Council of Chalcedon made the bishops of five of the most important cities of all in the ancient empire—Constantinople, Ephesus, Alexandria, and Jerusalem in the East, and Rome in the West—patriarchs, and the patriarch of Constantinople, the capital of the Byzantine Empire, was called ecumenical or universal patriarch; with this title, he is still the chief dignitary of the Eastern Orthodox Church. On the other hand, the patriarch of Rome came to be called the pope. He had long been looked upon as the chief arbitrator of disputes and heir of the church which, having been associated with the apostles Peter and Paul themselves, had an apostolic tradition of unquestionable soundness. Indeed, it was said by many in the West especially that the pope, as successor to Peter as bishop of Rome, was heir to those promises Matthew's Gospel records Jesus as giving to Peter:

> You are Peter, and on this rock I will build my church, and the powers of death shall not prevail against it. I will give you the keys of the kingdom of heaven, and whatever you bind on earth shall be bound in heaven, and whatever you loose on earth shall be loosed in heaven. (Matt. 16:18-20)

Furthermore, in the confusion that attended the collapse of the empire, the popes, particularly strong popes such as Leo (r. 441–61) and Gregory (r. 590–604), emerged as dominant figures in both church and secular affairs, beacons of stability and hope in a dark and terrifying world. It is not surprising that, by the Middle Ages, their sovereignty over the church in the West was firmly established.

One extremely important social development in Christianity was monasticism. In order to serve God better, and in search for security and purity in a corrupt and chaotic society, young men—and not long afterward, women—left society to remain unmarried and form communities focused on the worship of God. It started in Egypt in the late third century when men such as Anthony and Pachomius went into the desert to pursue lives of prayer as hermits. Soon they were followed by disciples and communities grew up, and before long the idea had spread throughout the Christian world. Benedict (c. 529) established the Benedictine monastic pattern, which became normative for the church in the West. Quickly monasteries became centers both of missionary work and the preservation of learning, and also orphanages, hospitals, and way stations.[18]

Parallel to monasticism was the general idea of celibacy for the clergy. There was a widespread feeling, based both on the examples of the unmarried Jesus and Paul the apostle and on lingering aversion to the "passions" derived from Greek philosophy, that the celibate life was holier and closer to perfection than the married. The actual situation in the early church was mixed, however. In the East, the pattern which obtains in Orthodoxy to this day, that bishops should be celibate but the ordinary clergy may be married, was established at least by the time of the general councils. In the West, partly in response to the social disruptions, regional

---

[18]See Helen Waddell, *The Desert Fathers* (Ann Arbor: University of Michigan Press, 1957); Justin McCann, *Saint Benedict* (Garden City, N.Y.: Doubleday Image Books, 1958); and David Knowles, *Christian Monasticism* (New York: McGraw-Hill, 1969).

churches and finally the papacy enjoined celibacy for all clergy, and this was observed (at least officially) everywhere in the West by the Middle Ages.

Patterns of popular Christian worship also evolved strikingly. One feature was devotion to the Blessed Virgin Mary, mother of Jesus Christ, and to other saints. It had roots in the early church's veneration of martyrs and in Christian belief that all who are in Christ, whether in this life or the next, are one family and so able to communicate with and help one another. Now this area of the faith grew and expanded; shrines and altars to saints and festivals for them appeared in both East and West; statues in the West and icons (sacred paintings) in the East, as well as relics from them—bones, clothing—came to focus this devotion. The cultus, especially for the vast illiterate masses now Christianized, provided a deeply felt color and warmth. With it also came pilgrimages, journeys for the sake of devotion to Jerusalem and other holy places.

Christian life now had two basic emphases: the winning of eternal life in heaven and the avoiding of hell, after death; and following Christian moral teachings here. Although the Last Judgment, typically portrayed on the rear wall of medieval churches, was much regarded, like death it was chiefly seen as a narrow portal to heaven. Heaven was gained through the sacraments (baptism, holy communion, and the "last rites" especially) and by prayer, penitence for sins, and a moral life. Morality included doing those things that would make earthly society just and stable, a worthy prologue to heaven. Thus Christian moral teaching helped to make the medieval world, which idealized itself as an unchanging human estate lying between the time of Christ and the Last Judgment.

MEDIEVAL CHRISTENDOM

We lack space to trace the history of Christianity through the Middle Ages. Let us take a look instead at the religious life of a medieval peasant, who would be typical of the vast majority of people in Europe between 800 and 1500, and in many places until much later. His life would center around the village where his fellow peasants lived, the manor or castle of the lord, and the church. In some cases the lord would actually be a bishop or monastery; usually it would be a hereditary feudal lord, who would spend much of his time leading his knights in combat with the neighboring lords and their knights, and who would probably name the priest of the church.

All would be illiterate or virtually so; the peasants and probably the lord and his household would consider reading beyond or beneath them; the priest might be uneducated even in theology, and might have just enough letters to recite the service in a Latin he could hardly understand. Education grew gradually more general among both clergy and genteel laity as the Middle Ages wore on, but for the most part only bards, monks, lawyers, tradesmen, and Jews had anything that resembled learning.

All that would be beyond the horizons of the peasant. As a serf, he was bound to the soil of the manor. He had never been more than a few miles from the village where he had been born and would live and die in sight of its church spire. The village was a shabby affair of mud, wattle, and thatch; above it loomed the imposing but grim castle or manor house of the lord. In theory, the serfs were obligated from birth to the service of the lord in the castle, although they had plots of their own as well as the lord's fields which they worked. The lord could employ them, tax them, and judge them at law as he saw fit. They could not marry without his consent, nor leave the estate. In practice, however, the relationship was complex and mitigated by custom, for the lord was also dependent on the serfs and lived close to them in an isolated community. Lord and peasant shared feasts in the great hall, and all but the greatest lords had to work alongside their peasants at harvest, and were hungry with them during the cruel medieval winter if that harvest was poor.

The center of this community was the parish church. This stone building was an island of relative grace and color in a drab world. It would have vivid paintings and windows showing supernal things: a radiant saint, the wondrous Mother of God with her warm open arms and compassionate look, Christ judging high and low alike on the dreaded Last Day. At the front would be the richly decked altar, with its hangings, glowing cross, and flickering candles. A scent of incense might hang in the air. Manifestly this place was of some different order from the cold, heavy castle with its endless fighting, and the too often hungry, sick, and overworked village. It was clearly the portal of another world of supernal terror and joy, a magic lens that enabled a richer level of perception.

On Sunday bells from this church would ring out, and the lord and his family and knights would gather together with the peasants in the church for mass, generally at 9 A.M. The priest in his vestments would stand before the altar and, with many bows and elaborate gestures, wavings of incense and strikings of bells, would celebrate the mass. It was the same offering and blessing of bread which the early Christians had done in their catacombs and upper rooms, but the priest would be muttering now in an old and sacred tongue the words that made the wafers of bread and cup of wine the Body and Blood of Christ, for the saving of souls in the parish. He might also give a sermon. Priest and church were supported by glebe lands, fields of the manor set aside whose revenues went to this cause.

Besides Sundays, numerous festivals of saints broke the tedium and hard work of village life. Then would come special services, dancing, fairs, and traditional practices—some of them, like the Procession of the White Lady of Banbury cited in Chapter 2, having clear pre-Christian background, but no less delightful to the peasants for that.[19]

There were other breaks in the rhythm too. Not the peasants, but merchants and tradesmen were able to make pilgrimages to shrines where miracles were said to take place, like Chaucer's pilgrims to Canterbury. In other ways, too, the pattern of medieval life was often broken, for the Middle Ages were by no means the static "Age of Faith" sometimes imagined. Changes and dissidents there were always.

---

[19]See George G. Coulton, *Medieval Panorama* (New York: The Macmillan Company, 1938): and two works of readable history by H. Daniel-Rops: *The Church in the Dark Ages,* trans. Audrey Butler (New York: E. P. Dutton, 1959), and *Cathedral and Crusade: Studies of the Medieval Church 1050–1350,* trans. John Worthington (New York: E. P. Dutton, 1957).

The vicissitudes of war and weather—and often disease—swept continually through the villages.

For there were big events and important people in the Middle Ages as well. Rumors, at least, of the Crusades, that remarkable combination of bloodthirstiness and piety, would be in the air. The Crusades expressed the very spirit of medievalism, but helped to bring that age to an end by opening up contact with new ideas from the East, and from the Greek culture better preserved there—as well as leading to deep-seated enmity between Christian Europe and Islam, and between Eastern and Western Christianity as well.

In the year 1054, before the Crusades started (in 1095), came the formal rupture between the Eastern Orthodox and Western (Roman) Catholic churches. The official reason was the *filioque* question, whether the Holy Spirit proceeds from both God the Father and God the Son (as the Western version of the Nicene Creed stated), or from the Father alone (as the Eastern version had it), and a few other theological and ecclesiastical issues of similar quality. But the real issue was the growing authority of the papacy in the West (the word "filioque,"—"and the Son"—had been added to the Western Nicene Creed by authority of the pope, not of a general council), and even more perhaps by wide cultural differences emerging between western Europe and the Byzantine East. The split was effectively made irrevocable by the Crusades; the sack of Constantinople by soldiers of the cross in 1204 left a bitter legacy which made lasting reconciliation impossible.

The greatest Western religious thinker in the Middle Ages was Thomas Aquinas (1224–74), the major figure of the style of philosophy known as scholasticism. Influenced by the Aristotelianism of the Muslim thinker of Cordova, Averroës, Thomas was concerned to distinguish betwen the realm of nature where reason holds sway, and the realm of faith where revelation adds its gifts; the existence of God, shown by nature, is (he stated) knowable through reason alone. The result of this philosophical and theological labor was a vast synthesis of Aristotelian science and philosophy, Christianity, and medieval experience, which summed up the vision of that age and has been the most important intellectual force in Roman Catholicism down to the present. In it, all beings under God—angels, mankind, matter, sound reason, and sure revelation—have their logical places and reasonable duties in reflecting God's glory, a vision expressed more poetically but no more powerfully in the *Divine Comedy* of Dante Alighieri.

The Middle Ages teemed with new religious movements, increasingly so as time advanced. Most were reactions to the church in favor of "Gospel simplicity" and "inwardness." They favored asceticism, fervent religious feelings, and freedom of movement for religious persons in contrast to the comparative wealth, objective worship of shrine and sacrament, and rootedness in feudal, village, and agricultural patterns of the conventional church. The dissident movements were, significantly, strongest among the craftsmen and tradesmen of the burgeoning towns, although sometimes they swept through countryside districts on a wave of social protest. They were a combination of the age-old "holy man" ideal and the modern severing of religion from its rural roots; both motifs contrast with the medieval alliance of religious and feudal concepts, and of Christianity and agricultural religion.

Some of these movements, like that of Francis of Assisi and his friars, remained within the orbit of orthodoxy. Francis, the "Little Poor Man," lived and inspired many others to live a life of Christian perfection marked by poverty, universal love, and a new personal devotion to the human Christ in the manger and on the cross; his order of friars, or "brothers," wandering, begging, and relatively free from control by bishop or parish priest, transmitted this experience throughout Europe and soon enough to Latin America and the Orient.

Other such preachers, however, were considered heretical. Some, like the Albigensians or Cathari who were the object of brutal persecution in the thirteenth century, were, indeed, inspired by ancient Manichaeism as well as the new ideas of simplicity and inwardness; the Albigensians so honored spirit above flesh that they held self-starvation a noble thing. Others, like the Waldensians, Lollards, and Hussites, were more concerned to conform Christian life to the Bible according to their lights. The important thing to note is that these protests were challenges to the medieval order by a new, sometimes cantankerous but always deeply felt, individualism and rejection of the old corporate village faith of parish church and succession of agricultural festivals.[20]

THE REFORMATION AND LUTHER

The next development was the Reformation, which carried all these trends to their natural conclusion—a new style of Christianity. Perhaps the onset of change was abeted by the Black Death, or plague, which swept across Europe, wiping out something like a third of the population during 1348–50, disrupting traditional patterns of society, leaving many parishes without clergy, and on a deeper level going some ways to discredit the traditional faith and church. (People asked themselves, "Why do good and bad alike succumb to the plague? Why does the traditional church and Christian life not protect us?")

At the same time, the prestige of the papacy as the unifying force in Europe and Christendom was greatly weaked by the abduction of the pope by agents of the French king in 1309, and his and his successors' residence in Avignon, France, under French domination 1309–77. Above all the papacy's image was tarnished by the resultant great schism of 1378–1417, when two (and for a time three) "popes" existed, one in Rome and one in Avignon, each claiming to be the true ruler of the church and each holding the allegiance of several nations.

Against this background, groups such as the English Lollards, followers of John Wycliffe, began around 1380 to demand such reforms as abolition of clerical celibacy, of the use of images, of prayers for the dead, of pilgrimages and elaborate vestments. They demanded that the clergy should chiefly preach and that the scriptures should be freely available to all in the vernacular language. In Bohemia and Moravia the Hussites, followers of John Hus (who died at the stake in 1415) made

---

[20]On spiritual dissidents in the Middle Ages, see Steven Runciman, *The Medieval Manichee* (Cambridge: Cambridge University Press, 1960); and Norman Cohn, *The Pursuit of the Millenium* (New York: Oxford University Press, 1970).

One God, Many Words and Wonders

similar demands, particularly asking that the church should manifest poverty and church lands be expropriated.

It was not until the sixteenth century, however, that new ideas came into their own at a time of the slow decline of feudalism, the rise to prominence of townsmen, and the corresponding shift of Christian emphasis (even in Catholic mysticism) from cosmic and sacramental religion to preoccupation with inner motivation and experience. It would be an oversimplification to say that these changes caused the Reformation. The modern mind was also shaped by Renaissance businessmen and intellectuals in Catholic Italy, who shared many of the new attitudes yet did not become Protestant. But certainly social changes and the Reformation went together.

The Reformation was overtly focused on spiritual and theological issues, however. The man who by far most influenced its course, Martin Luther (1483-1546) was little concerned consciously with these matters of social history, for he was a scholarly monk of the Augustinian order since the age of 21, though his father—a strict, pious, enterprising civic leader engaged in the mining business in the small German town of Eisleben—was surely typical of the kind of man the Reformation would help to supersede knights, lords, and peasants. Nonetheless, it was Luther's deeply inward spiritual struggles which defined the issues, language, and direction of the Reformation.

In his monastery Luther experienced grueling anxiety. His problem was that he felt himself a sinner, however blameless a life he lived as a monk. So long as he thought of it in terms of how much he had to do, what standards he had to meet, what religious acts he had to perform, and what devout feelings he had to feel, he could only live, it seemed, in a cruel uncertainty, which would virtually lead to madness if one were really serious about it—and Luther was nothing if not serious. He felt trapped; he was commanded to love God, but how could one love a God whose demands left one in such anguish? Could he ever know if he had done enough?

Then, in studying the Scriptures, Luther came to the lines "The righteous shall live by faith" (Habakkuk 2:4, Romans 1:17). This saying provided a sunrise of new awareness. He realized to the depths of his being that what set a person in right relationship with God was not the things he had been trying before, but simple faith—sincere belief, trust, and intention—and this as a matter of inner attitude was available to anyone at any time. In fact, it is not really a matter of what we do at all, for faith is first of all a gift—a grace (from *gratia,* meaning "free")—from God, always free, always poured out in love, to which we only respond with sincerity of faith. When Luther realized this, all else appeared superfluous and likely to confuse. For this reason he insisted also on the principle of *sola scriptura,* the Bible alone as guide to Christian faith and practice, for he felt that salvation by grace through faith *was* the clear and central message of the Scripture, and that its obscuring had come about through overlays of human philosophy and ecclesiastical tradition.

Luther's new understanding of Christianity first brought him into conflict with its medieval version over the issue of indulgences. Indulgences were related to the doctrine of purgatory, a universally held medieval belief that there was an intermediate state, purgatory, between heaven and hell for those who died neither saints nor hopeless sinners; there souls would suffer purging fires for a long or short time, until they had been cleansed of evil and justice was satisfied, and then could await entry into the presence of God. Indulgences were certificates issued by the pope, under his power of binding and loosing, affirming that because the recipient had done an adequate number of acts of penitance and devotion, so many days—or all—of his prospective suffering in purgatory had been remitted. This remittance was held to be made possible by the transfer to the penitent of something of the superabundance of merit attained by Christ and the saints; to this "treasury of merit" the pope held the spiritual key. Indulgences could even be obtained by one person on behalf of another, living or dead.

This profoundly medieval doctrine was not without its attractive side; it was a concrete way of stating the benefits accrued from such extra and innocent religious acts as pilgrimage, and it suggested, in the exchange of merit idea, that Christians deeply share in one another's lives and can bear one another's burdens. It was an implementation of the communion of saints. (Indulgences are still made available in the Roman Catholic Church.) But in Luther's day indulgences were being widely distributed in Germany with little consideration but for the donation of money customarily given by the recipient; in effect they were being used as a means of church fund-raising, and a special drive was on to raise funds for the building of St. Peter's cathedral in Rome. Moreover, the theology behind indulgences went very much counter to Luther's new inner discovery of salvation by grace through faith only; the use they were being put to raised the hackles of nascent German nationalism, for thinking Germans felt they were being exploited for the sake of interests south of the Alps.

On October 31, 1517, Luther posted 95 theses, or points for debate, on the door of All Saints Church in Wittenberg, which served as the university's bulletin board. It was the eve of All Saints' Day, when many relics of the saints (a comparably questionable matter with Luther) would be exposed for veneration in that church. In the famous 95 Theses Luther spoke against abuses of indulgences, relics, and the like, but the tone was not extreme nor did he question papal authority or the doctrine of purgatory as such. He stressed the supreme value of inwardness, however, sharing the sufferings of Christ more than prematurely trying to take advantage of heaven: a theology of the cross rather than a theology of glory.

This challenge started as a theological dispute, but quickly escalated beyond what one would normally expect of such arguments among monks. Luther was engaged in a course that finally led to his rejection of papal authority as its logical outcome, and this in turn produced his excommunication by Rome in 1521. Public opinion in Germany tended to take Luther's side. Spurred on by his pamphlet "Address to the Christian Nobility of the German Nation," a sense of German national pride and identity, long smoldering under cultural and spiritual domination from southern Europe, was enflamed. When Luther was summoned before the Imperial Diet at Worms to defend himself, he may not actually have used the famous words, "Here I stand; God help me, I can do no other," but that was what he meant, and the defiance of resented authority deeply stirred many a German knight. But this did not please the young Holy Roman Emperor Charles V, who desired to continue the alliance between his throne and that of the pope.[21]

The test of inward faith, rather than rites, sacraments, or pious deeds, was congruous with a longstanding German mystical bent. The precise theological points at issue may have mattered less to the knights and people at large than to scholars, but the common folk grasped the implication that the new teachings meant all persons were fully equal before God. When Luther's German Bible and simplified services in the vernacular soon appeared, people well understood both the new orientation toward inward faith and the implicit Germanic self-affirmation.

Luther had hoped to see the church purified, and Christians everywhere find new inner freedom and peace. It was a cause of grief and bitterness to him that one of the most conspicuous results of reform was conflict—theological, political, and military. In the following century this escalated into the devastating Thirty Years' War, finally settled at the Peace of Westphalia in 1648. Scandinavia, most of northern Germany, and small minorities elsewhere were thereafter Lutheran.

CALVIN

The most important reformer after Luther was John Calvin (1509–64). He was a Frenchman, but is associated mainly with Geneva in Switzerland. As a young man he was a Renaissance humanist, but in 1533 he was converted to the Protestant movement that Luther had spearheaded. He immediately wrote his theological masterpiece, *Institutes of the Christian Religion*. The brief first edition was published in 1536, but Calvin kept revising and expanding it until the definitive edition of 1559.

After 1541 Calvin lived in Geneva, which had recently thrown out its ruling bishop and become Protestant, and had invited him to take over leadership. Reluctantly (he much preferred a quiet scholarly life) he accepted, and during his stay he made Geneva a kind of holy community of the faith as he interpreted the latter's demands, dominated by himself and other clergy, enforcing strict moral rectitude and correct belief in church and city government alike.

Calvin's theology is based on a strong contrast between the infinite greatness and power of God, and the sinfulness of mankind. God's glory fills the universe; the division between the sacred and the secular is done away, for all is sacred, and all that happens is due solely to his will, from life and death to the smallest seemingly accidental events here below. Nonetheless mankind is in rebellion against God; God permits this in order that his mercy may be shown in the salvation of those whom he chooses, while divine justice is affirmed by the punishment of the rest. Those whom

---

[21]A readable life of Luther is Roland H. Bainton, *Here I Stand* (New York: Abingdon-Cokesbury Press, 1950). For the entire period see Harold J. Grimm, *The Reformation Era 1500–1650* (New York: The Macmillan Company, 1973).

God chooses for eternal life do not have any merit of their own; they are recipients of his grace which, as Luther (following Augustine) had emphasized, must come before anything right that humans can do. The elect, those chosen through grace, will be marked by righteous life and a seemingly spontaneous and persevering predilection for true religion. Calvin's theology also emphasizes mystical union of the Christian with Christ.

Calvin stressed, like Luther, the importance of the Bible alone as the normative guide for Christians. In church organization, he made much greater changes than did Luther; doing away with bishops, he gave considerable place to local control and boards of elders or presbyters. The sacraments of baptism and holy communion were greatly simplified in administration and, in practice, given much less importance than the preaching of the Word of God, the chief means by which people are called to faith and grace.

The theology and style of church life left by John Calvin has been much criticized; and indeed, when Calvinism appears without the panoramic world vision and God-intoxication of its best men and women, it can easily become harsh and rigid. Calvinism's positive role in the making of the modern world must be appreciated. Calvinism contributed immensely to the development of modern democracy: indirectly through its new emphasis on the equality of all before God, for the elect might be found in any social station; and directly through the model of its presbyterian or congregational forms of church organization, which gave many sorts of people experience in decision-making responsibilities, and did not fit as well with feudalism or absolute monarchy as did bishops. Calvinists insisted, as did other Protestants, that everyone should be able to read the Bible for himself, and this gave much impetus to education. Finally, it can be noted that Calvinism appealed especially to the rising business class in western Europe; its stress on the elect's sense of inner call, commitment, and righteousness in the midst of work in the world rather than sacerdotalism or monasticism, and its stern ethics with their self-denial, hard work, and individual responsibility, contributed much to the psychology which made this class prosperous and, in fact, for several centuries second to none in worldwide influence. Sometimes this happy destiny was seen as in itself a sign of divine election and favor.

Today, churches known as Reformed, Presbyterian, or Congregational are from the Calvinist tradition, although Calvin's original message has been varyingly modified in them over the years. Calvinism became dominant in Holland, Scotland, and parts of Germany and Switzerland; the Puritan movement in England and America was Calvinist as well, and has had tremendous impact on life in those countries and their spheres of influence. Minority Protestant churches in France, Hungary, and some other parts of Catholic Europe are also Calvinist in background.

THE ENGLISH REFORMATION

In England the Reformation took yet another form. It is natural that this country of Wycliffe and the Lollards, and of emerging nationalism as well, should have harbored many people who responded enthusiastically to news of the events in Germany. Yet the English character has always exhibited a sense of pragmatism, moderation, and appreciation of tradition as well as thirst for reform. All of this is evident in the English Reformation. Significantly, it did not receive its impetus from a wholly engaged reformer like Luther or Calvin, but from a rather sordid political matter. The king, Henry VIII, had been an enthusiastic defender of the old faith against the reformers, but in the early 1530s desired to divorce his queen, Katharine of Aragon, since she had been unable to give him a living male heir. This step required a dispensation from the pope which the latter, Clement VII, was unwilling to authorize. Therefore Henry called upon Parliament to sever relations with Rome and make the king supreme head of the church in England; the resultant Act of Supremacy was passed in 1534. Henry was divorced and married again, not for the last time.

Although strained relations between Rome and England were no new thing, undoubtedly the continental reformation created an atmosphere conducive to taking this final step. But those who desired a more thoroughgoing reformation were initially disappointed. True, the monasteries, convents, and pilgrimage shrines were dissolved promptly and their wealth divided among Henry's henchmen, but otherwise little changed; most of the same bishops remained in their sees, and the same celibate priests in their parishes, saying the same Latin mass. The king rigorously enforced Catholic doctrinal orthodoxy.

But after Henry VIII died in 1546, the dike could no longer hold. Calvinist influence now pouring in from Geneva overbalanced the conservative side. A new form of worship in the English language, the *Book of Common Prayer,* was produced in 1549; essentially, it perpetuated the basic structure of the old Latin forms but with substantial concessions to Protestantism on sensitive issues, such as its formal elimination of devotion to saints. It was over a century before the religious situation in England was fully stabilized, but the essential outline of its official form, the Church of England, was already apparent in the Prayer Book of 1549: continuity of church structure from the Middle Ages; English language worship, which was Catholic in outline but designed to be nonoffensive to moderate Protestants; a pragmatic mentality (which emerged more slowly) allowing for some divergence of theological opinion among individual clergy and members, especially between the Catholic and Protestant traditions which meet in the Church of England.

A minority in England maintained allegiance to the Church of Rome. Over the next two centuries, others separated themselves into more fully Protestant groups: Puritan (Calvinist), Baptist, Quaker, Methodist.

RADICAL REFORM

Outside the great movements of Luther and Calvin, and that in England, and generally without the support of rulers, the Reformation stirred up the zeal of many who wanted much more far-reaching changes in the church, and often also in society. These movements typically stressed the need for personal conversion experiences, moral perfection, and a close following of the New Testament both in faith and social life. They varied from Anabaptists (indirectly the forebears of modern Baptists in England and America) who rejected the baptism of infants, insisting that Christians should have a personal conversion experience and be baptized only after it; and Mennonites, who were perfectionists, pacifists, and often communalists; to rationalistic Unitarians such as Michael Servetus, who denied the doctrine of the trinity and was burned at the stake in Calvin's Geneva.[22]

Let us now survey the three main branches of Christianity today, Eastern Orthodoxy, Roman Catholicism, and Protestantism.

EASTERN ORTHODOXY

The branch of Christianity called Orthodox is the dominant religious tradition of Greece, the Balkans, and Russia; there is a scattering in other parts of the Near East, and of course it is found wherever immigrants from its homelands have come, including the United States. (A Russian Orthodox cathedral was established at Sitka, Alaska, as early as 1794.) The Orthodox churches, about 160 million strong, are often called "Eastern" because their center of gravity is in eastern Europe, although this faith is of worldwide importance. They are sometimes called Greek Orthodox, since the cultural and historical background is Greek; the tradition took its definitive form in the culturally Greek Byzantine Empire. But the majority of Orthodox are now Slavic rather than Greek. The Orthodox churches of various nationalities commonly go by that name, such as Russian Orthodox, Serbian Orthodox, Rumanian Orthodox.

Orthodoxy likes to speak of itself as the oldest Christian church, and indeed geography makes its churches continuous with those that Paul and other apostles founded or visited in places like Thessalonika, Corinth, and Cyprus. But the ritual and ethos of the present-day Orthodox churches is essentially the form in which it crystallized in the Byzantine period before the fall of Constantinople to the Turks in 1452. Since then, most Orthodox lands spent long centuries under Muslim or Mongol rule, just as most of them are now under Communist regimes cold toward church and religion. This history, so different from that of Christianity in the West, has inhibited outward development but has given Orthodoxy a deep relation to the national culture of several countries, and often a very rich inner spiritual life.

The word "orthodox" has varying usage and connotations in English. For the people of the Eastern churches it is an attractive and strong word, not primarily suggesting negative and narrow attitudes. They believe, of course, that their churches alone preserve the correct or orthodox tradition of Christian teaching and life from earliest times. But they also like to point out that in Greek "orthodox" can mean both "right teaching" *and* "right glory." The combination of these two gives insight into the world of Orthodox life.

A highly conservative mood informs the standard doctrinal teaching of the Orthodox churches. It is held that only a general council can officially define doctrine, and only seven are recognized: Nicaea, Constantinople, Ephesus, Chalcedon, and three more. Moreover, Orthodox thought has been deeply influenced by Platonism with its assumption that what is most real and true is unchanging. Thus, central to Orthodoxy is the reality of the trinity, God as three in one, an eternal

[22]See George Huntson Williams, *The Radical Reformation* (Philadelphia: The Westminster Press, 1962).

One God, Many Words and Wonders

mystery that undergirds the world. Next is the eternal reality of the incarnation of God in Christ, not only a historical episode but an eternal involvement of God in the material world, through struggle and suffering making the children of earth divine, manifesting true glory.

On the one hand, this attitude has led to an exaltation of timeless contemplation, exemplified by devout Orthodox monks like those living virtually out of history on Mount Athos in Greece, whom all serious Orthodox regard as ideals and as unseen givers of life to the church. The goal, Orthodox say, is to be deified in the sense of becoming "partakers of the divine nature," actual sharers in God's own life; contemplation raises us to this level.

Yet on the other hand, Orthodoxy greatly celebrates Christ's resurrection and the anticipated last day when God will make the new heaven and earth and be all in all. These represent the triumph of God's suffering work in the world as he makes it visibly what the contemplative knows inwardly it is, infused with divinity.

The worship side of Orthodoxy richly expresses these ideas. For one used to the plainness of much western Christianity, a first visit to an Orthodox church can be an overwhelming experience. The service is long and may be in an unfamiliar tongue. But few will be untouched by the glowing color and the soaring, exotic music. The Divine Liturgy, as the main Sunday service is called, is also at heart the early church's offering and blessing of bread and wine. The ornate vestments shimmer richly, incense is swung into the music-laden air over and over, the book of the Gospel and the elements of bread and wine are brought out in procession.

Across a partition (the *iconostasis*) before the altar, and at the church entry and elsewhere, will be seen the icons, vividly colored stylized paintings of Christ and the saints. These, which the faithful reverently kiss and before which they burn candles, have a very special meaning in Orthodoxy. Made according to holy traditions, they are seen as radiating the divine glory of the subjects and so are like peepholes into eternity and means of raising oneself to it. In fact, the whole Divine Liturgy is seen as an experience of moving up into another plane, or conversely a breakthrough of heaven to earth. The entire intricately wrought interior of the building may be backgrounded in gold, representing eternity.

The concept that the church makes available here on earth these experiences of the Other Side helps one understand the activity of people in Orthodox worship. People will often be coming and going throughout the long service, or getting up to pray and light candles, perhaps with prostrations, at various icons on their own. The sense of individual freedom suggests the church is more like a home than an institution. At the same time, Orthodoxy inculcates a deep sense of community within which this freedom is possible. A sense of simple belonging to the Orthodox community is an interior identity that goes beyond any particular forms of outward expression; there is much that is important and traditional in matters of worship, fasting, and so forth, yet they hardly stifle the homey and spontaneous tone with legalism.

Something of the same feeling permeates other of the Orthodox forms of social expression; particularly was this the case in old Russia. No country except India has had as many wandering holy men as Russia before the Revolution; in some ways the Orthodox Christianity of "Holy Russia" was far more Asian than western in religious style. The *startsi,* holy monks or hermits, more often laymen than priests, familiar to readers of Dostoevsky, were venerated counselors and givers of blessing. Some remained in one place, some were perpetual pilgrims who wandered about the vast land, and even as far as Jerusalem, with nothing but the clothes on their back and perhaps a sacred book or two, begging, remaining silent unless pressed to teach. There were also the "Holy Fools," perhaps idiots, madmen by conventional standards, or cripples, who might babble nonsense, meow like a cat in church, or castigate a czar for his sins, yet before whom even nobility might bow with humility, for they were seen as embodiments of the suffering Christ and of the irrational side of God here on earth.[23]

[23]Two books that provide real insight into the soul of Eastern Orthodox spirituality, especially in old Russia, are Jon Gregerson, *Transfigured Cosmos* (New York: Ungar, 1960), and *The Way of a Pilgrim, and The Pilgrim Continues his Way,* trans. R. M. Franch (New York: The Seabury Press, 1974).

Service in a Russian Orthodox church in Alaska. Note the swinging incense pot and the icons or holy pictures.

Thus, Eastern Orthodoxy has quite distinctive forms in the three areas of religious expression: theological emphasis on God in trinity and incarnation as eternally unchanging yet present all through the world, even in the lowliest, and always breaking through it in mystery and glory; a worship which expresses that glory; and social forms making room for tradition, homeliness, and spontaneity in individuals within a mystical community.

ROMAN CATHOLICISM

The Roman Catholic Church, the communion of Christians who recognize the supreme spiritual authority on earth of the bishop of Rome, the pope, and who share much else as well, is the largest Christian body. Some 600 million people are within its spiritual, or at least cultural, orbit; it is the dominant religious tradition in most of southern and central Europe, Ireland, and Latin America, and is an important minority in North America, Australia, and parts of Africa and Asia.

For many people both within and outside it, the Roman Catholic Church means an institution of monolithic uniformity and highly authoritarian direction. If this was ever true, and it never has been entirely, it is not today. Since the Second Vatican Council of 1962–65, this church has known considerable ferment and experimentation; whatever it becomes, it can surely not go back to what it was before. In the late 1960s and 1970s, I have witnessed a very informal mass—with guitars, the congregation standing around the altar, and pentecostal "speaking in tongues"—in Los Angeles; a highly traditional Latin mass in Communist-ruled Budapest; a dignified yet reformed mass in Japanese at Ise, not far from the great Shinto shrine, in which members of the congregation read various parts of the service. The Roman Catholic experience has never really been monolithic—even traditional worship does not have quite the same "feel" in Austria and Ireland, or Brazil and Belgium—but now its variations are becoming more spontaneous and individual, less merely differences in national "style" and background folk culture.

But one thing outwardly links this realm together: acceptance of the pope as symbol and guarantor of Christian unity. Even this sign has varied in appearance through the centuries, popes being weak and relatively little noted in some centuries, in others great potentates who played major roles in international politics, lavishly patronized art, or exercised near-absolute control over the church. Now understanding of the papal role, like much else, is changing. But its profoundest meaning, as a token of the catholicity or universality of the church, is likely to abide. With the papacy goes another characteristic which is also changing in nature, yet is deeply ingrained in the Latin past and Catholic present—an acceptance that some uniformity and centralized authority are good in the church, not only for practical reasons, but also because of the opportunity they provide for love and negation of egocentricity.

The papacy is far from being the only distinguishing mark of the Roman Catholic Church, however, and many today would argue it is not one to be overemphasized, even though in some ways it symbolizes much that is distinctive about the Roman Catholic experience. Here are some other general, principial characteristics.

1. Affirmation of appearances. This attitude, shared with Eastern Orthodoxy and many Anglicans and Lutherans, affirms the appropriateness of colorful visible ceremonies, vestments, and images. It affirms by them the presence of the numinous in the church, and the necessity of the church appearing to the world as a visible, organized community. This attitude is closely related to the sacramental principle—belief that definite, ceremonial acts like baptism, holy communion, and ordination are channels of God's grace and power. The fundamental assumption is that God's work is not wholly invisible and unpredictable, but that God does work through specific matter, people, and institutions; that the incarnation of God in Christ authenticates this experience and God's promises confirm it. For Roman Catholics, the affirmation of appearances and the sacramental principle are ways of emphasizing that the world was created good, and the church a visible and specific work of God on earth through which he comes to the world in the things of the world.

2. Organization and authority on a legal model. This church has a clear chain of command, and definite regulations regarding devotional practices, celibacy of clergy, and moral questions such as divorce and birth control. The legal attitude is an inheritance of Roman law and organization, to which is added a belief that Christ gave to his church a definite teaching authority.

3. A growing institution. Together with organization and authority, there is another side too: a conviction that the Christian fellowship, the church, is an organic, growing, and so changing institution. The papacy and other organs of the church's teaching authority have power to direct this growth, yet it is believed to move under the guidance of the Holy Spirit, who is always helping Christians to understand and manifest better the truth given them. Changes in rite and custom, and clearer definitions of what perviously had been latent or unclear in doctrine (although doctrine itself does not change), accompany its pilgrimage down through the ages. Papal infallibility, itself defined by the First Vatican Council in 1870, means that the pope is preserved from error when he exercises this defining function in a formal way.

The Roman Catholic Church, then, is an institution highly visible, sacramental, legal, and yet changing. While it certainly claims continuity with the church of the early centuries and the Middle Ages, it is equally not the same in all respects now as then. Let us look at some specific characteristics of present-day Roman Catholicism.

First some essential doctrines. God is said to be accessible to reason. Faith means intellectual assent. In other words, one can know by reason that there is a God apart from the Christian revelation, and faith is recognizing in the mind that this is so. This is all significant for it indicates the partnership of religion and philosophy, and the belief, important to many Catholic attitudes, that there are basic truths upon which the Christian faith builds. The added revelation which comes through Christ is mediated through both scripture and tradition, the Bible and the church's lore interacting to cast light upon each other. Its basic points are the trinity and the incarnation of God in Christ.

The Roman Catholic Church makes much of the Mother of Jesus, the Blessed Virgin Mary. This is fundamentally because her role guarantees the incarnation, but also because she is seen—in her acceptance of God's request that she bear his incarnating son—as a representative of the human race as it was before sin came. She is humanity responding perfectly to God's will, and receiving the fullness of God's grace and reward. This is the meaning of the papally defined doctrines of the Immaculate Conception (1854), that Mary was herself conceived without original sin (Immaculate Conception is not to be confused, as it often is, with the virgin birth of Christ); and of her bodily assumption into heaven, defined by the pope in 1950, which makes her an exemplar of the resurrection and heavenly reward of all the redeemed.

St. Alphonso Liguori (1696–1787) said "What Jesus has by nature, Mary has by grace." The prerogatives of Mary, distinctively Christian even if corresponding to the paradigm of the pre-Christian Mediterranean goddesses like Isis and Cybele and answering to the natural desire of many for feminine as well as masculine principles in religion, have made devotion to Mary immensely popular; her power in heaven is held to be immensely great, and her benevolence virtually unconditional. Marian piety has reached a high pitch in the last hundred years or so with the two

First Communion, during mass in a Roman Catholic church.

above-mentioned definitions. They were paralleled by widespread belief in appearances of Mary to heal and prophesy at such places as Lourdes in France and Fatima in Portugal, now extremely popular pilgrimage centers, with their holy grottos or wells, their appealing statues of the Mother of God appearing to artless peasant children, their dramatic torchlight processions, their ongoing miracles. But post-Vatican II emphases have now somewhat reduced interest in this whole Marian complex.

Other significant doctrines include purgatory, already mentioned, and the canonization of saints, a process by which the pope (anciently, any bishop) declares that a given person of "heroic sanctity" is in heaven and so able to intercede on behalf of those who call upon him or her before the throne of God.

Worship is centered on the seven sacraments, although by no means limited to them. These include the initiatory rites of baptism and confirmation, and the mass. This last, the ancient offering of bread and wine, was until fairly recently always said in Latin, except in certain churches using rites similar to those of the Eastern Orthodox. The priest stood at the altar in stately vestments, his back to the congregation, and at the supreme moments when the bread and wine became the Body and Blood of Christ, knelt and then elevated them, to the accompaniment of bells. At a "high mass" there would be a sermon, incense, and chanted music during the rite. Members of the congregation could follow the Latin service in a book with translations; even if they did not, the rich atmosphere, so expressive of numinous "otherness," and of the contrast between the sacred and the ordinary, would be conducive to prayer and meditation. Now, the use of the ordinary language and a rather more informal mood, with the priest standing behind the altar facing the people as the host at a banquet, suggests something different, the church as a family of love where the talents of all have a place.

Another sacrament is penance, the forgiveness of sins. One is expected periodically to make a private confession of his or her sins to a priest, generally in the small boxlike structure in churches called the confessional. The priest has authority to impose a penance—commonly a set of prayers to say—and to give absolution, or impartation of God's forgiveness for the confessed wrongs.

Marriage is another sacrament, for it is a gift of God and a means of grace. The Roman Catholic church therefore has rules governing its members' marriages; since the marriage bond is sacramentally permanent, divorce is a difficult matter which requires legal procedures within the church, marriage to non-Catholics is regulated, and there is disapproval of abortion and "nonnatural" means of birth control.

The two other sacraments are holy orders, ordination to the priesthood; and extreme unction, the anointing with oil which is part of the "Last Rites" given to the dying.

Roman Catholicism is abundant in spiritual life apart from the sacraments. Devotion to the Blessed Virgin may take the form of the rosary with its repeated Hail Marys, or novenas, special sets of prayers on successive days, or pilgrimages to shrines. Sometimes the Virgin of a particular church or shrine, especially in Europe or Latin America, is thought of almost as a unique individual; one may see on the walls votive tablets inscribed with messages such as "thanks to Our Lady of _____ for healing," or peasants may express a rivalry between their own Virgin and the Virgin of a neighboring town. There are devotions to the Immaculate Heart of Mary pierced by swords, and to the Sacred Heart of Jesus. The whole Communion of Saints is seen as a close family, and the faith interacts with popular culture particularly as the nationality and style of each saint permeates his or her cultus. Today, creative diversity continues to emerge; the charismatic movement, for example, enriches Roman Catholicism with pentecostal spontaneity and "speaking in tongues."

Roman Catholic social expression is complex and highly organized. At the head of the church is the pope, whose seat is at the Vatican City, a tiny independent state of which he is sovereign in the heart of Rome. He is elected by the College of Cardinals, an assembly of some seventy prominant archbishops, bishops, and a few others who have been named by a previous pope to this dignity. The pope is assisted by the curia, a cabinet and bureaucracy whose department heads are generally cardinals. Beneath the papacy the church is divided into provinces, headed by archbishops, dioceses headed by bishops, and local parishes under their parish priests. Today bishops are generally appointed by the pope and parish priests by the bishop, although other arrangements (often with the state having a role) have obtained in the past and do today in some places. Today there is some demand for changes in methods of appointment.

Parallel to this hierarchy are the orders of monks and nuns, persons who have undertaken not only the celibate state but also vows of poverty and obedience; they usually live communally in monasteries and convents, devote much time to worship together and private meditation, and are engaged in educational, missionary or charitable work, if it is not an "enclosed" order whose task instead is a combination of manual labor, study, corporate prayer, and contemplation. The great orders, such as the active Franciscans, Dominicans, and Jesuits, and the more contemplative Benedictines and Cistercians (including Trappists), and their distinctive traditional garb, are well known. Today the "religious life," as this way is called, is also undergoing considerable modification, but it remains a bulwark of Roman Catholicism.

PROTESTANTISM

The term Protestantism is generally taken to include all non-Roman Catholic and non-Eastern Orthodox churches which directly or indirectly derive from the sixteenth-century Reformation in northern and western Europe. We have already looked at this event and some of its principles. For although the vast swarm of Protestant denominations may suggest almost chaotic variety, they do have in common certain basic attitudes traceable to the Reformation. Even points upon which they differ tend to fall into certain predictable categories. Churches of the Reformation tradition vary from some Anglican and Lutheran churches with worship and doctrinal emphases similar to those of the Roman church, to silent Quaker meetings and pentecostalist groups with their spontaneous shouts and "tongues." But apart from a few exceptions on the extremes, Protestant worship could not be mistaken for any other.

So far as theoretical expression is concerned, the central emphasis for most informed Protestants remains justification by God's grace through faith in Christ, and all that it implies. The important thing is that one's consciousness and feelings be centered on God, open to his will and grace. What is of value, then, is what evokes and expresses this centering. Thus, Protestantism in doctrine and story alike is inclined to apply the principle of parsimony: cut away everything not essential to hearing and receiving the word of God in the scriptures; cut away all that might distract from one's personal relationship to God.

This simplification motif is clearly evident in worship. Protestant worship has generally become stylized: the typical service contains hymn, scripture, prayer, sermon, the offering (often quite formal and ritualized), benediction, and a closing hymn. The main participation of the congregation is in singing, although in some churches the people offer prayers as well. Otherwise the minister, as a trained religious specialist, is the principal communicator of the mainly verbal experience.

For the power of words to communicate saving concepts, imagery, or emotions (rather than mantic spells whose very sounds have power) is central; the scripture and sermon and hymns contain "the words of eternal life." Compared to the value given what is communicated through reading and hearing words and music, communication through other media is relatively distrusted by Protestants.

In social expression, the ideal is generally recovery of the New Testament church, since seldom (except in Anglicanism) is post-New Testament tradition given much acceptance. However, the New Testament scriptural paradigm means different things to different wings of Protestantism, and there is a considerable variety in modes of government. Some are ruled by bishops, some by boards of presbyters, some by the local congregation. In practice, the historical situation has also influenced structural form. After the Reformation, Protestantism had state church status in a number of countries; this meant that its organization had to fit in with the laws of the realm. On the other hand, groups such as the Puritans in England who rebelled against that situation, being small and fairly powerless, had to focus on the local church as the important entity. In America after the Reveolution, and particularly on the frontier, Protestantism was independent of the state and highly fluid. This led to a wealth of new forms of expression, which usually were rooted in the authority of the local group or the charisma of the traveling evangelist.

The scope of Protestantism can be comprehended by stressing first its common themes, and then by examining the poles existing in the expression of each.

In terms of theoretical expression, we have noted the centrality of salvation by God's grace through faith. But there are poles regarding the means of receiving grace and expressing faith: in the Lutheran and Reformed traditions, the means is preaching and reading the scriptures primarily; in Anglicanism, the sacraments may be equally important as objective means of grace; among pentecostals and others at the opposite end of the spectrum, charismatic personalities, revivalists and healers, may in practice be primary means of grace. Similarly, the expression of grace ranges from an emphasis on the ethical life and good works (and here there is polarization between those who stress personal morality and those who stress Christian responsibility for society as a whole), to an emphasis on spiritual states and their expression through conversion, inward joy, and ecstatic phenomena like "tongues"—although of course the two sides are not necessarily incompatible.

The other major Protestant position, the sufficiency of scripture alone, has expression ranging from those who stress that the Bible must judge church life, to those, particularly some Anglicans, who like Roman Catholics and Eastern Orthodox would emphasize the importance of interpreting scripture within the context of church tradition. (That is something everyone probably does to some extent, since it is inevitable that one will bring to one's understanding of those books written long ago and far away one's own experience in church life and language).

There also is a difference between fundamentalists, who insist on a "literal" rendering of such points as the virgin birth and miracles of Jesus, and "liberal" interpretations which hold that Scripture must be interpreted in a way consistent with present-day historical and scientific knowledge. This distinction means in effect that fundamentalism often functions as a vehicle of resistance to current culture, forming sects, while liberalism tries to relate Christianity to the current scientific and scholarly world view.[24]

A continuum is also seen in styles of worship: they range from the solemn and formal services of Anglicans, Lutherans, and Reformed, to the folksy worship of many Methodists and Baptists, and the often ecstatic meetings of Pentecostals. The most formal expression has generally been that of the "state church" Protestants of Europe and their American counterparts. But the recent growth of informal, "experimental" services and of charismatic or pentecostal phenomena all through Protestantism has changed this pattern.

Protestant social organization has in common the tacit or explicit assumption that the whole of the Christian church cannot be seen visible and entire in the world today; it is at best only the sum total of many Christian bodies, and its true membership, some would say, cuts across all sorts of lines and is known only to God. Thus all visible Protestant bodies are particularized, limited in their base to certain culture areas. They stress local or regional control, although this may mean anything from a state church to an independent congregation. Types of organization vary widely between churches that come out of the state church tradition, whether the Church of England or state Lutheran and Reformed churches in Germany, Scandinavia, or Holland, or their American branches, and those independent movements that sprang up as alternatives to them and usually had, at least originally, sectarian characteristics: charismatic leaders, local control, strict moral codes, and greater stress on subjective feelings.

The fluid Protestant style of Christianity is not restricted to northern Europe and America, but is as international today as any religious movement in the world. Its rapid geographical expansion began in the missionary enthusiasm of the nineteenth century, when the major Protestant nations were vigorous and expansive, and has continued into the twentieth. Today, missionary-sending from Europe and America is less central to world Protestantism, although still important. But indigenous

---

[24]See the concluding chapter of Robert S. Ellwood, Jr., *One Way: The Jesus Movement and Its Meaning* (Englewood Cliffs, N. J.: Prentice-Hall, Inc., 1973).

A Protestant service of worship.

Protestant churches, some quite independent and some tied to older denominations, exist today nearly everywhere the missionaries went. Missionary educational work has been a very important factor in the emergence of new nations in many parts of the world. (Nineteenth- and twentieth-century Roman Catholic missionary work, of course, is of equal significance.) Today, in some parts of the "Third World," especially Africa and Latin America, churches of broadly Protestant lineage founded by local prophets or pentecostalists are the most active Christian force. They represent a quite different Christian style from that of staid "main line" denominations, although one more similar to the radical reformers and the American frontier. Above all, they relate Christianity to local cultures in ways that European and American churches usually cannot.

AMERICAN DENOMINATIONALISM

We will now turn to American religion and its special style of spiritual life. The American Main Street, lined with big voluntarily supported Catholic, Protestant, and Jewish places of worship, really represents a map of the invisible world that is quite distinctive within both the Judaeo-Christian tradition and the religious world as a whole.

One God, Many Words and Wonders

Because of the special nature of religious history in America, denominationalism is a key to understanding it. Even Judaism, Roman Catholicism, and Eastern Orthodoxy—all very important in American religious life—have had in practice to fall into the style of social expression it creates.

The basic facts in American religious life are: 1) immigration by peoples of numerous religious cultures, and 2) the emergence of a new society with a need for cohesion and a sense of creating a new political and spiritual way of being in the world. These facts have created pluralism rather than a single official or heavily dominant religious institution, as obtains in most other societies. Yet they have also meant that most groups have found themselves affirming common American ethical and social ideals—democracy, patriotism, social concern—together with their distinctive doctrines and worship.

The general history of religion in America reflects these centrifugal and centripedal drives. In the colonial period, immigrants of diverse religious backgrounds settled in different areas, often in order to find a religious haven: Puritans in Massachusetts, Baptists in Rhode Island, Quakers in eastern Pennsylvania, Lutherans in western Pennsylvania, Roman Catholics in Maryland, Anglicans in Virginia and the southern seaboard. During 1720–40 the movement for a deeper, more intellectually serious and also more feeling-oriented Christianity called the Great Awakening swept across parish, denominational, and colonial lines. The first vital expression of the American centripedal force, it paved the way for the Revolution in that it gave the populations of the thirteen colonies a new sense of being a distinctive American people with their own spiritual concerns, rather than just transplanted Europeans.

The Revolution, of course, brought the sense of national unity to a high pitch, and culminated religiously in the First Amendment to the Constitution, which made the United States of America the first society in the history of the world to have, not only religious toleration, but genuine legal freedom and equality for all faiths, and the absence at the national level of any official religious endorsement or support. In this situation, many there were who felt that, forced to stand on its own in a new society and shorn of feudal trappings, religion would wither away, or (as the concurrent Unitarian movement in New England suggested) become very "rational." But such was not to be.

Instead, during the period of westward expansion, nation building, and belief in a special American "manifest destiny" both geographical and spiritual, religion flourished in a cornucopia of forms. Evangelical revivals swept the frontier. They brought tremendous growth to the Methodist and Baptist churches, and produced new denominations like the Disciples of Christ. New movements such as Spiritualism and the Latter-Day Saints originated in upstate New York. There were utopian communes and numerous colleges planted in the name of religion. In an expansive era, the centrifugal and centripedal drives reinforced each other without great tension—and showed that religious pluralism, with absence of state interference or support, far from weakening religion can liberate it to flourish brilliantly.

But this primal "era of good feeling" was not to last. Just as Eden ended with discovery of sin, so the optimism of the first decades after independence was darkened by the confrontation with the shadow side of American life—slavery. The middle decades of the nineteenth-century were rent by controversy over slavery, and denominations were divided by it on north-south lines, so that we came to have northern and southern Baptists, Presbyterians, and Methodists (the Methodists were reunited in 1939). After the Civil War, most of the freed slaves entered exclusively black churches. For many decades, black churches were the only important institutions controlled by blacks, and their ministry the only profession generally available to them. Out of the black churches came a distinctive style of religious life characterized by close community feeling, a free spiritual expression in which as important a worldwide movement as pentecostalism is rooted, and leaders in the Civil Rights movement such as Martin Luther King.

During the same years, and up until 1920, new immigration vastly increased American population with a mixed multitude. During the one decade of the 1840s, American Roman Catholicism grew by immigration from a small minority to the largest single church in the nation—a position it has held ever since. Jews, Eastern Orthodox, and German and Scandinavian Lutherans also immigrated in the millions during the latter half of the century. All this was in the context of great social change: the growth of cities, industry, widespread education, and life based on modern technology. The older Protestantism tended to react in two ways: a conservatism which came to be known as fundamentalism and which sought to preserve the religious values of frontier revivalism and religious surety in a changing world; and the more liberal "social gospel" movement, which strove to correlate religion to new ideas in science and society, and to recover the old dream of making America into a new "people of God" through social reform.

The strands of this history are expressed in the panorama of American denominations. They are far from the whole story of American religion; the centrifugal "civil religion" drive toward a common American ethic and vision cuts across them, and important issues like fundamentalism versus the "social gospel" have polarized denominations from within as well as found expression in distinctive denominations. Indeed, "one issue" denominations without concomitant ethnic or sociological roots have not generally been very successful, and it seems that now the day of forming major new denominations is long since past—although the countervailing "ecumenical" drive toward unifying them has had only limited success.

But American denominational pluralism is an important phenomenon. Derived from the unique history of colonial settlement, the frontier flux, the slavery controversy, and immigration, it is as distinctive in its way as Tibetan Buddhism. No other society, except to some extent British commonwealth nations such as Canada and Australia which have had a superficially comparable religious history, approaches this particular form of sociological expression of religion.

The denomination in America is a voluntarily supported religious group for which its members feel responsible, and which feels in practice primarily responsible for them rather than as a denomination for the total spiritual life of the nation. (All this is quite different from most traditional religion and old world Christianity.) The religious nation is seen as a composite of denominations, all legally and (in the minds of many) spiritually coequal. ("It doesn't matter what church you go to so long as you go.") They are sometimes competitive, sometimes cooperative; the complex webs they form are the strong outline of the map of the invisible world in America. Because this pattern is so different from that of Europe, and so rooted in

One God, Many Words and Wonders

the relatively brief American past, it largely accounts for the lack of a sense of the long ancient and medieval Christian history so characteristic of American churches.

Here is a glance at important Protestant denominations or traditions that express this map. Membership approximations are for the mid-1970s.

The Methodist family includes the United Methodist Church with some ten and a half million members; the Free Methodists, which are a conservative group split from it; and the predominantly black American Methodist Episcopal Church and American Methodist Episcopal Zion Church. Methodism stems from the eighteenth-century preaching of John Wesley and others in England. In an age when official Christianity was generally indifferent to the needs of the poor, Wesley brought them a faith based on conversion experience and holiness of life (he taught the "holiness" doctrine that a person who had genuinely accepted Christ and received the Holy Spirit could aspire to lead a sinless life). In America Methodism greatly flourished on the frontier, although in the process of becoming a dominant faith, especially in the small towns of the South and Midwest, it inevitably has become more moderate or liberal. In reaction to this, groups such as the Free Methodist Church and Church of the Nazarene broke with Methodism around the turn of the twentieth century to keep intact the original Wesleyan conversion and holiness doctrines as they understood them.

The largest single block of American Protestants are the Baptists. The Southern Baptist Church has some twelve million members; it is virtually a way of life in parts of the South. The northern-based American Baptist Church has one and a half million members. Two predominantly black National Baptist churches total some eight million, and there are other smaller Baptist groups. All Baptists in America derive from seventeenth-century movements in England, inspired by "radical reformation" Anabaptists on the continent, which stressed that baptism should not be given to infants, but should be a sign following adult conversion. Baptists have always stood for religious freedom and have opposed state churches; they have tended to be conservative regarding scripture and personal morality.

There are three major Lutheran churches in America, the American Lutheran Church (two and a half million members); the Lutheran Church in America (three million), and the Lutheran Church—Missouri Synod (two and eight-tenths million). The last is widely recognized as the most conservative. Although the Lutherans represent American expressions of the state churches deriving from Luther's wing of the Reformation, unlike Methodists and Baptists who derive from European dissident movements, they were in practice heavily influenced by nineteenth-century pietistic movements, which explains differences between European Lutheranism and the more conservative American Lutheranism. Lutheran worship is generally stately and attractive, with majestic music and learned preaching; Lutheran people in America, largely of German and Scandinavian descent, are conspicuous in their loyalty to the church and its worship.

The Church of England, the state church separated from Rome in the days of Henry VIII, is represented in America by the Protestant Episcopal Church, with some three and two-tenths million members. It was dominant in much of Colonial America, but great numbers of its nominal members were swept away by the frontier Methodist and Baptist movements after the American Revolution. But Episcopalianism managed to recover strength, and now represents a tradition with the colorful, rather ceremonial worship and theological tradition of the Church of England.

The Presbyterian churches in America (the United Presbyterian Church with three million members, the southern-based Presbyterian Church in the United States with one million, and a few smaller ones) represent the tradition of the state Church of Scotland and its affiliates in England and Ireland. Their theological heritage is Calvinist, their worship simpler and closer to the central Protestant structure than the Episcopalian. They have always emphasized a high level of education and preaching among the clergy.

Also in the Calvinist lineage are two groups representing wings of the Reformed Church in the Netherlands: The Reformed Church of America (370,000 members) and The Christian Reformed Church (285,000).

A Calvinist background is also found in the United Church of Christ, with some two million members. The UCC is a merger of the Congregational Church, whose heritage is the Puritan settlers from England in New England, and the German Evangelical and Reformed Church. By and large congregationalism and the UCC have moved away from the proverbial (though often misunderstood) narrowness of the Puritan to a liberal stance which permits no small diversity of expression. Its congregational organization allows each local church to elect its own minister and draw up its own statement of belief.

A numerically small but significant denomination of New England congregational background is the Unitarian-Universalist church (265,000 members), a union of two very liberal bodies. It professes absolute freedom of belief; most of its members would reject such doctrines as the trinity and the divinity of Christ, and many would reject belief in the traditional God in favor of religion centered on human needs and ends.

Another small but important tradition is that of the Religious Society of Friends, commonly called the Quakers. Starting from the ministry of George Fox in seventeenth-century England, Quakers rejected a paid ministry, sacraments (they do not baptize or give holy communion "outwardly") and structured worship. A Quaker meeting consists of worshippers sitting in silence until someone feels moved to speak, which he or she may then do freely. Quakers first settled Pennsylvania; now the several Quaker denominations have about 200,000 members together. Some are still nonministerial and "unprogrammed"; these tend to be liberal socially and theologically. Others, usually more conservative in temper, have ministers and organized worship services.

A large number of denominations have originated in America. These are all further from European traditions, as one would expect, than the churches cited. There are the Churches of Christ, two and four-tenths million, and the Christian Church (Disciples), one and three-tenths million, which emerged as frontier endeavors to recover the New Testament church, and are now moderate to fairly conservative evangelical churches. Pentecostalism, so dynamic worldwide that it has been called a Christian "third force," started in America and is represented by a variety of churches: several called Church of God, the Assemblies of God, the Pentecostal Holiness Church, and others. They emphasize the value of "speaking in tongues" as a sign of conversion and receiving of the Holy Spirit; worship life is spontaneous, immensely alive, and full of the expectation of miracles.

Other American movements include the Church of Jesus Christ of Latter-Day Saints (the Mormon church), with some three and two-tenths million members worldwide but mostly in America, based on the teachings of Joseph Smith, whom his followers believe found golden plates in upstate New York telling, among other things, that Jesus came to ancient America; the Church of Christ, Scientist, founded by Mary Baker Eddy, which emphasizes that God is all and therefore there is no disease save in distorted mind; and the Seventh-Day Adventist Church (435,000 members), which stresses that Christ will return again very soon, and also that Christians have an obligation to keep much of the Law of Moses, including worship on Saturday, the old Sabbath. There are churches in the New Thought tradition, such as the Unity churches and the Church of Religious Science, theologically liberal and stressing the power of mind to solve problems and bring joy. Spiritualist churches focus on communication by mediumship with the spirits of the departed to assure believers of immortality.

American Protestantism is indeed diverse. Not only do the denominations differ widely, but even within a single denomination one may find some members asserting that God is dead and that our concerns must be entirely secular, while others see visions and find God's hand at work among them in signs, miracles and tongues. Yet the diversity is not infinite, and what holds it together is really more basic than its diversity: there is everywhere a fundamental belief in the importance of right inwardness, whether one means by that intellectual integrity, powerful conversion feelings, the Holy Spirit giving supernatural gifts, or positive thinking. There is a definite congregation and a weekly worship service (not the case in all religions), which usually focuses on singing, preaching, and prayer. A Unitarian and a Pentecostal church might seem quite different to an outsider, but the outsider would have no trouble in comprehending that they are related in a way neither is to a Zen monastery, Hindu temple, Muslim mosque, or even a Rumanian Orthodox or Italian Roman Catholic church. American Protestant churches represent numerous fine gradiations of doctrine, worship, and sociological grounding, but all these are finally within only a certain portion of the much broader spectrum of human religion as a whole.

Islam

THE MEANING OF ISLAM

Approximately half a billion of the world's population adhere to the faith of Islam. It is the youngest of the world's great religions. Despite important variations within Islam, it is also the most homogeneous and self-consciously an international community of the three giant cross-cultural faiths, Buddhism, Christianity, and Islam.

Islam is a community which does indeed cut across many cultures. Non-Muslims often envision Islam as the faith of romantic (and now tremendously oil-wealthy) Arab sheiks and caravaneers, but only a minority of Muslims are Arab, and only a tiny minority are wandering desert dwellers. The largest single Muslim nation is lush and tropical Indonesia, where the faith of Muhammad is superimposed on a very East Asian culture. Other Muslims in great numbers are farmers and craftsmen in India and Pakistan; modern businessmen in the cities of Turkey, Iran, or Malaysia; blacks in sub-Saharan Africa, where Islam is growing rapidly. Even in the Arab countries where Islam originated, the population is largely urban or engaged in intensive, sedentary agriculture in fertile strips like those along the Nile and the Two Rivers. Normative Islam in fact has always been preeminently a faith of citified, mobile, international-minded people, sometimes conquerors but more often urban businessmen, and through them has spread from culture to culture.

Partly because of this base, Islamic culture has a quite visible unity as well as great diversity. From Morocco to Java, the Muslim mosque presents a distinctive atmosphere. Few would mistake a mosque for a church, synagogue, or Hindu temple. The mosque, a place of prayer to the infinite Lord, has no picture, image, altar, flowers, or candles—only a vast, clean, cool, austerely beautiful empty space. The floor may be spread with rich carpeting, and the walls and ceiling or dome with the delicate, fantastic tracery of arabesque. But nowhere will realistic representational art be found. Only a bare niche in the wall serves to orient prayer in the direction of Mecca; only a modest affair like a seat atop a staircase serves as pulpit.

On the streets of a Muslim country, the pervasive influence of the religion is felt too. Five times a day—sunrise, noon, mid-afternoon, just before sunset, at dark—a crier called a muezzin (nowadays, he is often replaced by a recording and a loudspeaker system) summons the faithful to prayer from the minaret, the tower attached to every mosque. His plaintive cry, which sometimes irritates tourists (especially at dawn) and sometimes thrills them, replaces the bells of Christendom. Then countless believers fall to the ground in prayer, virtually in unison, in shops, homes, streets, wherever they are, as well as in mosques.

In the markets, veiled women are not seen as much as formerly, but are still common in some parts of the Muslim world. Although the Muslim prohibition against alcoholic drink is not always strictly observed, it is in coffee shops and teahouses rather than pubs or bars that one sees the men gathered of an evening to discuss the affairs of the day. Finally, if one is at all familiar with the local language, he will be struck by the frequency of expressions like "If Allah wills" in daily conversation.

For the heart of Islam is submission to the total will of Allah, or God. ("Allah" is not the name of a god, but simply means "The God"—the one and only God.) God's will for man, Muslims believe, was most fully given in the Koran, the book revealed through the prophet Mohammed. Islam means "submission" and the name tells us that the central idea of this faith is simply full and complete submission to the will of God; an adherent of the faith is called a Muslim, one who has made the submission.[25]

So it is that the muezzin in his five-times-daily cry says:

> Allah is great! Allah is great!
> There is no God but Allah,
> And Muhammad is his prophet!
> (*At dawn, he here adds:*
> Prayer is better than sleep!
> Prayer is better than sleep!)
> Allah is great! Allah is great!
> There is no God but Allah!

That is the central motif of Islam—the greatness of God alone. Because Allah is great and sovereign, all the world and all the affairs of mankind belong only to him. For this reason Islam does not lavishly embellish the "religious" sphere with rites and symbols and priesthood; if Allah is truly great, Islam says, he can be worshipped anywhere by anyone in the simple forms prescribed by the Koran and tradition. If God is truly sovereign, what he has commanded for all of society—law, ethics, government—is just as important as the religious commandments, and inseparable from them. For this reason Islam is experienced as a total and indivisible way of life. It is deeply consistent with the basic premise of the faith—the absolute sovereignty of God over all situations and over every atom of the universe—that

[25]Formerly, the religion was often called Muhammadanism and its followers Muhammadans by occidentals, in analogy to Buddhism or Christianity. But Muslims object to this label and never use it themselves, saying that they do not worship or idolize Muhammad, but rather submit to God's will as revealed in his prophetic ministry. Today these feelings are rightly respected and the proper terms Islam and Muslim generally used.

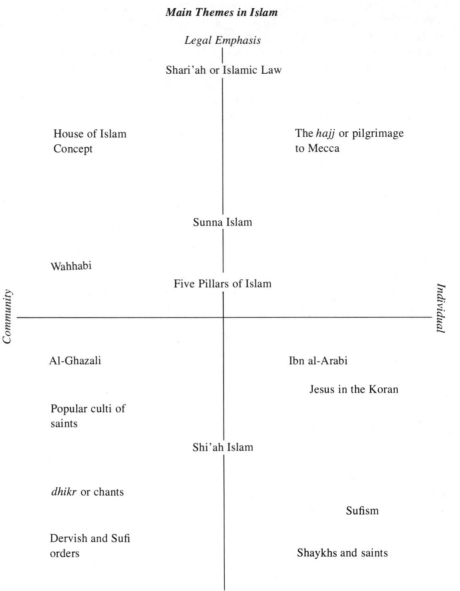

Main Themes in Islam

Legal Emphasis

Shari'ah or Islamic Law

House of Islam
Concept

The *hajj* or pilgrimage
to Mecca

Sunna Islam

Wahhabi

Five Pillars of Islam

Community

Individual

Al-Ghazali

Ibn al-Arabi

Jesus in the Koran

Popular culti of
saints

Shi'ah Islam

dhikr or chants

Sufism

Dervish and Sufi
orders

Shaykhs and saints

Sainthood Emphasis

Thematic Chart VIII.   Like most spiritual traditions, Islam seeks both to create community
and come to terms with the diversity of individuals. It also is polarized in practice between
two models of the spiritual path, each of which has its own community-forming and
individual-expression style: the way of the law-follower and the way of the saint.

whenever feasible Muslims not only establish Muslim worship, but create Muslim societies under Muslim rulers based on Koranic law. Modern conditions have often mandated reinterpretations of this ideal. But the Koran remains the fountainhead of true law and true culture, and a summons to submission in every area of life, the "secular"—political, economic, family life—as well as in such conventionally "religious" matters as how one says one's prayers.

MUHAMMAD

At the core of Islam lies the experience and faith of Muhammad himself. He lived in Arabia 570–632, and was born and raised in the city of Mecca, a commercial center, and even before him a city sacred to the Arabs. Its holy sanctuary, which drew numerous pilgrims, was the home of many polytheistic gods—of moon, stars, and the days of the year chiefly—and the resting-place of a sacred black stone, probably meteoric, considered to be from heaven. The area around this place of worship was a neutral zone where representatives and merchants of many tribes, often warring, could meet in peace.

Muhammad came from a poor but respected merchant family which was part of the prestigious Quraysh tribe, custodians of the sacred places of Mecca. According to tradition he became a camel driver as a young man. When he was twenty-five he entered the service of Khadijah, a wealthy widow much older than he. Before long he married her, and she bore his daughter Fatima.

Muhammad was always a serious, thoughtful, and rather withdrawn man. But until he was about forty his life was not outwardly much different from that of the other merchants of the sacred city. At that age, however, he found himself going into the mountains more and more to devote himself to meditation.

About the year 611, Muhammad began to have a remarkable series of experiences in these solitary meditations in mountain caves. A mysterious darkness would come over him, then the luminous figure of the archangel Gabriel would appear and recite words to him, which he could remember clearly. These words were first of all about the unity of God—that there is but one single God, "Lord of the worlds," who abominates idolatry and will judge the earth on a day of fire and anxiety; this God calls upon all men to accept his sovereignty.

For ten years (611–21) Muhammad implored his fellow Meccans to obey this call to acceptance of the oneness of God, but with little success. Indeed, it seemed to many that his fervent message threatened the lucrative polytheistic cultus, and Muhammad found his position in Mecca untenable. In 622 he accepted an invitation from the city of Yathrib (now Medina) to teach there. His journey to Yathrib, called the *hejira,* is the date from which the Muslim calendar starts; it marks the beginning of Muhammad's public and organizational work on a large scale.

It may be helpful to consider for a moment the context of this work. The Near East in Muhammad's day was dominated by the political, economic, and ideological rivalry of three great powers: the Byzantine and Ethiopian empires, which were

Christian, and the Persian, which was Zoroastrian but harbored influential minorities of Jews and non-Orthodox Christians. The Byzantine and Persian empires, archfoes, fought interminable and debilitating wars, which usually ended in standoffs.

In this situation, Arabia was by no means the barbaric backwater sometimes imagined. But it was nonaligned, a no-man's-land between superpowers. There were Christians and Jews in Arabia who were thought to lean respectively to Byzantium and Persia. But the wily merchants of Mecca and Yathrib, well aware of world affairs through trading contacts in the great imperial cities, realized that their well-being required them to avoid overdependence on either side.

Yet many were also well aware that the religions of the great powers were more "modern" than their own polytheism. Belief in a sovereign deity, whether the Christian God or Ahura Mazda or the God of the Jews, was clearly the new progressive thing upon which great civilizations were being built. Moreover, "new occasions teach new duties," and the prosperous, individual-enterprise Meccan merchants found the old sense of identity and immortality in the tribe breaking down deep within them. A new doctrine and ethic, emphasizing mercantile values, individual responsibility, and the sacredness of the individual betokened by personal judgment and immortal life, was called for. The new teaching might draw from Zoroastrianism, Judaism, and Christianity, or at least parallel them, in its idea of one God and moral choice. But it had to be politically independent of other ideologies. Some Arabs, called Hanifs, had already moved in this direction; they are not fully understood, but apparently were pious though not highly organized people who shunned the worship of idols and affirmed a generalized monotheism. Other Arabs to the north were Christian. But in this situation there lacked an Arab prophet, one who as an Arab would bespeak the common national and spiritual concerns of the Arabs.

That is what Muhammad did visibly in the ten years that remained to him, and he did it so well that his words carried conviction far beyond the Arab world. Using Medina as a base, he brought all Arabia, including Mecca, under his control. He became at once the religious leader of the Arabs, and their political ruler and military commander. Right up to the end of his life, which occurred just after his return from his triumphal progress to Mecca in 632, the strange revelations continued. Together they make up the text of the Koran, the Holy Scripture of Islam.

THE KORAN

Unlike the Judaeo-Christian Bible, the Koran is not a collection of diverse material from over a thousand years. It was all delivered in a period of no more than twenty-two years through one man in strange private sessions with God and his angel. It is not a book of history, or a life of Muhammad, or a philosophical treatise. It is a book of proclamation: proclamation of the oneness and sovereignty of God, of his coming judgment, of man's need to submit to him. In passing it also presents a Muslim view of previous religious history, especially of the earlier prophets like Abraham, Moses, and Jesus. From time to time it gives instructions to the faithful upon which Muslim law is based.

To Muslims, the Koran is a miracle, the most convincing miracle of all as validation of their faith. It is said to be untranslatable, but to be in the original Arabic of exquisite, incomparable beauty of rhythm and expression. That one man, and he illiterate according to tradition, could be the merely human author of "the Glorious Koran, that inimitable symphony, the very sounds of which move men to tears and ecstasy,"[26] seems to them incredible. The Holy Koran, they deeply believe, is the full and complete message of the infinite divine mind to mankind. Thus it is not only studied, but chanted, memorized, and recited on all sorts of occasions, venerated both as words and as a book. Even its way of speaking is divine; it represents the personal *style* of Allah and so transmits something of God's essence. Its very choice of rhythm, metaphor, and rhetorical method, in other words, reveals something of how God thinks and feels, just as do its contents. So significant is the Koran to Islam that it makes a distinction between other religions that have comparable scripture—even if not equal to the Koran—and the "idolatrous" religions that do not. The former, especially Jews and Christians, are called "People of the Book" and considered of higher status and closer kinship to Muslims.

Admittedly, it is usually not easy for those who are neither Muslims nor Arabists to appreciate, on the basis of translations, the rapturous terms in which the Koran is praised. Even allowing for what of rhythm and allusive eloquence is presumed to have been lost in translation, one may feel an initial disappointment. The book seems disorganized, repetitious, platitudinous, in some instances bizarre.

It is necessary to bear in mind always the Koran's purpose—to proclaim the oneness and sovereignty of God. It does not develop a philosophy or tell a story because those are not its purposes. The Koran is intended only to state one basic truth; it repeats itself to reinforce that one simple truth. As A. J. Arberry has put it, it is like being surrounded by a gallery of paintings on the same subject.[27] If the accounts of some matters common to other faiths, such as the lives of Abraham or Jesus, seem twisted as they appear in the Koran, it must be remembered that Muslims are not, after all, Jews or Christians. They are under no obligation to regard the versions the latter consider authoritative to be fully authentic or complete.

The Koran begins with the following prayer, which well sums up its basic spirit and message:

> In the Name of Allah, the Compassionate, the Merciful
> Praise be to Allah, Lord of the Creation,
> The Compassionate, the Merciful, King of Judgment-day!
> You alone we worship, and to You alone we pray for help.
> Guide us to the straight path,
> The path of those whom You have favoured,
> Not of those who have incurred Your wrath,
> Nor of those who have gone astray.[28]

---

[26]Mohammed Maramduke Pickthall, *The Meaning of the Glorious Koran* (New York: Mentor Books, n.d.), p. vii.

[27]A. J. Arberry, *The Holy Koran* (London: George Allen and Unwin, 1953), p. 26–27.

[28]N. J. Dawood, trans., *The Koran* 4th rev. ed. (Harmondsworth, England: Penguin Classics, 1974), p. 15. Copyright © N. J. Dawood, 1956, 1959, 1966, 1968, 1974. Reprinted by permission of Penguin Books, Ltd.

The book continues to describe the wonders of creation; how God made mankind from the union of the sexes, out of clots of blood, and through the mysterious development of the embryo. It exhorts men not to deny but to show gratitude for this panorama of mercy and marvel, for when the judgment comes, wrongdoers will not be asked about their sins, but will be known by the expression on their faces. The deniers of the Lord's blessings then will suffer in hell, but those who have regard for the divine majesty will find themselves in surroundings fit for heroes: gardens of flowing springs, lush fruits, and dark-eyed damsels. Like the paradises of most religions, this one has the brightly colored, gemlike, antipodes-of-the-ordinary quality of dream, poetry, and sensuous youthful joy. But the deeper meaning of the Koran's message is less reward and punishment than the inescapable fact of Allah himself:

> Roam the earth and see how Allah conceived Creation. Then Allah will create the Second Creation. Allah has power over all things; He punishes whom He will and shows mercy to whom He pleases. To Him you shall be recalled.

> Neither on earth nor in heaven shall you escape His reach; nor have you any beside Allah to protect or to help you.[29]

And again:

> To Allah belongs the east and the west. Whichever way you turn there is the face of Allah. He is omnipresent and all-knowing.[30]

The fundamental faith of the Koran, then, is consistent monotheism. It is expressed in the coming judgment, the absolute sovereignty of Allah over all things, both the making and fortunes of the present world and over the issue of who will be brought into joy in the Second Creation. That Muhammad is the envoy of God, and the last or seal of the prophets, is not in Muslim eyes an addition to consistent monotheism, but the way God guarantees that this truth shall be known:

For Muslims believe that Islam is the ultimate religion, the "super-religion." It is the religion of Abraham, the primal monotheism of the beginning, come back in finalized form. It is the ultimate form of religion because it is in fact the simplest and clearest. It is just the essence of religion, plain and perfect submission to the absolute God in all areas of life.

The Koran indicates that before Muhammad a series of prophets, all to be greatly honored, labored to call men back to this perfect islam, or submission. They included Abraham, Moses, Ishmael, Idris (Enoch), and Jesus. But it was through Muhammad that the final, complete message came, superseding all that went before—it was the culminating message of God for mankind.

The role of Jesus in the Koran and in this series usually puzzles Christians. The Koran makes Jesus the greatest before Muhammad. He was called to preserve the

[29]Ibid., p. 194.

[30]Ibid., p. 336.

One God, Many Words and Wonders

Torah of the Jews, and was a wise teacher of deep inward holiness. (This last quality has made him especially beloved of the esoteric mystics of Islam.) Jesus has, to say the least, been far more highly regarded by Muslims than Muhammad has been by Christians.

The Koran accepts the virgin birth of Jesus, and calls Mary the greatest among women, but makes Jesus born under a palm tree rather than in a stable. It mentions the Last Supper, but it denies that Jesus was actually crucified. It says instead that people only thought he died on the cross; instead, he was taken directly to heaven. It affirms that Jesus will come again at the end of the world to establish everywhere the Muslim religion, and has Jesus predict the coming of Muhammad, but denies that Jesus is the "Son of God."

However different the life and meaning of Jesus may here appear, in looking at Islam and the Koran Christians may, in the words of Seyyed Hossein Nasr, "come to understand how the sun of their own spiritual world is also a shining star in the firmament of another world."[31]

One of the loveliest passages of the Koran reads:

> God is the light of the heavens and the earth.
> The likeness of His light is as a niche,
> Wherein is a lamp, the lamp in a glass, the glass like a glistening star, kindled from
>   a blessed tree,
> An olive neither of the east nor of the west,
> Whose oil would almost shine had no fire touched it.
> Light upon light: God guides to His light whom he will:
> God brings similitudes for men and God has knowledge all things.[32]

In all ways then the light of God is added to light; the final revelation is not inconsistent to what was presented in earlier prophets, even though the other "People of the Book" may have distorted their heritages. But Islam gives the final luster of a perfect glass to the light of God agelessly hidden in the lamp of the world.

All the way through, then, the central message of Islam is oneness: the unity of the line of true prophets, the oneness of final prophet and book, the oneness of the People of God, the one submission to be made, finally the supreme oneness of God.

Islamic submission to oneness is expressed in part through avoidance of *shirk,* idolatry, or putting other gods beside the One. It is typified by the avoidance of images, and often of any representational art, in Muslim religion and culture. This is not a condemnation of the world of created things, for Islam has little asceticism of that sort. It extolls the joys of marriage and the table, and paradise itself is described in sensual terms. But these are gifts of God, to be accepted and enjoyed for themselves with gratitude. They are not to be worshipped or even artistically re-created as symbols for God, who needs no such help.

The submission of Islam is not just a private, personal matter. It is not meant to

---

[31]Seyyed Hossein Nasr, "Jesus Through the Eyes of Islam," *The Times* (London), July 28, 1973.

[32]Kenneth Cragg, trans., *The House of Islam* (Belmont, Calif.: Dickenson Publishing Co., Inc., 1969), p. 39. Reprinted by permission of the publisher.

be the sort of following of inner "leadings" which often merely indulges whims and sanctifies self-inflation. To be sure, Islam has not lacked colorful but dubious figures who have claimed special divine calls. But the tradition has tried hard to combat the human proclivity to mix piety and egotism through the *shari'ah,* or law. Islam makes the Koran not only a book of God's self-revelation, but also a source of practical regulations covering such matters as marriage, almsgiving, relations with non-Muslims, and punishment of criminals.

Shari'ah is the Koran as it is explicated and expanded by recognized jurists, who depend in this process upon *hadith,* traditions about the extra-Koranic sayings and examples in the life of Muhammad and the early community. Through the use of analogy, and by determining consensus, they decide how Koranic law is to be applied to concrete cases before them. *Sunna,* the laws binding on Muslims in all areas of life, is the product. Muslim law, then, provides an obligatory and objective measurement of whether a person really submits to God, or only says he does but loves more the idols of his own fantasies.

The submission is made even more objective by the concept of the community or house of Islam, a ready-made political, economic, and juridical, as well as purely "religious," unit in the world. Insofar as the shari'ah ideal is actualized in it, willing participation in the House of Islam and following its norms is one with Islamic submission to Allah. For the ideal of submission in all areas of life logically implies joining oneself to others who make the same submission; doing so is a test of real sincerity. (As the New Testament also recognizes, it is easy to think one loves God, but to dislike others who also love God.)

Out of the community ideal of Islam comes the concept of *jihad,* or holy war, which is designed to bring regions of unbelief into the House of Islam. Since Islam in principle is a state as well as a religion, presumably only an absolute pacifist would be able to reject the theory of jihad out of hand, since other states also fight to defend or expand their ways of life. However, many Muslims interpret the jihad as allegorical of the spiritual struggle.

HISTORIC ISLAM

In 632, the year of the prophet's death, all these themes were coalescing to form the new faith of the newly unified Arab people. Returning from his triumphal pilgrimage to Mecca, Muhammad preached a farewell sermon, and shortly after died with his head in the lap of Aisha, his favorite wife. He was mourned, yet his death came at a propitious moment.

Through a brilliant combination of diplomacy and militancy, Muhammad had united Arabia under his command. He was the charismatic hero of the hour; he died before his hour of supreme glory had had a chance to pall.

His religious mission was apparently fulfilled; the revelations which quickly became the Koran were adequately rounded off. Unlike other religious founders, Muhammad died a popular hero among his people, a ruler, a successful diplomat, politician, and general. He was a mystic visionary also, but there was nothing ethereal about him. Instead he seemed to his people a man larger than life in many senses: warmhearted, full of cheerful humor, a planner of stratagems, a marshall who rode into battle with his troops and held his following together by the force of his personality when all seemed darkest—yet also a seer deep in prayer and vision alone in the desert, a rock of convinced faith and principle, and a princely lover of women. From this complex and extraordinary man came the Islamic faith, a faith which seems at once made for humans as they are, with their needs for politics, laws, wars, and sexual expression—and made for God as he is at his most magnificent, personal, creative, sovereign, and glorious, calling humans to total submission.

Inspired by fresh memories of Muhammad striding through Arabia, at the moment of his death the Arabs were ready to carry Islam out of his native land, and this they did under new leadership with a rapidity which ever since has amazed the world. The caliphs (emperors) who were successors of Muhammad within a century ruled from Spain and Morocco to the Indus in the East. They came near to conquering Europe, but were finally stopped by Charles Martel at the battle of Tours in 732. The weary Byzantine Empire reeled before their sway and lost vast provinces— once-Christian Egypt, Palestine, Syria, and part of Asia Minor. The Persian Empire collapsed entirely and passed to Muslim faith and sovereignty. After 750 Baghdad was the seat of the caliph who ruled all this realm except Spain; that imperial city typifies the fact that early expansive Islam was fundamentally a faith of urban merchants and men of affairs.

The years of the Baghdad caliphate (750–1258) and of the Cordova caliphate in Spain (755–1236) were the glorious years of early Islamic civilization. These centuries were the Dark Ages in Europe, but in the caliphates art, science, and philosophy matured, thanks in part to Muslim revival of ancient Greek wisdom and transmission west of lore from India. Modern mathematics has roots in the Arabic system of numbers and the zero, which the Muslims may have borrowed from India but whose use they explored. The Greek classics, including the philosophy and science of Plato and Aristotle, came back to Europe in the late Middle Ages and the Renaissance by way of the Muslim world. Muslim philosophers of the Baghdad caliphate such as Avicenna (980–1037) and of Cordova such as Averroës (1126–98) had no small influence on Christian and Jewish thought. Averroës, for example, searched out profoundly the relationship of reason and revelation, and held that both are valid ways of knowing, a quest upon which the works of Maimonides and Thomas Aquinas are partially built.

After the wars with Christian Europe called the Crusades, which engendered bitter feelings and much misunderstanding between the two faiths not yet healed, and the fall of the caliphates, Islam broke down into smaller units. Most of the Arab lands ended up as parts of the Turkish-ruled Ottoman Empire (though the Turks are not Arab). The Turks finally took Constantinople (modern Istanbul) and ended the lingering death of Christian Byzantium in 1452. Farther east, Persia and the Moghul Empire in India became splendid Islamic civilizations.

But gradually, it seemed, the Muslim world grew stagnant. By the nineteenth century most of it was under European influence or dirent colonial rule. The reasons for this decline from the brilliant and dynamic early life are complex. In part it was due to external factors: the incursions of conquerors like Genghis Khan, the European advances in technology and world exploration. Internally, the growing power of the law, shari'ah, as it came, case after case, to dominate more and more areas of life had a stultifying effect. The control of law believed to have divine sanction inevitably made society static, putting a premium on conformity rather than innovation and new ideas.

In the twentieth century, however, Islam has shown a new burst of life. It has served as a vehicle for nationalism from North Africa to Indonesia, and has recovered something of its old dynamic sense of the unity of the diverse peoples who are followers of the Meccan prophet.

Thus the roles of Islam as both political and spiritual forces in the world are by no means over. The new shapes of oil economics and geopolitics are, in the last decades of the twentieth century, giving parts of the Islamic world a leverage and comparative prosperity they have hardly known since the Middle Ages. At the same time, in recent decades many Muslim nations have modified Islamic law with legal codes borrowed from elsewhere and have made pragmatic revisions of it in the light of modern conditions, although practice varies from the thorough-going secularization of Turkey under Kemal Ataturk to Saudi Arabia, where traditional law largely remains in force. (Thus the traditional law which allowed a man up to four wives if he treated them equally and to divorce a wife virtually at will is no longer observed in much of the Muslim world.) Out of this combination of new power, prosperity, and flexibility we may well see creative new forms of Islamic faith and culture emerge.

THE FIVE PILLARS
OF ISLAM

Let us examine some aspects of traditional and normative Islamic life. These center around the Five Pillars of Islam: the confession of faith, prayer five times a day, giving of alms to the poor, fasting in the month of Ramadan, and the *hajj,* or pilgrimage to Mecca.

The first of the five pillars is to say, "There is no god but God (Allah), and Muhammad is the *rasul* (prophet or envoy) of God." This statement sums up in a few words the simple Muslim faith. The basic concept of the oneness of God has been discussed. When Muhammad is called the rasul or envoy of God, it means exactly this—that he is God's appointed spokesman, the mouthpiece through which God chose to deliver his call for submission and his final commandments to the world. True, Muhammad is also considered a paragon of virtue and fountain of wisdom, so that his sayings and acts as transmitted by tradition are basic precedents in Muslim law. But he is not a saint, a seer, wonder-worker, divine incarnation, or even profound mystic like the Buddha or peerless philosopher like Confucius. It was emphasized that Muhammad's birth was biologically normal, and that he performed no miracles except the delivery of the Koran itself. The Koran attributes virgin birth to Jesus, and miracles to earlier prophets—Moses changed a staff into a serpent;

One God, Many Words and Wonders

Jesus is said by the Koran not only to have been taken up into heaven, but also to have caused some clay birds to come to life and fly away. These are appropriate to the son of Mary, for he is the prophet of mystic and marvelous holiness; similar powers are recognized, as we shall see, in numerous Muslim *wali,* or saints. But Muhammad's own calling was not to this sort of thing, but simply to be the spokesman of God. His miracle is the Koran itself; its production by a man like him in enigmatic circumstances, and the wonderful emergence of the Islamic community around him, are considered sufficient evidence of his authority; Muhammad needed dispense no other, more trivial, miracles as calling-cards.

The second of the pillars is prayer. The Muslim is to pray five times a day. As we have seen, in Muslim communities the voice of the muezzin from the minaret calls the faithful at the appointed times. Each prayer period begins and ends with standing upright, and includes bowing and prostration. It is preceded by washing as a ritual of self-purification. Water is available for this purpose at mosques and oases, and if it is not at hand sand may be used. The heart of the five-times-daily prayer is the opening chapter of the Koran, already quoted, beginning "In the Name of Allah, the Compassionate, the Merciful . . ." the faithful pray that they may be guided in "the straight path," but it may be noted there is no prayer for individual needs or favors; the Muslim knows that one's relation to Allah should be one of faith, praise, gratitude, and obedience, and that God knows one's specific needs before one can ask.

The third pillar is almsgiving. The fundamental obligation is to give ten percent of one's wealth to the needy within the Muslim community; expanded, it covers good works and comradely attitudes in general, a helping hand and friendly smile for one's neighbor. This pillar reaffirms the social and ethical dimensions of Islam. The Muslim faith strives to remember it is a community of submission and service, working for a more just world, not just a personal path to salvation. Strictly speaking almsgiving should be done out of religious commitment rather than compulsion (although it was collected, from Muslims only, as a tax in traditional Islamic states). But many modern reformers have seen in the almsgiving principle a rationale for social welfare programs or socialism as an application of the Islamic community ideal under contemporary conditions.

The fourth pillar of Islam is the fast of Ramadan. Ramadan is a month of twenty-eight days in the Muslim calendar; during this period the faithful are neither to eat nor drink between daybreak and dark, but to spend these hours in prayer, frequenting the mosques. Commonly, family and friends will gather at night to dine as soon as it is permitted, and there are traditional Ramadan dishes. Often the meal will be combined with reading aloud from the Koran and prayer, and will continue far into the night. The daylight hours will be for rest and further prayer. At the end of Ramadan there is, as one might expect, an explosive celebration, which commences when the first sliver of a new moon indicates the end of this odd reverse time and the beginning of the next month.[33]

---

[33]A vivid account of Ramadan, and of much else of Islam in an Iraqi Shiite setting, may be found in Elizabeth Warnock Fernea, *Guests of the Sheik* (Garden City, N. Y.: Doubleday Anchor Books, 1969).

Because the Muslim calendar is lunar, the occurrence of Ramadan moves progressively through the seasons. When it falls in the short, cool days of midwinter it is relatively easy to endure, but amidst the long summer days of a hot, dry climate, going without food or even a sip of water provides a stern test of Muslim loyalty. Understandably, some partially successful attempts have been made in recent times to reinterpret Ramadan in view of the exigencies of modern urban life. For innumerable devout Muslims, however, Ramadan remains a strenuous test of faith, softened by support from culture and tradition and the "we're all in it together" mood of a Muslim society's observance. For many, too, the opportunity for a deepening of one's life of prayer and Koranic study is genuinely welcome.

The fifth pillar is one known to almost everyone who has heard anything about Islam: the pilgrimage to Mecca called the hajj. Mecca, the immemorially holy city and birthplace of Muhammad, is the focal point of Islam. As though aligned along rays to a sun, Muslims at prayer face toward this vale in the Arabian Desert, and once in a lifetime their feet are to take them down that ray to the holy place. Every year a million or more Muslims gather at Mecca in the month of pilgrimage; this assembly affords like nothing else that sense of unity and identity for which Islam is justly famous.

Not all Muslims, of course, make the pilgrimage even once. Minors, the elderly, the infirm, and those without financial means are among those exempted from the obligation. For those who do go on the hajj, the rewards are substantial, not only in spiritual fulfillment, but in prestige within the Islamic family. Back in his home community, wherever it lies between Mauritania and Indonesia, the returned pilgrim may add the title hajji to his name, and will be afforded special honor.

The pilgrimage is properly made in Dhu-l-hijja, the last month of the Muslim calendar and the month when Muhammad first began to receive the Koran. The pilgrimage is thus a meeting of sacred ultimates—a return just before the beginning of a new year to the place of the creation of the world and where Islamic time began.

Muslim belief about Mecca and the hajj combines the city's pre-Islamic role as a sacred center, a sanctuary for combative tribes, and a place of polytheistic worship, with beliefs about Abraham and the revelation through Muhammad. According to traditional Muslim belief, Mecca is the navel of the world, the spot where creation began. Abraham (Ibrahim in Arabic), the primal prophet of the original pure monotheistic religion, was then called by God to proceed from Palestine to the valley where Mecca is now located.

This he did, together with Hagar his wife and Ishmael (Ismail) his son, forefather of the Arabs. On one occasion, Hagar was lost in the desert with Ishmael and ran desperately about looking for water for the infant, until she found that a well had sprung up where Ishmael had struck the sand with his heel. Later, Abraham under God's instructions built the cubical shrine at Mecca, with the help of Ishmael. In the corner of the kaaba was placed the black stone brought from heaven by the angel Gabriel. On another occasion, in a variant of the account of the sacrifice of Isaac in the Judaeo-Christian Bible, Abraham was commanded by God to sacrifice his son Ishmael. As they went to the place of sacrifice, Satan three times appeared to Ishmael and tempted him to reject his father's demand, but Ishmael kept faith and refused. At the last moment, a ram was substituted for the boy. (The great Dome-of-the-Rock mosque in Jerusalem also commemorates this event, and the almost-sacrifice of Isaac.)

The kaaba is now the center of the great open-air mosque of Mecca, and is the real focal point of all Muslim worship. Other mosques have a niche in a wall facing in the direction of Mecca; this mosque, because it *is* the focal point, is circular with the kaaba, or Holy House, at its center. The kaaba itself is covered with black and gold felt and has a gold-encrusted door, seldom opened. Around it are wide tracks where pilgrims circumambulate the shrine, and beyond these platforms for prayer.

In Muhammad's day the kaaba contained three hundred and sixty images of heathen gods, so far had the faith of Abraham declined, but the prophet had these destroyed. Now the kaaba holds nothing but a few lamps. Yet for Muslims, whose faith is in the infinite God alone, for this the shrine is all the more holy. The kaaba is said to be an exact replica of the house of God in paradise above, around which angels circle as the faithful on earth circle the earthly kaaba. Heaven, tradition says, is closer to earth at Mecca than anywhere else, so prayers are heard best from there. Nothing comes between the kaaba and the abode of Allah; airplanes are not allowed to pass over it, and it is said that even birds will not fly above the Holy House. Nearby is Zamzam, the well of Hagar and Ishmael, reputed to have curative powers.

Interestingly, Muhammad developed his teaching about the Meccan pilgrimage during the time he was at Medina, when it was by no means clear that he would ever be reconciled to his home city. The teaching may, of course, have had political motives aimed at appeasing his kinsmen. Yet it also suggests that for the exile Mecca had the quality of many pilgrimage centers of being "the center out there"—a place remote from the center of present action on the worldly plane, yet a place of access to ultimate origins and ultimate goals. So has Mecca ever been.[34] Indeed, after the time of Muhammad Mecca's role as a commercial center declined, and the holy city has since depended economically almost entirely on its sacred role.

The carrying out of the hajj is marked by many careful rituals. As he approaches the city, probably from the seaport and airport city of Jiddah on the coast, the pilgrim stops to separate himself from the ordinary world by ablutions, as before prayer. He then dons special white garments; thereafter until the rites are completed he must abstain from killing man, beast, or plant, from sexual activity, and from cutting hair or nails.

Upon arriving at the sacred site, he kisses (or if that is not possible because of the crowd, touches) the sacred black stone. He then circumambulates the kaaba seven times.

Next he runs seven times up and down a colonnade between two hills about four hundred and fifty yards apart. The usual explanation is that this commemorates Hagar's running about looking for water for Ishmael.

Then the pilgrim proceeds outside Mecca to Mina, where he probably finds quarters in a vast tent city with a temporary population of a million or so; this

[34]For an illuminating discussion of pilgrimage, which indirectly casts much light on the meaning of the hajj, see Victor Turner, "The Center Out There: Pilgrim's Goal," in *History of Religions*, 12, no. 3 (February 1973), 191–230.

gathering in itself gives him an experience of the power and unity of Islam. The next day he and the other pilgrims all proceed to Mount Arafat, upon which they must stand between noon and sundown. There, seated on a camel, Muhammad gave his farewell sermon on his own last pilgrimage to Mecca.

This "standing at Arafat" is the culminating act of the hajj, and the one act that cannot be omitted. It is the archetypal assembly of the faithful as a united army drawn out of all kindreds and tongues in submission to God. It is said to bring to mind the gathering of all peoples for judgment on the Last Day, and repeats the first assembly which Muhammad himself commanded so heroically.

After this, the final rites represent a process of desacralization. Returning to Mina, the pilgrim throws rocks at three stone pillars said to represent devils, recalling the three temptations of Satan which Ishmael rejected.

On the last day of the formal sacred pilgrimage time, the pilgrim will sacrifice a ram or goat in a certain field; part of the meat is supposed to be given to the poor. On the same day, throughout the Muslim world, an animal is similarly sacrificed. Its head is pointed toward Mecca, and as the Muslim cuts its throat, he says, "In the name of Allah." This recalls the ram substituted for Ishmael in Abraham's rite.

Next, in Mecca, the pilgrim has his hair cut. The hair, a token of oneself, is left behind as a sign of his dedication. He circumambulates the kaaba a final time.

Most pilgrims then proceed on to Medina, although this is optional. There, in this second most sacred city of Islam, they visit Muhammad's mosque and tomb. Many Muslims desire to come to Medina to die and be buried there with the prophet and his family.

The hajj is a collection of diverse traditional acts. Some may seem very Islamic and meaningful, some like the running and stoning of the "devils" rather primitive and bizarre. Yet Muslims find them all spiritually significant, though none more so than the mere fact of the pilgrimage itself. Many Muslims, including the most mystical, have found deep inward meanings in all the traditions; stoning the pillars, for example, is made to represent the striking down of sinful desires within the self.

Perhaps the best explanation is that of the great medieval theologian al-Ghazali.[35] He pointed out that the hajj is meant to be a supreme act of islam, of submission and self-abnegation. That in it which is less than rationally appealing or satisfying to refined feelings can do much to purify out the egotism which so easily lingers in a heart that considers itself refined. The hajj is an act of sheer devotion, and of sheer identification with the inscrutable mind of God and with the Islamic tradition. It affirms that at the center of true religion is finite man facing the infinite mystery of God, not the satisfaction of human inclinations.

SUNNA AND SHIAH

Let us now examine some of the variations within Islam. The most important today is between the Sunna and Shiah traditions. Sunna is the normative Islam of most places. Shiah is the official Islam of Iran, is dominant in southern Iraq, and is represented by minorities in Lebanon, Pakistan, India, Yemen, and elsewhere.

[35]G. E. von Grunebaum, *Muhammadan Festivals* (New York: Henry Schuman, 1951), pp. 44–47. The entire discussion of the hajj in this book, pp. 15–49, is very useful.

The kaaba in Mecca, with pilgrims circumambulating it.

In Sunna the fundamental authority is shari'ah, Muslim law. It is interpreted not by a single individual, but by consensus of learned men who base their decisions on tradition, hadith, and analogy. Although the University of Cairo has long been considered the most venerable repository of such learning, Sunna is more or less decentralized. Its tone is one of putting most emphasis on the basic Five Pillars of Islam, and on a rather formal—though deeply felt—style of devotion. Its legal bent stresses putting all of life under God and the Koran. Different schools of law interpretation obtain within Sunna, though they are not competitive but recognized alternatives. Sunna also embraces some submovements; one is Wahhabi, dominant in Saudi Arabia, a conservative, puritanical reform dating from the eighteenth century.

Shiah is different in tone and more complex. Shiites believe that after Muhammad there was intended to be a succession of *Imams,* divinely appointed and authoritative teachers of Islam, to guide the faithful. The first was Ali, Muhammad's cousin, and after him Ali's eldest son, Hasan, and then Ali's second son, Husain. There were then nine others in family succession, down to the twelfth, who was born in 869.

All of these, except the last, died mysteriously and are said by Shiites to have been killed at the instigation of various caliphs. From the Shiah point of view, the caliphates represent dark usurping powers seeking to destroy the true spokesman in each generation of the house of the prophet of God. The twelfth, known as the *Imam*

Zaman, or Mahdi, the Imam for All Time, is said to be still living, but invisible. In the fullness of time he will reappear to bring justice to the earth. Subsects of Shiah recognize only part of the lineage, or variations on it. Understandably, colorful claimants to the title of Mahdi have appeared from time to time in Muslim history.

Shiah devotion puts most emphasis on Husain, the third Imam and the most worthy and tragic of all. In the sixty-first year after the hejira, he and his companions were killed by the forces of the Caliph Yazid in a great battle at Karbala, in southern Iraq. The death of this splendid young hero has been made by Shiah into an event which demands eternal recompense by fervent mourning and reenactment. Husain's shrine at Karbala is a mighty place of pilgrimage.

The death of Husain is celebrated by Shiites in the first ten days of the Muslim year, the festival of Muharram. During these days Shiah communities go wild with religious fervor. At the end of the old year, black tents are set up in the streets with memorial arms and candles to remind passersby of the martyr. On the first day of Muharram, the devout cease from bathing or shaving. The story of Husain is vividly recited from pulpits in the tents; the listeners respond with wailing and tears. Even more startlingly, groups of men will roam the streets venting their anguish by inflicting sword wounds on themselves, dragging chains, dancing wildly, and pulling out their hair.

The climax of this remarkable commemoration of a hero's death is on the tenth day of Muharram. The battle of Karbala and the death of Husain are enacted in a colorful passion play, with horsemen in bright costumes charging and recharging each other, battering each other in sport with wooden staves. The crowd becomes more and more excited; finally Husain is taken, and is seen to suffer excruciatingly from thirst while the cruel foemen make sport of him. At last he is beheaded.

The play then culminates in a funeral procession through the streets with the bloody and gruesome model of the severed head. By now frenzy has reached a great pitch. Rage and violent mourning combine; in the heat of the wailing for Husain, a self-announced Sunna Muslim might well not be safe in the midst of an impassioned Shiah crowd.[36]

The atmosphere of Shiah, as reflected in the Muharram and the beliefs about the mysterious martyred or hidden Imam, is clearly different in tone from Sunna. The Shiah world, far from being one in which submission to the revelation of Allah steadily and progressively triumphs, is a darker sphere where treachery and deception and cruelty are all too likely to prevail on the outer plane. Heroes and true prophets of God suffer and die in anguish, while ruthless imposters sit upon thrones; the number of true faithful is small compared to that of frauds, and the faithful are known chiefly by the fervor of their righteous wailing for the evils of this hard world, and the keenness of their hope in God's inward, invisible plans. The tense, nervous, suspicious emotional tone of Shiah communities, particularly where they are minorities and during Muharram, has often been noted.

Undoubtedly it is no accident that Shiah began in the Valley of the Two Rivers,

[36]See the account in von Grunebaum, *Muhammadan Festivals,* pp. 87–94. Fernea, *Guests of the Sheik,* contains a colorful firsthand account of the first ten days of Muharram, pp. 216–66.

One God, Many Words and Wonders

where anciently New Year's (which Muharram really is) had included rites of battle with chaos by the hero Marduk, and wailing for the dead Tammuz, as we have seen. Shiah is strong in formerly Zoroastrian Iran, with its belief in a cosmic bottle of good and evil, a hidden coming prophet, and an apocalyptic reversal to which the faithful looked forward. Christian and Manichaean influences on Shiah cannot be excluded either, for Husain emotionally becomes virtually a suffering savior.

ISLAMIC MYSTICISM

A discussion of Islam would be superficial if it dealt only with its outward, official history and practices, and left out the mystical wing, which has frequently given the faith of Muhammad another face. This tradition is known to the West as Sufism, and its practicioners as Sufis. Their God is the same God as that of the Koran and the tradition. But they seek not only to follow his external commandments, but to know him initimately and even to lose themselves in love and self-abnegation into the depths of his being. Around the Sufis' mystic quest have clustered a number of auxiliary practices, many of great beauty: spiritual masters, parables and wisdom tales, spiritual fraternities, schools of meditation, techniques of attaining ecstasy through music, chanting, and dance.

Sufis believe their approach is grounded in the inner experience of the prophet himself. Muhammad clearly prayed deeply and knew God intimately, even to trance and rapture. Certain verses of the Koran support the quest for mystical awareness of God everywhere: "To Allah belongs the east and the west. Whichever way you turn there is the face of Allah."[37]

Another suggests the esoteric side of things: we are told that Allah took his servant from a holy shrine to a farther shrine to reveal certain divine signs.[38] According to some traditions, this last passage refers to God's mysteriously transporting Muhammad in a single night from Mecca to Jerusalem, and then taking him up into heaven to show him sights not seen by other mortals; accounts of this journey at second hand probably helped inspire Dante's *Divine Comedy*.[39]

Thus Sufis believe not only that their way is that of Muhammad himself, but many of them also that—just as in a sense Muhammad's declaration was but a restoration of the true primordial faith of Abraham and of Eden—Sufism is really a timeless path known to the wise in all generations.

Doubtless there is truth to this, represented historically by the parallels and possible influence between Sufism and Asiatic shamanism, Greek Neoplatonism, Christian monasticism, and the lore of Hinduism and Buddhism. But within Islamic history, although there had long been spontaneous examples of mystics, Sufism became visible as a movement about a century after Muhammad. Like Shiah but in a different way, Sufism was a reaction against the luxury and corruption, the loss of

[37]Dawood, *The Koran*, p. 336; verse cited above, note 30.

[38]Ibid., p. 228.

[39]See J. R. Porter, "Muhammad's Journey to Heaven," *Numen*, XXI, fasc. 1 (April 1974), 64–80.

original desert simplicity and pure faith, which many serious Muslims saw overtaking the now triumphant Islamic world of the caliphates.

The origin of the word "sufi" is disputed, but the majority of scholars attribute it to the Arabic word for wool, *suf,* alluding to the coarse wool garments ascetics seeking a more inward way wore as a mark distinguishing them from those content with outward conformity to Islam.

Sufi inwardness made of greatest importance one's personal relation of faith and love to God, a love which was its own reward. Never has this attitude been more eloquently expressed than by the mystic Rabi'a al-'Adawiya of Basra (d. 801), a former slave who had been trained as a flute player. At night she would pray thus:

> Oh my Lord, the stars are shining and the eyes of men are closed, and kings have shut their doors, and every lover is alone with his beloved, and here am I alone with Thee.

She said also:

> I saw the Prophet in a dream, and he said to me, 'O Rabi'a, dost thou love me?' I said, 'O Prophet of God, who is there who does not love thee? But my love to God so possessed me that no place remains for loving or hating any save Him.'

And again:

> It is a bad servant who serves God from fear and terror or from the desire of a reward. . . . Even if Heaven and Hell were not, does it not behoove us to obey Him?[40]

This is a pure Sufi spirit echoing down through the ages. As time went on, this sheer love of God came to be more and more organized, with particular practices and doctrines and societies shaping the lives of those who followed its path.

Thus Abu Yazid al-Bistami (d. 874) described the stages of the spiritual life leading up to *fana,* complete passing away of the separate individual self into God. The fana state was often manifested in ecstatic spiritual intoxication; in that state al-Bastami, hardly knowing whether it was he or God in him whose words they were, did not shrink from expressions like, "I am your Lord," "Praise be to me, how great is my majesty," or "My banner is greater than that of Muhammad." The conventional were duly shocked.

Finally, in 922, one of these God-possessed persons of uninhibited rapture, al-Hallaj, was executed at Baghdad for saying, "I am the Truth"—"Truth" being an attribute of Allah. The tragic Al-Hallaj had taken Jesus, in Islam the exemplar of the inward mystic, as his model of the God-incarnate man, and appropriately al-Hallaj was crucified.

At the same time, a reaction in favor of a more orthodox Sufism set in. Junayd of Baghdad (d. 911) emphasized that the claims of mystical experience cannot be

---

[40]From Margaret Smith, *Rabi'a the Mystic* (New York: Cambridge University Press, 1928), pp. 22, 99, 100. Reprinted by permission of the publisher.

given priority over normative moral and customary demands of religion, and that the nature of love itself demands that, even in the mystic's "identity" with God, there be also a difference betwen him and God.[41]

The great al-Ghazali (d. 1111), who had been a conventional Muslim scholar until he experienced, and then sought to interpret, the mystic path, made Sufism a respectable part of Islam. He interpreted Sufi inwardness as an attitude to accompany the outward acts and bring them to life, as we have seen in his treatment of the hajj.

The philosopher and Sufi master Ibn al-Arabi (d. 1240), a spiritual follower of al-Ghazali, moved in the direction of a pantheist philosophy as the intellectual expression of what the Sufi "knows" and enacts. For him, God was not only the source of all, but the sole reality. Within the divine, however, are gradations; between man and the divine heart is a realm of images that reflect in the human imagination—angels, the Day of Judgment, and so forth—and on these images religious visions and events are grounded.

The Sufi way has made much of *shaykhs,* spiritual teachers and masters, and *wali,* saints. Drawing initially from Shiah sources, Sufis also have talked of hidden holy ones, and of a coming Mahdi or apocalyptic teacher-savior. According to Sufism, the saints are different from the prophet Muhammad, but in their own way nearly as great. For a Sufi to attain *waliya,* sainthood or being a "friend of God," was as good a goal as outward Islam, submission.

Indeed, by the tenth and eleventh centuries the twin goals of sainthood and submission came together, as the notion gained force in Sufi circles that one should submit to one's shaykh or spiritual guide. The *shaykh,* called farther east around India a *pir* or *murshid,* was more or less an Islamic parallel to the Hindu guru. The very self-abnegation of submitting to his commands "as a dead body in the hands of its washers" was an experience of egolessness and bore its own spiritual reward, whether the guide was wise or not.

Many were wise, but their wisdom was expressed in peculiar tales and gnomic wisdom. We are told, for example, that a certain man fell down in a seizure in a street of perfume sellers. People tried to revive him with various of the sweet odors of the tradesmen, but to no avail. Finally someone thrust sharp, pungent, ammonious ordure before his nose, and he arose. It is only by the different, even if it is merely diconcerting, that the walking dead can be brought to life.[42] The methods of differentness have the shaykhs employed, with their paradoxes and their chanting, dancing, and trances.

Since the labors of al-Ghazali, Sufi masters generally have emphasized doing the normative devotions of Islam, but with a special mind to the inward as well as the outward aspects. But beyond that, there are special ecstatic techniques for knowing God which the shaykhs taught: practices like *dhikr* (or *wird*), reciting the beautiful names of God on beads, or even whirling dances like those of the der-

---

[41]See the profound discussion of Junayd in R. C. Zaehner, *Hindu and Muslim Mysticism* (New York: Schocken Books, 1969).

[42]Idries Shah, *Tales of the Dervishes* (New York: E. P. Dutton & Co., 1970), p. 143.

vishes, or feats of shamanistic fervor like rending garments, eating glass, cutting oneself without pain, to show one's divine absorption.

Practices like these were developed by the great Sufi orders, which spread across Islam after the tenth century. They still exist, although since around 1900 their power has diminished. For the most part they were not celibate monastic orders, although in some instances an inner core of devotees or leaders might—whether officially married or not—exemplify a level of commitment comparable to that of monks or abbots in other faiths. But for the bulk of lay adherents, the orders were more like lodges: one would receive a formal initiation by a shaykh or pir of the order, and then would practice its devotion corporately and privately. Some Sufi orders, especially in the Turkish Empire, had political and revolutionary overtones. Some have been suppressed by modern Islamic governments because the whole Sufi attitude was considered by modernizers to inculcate a medieval, superstitious, non-productive mentality. Ironically, at the same time Sufism has been discovered and much appreciated by many outside of Islam.

Sufi orders with their saintly masters were and are a great proselytizing force for Islam. It was primarily in their gentler, more mystical form that Islam entered India and Indonesia; it is easy to speculate that, apart from its empathetic presentation by such mystic saints, Islam might have had but little success in these cultures, so differently oriented from Arabia. Today Sufi orders are having great success in spreading Islam in Africa.

The prestige of the shaykh made much of Islam into a cult of personalities. Shaykhs became saints, wali, who had cosmic as well as temporal meanings. It was said to be the saints who kept the world together generation after generation. In an invisible hierarchy were varying degrees of saints: "successors," "pegs," "pillars," and finally *qutbs,* "poles" or "axes" of the universe. These last, according to a popular tradition, are of a certain definite number in every generation, and when one dies he is replaced by another. They are the true pivots upon which the world in its inner life turns. They may not be known to the general public—indeed, a saint in his humility may not even know himself that he is a saint, much less an axis of the world—but should he fail in the mysterious work his inward sanctity enables him to do, the social order and the earth itself would fall apart. Finally, Sufis spoke of the enigmatic leader and guide of the saints themselves, al-Khidir, "the Green One," a generally invisible but immortal and ever-youthful guide who appears at time of need to the dreams or waking sight of the sincere questor on the mystic path.[43]

The Muslim public knew well the reputations of the more visible saints. They flocked to their presences and, after their deaths, to their tombs. In the heyday of popular Sufism, the twelfth through nineteenth centuries, legends of saints were rife, and pilgrimages to their holy places rivaled Mecca in popularity. Many of them are still much frequented. In Shiah areas, the shrines of Imams, like that of Husain himself at Karbala in Iraq, are thronged. Countless village mosques contain the tomb of a local saint, unmarked by image or picture but well known and visible because of its coffin shape, inscription, and the many colored flags on the building.

[43]See the discussion of Muslim saints in Fazlur Rahman, *Islam* (Garden City, N. Y.: Doubleday Anchor Book, 1968), pp.162-65 and in von Grunenbaum, *Muhammaden Festivals*, pp. 67-84.

In the valley of Bamian in Afghanistan, famous for its ancient Buddhist monastic caves, but whose population is now strongly Muslim, I came across a shrine of an "ice-burning saint." According to the local legend, this mystic had once come with his disciples into the valley and begged for fuel with which to cook food for himself and his band. But the villagers, not recognizing him for what he was, hardened their hearts against his request. The saint then sent a disciple into the nearby mountains to get some ice, and by a miracle he caused the ice to burn, and used it for firewood. Thereupon the awestruck villagers believed in him and besought the holy man to stay, which he did. When he died, the shrine was built over his tomb, a modest domed edifice of mud with a wall around it, all festooned with red banners. I saw bearded men of the village circumambulate the tomb inside the walls muttering dhikr as they went; in setting out, each stooped to pass under a table holding a large book, presumably the Koran.

One sensed here both the devotional power of popular Islam, and the basic similarities of the central Asiatic myths and culti of men of power, whether in shamanistic, Hindu, Buddhist, Muslim, or Christian forms . . . for the wizard saint has been a constant in all the many faiths which have swept across the wild mountains, deserts, and forests of that vast area of the earth.

Islam generally believes that the saints have power to perform miracles. Muhammad did not, except the miracle of the Koran itself. But the saints, like Jesus who is their esoteric model, have a different calling from that of the public envoy of God, one at once more arcane and more popularly appealing. They must work wonders to show the transcendence of spiritual attainment over the material, and do works of mercy which help hold the universe together. They are masters of the realm of archetype and dream that lies above this world and below God, as written in the philosophy of al-Ghazali and Ibn al-Arabi. The *baraka,* or numinous power of the saints, rests eternally over even their tombs and relics, and for this reason pilgrims to these sites are often healed and blessed.

This then is Islam—a faith which appears highly unified and monolithic from outside, and which is in some ways, yet which also has a rich diversity of traditions and expressions. It is a faith grounded in the revelation through Muhammad and his holy places and prayers. Yet it is also the faith of numerous other "Friends of God" in Muhammad's following, the saints. It is a faith in which the Arabic Koran has an absolutely central place, yet into which many cultures and customs have been drawn.

EIGHT

RELIGION PAST, PRESENT, AND FUTURE

Concluding Reflections

We have surveyed an array of religions of mankind past and present. We have encountered a remarkable diversity among them, yet we have also noted what they all have in common. Most fundamentally, they all put under a culture a map that traces roadways of meaning between the highest and the most tragic moments of one's life, and between these and the brightest fixtures in the stories and shrines of one's people. Whether in the architecture of the temple or the voice of the prophet, the broad security of religion based in the general culture or the exciting intensity of small withdrawal groups, religion makes this map and constructs these roads into one's personal story and through one's inner weather.

Some of the religion we have looked at—perhaps most or all in the eyes of many—seemed very much rooted in the past, if not irrevocably locked there. The past may give it a romantic patina, or sprinkle it with the dust of something grisly that we are glad is gone, but it is still in the past. We may in wistful moods wish we could revisit the living temples of ancient Greece, or hear the Buddha speak, but we do not expect their like will be seen again, unless all things do recur in infinite time and, as a poet says of the wonders of Mycenae:

> It may be that no splendor passes evermore from Earth,
> But that, through endless incantations—subtle, strange, divine—
> It knows in far-off time and space a new resplendent birth:
>
> In what age, in what world, shall this proud lion find again—
> Deep in the sea of stars—his race of gods and godlike men?[1]

But on a shorter scale, it may indeed seem that much of mankind's religion is trapped beyond renewal in the past, and that even living religion—of which there is much in the world today—is a carry-over from the past into the present, relating modern experience to ancient maps.

Is religion then an anomaly which cannot be expected to survive much longer? At least since the eighteenth century eminent voices have predicted the withering

[1]"Golden Mycenae," in Donald S. Fryer, *Songs and Sonnets Atlantean* (Sauk City, Wis.: Arkham House, 1971). Reprinted by permission of the publisher.

away of religion. This is not a book of prophecy, and will not attempt to foretell the future. But we can indicate that the relation of religion to its times is usually more complex and mysterious than appears on the surface.

Religion always comes into a present as something out of the past. Both the temple and the voice of the prophet, in differing ways, point to a world simpler and more pristine than the ambivalent world of the day. In this simpler world of mythic time, or of scripture or vision, the works of the gods are more evident and moral values clearer. For religion to appear today as something from the past, which is somewhat out of joint with the present, is nothing exceptional in itself. Nor is it any new thing for prophets to appear who proclaim that at least the extant religion is ready to be superseded. So spoke the Buddha in effect of the old Brahminism and its rites, and Muhammad of the old gods of stars and moon.

In all the countless religious changes earth has seen, the religious quest has finally been renewed, but it has not seldom changed course and set out in unexpected directions. Often its new forms have at first hardly seemed like "religion" at all, compared with the older elaborate structure. At first the Buddha's methods may have seemed more like an ancient version of psychotherapy, and the cause of Muhammad like a radical political movement, than something which would someday have its equivalents to heavens of gods and the temples of the Nile. These and other new movements seemed more like breaths of fresh wind, which swept away all the old gods and cleaned the skies, leaving None or only One.

But the "Death of God" is no new thing; God or the gods have died many times, but a new God or new gods are soon born and arise to fill the vacuum. Their names may hardly yet have the glow of the old and holy, and they may come from segments of society little involved in the religious commerce of the previous age. The Buddha was of Kshatriya rather than Brahmin caste, Muhammad was from Arabia rather than one of the main religious powers, Jesus was from Galilee. But it is often something that appears "noncompetitive" in the power structure of the day which bears the future, like obscure tiny furry mammals in the age of giant reptiles.

Religion is changing today. It is not changing at as fast a rate as it has at some periods in the past, for there are no great new movements afoot which look like they might replace Buddhism, Islam, or Christianity in the manner these did their predecessors. Moreover, conservative as well as innovative forces are at work in all faiths. Even the vaunted modern technology, which some have said will create a new secular world in which religion can no longer have a place, works both sides of the street. The urbanization and industrialization it has brought have indeed disrupted the traditional religion-based lifestyles of millions, but technology has also greatly facilitated such traditional religious practices as pilgrimage (now via jumbo jet) to Rome or Mecca, the publishing of scriptures for a mass readership, and missionary preaching by means of radio and television.

But we can be sure that new religious forces will emerge—unless, as some religionists predict, this world is soon terminated—whether under old or new names. There may be unexpected revitalization of old motifs. New and unexpected religious meaning may be found in some very new experience, like space exploration, which now seems nonreligious in any traditional sense. New religious ventures have both old roots and new graftings in surprising combinations.

The crescent Earth, as seen by astronauts on the Moon, rises over the lunar horizon.
The exploration of space may influence future developments in religion.

If the more dismal current predictions about the future prove themselves, and our planet becomes a morass of overpopulation and falling living standards, we can expect a situation of outward hopelessness to lead some to the mystical inward quest, some to elaborate cults and rites which provide a vivid alternative world, and some to semi-religious revolutionary ideologies. Or, the world may fall into the new medievalism of some overarching religio-social system with new (perhaps "scientific") equivalents of priest, salvation, and miracle. An overpopulated, "steady state" society is likely to sanctify the static, hierarchical structure it calls into being with sacred forms.

But if the grievous present problems are solved by technology and the world manages improving conditions of life and perhaps continual space exploration, the religious outlook will be quite different. The religious spirit of prosperous and expanding peoples, especially those able to expand geographically into new territories, like ancient Israel and nineteenth-century America, contrasts much with that of poor and restricted times. For the former, religion presents the vision of an expanding corporate future destiny, achieved by exhilarating work and struggle but eminently worthwhile, toward which God beckons his people. In the latter situation, religion offers instead inner space to explore and inner exhilarating attainments through mystical and salvation and counterculture experiences.

In the future, one or the other possibility may (or may not, if the gulf between wealthy and poor nations holds) emerge worldwide. One feels that whether or not space exploration is richly developed will say far more about the religion of the future than many now acknowledge—not so much because of anything we may find in space, as for what it symbolizes about the exploring culture's view of human nature and destiny. For religion lives by symbols; it perpetuates old sacred symbols from the past, but also has a way of discovering the sacred side of the new symbols, to make them parts of a new spiritual world where everything comes together.

In the present book, however, our task has been the fascinating historical and descriptive one. We have tracked out some of the ways religion has followed down the years, and we have found that just to be in the presence of all this variegated richness is in itself an awareness-expanding, even a religious, experience. To feel this way before the past and present is a good prelude for turning to the future.

Bibliography

The following list is by no means exhaustive; in many of the categories there are hundreds, or even thousands, of valuable books. What I have tried to do is suggest a few books in each category, not so much for research as for further general familiarization with broad areas. Most of them are written at a level accessible to beginning or middle level students. Most are either presently in print or should be available in larger libraries. Books footnoted in the text are also generally recommended.

In many cases these books have gone through a number of editions; the date given below may not represent the earliest or latest printing. Books marked with an * are available in paperback; however, the edition cited is not necessarily the paperback edition.

Most of these books, especially the introductory textbooks on specific faiths, contain excellent bibliographies. For further reading material the student is referred to them, and to Charles J. Adams, *A Reader's Guide to the Great Religions* (New York: The Free Press, 1965).

Introduction

***Bettis, Joseph Dabney,** ed., *Phenomenology of Religion*. New York: Harper & Row, 1969 A collection of basic papers by leading philosophers on "description of the essence of religion."

***de Vries, Jan,** *The Study of Religion: A Historical Approach*. New York: Harcourt, 1967. A summary of the modern history of academic religious studies.

***Eliade, Mircea,** *Cosmos and History*. New York: Harper Torchbooks, 1959. A good basic approach to the history of religions; compares concepts of time in different types of religion.

*————, *From Primitives to Zen*. New York: Harper & Row, 1967. A useful collection of texts and description arranged thematically.

*————, *Patterns in Comparative Religion*. Cleveland: Meridian Books, 1963. A substantial cross-cultural treatment of basic religious symbols and themes, such as sun, moon, and agriculture.

*————, *The Sacred and The Profane*. New York: Harper Torchbooks, 1961. An excellent basic introduction to the history of religions, elucidating such matters as the meaning of the temple, the festival, initiation, and myth.

King, Winston L., *Introduction to Religion*. New York: Harper and Row, 1954. A very competent survey, combining an informed theoretical perspective with much information on particular religions.

*van der Leeuw, Gerardus, *Religion in Essence and Manifestation,* 2 vols. New York: Harper & Row, 1963. A classic thematic study containing a succinct statement of the phenomenological method.

*Lévi-Strauss, Claude, *Structural Anthropology.* Garden City, New York: Doubleday and Co., 1967. An important modern anthropologist's treatment of how myth, ritual, and shamanism create symbolic worlds.

McCasland, S. Vernon, Grace E. Cairns, and David C. Yu. *Religions of the World.* New York: Random House, 1969. A useful textbook, encyclopedic in scale.

*Otto, Rudolf, *The Idea of the Holy.* London & New York: Oxford Univ. Press, 1958. A classic statement of the experience of the "numinous" from which religion begins.

*Smith, Huston, *The Religions of Man.* New York: Harper & Row, 1958. A very readable and insightful survey.

*Spencer, Sidney, *Mysticism in World Religion.* Baltimore: Penguin Books, 1963. The most authoritative survey of this area.

*Streng, Frederick J., *Understanding Religious Man.* Belmont, Calif.: Dickenson Pub. Co., 1969. A good introduction to methodology in religious studies.

Turner, Victor W., *The Ritual Process.* Chicago: Aldine Pub. Co., 1969. A highly stimulating set of essays on the meaning of rite and symbol.

*Wach, Joachim, *The Comparative Study of Religion.* New York: Columbia Univ. Press, 1958. A brilliant treatment of the major concepts and problems in comparative religious studies from the author's point of view.

*——, *Sociology of Religion.* Chicago: Univ. of Chicago Press, 1944. A classic statement of the different kinds of religious groups, leaders, and forms of expression.

*Weber, Max, *The Sociology of Religion.* Boston: Beacon Press, 1963. A collection of basic writings by one of the seminal thinkers in this area.

Primitive Religion

Albright, W. F., *From The Stone Age to Christianity.* Baltimore: Johns Hopkins Univ. Press, 1957. A standard survey from the point of view of Palestinian archaeology but casting much light on prehistoric religion in general.

Caillois, R. *Man and the Sacred.* New York: The Free Press of Glencoe, 1960. A sparkling essay, including treatment of such topics as the sacred meaning of play and war in archaic societies.

*Comstock, W. Richard, *Religion and Man: The Study of Religion and Primitive Religion.* New York: Harper and Row, 1972. An authoritative and readable survey of basic concepts and data.

*Eliade, Mircea, *Shamanism: Archaic Techniques of Ecstasy.* New York: Pantheon Books, 1964. A masterful overview of the data and its meaning from the perspective of a historian of religions.

*James, E. O., *Prehistoric Religion.* London: Thames and Hudson, 1957. An orderly overview of the data.

*Leslie, Charles, ed., *Anthropology of Folk Religion.* New York: Random House, 1960. A collection of fascinating essays on topics ranging from the Krishna cult in India to Haitian voodoo.

Maringer, Johannes, *The Gods of Prehistoric Man.* New York: Alfred A. Knopf, 1960. Authoritative summary of what is known about the religion of Stone Age man.

*Lowie, Robert H., *Primitive Religion.* New York: Grossett & Dunlop, 1952. A classic text.

*Radin, Paul, *Primitive Religion.* New York: Viking Press, 1937. A book providing an important perspective; it emphasizes the place of individual differences and doubt among primitive people.

*Redfield, Robert, *The Primitive World*. Ithaca: Cornell University Press, 1953. A basic book by a great anthropologist; gives much attention to religion.

India—General, Ancient

*Basham, A. L., *The Wonder That Was India*. New York: Grove Press, 1959. A masterly survey of classic Indian society with much attention to religion.

*Coomeraswamy, Ananda, *The Dance of Shiva*. Bombay: Asia Pub. House, 1948. A brilliant insight into the classic Indian mind through the gateway of art; invaluable for understanding of the religion in depth.

Danielou, Alain, *Yoga: The Method of Reintegration*. New York: Univ Books, 1955. A concise and useful summary of the basic yoga texts.

*Deutsch, Eliot, *Advaita Vedanta: A Philosophical Reconstruction*. Honolulu: East-West Center Press, 1969. A splendidly readable introduction to India's most prestigious philosophical tradition.

*Eliade, Mircea, *Yoga: Immortality and Freedom*. New York: Pantheon Books, 1958. An invaluable overview of yogic concepts and literature.

*Hopkins, Thomas T., *The Hindu Religious Tradition*. Encino, Calif. & Belmont, Calif.: Dickenson Pub. Co., 1971. A useful introductory text; particularly valuable for its treatment of Vedic ritual.

*Lanroy, Richard, *The Speaking Tree: A Study of Indian Culture and Society*. London, New York: Oxford University Press, 1971. A substantial, valuable interpretation, particularly for its psychological insights.

Morgan, Kenneth W., ed., *Religion of the Hindus*. New York: Ronald Press, 1953. A collection of papers by Hindus written on a nonspecialist level; a good introduction to Hinduism.

*Organ, Troy Wilson, *Hinduism: Its Historical Development*. Westbury, N. Y.: Barron's Educational Series, Inc., 1974. A reliable history, emphasizing the development of intellectual concepts.

*Prabhavananda, Swami, and Christopher Isherwood, *How to Know God: The Yoga Aphorisms of Patanjali*. New York: Mentor Books, 1969. An easy-to-read version of the basic yoga text with commentary.

*———, *Shankara's Crest-Jewel of Discrimination*. New York: Mentor Books, 1970. The most accessible text of the nondualist tradition and a good introduction to the classic Indian metaphysical mind.

*———, *The Song of God: Bhagavad-Gita*. New York: Mentor Books.© 1951 Vedanta Society of Southern California. The most readable translation of this classic text, with an introduction by Aldous Huxley. Oriented toward an Advaita interpretation.

*Prabhavananda, Swami, and Frederick Manchester. *The Upanishads: Breath of Eternal*. New York: Mentor Books.© 1948, Vedanta Society of Southern California. A splendidly poetic and readable introductory translation of the most important of these basic texts. Oriented toward an Advaita interpretation.

*Zimmer, Heinrich, *Myths and Symbols in Indian Art and Civilization*. New York: Harper Torchbooks, 1962. A rich study; myth and symbol are as important as philosophy for understanding India.

*———, *Philosophies of India*. New York: Meridian Books, 1956. A brilliant and readable work by a scholar who understands the Indian tradition in a profound, if romantic, way.

Jaini, J., *Outlines of Jainism*. Cambridge, Mass.: Cambridge Univ. Press, 1916. A useful summary.

Stevenson, Mrs. Sinclair, *The Heart of Jainism*. London: Oxford University Press, 1915. Still the most readable overview, although dated and written from a Christian perspective.

Hindu Gods

****Coomeraswamy, A., and Sister Nivedita.** *Myths of the Hindus and Buddhists*. New York: Dover, 1972. An elementary retelling; well-written and cumulatively gives a good insight into India.

Danielou, Alain, *Hindu Polytheism*. New York: Pantheon Books, 1964. A massive summary of data about the gods, mostly through selective translations of classic texts. Well-illustrated.

****Singer, Milton,** ed., *Krishna: Myths, Rites, and Attitudes*. Chicago:. Univ. of Chicago Press, 1968. A good, rather scholarly collection of papers on Krishna and his cultus.

Sikhs

Clark, John Archer, *The Sikhs*. Princeton: Princeton Univ. Press, 1946. The most accessible summary of Sikh history, belief, and practice.

Singh, Trilochar, and others. *Adi Granth: Selections from the Sacred Writings of the Sikhs*. London: George Allen & Unwin, 1960. A readable translation.

Modern India

Brent, Peter, *Godmen of India*. New York: Quandrangle Books, 1973. A fascinating picture of the role of "God-realized" holy men in India today.

****Erikson, Erik H.,** *Gandhi's Truth*. New York: Norton, 1969. A brilliant if controversial "psycho-biography" of the most famous man of twentieth-century India.

Isherwood, Christopher, *Ramakrishna and His Disciples*. New York: Simon & Schuster, 1965. A very sympathetic picture of the influential saint of the last century who through his followers continues to shape modern understandings of Hinduism.

Buddhism—General

****Burtt, E. A.,** *The Teachings of the Compassionate Buddha*. New York: Mentor, 1955. A valuable set of excerpts from translated scriptures.

****Ch'en, Kenneth K. S.,** *Buddhism: The Light of Asia*. Woodbury, New York: Barron's Educational Series, 1968. A good introductory text, particularly for its country by country historical survey and its treatment of Buddhist cultural influence.

****Conze, Edward,** *Buddhism: Its Essence and Development*. New York: Harper Torchbooks, 1959. A masterful and vivid essay emphasizing Buddhist doctrine. Especially good on Mahayana.

**————, *Buddhist Meditation*. New York: Harper Torchbooks, 1969. A collection of texts on this topic; good editing.

**————, *Buddhist Scriptures*. Baltimore: Penguin Books, 1959. Another useful collection.

*———, *Buddhist Thought in India*. New York: Harper Torchbooks, 1962. A brilliant intellectual history, written with feeling, insight, and style.

*———, *Buddhist Wisdom Books*. London: Allen & Unwin, 1958. Translations of two basic texts.

*Coomeraswamy, Ananda,** *Buddha and the Gospel of Buddhism*. New York: Harper & Row, 1964. A sensitive essay from a Hindu point of view.

*de Bary, Wm. Theodore,** ed., *The Buddist Tradition in India, China, and Japan*. New York: The Modern Library, 1969. A useful collection of translated texts with good introductions.

Gard, Richard, *Buddhism*. New York: G. Braziller, 1961. A good introductory collection of translated texts and excerpts from studies.

Morgan, Kenneth, *The Path of the Buddha*. New York: Ronald, 1956. A series of interesting essays by modern Buddhists written for the general reader.

*Robinson, Richard H.,** *The Buddhist Religion*. Belmont, Calif.: Dickenson Pub. Co. 1970. A vivid introductory textbook.

Schecter, Jerrold, *The New Face of Buddha*. New York: Coward-McCann, 1967. A reporter's observation of Buddhism and modern politics in Southeast Asia, China, and Japan.

*Streng, Frederick J.,** *Emptiness: A Study in Religious Meaning*. Nashville: Abingdon Press, 1967. A scholarly and stimulating study of Nagarjuna's philosophy of the void.

*Swearer, Donald K.,** ed., *Secrets of the Lotus: Studies in Buddhist Meditation*. New York: The Macmillan Co., 1971. An unusual combination of lectures by modern Buddhist meditation masters and accounts of experiments with Buddhist meditation by American students.

Thomas, E. J., *The History of Buddhist Thought*. New York: Barnes & Noble, 1951. A standard scholarly resource.

The Buddha

*Percheron, Maurice,** *The Marvelous Life of the Buddha*. New York: St. Martins, 1960. A popular account of the traditional story.

*Rahula, Walpola,** *What the Buddha Taught*. New York: Evergreen Press, 1962. A competent summary for the general reader by a modern Buddhist monk.

Thomas, E. J., *The Life of the Buddha as Legend and History*. London: Routledge and Kegan Paul, 1924. A scholarly evaluation.

Buddhism in Southeast Asia

King, Winston L., *A Thousand Lives Away*. Cambridge, Mass.: Harvard Univ. Press, 1964. A fascinating description of Buddhism in modern Burma.

*Lester, Robert C.,** *Buddhism in Southeast Asia*. Ann Arbor: Univ. of Mich. Press, 1973. A clear, competent summary.

Tantra

*Bharati, Agehananda,** *The Tantric Tradition*. Garden City, N. Y.: Doubleday and Co. 1970. A splendid, if sometimes technical, exposition of this often murky field.

*Blofeld, John,** *The Way of Power*. London: George Allen & Unwin, 1970. A very clear statement. Sympathetic, emphasizes the Tibetan usage.

*__Rawson, Philip S.,__ *Tantra: The Indian Cult of Ecstasy.* London: Thames and Hudson, 1973. A lavishly illustrated popular treatment emphasizing the Hindu tradition.

Religion in Tibet

*__David-Neel, Alexandra,__ *Magic and Mystery in Tibet.* New York: University Books, 1965. A fascinating first person account; not highly scholarly, but a stimulating introduction to old Tibet.

*__Evans-Wentz, W. Y.,__ *The Tibetan Book of the Dead.* New York and London: Oxford Univ. Press, 1960. A translation of a famous and popular work, with introductions by Carl Jung, Lama Govinda, and others.

__Hoffmann, Helmut,__ *The Religions of Tibet.* New York: The Macmillan Co., 1961. A survey particularly useful on Bon.

__Snellgrove, David,__ *Buddhist Himalaya.* Oxford: Bruno Cassirer, 1957. A survey by a first-rate scholar; includes some travel narratives.

__Snellgrove, David, and Hugh Richardson.__ *A Cultural History of Tibet.* New York: Praeger, 1968. A standard resource.

*__Willis, Janice Dean,__ *The Diamond Light of the Eastern Dawn.* New York: Simon & Schuster, 1972. An unusual account of Tibetan meditation methods by an American who has studied and practiced them. Easy to read.

Chinese Religion

__Baity, Philip Chesley,__ *Religion in a Chinese Town.* Taipei: The Orient Cultural Service, 1975. A valuable study based on field research in Taiwan.

*__Blofeld, John,__ *I Ching.* New York: E. P. Dutton & Co., 1968. The most readable translation of this classic.

__Bredon, Juliet, and Igor Mitrophanow,__ *The Moon Year.* Shanghai: Kelly & Walsh, 1927; Reprinted New York: Paragon Press, 1966. A report of Chinese religious and traditional customs centering around the festival calendar.

__Eberhard, Wolfram,__ *Guilt and Sin in Traditional China.* Berkeley and Los Angeles: Univ. of California Press, 1967. Analyzes popular morality books and fiction, together with popular concepts of heaven and hell; invaluable for understanding popular Chinese religious concepts.

*__Fung Yu-Lan,__ *A Short History of Chinese Philosophy.* New York: The Macmillan Co., 1960. A sound, well-written summary.

__Jordan, David K.,__ *Gods, Ghosts, and Ancestors: The Folk Religion of a Taiwanese Village.* Berkeley and Los Angeles: Univ. of California Press, 1972. An illuminating report of field research.

*__Thompson, Laurence G.,__ *Chinese Religion: An Introduction.* Belmont, Calif.: Dickenson Pub. Co., 1969. An excellent beginner's book which integrates all levels and periods of Chinese religion into a unified picture.

*————, *The Chinese Way in Religion.* Encino, Calif.: Dickenson Pub. Co. 1973. A valuable collection of translated texts and studies, with good introductions.

__Wolf, Arthur P.,__ ed., *Religion and Ritual in Chinese Society,* Stanford, Calif.: Stanford Univ. Press, 1974. A collection of anthropological studies on popular religion.

*__Yang, C. K.,__ *Religion in Chinese Society.* Berkeley & Los Angeles: Univ. of California Press, 1961. Advanced, but a landmark treatment of the sociology of religion in China.

***Bahm, Archie J.,** *The Heart of Confucius*. Harper & Row, Pub., 1971. Simple translations of two basic Confucian texts, *The Mean* and the *Great Learning,* with an introduction which gives useful explanations for beginners of basic Chinese philosophical terms.

***Ch'u Chai, and Winberg Chai.** *Confucianism*. Woodbury, N. Y.: Barron's Educational Series, Inc. 1973. A useful introduction to Confucian philosophy from an intellectual history point of view.

***Creel, H. G.,** *Confucius and the Chinese Way*. New York: Harper Torchbooks, 1960. A standard book on the life, thoughts, and influence of Confucius.

***Fingerette, Herbert,** *Confucius—The Secular as Sacred*. New York: Harper Torchbooks, 1972. A brief but stimulating interpretive essay.

***Ware, James R.,** *The Sayings of Confucius*. New York: Mentor Books, n.d. A readable translation of the Analects.

Taoism

***Blofeld, John,** *The Secret and Sublime: Taoist Mysteries and Magic*. London: George Allen & Unwin, 1973. A personal, anecdotal narrative giving a lively picture of the Taoist world.

***Bynner, Witter,** *The Way of Life According to Lao Tzu*. New York: Capricorn Books, 1962. A free but very readable translation of the *Tao te Ching*.

Goullart, Peter, *The Monastery of Jade Mountain*. London: John Murray, 1961. A vivid, atmospheric account of Taoist life in pre-Communist China.

***Merton, Thomas,** *The Way of Chuang Tzu*. New York: New Directions Publishing Corp., 1969. A sensitive mystical interpretation of a seminal Taoist thinker.

***Rawson, Philip, and Lazslo Legeza.** *Tao: The Eastern Philosophy of Time and Change*. New York: Avon Books, 1973. A groundbreaking explication of Taoist philosophy and its expression in religion, art, and symbolism.

***Saso, Michael R.,** *Taoism and The Rite of Cosmic Renewal*. Pullman: Washington State Univ. Press, 1972. A rare scholarly account of Taoist religious ritual, with much insight into religious Taoism.

***Welch, Holmes,** *Taoism: The Parting of the Way*. Boston: Beacon Press, 1957. The best general introduction to all sides of Taoism.

Buddhism in China

***Blofeld, John,** *The Wheel of Life*. Berkeley: Shambala Press, 1972. An autobiographical book that offers, through the author's exploration of Buddhist China, rare insights into its manifold variety.

***Ch'en, Kenneth,** *Buddhism in China: A Historical Survey*. Princeton: Princeton Univ. Press, 1964. An authoritative introduction.

Welch, Holmes, *The Practice of Chinese Buddhism 1900–1950*. Cambridge, Mass.: Harvard Univ. Press, 1967. An excellent account of Chinese Buddhism before the revolution; especially good on the actual life of monasteries and temples and on popular devotional practices.

————, *The Buddhist Revival in China*. Cambridge, Mass.: Harvard University Press, 1968. Buddhism in modern China prior to 1949.

—————, *Buddhism Under Mao*. Cambridge, Mass.: Harvard University Press, 1972. A thorough study of Buddhism in Communist society.

*Wright, Arthur F.**, *Buddhism in Chinese History*. Stanford: Stanford Univ. Press, 1959. A brief, vivid, and reliable treatment of the introduction and assimilation of Buddhism in China.

Religion in Japan

Dorson, Richard M., ed., *Studies in Japanese Folklore*. Bloomington, Ind.: Indiana Univ. Press, 1963. Essays providing a good overview of Japanese folklore and folk religion.

*Earhart, H. Byron**, *Japanese Religion: Unity and Diversity,* 2nd. ed. Encino, Calif.: Dickenson Pub. Co., 1974. A fine introductory text, historically oriented.

*—————, *Religion in the Japanese Experience: Sources and Interpretations*. Encino, Calif.: The Dickenson Press, 1974. A useful collection of texts and examples of modern scholarship.

*Hori, Ichiro**, *Folk Religion in Japan*. Chicago: Univ. of Chicago Press, 1968. A collection of readable essays by a prominent Japanese scholar.

Kitagawa, Joseph M., *Religion in Japanese History*. New York: Columbia Univ. Press, 1966. An authoritative historical survey, emphasizing the modern period.

Smith, Robert J., *Ancestor Worship in Contemporary Japan*. Stanford, Calif.: Stanford Univ. Press, 1974. The best study of this important aspect of Japanese religion.

Buddhism in Japan

*Bloom, Alfred**, *Shinran's Gospel of Pure Grace*. Tucson: Univ. of Arizona Press, 1965. A highly insightful interpretation of Pure Land Buddhism.

*Dumoulin, Heinrich**, *A History of Zen Buddhism*. New York: Pantheon, 1963. A standard work, covering this tradition in both China and Japan.

Eliot, Sir Charles, *Japanese Buddhism*. London: Routledge & Kegan Paul, 1959. An older book but still useful as a reference, especially on the various denominations.

*Kapleau, Philip**, *The Three Pillars of Zen*. Boston: Beacon Press, 1967. A fascinating introduction to Zen methods and thought. Contains accounts of modern Zen experience.

*Saunders, E. Dale**, *Buddhism in Japan*. Philadelphia: Univ. of Pennsylvania Press, 1964. A useful historical survey.

Steinilber-Oberlin, E., *The Buddhist Sects of Japan*. London: George Allen & Unwin, 1938. A rather romantic appreciation of the doctrine and flavor of the various forms of Buddhism in Japan; not always reliable in detail, but beautifully written; helps one enter the Japanese Buddhist world.

*Suzuki, D. T.**, *Zen Buddhism*. Garden City, N. Y.: Doubleday and Co., 1956. One of many books by this well-known writer who has successfully communicated much of the Zen spirit to the west.

Shinto

*Kageyama, Haruki**, *The Arts of Shinto*. New York & Tokyo: John Weatherhill, Inc., 1973. A well-illustrated treatment which gives insights into some little known sides of Shinto.

*Ono, Sokyo**, *Shinto: The Kami Way*. Rutland, Vt.: Charles E. Tuttle Co., 1967. A basic introduction, representing the point of view of a leading modern Shinto scholar.

Ross, Floyd H., *Shinto: The Way of Japan*. Boston: Beacon Press, 1965. A readable introduction, in some places communicating a personal perspective.

Ellwood, Robert S., Jr., *The Eagle and The Rising Sun*. Philadelphia: The Westminster Press, 1974. An account of certain of the Japanese New Religions in America, with emphasis on occidental converts to them.

****McFarland, H. Neill,** *The Rush Hour of the Gods*. New York: The Macmillan Co., 1967. A well-researched, sometimes critical, overview of several of the groups.

Offner, Clark B., and Henry van Straelen. *Modern Japanese Religions*. Tokyo: Rupert Enderle, 1963. A carefully done study emphasizing healing in the New Religions.

****Thomsen, Harry,** *The New Religions of Japan*. Tokyo & Rutland. Vt.: Charles E. Tuttle Co., 1963. A readable basic report on the major new religions.

Egypt

Černý, Jaroslav, *Ancient Egyptian Religion*. London: Hutchinson's Univ. Library, 1952. A reliable basic reference.

****Frankfort, Henri,** *Ancient Egyptian Religion: An Interpretation*. New York: Harper Torchbooks, 1961. An essay aimed at understanding by a prominent scholar.

————, *Kingship and the Gods*. Chicago: Univ. of Chicago Press, 1948. A monumental comparative study of religion and the state in Egypt and Mesopotamia.

Lewis, Spence, *Myths and Legends of Ancient Egypt*. New York: Frederick A. Stokes, 1915. Dated, but useful for its presentation of mythical narratives.

Mertz, Barbara, *Temples, Tombs, and Hieroglyphs*. New York: Coward-McCann, 1964. A popular work on Egyptian archaeology and what it has discovered; a good first book on ancient Egypt.

Mesopotamia

****Contenau, Georges,** *Everyday Life in Babylon and Assyria*. London: E. Arnold, 1954. A solid, valuable general perspective.

Frankfort, Henri, *Kingship and the Gods*. Chicago: Univ. of Chicago Press, 1948. A monumental book on religion and the state in Egypt and Babylon.

Hooke, S. H., *Babylonian and Assyrian Religion*. Norman: Univ. of Oklahoma Press, 1963. A good short introduction by a leading authority.

****Kramer, Samuel N.,** *History Begins at Sumer*. Garden City, N. Y.: Doubleday and Co., 1959. A semipopular account of Sumerian civilization, including religion.

**————, *Sumerian Mythology*. New York: Harper Torchbooks, 1961. Fairly scholarly.

****Saggs, H.W.F.,** *The Greatness That Was Babylon*. New York: Hawthorn, 1962. A thorough overview of the civilization, with substantial chapters on religion, kingship, and literature.

****Sanders, N. K.,** *The Epic of Gilgamesh*. Baltimore: Penguin Books, 1966. A readable annotated translation.

Iran and Zoroastrianism

****Cumont, Franz,** *The Mysteries of Mithra*. New York: Dover Publications, 1956. A classic study of a cult of Iranian background which had an immense impact on the Greek and Roman world.

***Duchesne-Guillemin, J.,** *The Hymns of Zarathustra*. Boston: Beacon Press, 1963. Translation of the oldest parts of the Zend-Avesta.

*————, *Zoroastrianism: Symbols and Values*. New York: Harper Torchbooks, 1970. A short study by a prominent scholar.

***Masani, Rustom,** *Zoroastrianism: The Religion of the Good Life*. New York: The Macmillan Co., 1968. An account by a modern Parsi Zoroastrian. Idealizing but offers an unusual view of the religion from within. Easy to read.

Modi, J. J., *Religious Ceremonies and Customs of the Parsis*. London: Luzac, 1954. A useful reference.

***Zaehner, R. C.,** *The Teachings of the Magi*. New York: The Macmillan Co., 1956. An excellent summary, based on a standard catechism of Zoroastrian doctrine.

Greece

Dodd, E. R., *The Greeks and the Irrational*. Berkeley: Univ. of Cal. Press, 1951. A good account of such aspects of Greek religion as shamanism and magic by a solid scholar.

***Grant, Frederick C.,** *Hellenistic Religions*. New York: Liberal Arts Press, 1953. Translations of basic texts with good introductions.

***Guthrie, William,** *The Greeks and Their Gods*. Boston: Beacon Press, 1951. A useful reference.

***Hamilton, Edith,** *Mythology*. New York: Mentor, 1971. A well-written summary of the famous Greek myths; also includs a short section on northern mythology.

***Jonas, Hans,** *The Gnostic Religion*. Boston: Beacon Press, 1953. An important, scholarly summary of what is known about Gnosticism, with a philosophical interpretation of it.

***Kerényi, Carl,** *Gods of the Greeks*. New York: Grove Press, 1960. A readable account of the Greek gods and their myths.

Murray, Gilbert, *Five Stages of Greek Religion*. New York: Columbia Univ. Press, 1930. A classic study of the development of Greek religion.

***Rose, H. J.,** *Religion in Greece and Rome*. New York: Harper Torchbooks, 1959. A useful short text.

Rome

***Dill, Samuel,** *Roman Society from Nero to Marcus Aurelius*. London: The Macmillan Co., 1904. An old but very useful account, giving due attention to all kinds of religious life.

Ferguson, John, *The Religions of the Roman Empire*. Ithaca, N. Y.: Cornell Univ. Press, 1970. A fascinating summary of the developed Hellenistic faiths of the Roman world, both official and personal.

***Grant, Frederick Clifton,** *Ancient Roman Religion*. New York: Liberal Arts Press, 1957. A collection of basic texts in translation.

***Grant, Michael,** *Roman Myths*. New York: Scribner, 1971. A good reference.

***Ogilvie, Robert M.,** *The Romans and Their Gods in the Age of Augustus*. New York: Norton, 1970. A valuable short summary.

***Rose, H. J.,** *Religion in Greece and Rome*. New York: Harpers, 1959. A reliable summary and reference.

Chadwick, Nora, *The Celts*. Baltimore: Penguin Books, 1971. A good scholarly summary: limited material on religion, but useful for background.

McCana, P., *Celtic Mythology*. London: Paul Hamlyn, 1971. A colorful popular account.

Macculloch, John Arnott, *The Celtic and Scandinavian Religions*. London: Hutchinson's Univ. Library, 1948. An authoritative text.

Piggott, Stuart, *Druids*. New York: Praeger, 1968. A well-illustrated summary of scholarly data.

Rees, Alwyn, and Brinley Rees. *Celtic Heritage*. New York: Grove Press, 1961. A fascinating presentation of the Celtic world view.

Sjoestedt-Jonval, Marie Louise, *Gods and Heroes of the Celts*. London: Methuen, 1949. A short mythology.

Germanic Peoples

Branston, Brian, *The Lost Gods of England*. New York: Oxford University Press, 1974. Interesting, authoritative, and readable.

Davidson, H. R. Ellis, *Gods and Myths of Northern Europe*. Baltimore: Penguin Books, 1964. A good summary of the mythology with some insight into religious practice.

————, *Pagan Scandinavia*. London: Thames and Hudson, 1967. Emphasizes religion; a sound well-illustrated introduction.

————, *Scandinavian Mythology*. London: Paul Hamlyn, 1969. A vividly illustrated popular account by a realiable scholar.

Macculloch, John Arnott, *The Celtic and Scandinavian Religions*. London: Hutchinson's Univ. Library, 1948. A brief but reliable introduction.

Turville-Petre, E.O.G., *Myth and Religion of the North*. New York: Holt, Rinehart & Winston, 1964. A solid introduction; on Scandinavia only.

Old Testament

Albright, W. F., *From the Stone Age to Christianity*. Garden City, N. Y.: Doubleday & Co., 1957. A scholarly guide to Palestinian archaeology, emphasizing its relation to the Old Testament, and its meaning for philosophy of history.

Anderson, B., *Understanding the Old Testament*. Englewood Cliffs, N. J.: Prentice-Hall, Inc., 1957. A standard introductory textbook.

Buber, Martin, *The Prophetic Faith*. New York: The Macmillan Co., 1949. A study by a famous Jewish theologian.

Buck, Harry M., *People of the Lord*. New York: The Macmillan Co., 1965. A good beginning textbook on the Old Testament.

Gaster, T. H., *Dead Sea Scriptures*. Garden City, N. Y.: Doubleday and Co., 1964. A semipopular overview of these important finds and their meaning.

James, F., *Personalities of the Old Testament*. New York: Scribners, 1939. A colorful, well-written interpretation of leading Old Testament figures.

Larue, Gerald A., *Old Testament Life and Literature*. Boston: Allyn & Bacon, 1968. A standard introductory textbook.

*Pritchard, James B., *The Ancient Near East in Pictures*. Princeton: Princeton Univ. Press, 1954. A fascinating survey by a distinguished archaeologist.

Richardson, A., *A Preface to Bible Study*. Philadelphia: The Westminster Press, 1944. A valuable beginning introduction to serious study of the Bible, its world view and its times.

*Wright, G. Ernest, *God Who Acts*. London: SCM Press, 1952. An impressive statement of one interpretation of the biblical God.

Judaism

*Bamberger, Bernard J., *The Story of Judaism*. New York: Schocken Books, 1970. A valuable introduction.

*Finkelstein, Louis, ed., *The Jews: Their History, Culture, and Religion,* 2 vols. New York: Harper, 1949. A standard reference.

*Heschel, Abraham, *Between God and Man: An Interpretation of Judaism*. New York: The Free Press, 1965. The view of a very distinguished, moderately liberal modern Jewish thinker.

*Neusner, Jacob, *The Life of Torah: Readings: The Jewish Religious Experience*. Encino, Calif.: Dickenson Pub. Co., 1974. An anthology; emphasizes discussion of the commandments.

*———, *The Way of Torah: An Introduction to Judaism,* 2nd. ed. Encino, Calif.: Dickenson Pub. Co., 1974. A good introduction; emphasizes Jewish history and way of life.

Waxman, Meyer, *Judaism: Religion and Ethics*. New York: Thomas Yoseloff, 1953. A clear survey of Jewish practice and moral attitudes today.

*Wouk, Herman, *This is my God*. Garden City, N. Y.: Doubleday and Co., 1959. A popular statement of the meaning of Orthodox Judaism by a well-known novelist.

Jewish Mysticism

*Scholem, Gershom G., *Major Trends in Jewish Mysticism*. New York: Shocken Books, 1961. Quite scholarly; the definitive work, especially on the kabbala.

*Weiner, Herbert, *9½ Mystics: The Kabbala Today*. New York: Holt, Rinehart, and Winston, 1969. A fascinating, easy-to-read account by a modern rabbi of visits to contemporary centers of Jewish mysticism; provides an incomparable insight into their spirit.

Christianity

*Ahlstrom, Sydney E., *A Religious History of the American People*. (New Haven and London: Yale Univ. Press, 1972): A substantial but readable story of American religion, emphasizing periods and broad themes. Reliable and highly recommended.

Bellah, Robert N., *The Broken Covenant*. New York: Seabury Press, 1975. A study of American "Civil Religion": use of Christian-derived myths, salvation themes, taboos and the like in political and social life.

*Bettenson, H., *Documents of the Christian Church*. London and New York: Oxford Univ. Press, 1947. A standard reference for primary sources in church history.

Cragg, Kenneth, *Christianity in World Perspective*. London: Lutterworth, 1968. A provocative essay by a Christian theologian who is also a leading Islamicist on the world place of Christianity.

Fülöp-Miller, René, *The Saints That Moved the World*. New York: Crowell, 1945. A beautifully written account of five major Christian mystics.

Latourette, Kenneth Scott, *A History of Christianity*. New York: Harper & Brothers, 1953. A massive, well-written history from a Protestant missionary-oriented point of view.

*Niebuhr, H. Richard, *Christ and Culture*. New York: Harper Torchbooks, 1956. A classic study of different ways Christianity has related to its cultural environments.

*Rosten, Leo, ed., *Religions in America*. New York: Simon & Schuster, 1963. Questions and answers about the basic beliefs and practices of the major American religions and denominations; a good introduction.

*Tillich, Paul, *A History of Christian Thought*. New York: Harper & Row, 1968. A leading Protestant theologian's view of the topic.

*Underhill, Evelyn, *Mystics of the Church*. London: J. Clarke & Co., 1925. A semipopular account by a distinguished scholar; emphasizes Roman Catholic figures.

———, *Worship*. London: Nisbet & Co., Ltd. 1936. A view of Christian worship and its meaning which tries to be sympathetic to all traditions. Written before the modern liturgical movement, but a classic.

The New Testament

*Brox, Norbert, *Understanding the Message of Paul*. Notre Dame, Ind.: Univ. of Notre Dame Press ,1968. A readable, reliable book.

*Enslin, M., *Christian Beginnings*. New York: Harper & Row, 1938. A basic textbook by a distinguished if sometimes controversial scholar.

*Filson, Floyd V., *The New Testament Against its Environment*. London: SCM Press, 1950. Emphasizes the difference between early Christianity and its surrounding culture.

Goguel, M., *The Life of Jesus*. New York: The Macmillan Co., 1933. A beautifully written narrative by a distinguished scholar of liberal Protestant sympathies.

*Grant, Robert M., *A Historical Introduction to the New Testament*. New York: Harper & Row, 1963. A reliable guide to the indispensable background knowledge for New Testament studies.

Kee, H., and others. *Understanding the New Testament*. Englewood Cliffs, N. J.: Prentice-Hall, Inc. 1958. A standard textbook.

Reicke, Bo Ivan, *The New Testament Era*. Philadelphia: Fortress Press, 1968. A good historical introduction.

Riddle, Donald U., and Harold H. Hutson. *New Testament Life and Literature*. Chicago: Univ. of Chicago Press, 1946. A standard introductory textbook.

*Schweitzer, Albert, *The Quest of the Historical Jesus*. London: Adam & Charles Block, 1910. A very famous history of nineteenth-century New Testament research by one of the best-known and most controversial of twentieth-century scholars.

Spivey, Robert A., and D. Moody Smith Jr., *Anatomy of the New Testament*. New York: The Macmillan Co., 1969. A standard introductory textbook.

Gough, Michael, *Early Christians*. New York: Praeger, 1961. A valuable, well-illustrated survey oriented toward archaeology.

***Waddell, Helen,** *The Desert Fathers*. Ann Arbor: Univ. of Mich. Press, 1957. A good translation, with a beautifully written introduction. Gives a vivid picture of the earliest Christian monastics.

Wand, J. W. C., *A History of the Early Church*. London: Methuen and Co., 1937. A well-written work; traditional point of view.

Welsford, A. E., *Life in the Early Church A.D. 33 to 313*. Greenwich, Ct.: Seabury Press, 1953. A vivid, popularly written account; a good beginning introduction to the period.

Eastern Orthodoxy

Fedotov, G. P., *A Treasury of Russian Spirituality*. London: Sheed & Ward, 1952. A fine anthology of the mysticism of Eastern Christianity.

Lossky, Vladimir, *The Mystical Theology of the Eastern Church*. London: James Clarke and Co., 1957. Fairly scholarly, and a brilliant treatment of the topic.

***Ware, Timothy,** *The Orthodox Church*. Baltimore: Penguin Books, 1963. A good, solid introduction.

Zernov, N., *Eastern Christendom*. London: Weidenfeld & Nicolson, 1961. A sympathetic popular introduction.

Roman Catholicism

***Adam, Karl,** *The Spirit of Catholicism*. New York: The Macmillan Co., 1929. A profound but fairly simple essay, written from a personal point of view.

Bausch, William J., *Pilgrim Church: A Popular History of Catholic Christianity*. Notre Dame, Ind.: Fides, 1973. A modern treatment.

Brantl, George, *Catholicism,* New York: Braziller, 1969. A useful anthology.

Campbell, Robert, ed., *Spectrum of Catholic Attitudes*. New York: The Macmillan Co., 1969. An interesting collection of statements, giving a picture of the contemporary Catholic theological ferment.

***McKenzie, John,** *The Roman Catholic Church*. Garden City. N. Y.: Doubleday, 1971. A standard resource.

Rahner, Karl, *Teachings of the Catholic Church*. New York: Alba, 1967. A summary by a modern liberal Catholic theologian.

Protestantism

***Dunstan, Leslie,** *Protestantism*. New York: Braziller, 1961. A useful anthology of historical material.

Haverstick, John, *The Progress of the Protestant*. New York: Holt, Rinehart, & Winston, 1969. A lavishly illustrated popular history of Protestantism.

MacIntosh, Hugh Ross, *Types of Modern Theology: Schleiermacher to Barth*. New York: Scribners, 1939. A fine introduction to the most talked about modern Protestant theologians.

***Marty, Martin E.,** *Protestantism*. London: Weidenfeld & Nicholson, 1972. A survey of Protestant attitudes on a number of issues; good bibliography.

Nichols, James Hastings, *Primer for Protestants*. New York: Association Press, 1951. A well-done basic introduction to traditional Protestant attitudes.

*Niebuhr, H. R., *The Kingdom of God in America*. New York: Harper & Brothers, 1937. A seminal history of the interaction between Protestant attitudes and American history.

Pauck, Wilhelm, *The Heritage of the Reformation*. Glencoe, Ill.: Free Press, 1961. An authoritative historical statement.

*von Rohr, John Robert, *Profile of Protestantism*. Belmont, Calif.: Dickenson Pub. Co., 1969. A good basic textbook.

*Tawney, R. H., *Religion and the Rise of Capitalism*. London: John Murray, 1926. A statement of the often discussed thesis that Protestant and capitalistic attitudes have reinforced each other.

Islam

*Cragg, Kenneth, *The Call of the Minaret*. London and New York: Oxford Univ. Press, 1956. A brilliant and empathetic treatment of Islamic theology, with frequent comparisons to Christian concepts.

*———, *The House of Islam*. Belmont, Calif.: Dickenson, 1969. A splendid introduction.

*Christopher, John B., *The Islamic Tradition*. New York: Harper & Row, 1972. A brief introduction covering all cultural aspects of Islamic civilization.

Morgan, Kenneth, *Islam: The Straight Path*. New York: Ronald, 1958. A collection of popular papers by contemporary Muslims: a good introduction to the Islamic faith.

*Smith, Wilfred C., *Islam in Modern History*. New York: Mentor, 1959. Already a bit dated, but a valuable introduction to the ongoing life of Islam.

Watt, Wm. Montgomery, *What is Islam?* London: Longmans, 1968. An excellent overview by a distinguished Islamicist.

*Williams, John Alden, *Islam*. New York: Braziller, 1961. A useful anthology of Muslim literature.

The Koran

Arberry, A. J., *The Koran Interpreted*. 2 vols. New York: Macmillan, 1955. Probably the most readable and literary English version.

*Dawood, N. J., trans., *The Koran*. Baltimore: Penguin Books, 1968. Also recommended; a sound and accessible translation.

*Pickthall, Mohammed, *The Meaning of the Glorious Koran*. New York: Mentor, nd. An interesting translation by an English convert to Islam.

Islamic Mysticism

*Arberry, A. J., *Sufism*. New York: Harper Torchbooks, 1970. A brief, authoritative, and well-written introduction.

*Shah, Idries, *The Sufis*. Garden City, N. Y. Doubleday and Co. 1964. Attractive, moving, readable, much influenced by the author's own point of view.

*Smith, Margaret, *Readings from the Mystics of Islam*. London: Luzac, 1950. Beautiful translation of original sources.

*Trimingham, J. Spencer, *The Sufi Orders in Islam*. London and New York: Oxford Univ. Press, 1971. Scholarly; gives an incomparable insight into an important aspect of Islamic life.

Index

Church of Christ, Scientist, 311
Church of God, 311
Church of Jesus Christ of Latter-Day Saints
    (Mormon), 307, 311
Church of the Nazarene, 309
Church of World Messianity, 206
Circumcision, and initiation, 41, 43
Cistercians, 303
Clement of Alexandria, 280
Commensality, and caste, 101
Communion:
    in early church, 279–80
    Roman Catholic, 302
Communism, 296
Compassion, 131–32
Confucian classics, 157–58, 182
Confucianism, 156–64
    and Buddhism, 83, 174, 175
    foundation of, 22
    historicity of, 19
    in Japan, 191
    and Taoism, 164–65, 167, 168–69, 170–71,
    172
Confucius, 22, 157–59, 160, 162–63, 165–66,
    184
Congregational Church, 294, 310
Consciousness, aspects of, 77–78
Constantine, 283, 284
Conze, Edward, 112–13
Cordova Caliphate, 321
Creation stories, 12, 13
Crete, 227
Crusades, 289, 321
Cults, 16
Cumaean sibyl, 233, 234
Cybele, 235, 301
Cyrus, 217, 223, 225, 262

Daijo-sai, 43–44, 190
Dainichi, 127, 128
Daishi, Dengyo (Saicho), 194
Dancing:
    in agricultural myths, 54–55
    in Hasidic worship, 264
    and headhunting, 55–56
    and Krishna worship, 95
    on May Day, 31
    in Shinto, 149, 187
    Sufi, 331–32
Dante Alighieri, 289, 329
Darius, 226
David (King), 262, 263, 272
Death:
    and belief in soul, 35–40
    certainty of, 33
    Zoroastrian, 225
Decius, 281, 283
Delphic oracle, 229
Demeter, 57
Demian (Hesse), 2–3

Devotion, medieval, 23–24
Dharma, 67–68, 84, 86, 110
Dietary laws (Jewish), 269–70
Diocletian, 281–82, 283
Dionysus, 227, 230
Disciples of Christ, 307
Divination, 155–56
Divine Comedy (Dante), 289, 329
Doctrine, vs. myth, 12–13
Dogen, 202–3
Dominicans, 303
Dostoevsky, Feodor, 298
Dreams, 40, 169
Druids, 31, 238, 241
Dyaus, 71

Ea, 219, 220, 221
Easter, 20, 280
Eastern Orthodoxy, 286, 289, 296–99
Edda, 243
Eddy, Mary Baker, 311
Edwards, I. E. S., 212–13
Egypt:
    Christianity in, 285
    Great Pyramid, 39
    under the Greeks, 228
    imperial religion of, 21, 211–17
    Israelites in, 258, 261
    patriarchal revolution, 57
Eisai, 202
Eleusis, 231, 232, 235
Eliade, Mircea, 28–29, 46–47, 173
Ellwood, Robert S., 66–67
Enlightenment, paths to, 14
Enuma Elish, 221
Epics, 21
Epicureanism, 22
Eskimo shamans, 45, 46, 47, 48, 138
Ethiopia, 285
Ewe tribe, 49 (*illus.*)
Exodus (Hebrew), 13, 261, 268

Faith, and modernism, 23–24
Farmers (archaic), 52–57
Festivals:
    Egyptian, 214
    Jewish, 267–70
    Shinto, 186–87
    Wesak, 124
Fiji, 56, 63, 65–66
Fire, sacred, 71, 73
Flood stories, 220, 259
Four Noble Truths (Buddhist), 110, 112–13, 115
Fox, George, 310
France, 294
Franciscans, 191, 303
Francis of Assisi (Saint), 289–90
Freuchen, Peter, 45
Freud, Sigmund, 144, 159
Fudo, 195

Vajrayana Buddhism, 135–45
van Gennep, Arnold, 42, 43, 50
Varuna, 71, 224, 255
Vasubandhu, 132
Vedas, 70–71, 75, 77, 80, 95, 224 (*see also* Upanishads)
Vestal Virgins, 21
Vietnam, 119
Virgil, 234–35
Virgin birth, 301
Virgin Mary (*see* Blessed Virgin Mary)
Vishnu, 92–95
Vivekananda, 103
Void, 129–32, 175, 176
Voodoo, 16 (*illus.*)
Vritra, 71, 72

Wach, Joachim, 11
Wagner, Richard, 242
Waldensians, 290
Wang Shou-jen, 164
Wang Yang-ming, 164
Warriers, and Zen, 196–97
Wasson, R. Gordon, 72
Water, sacred, 101
Weber, Max, 9
Wesak festival, 124
Wesley, John, 309
Wisdom, 22–23
    Old Testament books, 263
    prajnaparamita, 130
Wisdom of Solomon, 22
Witchdoctors (*see* Shamanism)
Women:
    Eskimo taboos, 45

Women (continued)
    Hindu, 100
    and planting, 57
    role, in initiation, 42–43
Wotan, 242, 243, 244, 245, 246, 285
Wycliffe, John, 290, 294

Xavier, Francis, 191
Xerxes, 226

Yahweh, 259–60
Yantra, 90
Yap, 36, 40
Yemen, 326
Yidam, 143–44
Yin and yang, 161–62 (*see also* Tao)
Yoga, 6, 84–85, 173
Yogacara (*see* Mind Only Buddhism)
Yoga Sutras of Patanjali, 84–85
Yoni, 63

Zarathustra (*see* Zoroaster)
Zen Buddhism, 194, 196, 197, 201, 202–5
    and Mind Only school, 132, 133
    monasticism, 127, 128
    Rinzai vs. Soto schools, 202–3
Zend Avesta, 226
Zeus, 71, 227, 229, 230, 255
Zionism, 265, 270
Zohar, 264
Zoroaster, 22, 223–27, 254
Zoroastrianism, 22, 222–27
    and Islam, 316, 329
    and monotheism, 210, 250, 254, 255

1
Religions of the World

RELIGION OF THE MAJORITY
OF THE POPULATION

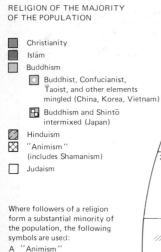

RELIGION OF THE MAJORITY
OF THE POPULATION

- Christianity
- Islām
- Buddhism
  - Buddhist, Confucianist, Ṭaoist, and other elements mingled (China, Korea, Vietnam)
  - Buddhism and Shintō intermixed (Japan)
- Hinduism
- "Animism" (includes Shamanism)
- Judaism

Where followers of a religion form a substantial minority of the population, the following symbols are used:

A "Animism"
B Buddhism
C Christianity
H Hinduism
J Judaism
M Islām
O Chinese religious blend (see above)

ATLANTIC

OCEAN

PACIFIC

OCEAN

EQUATOR

Tropic of Cancer

Tropic of Capricorn

80°
60°
40°
20°
20°
40°

2
Distribution of Religions by Major Regions c. 1970

Christiantity differentiated, thus

R Roman Catholic
P Protestant
OX Orthodox, Coptic, etc.

- Other religions or religion unspecified

- = 25 million persons

The area of a square is proportional to the total population and is divided into patterned ares that correspond to the proportion in that population of the religious groups

See Map 1 for key to symbols

WORLD POPULATION

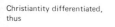

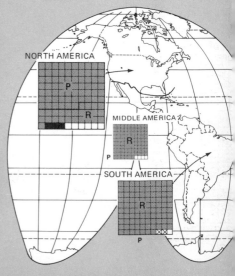

NORTH AMERICA

MIDDLE AMERICA

SOUTH AMERICA